PUBLICATIONS

OF

THE AMERICAN FOLKLORE SOCIETY

BIBLIOGRAPHICAL AND SPECIAL SERIES

GENERAL EDITOR, MacEDWARD LEACH

VOLUME VIII

1957

AMERICAN BALLADRY FROM BRITISH BROADSIDES

iii

American Balladry
From British Broadsides

A GUIDE FOR STUDENTS AND COLLECTORS OF TRADITIONAL SONG

by

G. MALCOLM LAWS, JR.

University of Pennsylvania

PHILADELPHIA

THE AMERICAN FOLKLORE SOCIETY

1957

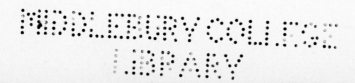

Library of Congress Catalog Card Number: 57-12600

Printed in the United States of America
By
The Kutztown Publishing Company, Inc.
Kutztown, Pa.

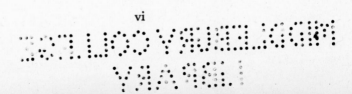

Dedicated to

PROFESSOR W. ROY MACKENZIE

to whose

scholarly, witty, and invariably illuminating

Ballads and Sea Songs from Nova Scotia

I am deeply indebted

Contents

Preface

Some years ago the statement was made in England that "there are no more folk-songs, only variants, to collect."[1] Though somewhat extreme, this remark serves to underline the fact that collectors of folksong eventually pass the point of diminishing returns. English collectors working in previously untried areas found that the bulk of their songs had already been recorded and printed by earlier investigators. Inevitable differences of texts and tunes were present, but they did not seem to justify the intensive labor necessary to place them before the public. As a result, little new material has appeared from the British Isles during the last twenty years. During the same period, the collecting and publishing of folksongs from America has continued vigorously. Imperceptibly we too have reached the point where we can predict about ninety per cent of the contents of any new regional collection. We have only to look at the collections from neighboring areas to know what to expect. Thus it is now possible to survey American folksong in something approaching its present entirety. The student of living folksong, like the student of living language, must be aware that the pasage of time will make some of his work obsolete, but he can take comfort from the thought that he is contributing to the history of his own era.

The present study concludes the general survey of living American balladry which Tristram P. Coffin and I have undertaken. It deals with all those currently traditional broadside ballads which have been imported from the British Isles but which are not included in Professor Francis J. Child's *The English and Scottish Popular Ballads*. The text includes descriptions of the ballads by types, an account of their origin in Britain and their distribution in America, an analysis of their relation to the Child ballads, and a discussion of their forms and variants. The latter part of the book is designed to assist collectors and scholars in identifying and studying the traditional broadsides. Appendix I contains a bibli-

---

[1] A. H. Fox-Strangways at a special meeting of the Folk-Song Society, 1931, reported in *JFSS* VIII, x.

ography for each ballad as well as sample stanzas and summaries of the ballad stories. Supplementary information about ballad publishers and ballad recordings is provided in additional appendices. Used in conjunction with the folksong anthologies to which I have made constant reference, this study should provide the reader with a fairly comprehensive concept of British balladry of the broadside type.

Still remaining to be studied or re-studied on a nation-wide basis are the American folksongs which for various reasons do not qualify as popular ballads. This large and unwieldy group includes nursery and play-party songs, nonsense songs, sea chanties, religious folksongs, temperance songs, sentimental parlor songs, and songs of various occupational groups, as well as a great number of primarily lyrical folksongs. All such songs have been excluded from this study although they are known to singers of traditional balladry.

Since the 18th century, practically every ballad editor has felt called upon to say a few nostalgic words about the good old days when balladry flourished. Each seems to have felt that he had rescued a few surviving pieces from oblivion and that a few more years would certainly sound the death knell of the traditional ballad. During all this time balladry has remained very much alive. Individual ballads sometimes die out of tradition, of course, but others take their place, and balladry continues to provide solace and entertainment for thousands. I would agree that the best days of balladry are over, and yet the singers still sing and the collectors record and publish. Hardly a year goes by without the appearance of one or two new regional collections, and there always seem to be more on the way. Of course all original collections are welcome both for their new material and for the variants which throw light on a subject full of obscurities, and no student of folksong would want the collectors to give up the chase. But the time has come for a shift in emphasis from field work to library work. The materials already collected are in desperate need of analysis, interpretation, and evaluation, and the study of folksong cannot advance properly until this need is fully realized and acted upon.

A book of this kind is in a sense a cooperative enterprise because it depends so largely upon the work of hundreds of indefatigable ballad collectors and editors over a period of many decades. The fieldwork necessary to gather a major collection requires unlimited patience, tact, skill, and energy. Transcribing and editing ballad texts is equally demanding and certainly less exciting. But the end result of this work in Canada and the United States is an unsurpassed body of permanently recorded folksong. Since to name the collectors and editors who have indirectly contributed to this volume would duplicate much of the bibliography, I must express my gratitude in this general acknowledgement and appreciation of their labors.

I am personally indebted to Mr. Clarence S. Brigham, Director of the American Antiquarian Society, who graciously lent me the microfilm of the Isaiah Thomas Collection; to Miss Carolyn Jakeman and other members of the staff of the Houghton Library at Harvard for making my summer visits to the library pleasant and rewarding; and to Mrs. Delphine O. Richardson of the University of Pennsylvania library for securing several scare items through Inter-Library Loan.

Professor MacEdward Leach, Secretary-Treasurer of the American Folklore Society, read the manuscript and offered a number of valuable suggestions. He has taken a keen interest in my project from the beginning and has been more than generous with his time, his books, and his advice. His friendship and his enthusiasm for ballad studies have done much to lighten the burden of this work. I am most grateful also to Professor Samuel P. Bayard of Pennsylvania State University, who kindly read the manuscript and recommended certain additions and changes which I was happy to incorporate in the final text. Finally my thanks go to Professor Tristram P. Coffin, who had announced his intention of making a survey of the ballads here covered but who generously yielded the subject to me when he undertook to compile the Index to the *Journal of American Folklore*.

Philadelphia
January, 1957

Chapter I

The Types of British Broadside Ballads Traditional in America

Since most widely read people come in contact only infrequently or casually with folksongs of any type, it may be well to begin this study with some brief definitions. The inclusive term 'folksong' includes all traditional songs, ballads and non-ballads alike, but the limiting word 'folksong' refers properly to lyrical rather than narrative pieces. By 'popular ballad' we mean a narrative song, usually anonymous, which depends upon oral tradition for its preservation. The ballad must tell a story; it cannot be primarily a lyric expression of emotion. In popular and literary usage the word 'ballad' has a confusing multiplicity of meanings, but we are concerned only with pieces of a type which has been familiar to folk singers for centuries. Having said that a ballad is a narrative song, I must admit that a ballad can be recognized as such whether or not it has ever been sung. In brief, a ballad has certain stylistic peculiarities which distinguish it from other types of verse. Thus the standard collection of British ballads, that of Professor Child, contains many pieces which may never have been sung, as do all the collections of British and American broadside ballad prints.

To confuse matters further, scholars have generally recognized a distinction between the style of the Child ballads and that of the typical broadsides, although both are called ballads and although specific pieces in both categories may or may not exist in tradition. Since the term 'popular ballad' is used in the title of Professor Child's compilation, which most of his contemporaries regarded as definitive, and since most poetic anthologies still present only representative Child ballads, some students have hesitated to accept as genuine popular ballads pieces which Child did not include or have handled them defensively or apologetically. One of the purposes of the present study is to emphasize the fact that all the ballads with which this book deals, whatever their origin, exist in

1

folk tradition, and disregarding aesthetic considerations, have at least as much right as the Child pieces to be called popular ballads.

My use of the term 'British broadsides' in the title requires further explanation. As generally used the term refers to printed journalistic pieces which were widely sold in the British Isles and elsewhere over a period of nearly four hundred years. Compositions of this type were largely ephemeral and topical. Many of the British broadside ballads have been preserved on their original single sheets in collections dating from the 16th, 17th, 18th, and 19th centuries. Such notable old collections as the Douce, the Pepys, and the Roxburghe contain thousands of examples of this type of balladry.[1] The word 'ballad' is loosely used in this connection since it may mean any song or series of verses, narrative or otherwise, which appeared on the penny or halfpenny sheets. The broadside ballad in this larger sense only infrequently achieved the status of folksong and much less frequently remained in living tradition. A small percentage of the printed broadsides, however, had sufficient appeal to be remembered and passed on from one generation to the next. These were subjected to those variations which creep into all folksong, and a few of them became almost indistinguishable in quality from some of the better Child ballads. Although the Child collection contains a substantial number of broadside ballads, these will be excluded from the present study.

Most of the ballads we are dealing with here can either be traced to British broadsides or are clearly in the broadside style. Hence the term broadside balladry distinguishes this class of songs from the native American ballads and from those of Child. All three types are widely distributed in American tradition. No ballad has been included which has not been recovered within the last half century or so from traditional singing in the United States or in the Maritime Provinces of Canada. A few imported ballads remain which do not seem to be of the broadside type. Instead of creating

---

[1] The major printed collections of primarily non-traditional broadsides are listed in the Bibliography near the end of this volume. For black-letter ballads, see under the Ballad Society; *Black-Letter Ballads;* Clark; *A Collection of Old Ballads;* Firth, *An American Garland; Osterley Park Ballads;* Ritson, *Ancient Songs and Ballads;* Rollins; and Roxburghe Ballads. For 18th and 19th century ballads, see under Ashton, Evans, Henderson, Hindley, Logan, and O'Lochlainn.

a fourth category for this handful of pieces, it has seemed best to include them here. Similarly a few ballads from Australia are included, but these are really transplanted Irish broadsides. The emphasis throughout this study will be upon traditional song, but in tracing these ballads to their original sources I must refer frequently to the broadside prints.

To quote a definition which I have used elsewhere, "a ballad is a narrative folksong which dramatizes a memorable event."[2] The memorable event can be almost any type of occurrence of sufficient substance to produce a short plotted narrative with a definite conclusion. The story almost invariably involves one or more human beings in whom the audience can take a personal interest. Of course simplicity and timelessness are helpful if the piece is to be remembered and widely sung. The ballad story usually advances chronologically in a series of four-line stanzas of simple diction. The method of the balladist is dramatic in that the emphasis is upon action and dialogue rather than exposition. Suspense is created as the narrative approaches its climax, and the audience takes part vicariously in the events recounted.

Among the folk, ballads are usually sung without accompaniment before a small group of friends in an isolated community. The singer tends to suppress his own personality and to let the ballad speak for itself. He rarely varies his emphasis to suit the subject matter, nor does he attempt to act out any part of the story. The concert style of singing, which emphasizes the personality, the technical skill, and frequently the acting ability of the singer, is foreign to the true folk singer. Inevitably professional performers acquire mannerisms which represent a departure from folk style; thus it is almost impossible to hear genuine folk singing except among the people to whom it is a traditional form of entertainment. In mining towns, fishing villages, lumber camps and mountain settlements, and on ships, farms, and Western ranches, balladry has quietly flourished while the urban population has been almost unaware of its existence. Only a small percentage of the people in ballad singing communities are singers, but the other members of the community or of the family constitute the appreciative audience without which folksong tends to fade away.

---

[2] *Native American Balladry*, p. 2.

During the 20th century so much emphasis has been placed on the importance of ballad music that it may not be amiss to observe that the ballad story still seems of basic importance to folk singers.[3] Of course a ballad cannot become a folksong until it is sung, but the evidence indicates that most singers regard the tune simply as a conventional vehicle for the story. Aside from the fact that many ballads are sung to more than one tune, musically talented collectors find that some "singers" cannot carry a tune at all, or deliver one piece after another in a monotonous chant. Then, too, the singer always seems to assume that the listener is concerned mainly with the story and that this must be sung to its conclusion no matter how repetitive the tune becomes after fifteen or twenty stanzas. Those who feel that I am slighting the music—and I admit that I am not equipped to do otherwise—should remember that most ballads of all types were composed without original tunes. This is certainly true of the British broadsides, which were almost always printed without tunes, although the publisher often named the tune to which the ballad might be sung. Thus ballad tunes are frequently far older than the texts and have no inevitable connection with them. That ballad tunes are often more beautiful than the texts is obvious to anyone who has heard some of these commonplace broadsides transformed by singing. Undoubtedly the musically inclined members of the folk appreciate the beauty of the traditional tunes, but this fact does not justify the conclusion that any ballads exist in tradition simply because their tunes are appealing.

A better understanding of American balladry as it is known among the folk will be gained by examining the well edited regional collections than by reading a general discussion of the topic. Among

---

[3] Cecil Sharp, whose primary interests were in music, had this to say on the subject: "It is a well-known fact that the folk-singer attaches far more importance to the words of his song than to its tune; that, while he is conscious of the words that he is singing, he is more or less unconscious of the melody." (*English Folk-Songs, Some Conclusions*, p. 18). Not all students of folksong agree with Sharp, however. Alexander Keith, for example, writes as follows: "In Aberdeenshire, at any rate, folk-singers are not liable to attach 'far more importance to the words than to the music. . . . Folk-poetry and folk-music are essentially and intimately related, and as a general rule the one is incomplete without the other." (*Last Leaves of Traditional Ballads*, pp. xlii-xliii).

the most recent collections is Alton C. Morris's *Folksongs of Florida.* Professor Morris's songs and ballads were contributed largely by native white Floridians whose ancestry can be traced to England, Scotland, and Ireland. The book contains 243 separate pieces; of these 34 are ballads to be found in the Child collection, and 32 are imported ballads without Child numbers. These in the latter group include such titles as "The Butcher Boy," "The Wexford Girl," "Charming Beauty Bright," "The Drowsy Sleeper," "Johnny Sands," "Captain Kidd," "The Miller's Will," and "The Romish Lady." Such ballads are, of course, the British broadsides with which this book is concerned. A larger gathering than that from Florida is Volume II of the *Frank C. Brown Collection of North Carolina Folklore.* This volume contains 314 titles of which 207 are listed as "The Older Ballads—Mostly British." The first 49 of these are Child ballads. At least 75 of the rest can properly be classified as British broadsides. Here one finds, in addition to those mentioned from Florida, such ballads as "Caroline of Edinburgh Town," "William Riley," "The Sheffield Apprentice," "Polly Oliver," "Johnny Doyle," "Green Beds," "The Dark-Eyed Sailor," and "Early, Early in the Spring." An examination of other regional collections will show that the British broadsides are invariably well represented, that the texts are usually good, and that the singers consider them on a par with the other pieces in their repertories. In fact, the broadsides frequently outnumber both the native American ballads and the Child pieces. In Chapter III I shall discuss the popularity of the broadsides in more detail, but enough has been said to show that no apology is needed for devoting a volume to this type of folksong.

No American collection of traditional ballads is devoted exclusively to the broadsides which originated in Britain. Instead these pieces are scattered throughout practically all the anthologies of American folksong. A collection containing only one text of each of these two hundred ninety traditional broadsides would fill a good sized volume, and the addition of variant texts would greatly increase its length. Since space limitations prevent the full reprinting of the ballad texts, the following analysis will give some indication of their subject matter. (More detailed information about each ballad is supplied in Appendix I). Of course no summary of a narrative can do justice to the original, although the loss in pieces of this type is less serious than in more significant works of art.

The broadsides are divided into eight major types: War Ballads, Ballads of Sailors and the Sea, Ballads of Crime and Criminals, Ballads of Family Opposition to Lovers, Ballads of Lovers' Disguises and Tricks, Ballads of Faithful Lovers, Ballads of Unfaithful Lovers, and Humorous and Miscellaneous Ballads. Arbitrary and imperfect as it is, this classification should make the identification and analysis of some of these pieces easier for collectors and editors. In general, I have grouped together ballads of similar subject matter without regard to their probable date or place of origin. The order of presenting the types has no significance.

Under War Ballads I include all pieces dealing primarily with military or naval action or with events related to it. In Ballads of Sailors and the Sea the emphasis is upon occurrences at sea or the experiences of the professional sailor ashore. Ballads of romantic love in which the hero is simply referred to as a soldier or sailor are not included in the first two classes. Criminal acts are committed in many ballads, but such pieces are excluded from Ballads of Crime and Criminals unless the interest is centered upon the criminal and he is looked upon as something of a professional. Most cases of murder, for example, fall more naturally into one of the four classes of love ballads. In the Ballads of Family Opposition to Lovers the action is usually precipitated by the disapproving relative, who is likely to be one of the main actors in the story. Opposition is mentioned in many other ballads, but mainly as a device for getting the story under way. In Ballads of Lovers Disguises and Tricks we have all those pieces in which lovers return unrecognized after long absences and those in which women dress in men's clothes to be near those they love. The trickery in the other ballads is usually some means of insuring a desired marriage. The next two classes deal with Faithful and Unfaithful Lovers. Stories of mutual devotion fall obviously into the first class, but in a number of pieces only one lover remains true. If the unfaithfulness of the other motivates the action, as in several murder ballads, the piece is classified among those of unfaithful lovers. The final group, Humorous and Miscellaneous Ballads contains quite a few pieces different in spirit or story from the rest. Here among others are anti-romantic ballads about marriage, some of them fabliaux, and comical Irish pieces, mainly from the variety stage. The remaining two dozen or so are included here simply because they do not fit well into any other category. The emphasis in the following discussion is primarily upon the subject matter of the stories in a large percentage of the ballads of each class. Other important topics such as origin, distribution, form, style, and variation will be deferred until later chapters.

War Ballads

The War Ballads are a small and not particularly impressive group. There is more of the spirit of actual battle in one such ballad as "Chevy Chase" than in all the broadsides in this category. "Erin Far Away," "The Drummer Boy of Waterloo," and "The Dying Soldier" are sentimentalized accounts of the death in battle of boys whose thoughts are with their families at home. In "Waterloo I" the fanciful broadside style is tempered by a realistic and ironic series of events. We follow the unwilling soldier from his impressment to his return home maimed for life. Again in "Patrick Sheehan" the hard lot of the wounded veteran is depicted. Blinded while serving in the English army, Patrick has no choice but to become a beggar soon after his discharge. Another Irish ballad, "The True Paddy's Song," treats the theme of the reluctant soldier with joyful good humor. The farm boy has an uneventful tour of duty because he refrains from shooting in the fear that the enemy will shoot back. Two ballads entitled "The Plains of Waterloo" (II and III) and "The Heights of Alma" purport to be eye-witness accounts of the major battles they describe. They are only moderately successful in combining the limited view of the single soldier with a summary of the larger events. Unfortunately none of these pieces is able to sustain much dramatic intensity.

Among the War Ballads I have included three pieces which reflect Irish resistance to English rule. "James Ervin" is the story of a boastful young Irishman who has been successful in thwarting his English captors. But the rebel in "Burke's Dream" has lost his freedom and can only imagine himself victorious. Betrayed by a woman he thought he could trust, the youth called "The Croppy Boy" is about to be hanged for his defiance of English authority. The ballad tenderly recounts his final moments on earth.

Among the most interesting of the remaining war pieces are two from the American Revolution. "The Sons of Liberty" is an Irishman's story of the fierce fighting of the American enemy. Perhaps it should have been included in *Native American Balladry* and labeled as a subtle piece of propaganda, but on the other hand it may reflect the admiration of the Irish for those who throw off the English yoke. At any rate the narrator seems sincere in his praise of George Washington and his brave soldiers. A ballad well above the average in dramatic impact is "Donald Monroe," which uses the Sohrab and Rustum theme in a Scottish story of emigration and rebellion. Unknown to their father, who has been in America for some years, his sons enlist in the British army so that they may see their parents. The father fights on the side of the rebels and unknowingly gives one of his sons his death wound. While the style of the ballad has little to recommend it, the plot is effectively handled.

The sea ballads of war also leave much to be desired both in quantity and quality. "The Battle of the Nile" is a tritely phrased account of the British naval victory as experienced by one of the crew, and "Nelson's Victory at Trafalgar" comments briefly on the events surrounding the death of the gallant admiral. "The *Little Fighting Chance*," another relic of the Napoleonic Wars, is a rollicking description of a fierce engagement ending in the capture of the French ship. Three pieces celebrating the victory of H.M.S. *Shannon* over the U.S.S. *Chesapeake* during the War of 1812 have been recovered from tradition. One of these is a fragment, and another may have been composed in Nova Scotia, from which province this meagre crop of sea ballads has come.

From Elizabethan times through the 19th century, every important military and naval event and many minor ones inspired an outpouring of ballads, as the *Stationers' Register* and the broadside collections show. And yet it is not surprising that few of these pieces are traditionally known in America. Unless they are universal in appeal or especially memorable, they are not likely to remain in tradition even in England. The typical folk singer has little historical sense and practically no interest in history as such. And ballads celebrating British military successes would have little appeal for American singers.

Ballads of Sailors and the Sea

Perhaps no group of ballads seems quite so authentic as that which recounts the hazards and hardships of the sea. Ranging from accounts of disasters in which hundreds lost their lives to the tragedies of individuals, they bring home to the reader or listener both the peril of the sailor and the anguish of his loved ones at home. Here in more than a dozen ballads are stories of storms and groundings, of missing men and men killed while whaling, of bitter cold and lightning, and even of the supernatural phenomena which sailors have told of for centuries.

Love is the central theme in a number of ballads of the sea. In several pieces a girl learns that her beloved sailor has been lost at sea, a fate extremely common in this most dangerous of occupations. All joy has gone from the life of the widow in "The Sailor and His Bride," and she would be glad to join her husband in death. In "Farewell, Charming Nancy" the girl watches her lover swept overboard in a storm and dies of shock and grief, and in "Thomas and Nancy," "Scarboro Sand," and "Susan Strayed the Briny Beach" death claims the pairs of lovers in much the same way. The ending of "A Gay Spanish Maid" is ironic as well as tragic. The girl's lover is the only one saved when his ship goes down, but she dies believing that he is lost. The bereaved young women in "The Sailor Boy I" and "Down by the Sea Shore" drown themselves when they hear that their sailor lovers are dead. These romantic and sentimental ballads fail to reflect the proverbial stoicism of seafaring men's loved ones. And yet by expressing the emotions caused by such tragedies, the balladists have struck chords of response among the folk, especially those who know the sea.

Two unusual ballads recovered in Nova Scotia, "Captain Burke" and "By the Ligtning We Lost Our Sight," tell similar stories of seamen who are struck blind by lightning while reefing sail during violent storms. In each the story is told by one of the victims, and the ballads may have been begging songs.[4] A passenger ship

---

[4] The introduction to the American broadside ballad "Bold Dighton" reads in part: "Sold by the Author only. . . . From Wounds which the Author received in Battle, he is unable to obtain a livelihood in the ordinary pursuits of life:—And it is hoped that every Generous American will be ready to participate in the Sufferings of the Unfortunate as well as to Applaud the Brave." (Mackenzie, p. 216).

bound for Liverpool is wrecked in "The Isle of Man Shore." In this a young husband is lost; he has saved his wife but has returned to the ship in a futile attempt to rescue his father. "Lady Franklin's Lament" makes use of the dream device once so beloved by writers of allegory. Instead of presuming to report the lady's feelings directly, the author uses a sailor's dream as a means of speculating upon the fate of Franklin, an explorer missing in the Arctic wastes. In "The Loss of the *Amphitrite*" a ship carrying female convicts goes down with almost complete loss of life. British naval vessels are the victims in three ballads, "The Loss of the *Ramillies*," "Ye Gentlemen of England I," and "The Bay of Biscay, Oh" ("Ye Gentlemen of England II"). The first disaster is by far the worst. Some five hundred men are lost when the ship breaks up. In the other two ballads storms do heavy damage to ships and crews.

"The Guilty Sea Captain" (A and B) and "The *Flying Dutchman*" are stories of the supernatural. In the former a captain proves a Jonah to his crew and is held responsible for the death of many of them in a storm. The A and B versions are somewhat different, but in both the captain eventually confesses that he is a murderer and hence the source of the trouble. "The *Flying Dutchman*" is a short and quite poetic tale of an encounter with that famous ghost ship. Another ballad of the supernatural is the light and fanciful piece called "The Merman." It tells of the happy fate of a sailor who was washed overboard, became the husband of a mermaid, and grew a tail.

The troubles of some of the toilers of the area are recounted in "The Greenland Whale Fishery" and "The Banks of Newfoundland." In the former a whale capsizes a boat and causes the death of five men, and in the latter the narrator and his companions almost freeze to death on a Yankee ship in the North Atlantic.

The following broadside ballads about pirates have been recovered from tradition in America: "The Flying Cloud," "The Bold *Princess Royal*," "The Bold Pirate," "Kelly the Pirate I," "Kelly the Pirate II," "High Barbary," "Bold Daniels," and "Captain Kidd." This is a small but select group. Several of the pieces are firmly established in tradition and are stirring and vigorous. The pirates of whom the balladists wrote usually operated in the Atlantic, the Carribbean, and the Mediterranean. They were frequently a menace to American shipping, and the East Coast of the United States contains many former pirate hideouts with their legends of buried treasure. The pirate ballads, however, seem usually to have been composed in England and to deal with both British pirates and the British ships they encountered. The best of these ballads, "The *Flying Cloud"* is unique in its length, its wealth of detail, and its dealing with both slavery and piracy, two colorful blots on human history. This story of a young man's career in crime seems too vivid not to have been based to some extent on actual events, but so far the origin of the piece has proved elusive. "Captain Kidd" is the confession of a man confirmed in evil and unable to change a course of life that leads inevitably to the gallows. It has something of the desperation of the last act of *Dr. Faustus,* though nothing like Marlowe's poetry. The unknown ballad composer was an artist of considerable talent and knowledge of the human soul.

"High Barbary," which has a spirited tune, tells a vigorous and stirring story of an English victory over a pirate ship. "Bold Daniels" recounts a similar triumph, this time off La Guayra on the Spanish Main. There is less British courage displayed in "The Bold *Princess Royal,"* probably because the merchantman is unarmed. In it the pirates use the device of saying they have mail to deliver, but the captain sees through the scheme and escapes. Another vivid ballad is "The Bold Pirate" in which the pirate captain suffers the maiming which Captain Horatio Hornblower occasionally worries about, that of having both his legs shot off.

It may be said that the crime does not pay theme is used fully in these pieces. There is nothing sordid about them, nothing to be compared, for example, to the ballads of seduction and murder to be discussed later. The highwayman on land and the pirate at sea are romantic figures, especially to those who have had no personal contact with them. But the moralistic balladists will not permit these outlaws final success. They are either sunk or captured, or their intended victims outrun them. But they have had their days of glory before the final debacle, and they have established reputations beyond those of ordinary men.

Humor, sometimes of a rather earthy kind, has crept into many ballads about the sailor ashore. Here some of the less attractive facets of human nature are convincingly displayed. Typical pieces tell of the returned sailor's treatment by tavern keepers and girls of the port. Of these "Green Beds" or "Johnny the Sailor" is the most popular. When Johnny pretends he has lost all his money, the innkeeper doesn't want her daughter to have anything to do with him. But when Johnny produces his gold, he is invited to share the girl's bedroom. Now it is Johnny's turn to refuse. He announces that he will go to a tavern to find girls and whiskey. Similar stories are told in "Will You Wed with a Tarry Sailor?" and "Jack the Jolly Tar II." In "Jack Tar" the sailor enjoys wine, women, and song until his money runs out, and then he is ejected. In "Tarry Sailor" Jack fares much better, though the morality of the piece is dubious. By substituting himself for the man with whom a girl has a midnight assignation, he is able both to enjoy his amours and to get revenge upon a landsman. Then there is the well known piece variously entitled "Home, Dearie, Home," "Jack the Sailor Boy," and "Bell Bottom Trousers." After spending the night with the girl who has lighted him to his tavern room, the sailor gives her gold and offers some gratuitous advice about the possible baby to come. But the sailor also has dealings with shadier women of the waterfront. In "Gold Watch" the girl he picks up and spends part of the night with sneaks away with the sailor's watch and money. And in "The Shirt and the Apron" the girl takes not only her victim's pay but all his clothes. Although not factual, these ballads are fairly accurate in spirit. The sailors are not individualized and they need not be, because their experiences are only too familiar to men of their profession. When the sailor appeared on shore after a long voyage, he wanted his pleasure and was proverbially willing to pay for it. The greedy landsman would try to take all he had in a short time and leave the sailor no choice but to return to sea.

BALLADS OF CRIME AND CRIMINALS

Most of the ballads about crime and criminals fall into well defined types: stories of encounters with unnamed highwaymen, songs about famous highwaymen and outlaws, laments of condemned men—or "good-nights," and ballads about transported convicts. The first group is full of excitement and adventure. In fact Professor Child, despite a certain prejudice against broadside pieces, included "The Crafty Farmer" among his ballads. "The Yorkshire Bite" and "The Highwayman Outwitted" are ballads so similar in style and substance to "The Crafty Farmer" that it is impossible to establish priority for any one of the three. In "The Yorkshire

Bite" (or Yorkshire trick) a boy is held up while returning to his master after selling a cow. He scatters the money on the ground, and, while the robber is retrieving it, rides away on the thief's horse with its saddle bags full of loot. "The Highwayman Outwitted" tells a similar story with certain striking differences in detail. In this the intended victim is a merchant's daughter. After she dismounts, the robber strips her and forces her to hold his horse, while he chases hers, which has run home. She jumps onto the robber's horse and rides home with his gold and diamonds. "The Three Butchers" is a bloody story of robbery and murder which is widely sung and which may have been in tradition for more than 250 years. In this the robbers use a naked woman as a decoy, and at her signal descend upon the men who have tried to help her. Johnson, the one brave butcher, kills eight of his adversaries but is himself done to death by the woman with a blow from behind. The girl in "The Undaunted Female" shows even more valor than the one in "The Highwayman Outwitted." While walking home, she not only kills a highwayman who has tried to rob her, but later, in the presence of a new male friend, finishes off three of the thief's companions after calling them from the woods with his whistle. It will be seen that in all these ballads the intended victims turn the tables on the robbers. Apparently the folk do not always identify themselves with the criminal.

In the ballads about famous highwaymen and outlaws, the central characters have certain heroic qualities. "Jack Sheppard" is a lively account of some of the high spots in the career of the 18th century highwayman celebrated in Ainsworth's novel. Two ballads about Dick Turpin, another notorious 18th century robber, are more firmly established in tradition. "My Bonny Black Bess II" is a sentimental monologue in which Turpin addresses his horse and praises her for her speed and loyalty. He shoots her as his own career ends rather than have her fall into a stranger's hands. In "My Bonny Black Bess I," he commits a holdup and then establishes an alibi by fast riding and trickery. In "Dick Turpin and the Lawyer," Dick who is travelling incognito, tricks a lawyer into revealing the hiding place of his money and later robs him. The impression left by these two ballads is that the robber's cleverness is much to be admired. The most effective folksong of this group is the Irish ballad "Brennan on the Moor." Before his career ends on the scaffold, Brennan has had a series of dangerous adventures and has always maintained his courage and good humor.

These almost legendary characters are replaced in another group of ballads by a series of rather pathetic and obscure young men whose short lives of crime are coming to an unhappy close. The best known of these is the lament usually called "The Boston Burglar" in America, though the burglar may come from other cities. This is only a slightly changed version of the ballad "Botany Bay," in which a convict is about to be transported to the Australian penal colony. In "Jack Williams" the young thief who has robbed to obtain money for his girl is also sentenced to Botany Bay, and he in "The Irish Mail Robber" meets the same fate. An even less fortunate group is represented in "The Rambling Boy" and "The Irish Robber" in which the defendants are sentenced to hang. Less realistic but more cheerful is "Gallows," a piece reminiscent of "The Maid Freed from the Gallows" (Child no. 95). In this the young man is saved at the last minute after his family and his priest have done everything possible to delay the hanging. His true love rides up in the manner beloved of melodrama, with his pardon signed by the king. "The Poacher's Fate" sounds as if it might be based on fact, since it is a rather circumstantial account of a youth who is shot by a keeper while poaching with some friends. Another story about the fate of poachers is "Van Dieman's Land," which describes the hardships of transported convicts who are sold to planters and yoked to plows.

In four other ballads which seem to have originated in Australia, transported Irish convicts, undaunted by their new surroundings, continue their illegal careers until they meet death by shooting or hanging. Three of them, "I Am a Wild Young Irish Boy," "The Wild Colonial Boy," and "Johnny Troy," display the criminals' charity. In the first ballad the outlaw is especially considerate: although he has killed five policemen, he lets a sixth escape for the sake of his wife and children, and when he is dying he reveals his identity so that a poor newsboy's mother may get the bounty offered for his capture. Among the incidents of Johnny Troy's career is that of taking pity upon an old man he intended to rob when he hears that his victim is a former convict and the father of a large family. The most famous ballad in this group is "Jack

Donahue." Jack dies in a gunfight with the police rather than face the gallows.

Finally there is the ballad about Jack Hall, which is sometimes called "Sam Hall" in American tradition. Jack is probably unique among ballad criminals in that he not only does not repent at the moment of death but curses all who have come to see him die. Usually the condemned man is in a softer and more sentimental mood. He grieves for the loved ones he must leave and if he is guilty is quite remorseful about his life of crime.

It could hardly be said that many of these ballads glorify crime. None of the criminals grows rich before dying penitent as did DeFoe's Moll Flanders. Many are penitent and not a few die, but one usually feels that they have come to a bad end. If they serve the purpose of bringing some excitement into the lives of those who hear them, the ballads also harp upon the theme that the wages of sin is death.

Ballads of Family Opposition to Lovers

The basic conflict in more than three dozen ballads of love results from the parents' strong disapproval of their child's choice of a partner. Parental hostility is rarely passive or verbal but takes the form of direct action to separate the lovers permanently. The sympathy of the balladist is always with the lovers; the parents are portrayed in various degrees of villainy, and no compromise between the generations is possible. The defeat of the opposition becomes second in importance only to a successful elopement and marriage. Family opposition seems invariably based on social and financial rather than moral considerations. We are led to believe that the loved one's motives are worthy and that he is of high moral character. Thus the attitude of the parents, or more rarely of other members of the family, is portrayed as reprehensible.

In a typical ballad of this type, a rich man's daughter falls in love with a youth of low social rank. The girl's parents then attempt to get rid of the youth, sometimes by arranging for a press-gang to perform a legal kidnapping and take the boy to sea.[5] In "The Jolly

---

[5] Frank Kidson had this to say on the subject: "But above all there are the press-gang songs. In nearly every case the story is to the effect that a farmer's son in love with a squire's daughter is, by the father's contrivance, pressed for sea. This is by no means an improbable circumstance,

Ploughboy" and "The Banks of Dundee" a father and an uncle use this device, though with only temporary success. The youth in "The Tan-Yard Side" is treated in the same manner and must travel far from his girl, while the unfortunate victim in "The *Nightingale*" dies in a shipwreck. Some of the families are more direct and brutal. In "The Bramble Briar" and "The Constant Farmer's Son" the rich girl's brothers lure her fiancé into the woods and murder him, much as the bridegroom is murdered in "The Braes of Yarrow" (Child no. 214). More frequently the girl's father attacks her lover or sends others to dispose of him. In "Lovely Willie" the father stabs Willie to death, and in "The Drowsy Sleeper" the youth avoids a similar fate by heeding the girl's timely warning. In "Edwin in the Lowlands Low" the innkeeper robs and murders his daughter's lover, though he is apparently unaware of the youth's identity. In the stirring ballad "The Bold Soldier" the young man is attacked by seven armed men hired by the girl's father to waylay him, but he fights so fiercely that the terrified old man yields his possessions as well as his daughter.

In various ballads, mostly Irish, parents attempt to have their daughters' suitors convicted of robbery or kidnapping.[6] In "Henry Connors", as a result of false evidence of thievery, the youth is sentenced to be transported, and in "Erin's Lovely Home" the young man is convicted of kidnapping the girl, though he was merely eloping with her. William Riley faces the same charge, but is freed by the girl's defense of him, and Mary Ackland and Mary Neal likewise win in court against their fathers. The record of parental viciousness continues with such tricks as intercepting the lover's letters and informing the girl that he is dead, as in "Early, Early in the Spring", forcing her to marry someone else, as in "Johnny

---

for, in the scandalous system of the impressment of seamen, the press was not solely confined to seaport towns: country villages were raided, and young men who had perhaps never seen the sea in their lives—ill-treated or maimed in the scuffle—were taken away at a minute's notice, possibly never to return. So recent was this that I personally know of men, living but a few years back, who had been victims of these village raids." (*JFSS* I, 41.)

[6] Parental objection in these cases seems to have been based on both social and religious grounds. In this connection see the note to "William Riley" (M 10) in Appendix I.

Doyle", or imprisoning her, as in "Charming Beauty Bright". The girls in the latter two ballads die of grief, as do so many of the young lovers in broadside balladry.

Ballads of Lovers' Disguises and Tricks

Some of the ballads of lovers' disguises and tricks are closely related to those in the previous section, since the tricks are frequently necessary to thwart disapproving parents. "Disguised Sailor" and "Jack Monroe" are representative of a large class of ballads in which the girl disguises herself in men's clothes and follows her lover to sea or to war.[7] In the former piece, the youth is pressed to sea by the rich merchant whose daughter he loves, and in the latter the lover goes to the wars of Germany followed by the girl. In most of these ballads the adventures of the disguised girl become of primary importance. Miss Gordie in "The Duke of Argyle" continues to fight in Egypt after her lover is slain, and the Scottish farmer's daughter is shot dead in "The Paisley Officer" while caring for her lover, who has been fatally wounded. The story of Jane Thornton, which is told in "Female Sailor Bold", is devoted mainly to an account of the girl's adventures on shipboard after she hears of her fiancée's death. Some of these heroines display remarkable seamanship on short notice. Only The Female Warrior takes the precaution of learning to sail before embarking on a British warship. She makes good use of her knowledge when the captain is slain, and defeats the French ship in a fierce battle. In "The *Lady Leroy*" a new twist is added to an old story. The girl in disguise purchases one of her father's ships for her elopement and soundly defeats the vessel which he sends in pursuit.

The outcome of these excursions into a man's world is not always predictable. Although the basic situations are tediously repetitious, the balladists have produced some original endings. In "The Noble Duke" the girl disguises herself as a duke, follows her lover to sea, and arrests him on a charge of stealing her treasure. "William Taylor" tells of a young woman who searches for her lover only to discover that he has acquired another love. The jilted girl shoots William dead and marries the ship's captain. Few ballads contain such a refreshing departure from sentimentality.

---

[7] See the notes to "Female Sailor Bold" (N 3) in Appendix I.

Sometimes it is the young man whose cleverness overcomes the opposition of a parent. In a ballad that sound like a medieval tale, the hero of "Love in the Tub" appeals to his prospective father-in-law's cupidity by offering to buy the contents of an apparently empty wine cask. Too late the merchant discovers that his daughter is hidden inside. In "The Lawyer Outwitted" the lover plans an elopement but takes precautions against being charged with kidnapping. The lawyer advises his young client to marry his fiancée quickly, after eloping on a horse provided by her. Eventually the lawyer learns that he was planning his own daughter's wedding.

Some ballad heroines take the initiative in effecting a desired marriage. In "Kate and Her Horns" the girl frightens her straying lover into a wedding by confronting him at night disguised as the devil and extracting from him a promise of loyalty to Kate. In "The Half-Hitch" the young lady's pretended fickleness works to her advantage. She so annoys her fiancé that he promises to marry the first woman he meets. She dresses as a disreputable beggar, forces him to keep his bargain, and makes him miserable for a while after their marriage before revealing her identity. This, of course, is the knight and the loathely lady motif in fairly modern dress. The lady in "The Golden Glove" decides that she loves a farmer rather than the squire she had planned to marry. While hunting in men's clothes, she leaves her glove at the farmer's cottage and then announces that she will marry the man who finds it. As might be expected, the farmer is a willing bridegroom.

Ballad lovers frequently test the devotion of the girls they have not seen for several years. No group of broadsides is more stereotyped than those in which the returned lover poses as a stranger and attempts to make love to the one who is waiting for him. She invariably spurns him, announces her loyalty to her absent lover, and describes him. This is the man's clue to report that her lover has been killed in battle or shipwreck. As the girl swoons, the youth reveals his identity, often by producing his half of a ring once broken as a pledge of fidelity. All is now well, and nothing is said either about the man's cruelty or the girl's poor eyesight. This story is repeated with minor variations in at least sixteen of the ballads sung in this country. In an occasional ballad of this class, an attempt is made to relate the incident to some contemporary event. Thus in "The Mantle So Green" William O'Reilly is said to have died at Waterloo, and in "The *Lady of the Lake*" the youth reports his own death in a recent shipwreck. One is inclined at first glance to consider these ballad stories extremely far-fetched. It is worth observing, however, that a century or two ago boys did go away to sea for years at a time. Communication with those at home was erratic or non-existent, and young lovers naturally worried about the devotion of their girls. Even the failure of the women to recognize their lovers seems less incredible when we recall that many a smooth-faced boy returned from sea a bearded man. But we need not take such ballads too seriously, since they were designed primarily as romantic entertainment.

BALLADS OF FAITHFUL LOVERS

The ballads of faithful lovers deal primarily with lovers' meetings and the events which result from them, or with acts which show exceptional devotion. Those with weak narrative and dramatic action have gained little currency in tradition, but enough of them have been recorded to show that the type is well known. In "The Gypsy Maid", "Ellen the Fair", and "The Lass of Glenshee", a fortune teller, a flower-seller, and a shepherdess attract the attention of wealthy men who fall in love with them at first sight and marry them shortly thereafter. Although surprised by the suddenness of their romances, the girls seem satisfied with their new status. In "The Sailor and the Shepherdess" and "Branded Lambs" young girls are successfully wooed in a pastoral setting, as is the young farmer to whom the rich lady is attracted in "Cupid the Plowboy". Other rustic romances are depicted in "Two Rigs of Rye" and "Robin Tamson's Smiddy". Pretty Betsey the Milkmaid finds herself in a predicament like that of Richardson's Pamela and is equally successful, first in warding off the squire's attempt to attack her and later in marrying him.

In several of the ballads the man visits the girl at her home with varying results, and in one the girl visits the man. In "Seventeen Come Sunday" the lover's visit is interrupted by the girl's justly suspicious mother; in "The Bonny Wee Window" Johnny's head becomes stuck in the window frame; and "When a Man's in Love" ends in marriage and a proposed emigration to America. "Rich Amerikay" tells much the same story as the last piece, except that here we have again the rich lady and the poor young man. The well known ballad "The Foggy Dew" tells the story of an illicit romance and the birth of a child. In some texts the father lives alone with his son; in others the parents are happily married. On first reading, "The Bold Fisherman" seems to be just one more slight ballad about the meeting of lovers. But Miss Lucy Broadwood has convincingly demonstrated that it may be interpreted as a piece of religious symbolism in which Christ is the fisherman and the bridegroom who takes the lady to his father's house.

But not all the ballads of faithful love end cheerfully. Many are filled with the tears of parting. Dark-Eyed Susan must part with her sailor William, and the girls in "Erin's Flowery Vale", "Jimmy and His Own True Love", "Soldier Boy", and several other ballads watch sadly as their lovers leave for foreign countries, the sea, or war. "Burns and His Highland Mary" is unique in presenting a poet and the young woman he wanted to marry as the central characters of a ballad. This piece retells the sad story which Burns himself had already immortalized. "A-Growing", a fine old ballad generally considered worthy of a place in the Child collection, is a widow's lament for her young husband, who has died before reaching manhood. In the supernatural Irish ballad "Molly Bawn", the man shoots his true love by mistake, but is saved from punishment by the appearance of the girl's ghost to plead for him at his trial. The women in "The Silvery Tide" and "Fair Fanny Moore" remain loyal to the men they love and are murdered by men whose advances they spurn. And finally the Sheffield Apprentice, by remaining true to Polly the chambermaid, signs his own death warrant. The rich woman who is his employer has him falsely sentenced as a thief when he refuses her offer of marriage.

BALLADS OF UNFAITHFUL LOVERS

In the pieces which I have designated "Ballads of Unfaithful Lovers", it is usually the disloyalty of only one lover which produces the conflict and hence the ballad story. Sometimes, as in "The Girl I Left Behind B" and "The Pride of Kildare", it is the girl who proves unfaithful. In each of these ballads the man accepts his fate, but in others he gives the girl a dose of her own medicine. Thus in "A Rich Irish Lady" the once rejected lover is delighted to hear that the girl is now dying of love for him and looks forward to dancing on her grave. Other men who have been spurned, such as those in "The Rejected Lover" and "Nancy I" are less ghoulish but no less adamant.

The fickleness of women may have a tragic outcome as it does in "The Lily of the West" when a distracted suitor stabs his rival to death. In "Oxford City" a servant poisons both the lady he loves and himself after she has said they are too young to marry. In "A Nobleman's Wedding" a bride dies of remorse for having broken her pledge of faithfulness to another man, and in "William and Nancy II" both lovers die of broken hearts after a brief reunion. William had sailed away leaving Nancy to marry someone else.

In more typical ballads than those just mentioned, one finds a grieving girl who has been cast off by the man who once professed love for her. Some of these pieces can be classified, in Professor Belden's phrase, as ballads of wayside seduction. The type is common to both the Child ballads and the broadsides, and the lament of the forsaken girl is equally familiar in lyric folksong. Among the best known of these ballads is "The Nightingale" or "One Morning in May". In thinly veiled symbolism we learn that the girl yields to the soldier in the hope of future marriage only to learn that he already has a wife. What was merely an interlude for him becomes a tragedy for her. The character of Rinordine is more mysterious in that he lives in hiding in a mountain castle, but the result of his chance meeting with the girl is the same. Other country girls are seduced in such ballads as "The Dawning of the Day", "Pretty Little Miss", and "Tripping Over the Lea". The emphasis in these pieces is upon the falseness of the men, and they usually end with a warning to other girls against deceivers. Though their narrative content is slight and unoriginal, they have a certain timelessness and poignancy.

The balladist may tell of events which follow the discovery of unfaithfulness. Sometimes the girls die of broken hearts, as in "Love Has Brought Me to Despair" and "The Bonny Irish Boy". In "The Butcher Boy", one of the most widely sung of all ballads, a jilted girl hangs herself, and in "Caroline of Edinburgh Town another girl plunges into the sea. Some of the girls die of exposure and despair, with babies in their arms, as in "The Fatal Snowstorm" and "Mary of the Wild Moor".

In the ballads, as in life, murder may be the outcome of a love which has become burdensome. *An American Tragedy* told a story already too familiar to ballad-makers here and abroad. Usually the man lures his pregnant fiancée to a lonely spot on the pretext of planning their wedding. He then announces that he will kill her. She pleads for her life and that of her baby, but he brutally murders her and attempts to conceal the body. The crime is soon revealed, frequently by supernatural means, and the murderer is executed. This story, with variations, may be found in "The Oxford Girl", "The Cruel Ship's Carpenter", "The Old Oak Tree", "James Mac-Donald", and "Pat O'Brien". In "The Old Oak Tree" the murdered girl's wounds bleed afresh in the presence of her slayer, and in "The Cruel Ship's Carpenter" the girl's ghost, carrying a ghostly baby, hounds the carpenter to death on shipboard. Revenge upon the unfaithful lover is the subject of several other ballads. Handsome Harry is pursued and drowned by the ghost of his victim, and the ghosts of male suicides in "A Gentleman of Exeter" and "Susannah Clargy" claim the girls who had promised to be true and had then become other men's brides.

Humorous and Miscellaneous Ballads

The ballads of married life are almost invariably unromantic and humorous. Some of them are closely related to the prose fabliaux of the Middle Ages in that they use infidelity as a theme and make the playing of tricks the main feature of the plot. In most of them one partner is ignominiously defeated, sometimes without realizing it. In ballads of this type, accidents, beatings, and even death are treated with rollicking good humor. The characters are rarely individualized; they may be considered embodiments of various unattractive but familiar human traits.

In the "Old Woman of Slapsadam" and its derivative "Johnny Sands", each member of the marital partnership would be glad to be rid of the other. The husband asks his wife's aid in committing suicide by drowning and then steps aside as she runs to push him into the water. She takes the fatal leap instead. The husband in "The Holly Twig" beats his scolding wife so severely that he sends her soul to hell. A little devil carries her away, and another husband is at peace. (This recalls "The Farmer's Curst Wife", Child no. 278). But the husbands are not always triumphant. The one in "The Rich Old Miser", after beating his bride without cause, is brought to terms when she applies the same treatment to him. The

Husband in "The Dumb Wife" has reason to regret his solicitude when a doctor cures the lady's dumbness but is unable to provide a remedy for a suddenly loosened tongue. And in the most enjoyable and popular of these pieces, Father Grumble's belief that he works harder than his wife is forcibly changed when he attempts to take over her chores for one day.

In ballads closer in plot to the fabliaux, the wives use various devices to keep their husbands from proving their infidelity, but in only one is the wife entirely successful. In "The Boatsman and the Chest" and "Will the Weaver" the husband first pretends ignorance of the whereabouts of his wife's lover. In the former he has a chest containing the lover carried with him to sea, and in the latter he builds a fire to smoke out his rival, who is hiding on the chimney pole. The husband's victory in "The Major and the Weaver" is less complete but still satisfying, if we ignore the moral aspects of the situation. The weaver dons the major's trousers by mistake as the latter hides under the bed. He decides that he is entitled to the trousers and the money in them, since he is sharing his wife with the major. "The Dog in the Closet" starts out rather like the other ballads with the husband correctly believing that he has his wife's lover locked in a closet. But when he returns with help, he is embarrassed to find only a dog where the lover should have been. Having made the substitution, his wife insists upon and receives an apology.

We now come to a series of comic Irish ballads which could hardly have been considered folksongs in the last century but have since attained that status. Various collections of American songs and ballads contain Irish narrative songs which have entered tradition largely by way of the variety stage and the comic songster. Many of these I have excluded because their stories are not told in the ballad manner but depend mainly upon humorous description and dialogue for their effect. But among the others are several which tell their stories with more simplicity and directness and without recourse to many verbal tricks. These, too, display the Irishman's extraordinary talent for good-natured portrayal of various aspects of the Irish character.

"The Monkey Turned Barber" tells of an Irishman who mistakes a monkey for the barber's elderly father. Pat asks for a shave, and the monkey reacts with dire results for the customer. In "The Love-of-God Shave" another Pat has a miserable time in the barber's chair for a different reason. He has asked for a shave on credit, and the barber, to discourage such people, tortures Pat with a rusty old razor until he runs from the shop. "Doran's Ass" is as pleasantly preposterous as "The Monkey Turned Barber". Still another Pat, this one dozing drunk along the roadside, mistakes Doran's ass for his true love and is terrified by the donkey's loud braying. The Irish custom of holding wakes also provides material for humorous stories. "Finnegan's Wake", which gave James Joyce a title, deals with the proverbial toughness of the Irish. Though Tim Finnegan has fallen from a ladder and cracked his skull, his family discovers that they are premature in holding a wake for him. Some whiskey is spilled on Tim, and he quickly revives. "The Irish Wake" is even more farcical. Pat's plan to collect his life insurance misfires because he carries it to its logical conclusion. During the wake Pat tries to lie still while his friends consume his whiskey, but later he is unable to stand the strain of hearing the earth fall on his own coffin and bursts from his grave. More realistic, though no less boisterous, is "Courting in the Kitchen". In order to save her job and perhaps her reputation, the girl turns against the man who has come to court her and has him arrested for robbery and assault. Such ballads as these, with their cheerful distortions of actuality, are highly entertaining, and they exhibit more technical skill and verbal originality than one usually finds in broadside balladry.

Another humorous ballad, probably English, has been frequently recorded from American tradition. This is the dialogue called "The Miller's Will" or "The Miller's Three Sons". After questioning his sons, the dying miller decides to leave the mill to the youngest because that youth would not take merely a peck or two from each farmer's bushel but would take three pecks and leave the customer one. The old miller is happy at the thought that larceny will continue on the same scale as before.

Other Irish ballads more conventional in subject matter and treatment fall into the miscellaneous group. One of the most beautiful is the supernatural ballad "The Lake of Cool Finn". The central event, the accidental drowning of a youth on a morning swim, is embellished and made vivid by a suggestion of some mysterious and supernatural force which causes the boy's death. He has time to warn his friend against following him before he disappears from sight. His sister learns in a dream that he has drowned. One justifiable complaint against the broadsides is that they have lost the suggestive power of the old balladry. In "The Lake of Cool Finn", among a few other pieces, that quality can be found.

Utterly outside the realm of poetry, though clearly within the ranks of balladry, is a piece called "Tom O'Neill". Tom almost has his career as a priest ruined when the rich girl he has rejected accuses him of fathering her unborn child. At the last possible moment Tom's name is cleared and the girl's plot is revealed by her partner, the actual father of the child. The story is sensational enough to hold anyone's interest, but the telling of it is miserably labored and inept.

A ballad displaying sectarian prejudice is "The Romish Lady", which dates at least from the early 17th century, though the oral tradition of American texts may not have nearly so long a history. The ballad tells of the troubles of a girl with Protestant inclinations who turns against Catholicism and refuses to follow the teachings of the priests. Reported to the authorities by her mother, she is imprisoned, tried before the pope, and at length burned as a heretic. The balladist's sympathy is obviously with the unfortunate girl, who dies nobly for a high cause. The appeal of such a piece to those suspicious of the Church of Rome is obvious.

A few ballads about sporting events have found their way into American tradition. "Creeping Jane" is the lively story of a slow horse with plenty of endurance which surprises everyone by winning her race. The Irish ballad "Skewball" adds a fanciful note by having the horse talk to its rider and accurately predict a victory. Oddly enough this ballad has turned up considerably altered in American Negro tradition.

From this point on the ballads become increasingly diverse in subject matter. "The Soldier's Poor Little Boy", "The Fisherman's Boy," and "The Farmer's Boy" are sentimental accounts of fortunate orphans literally or figuratively taken in out of the cold. From a material point of view, the farmer's boy is the most successful, since he not only inherits the farmer's lands but wins the hand of his daughter.

"The High Blantyre Explosion" and "The Miner's Doom" are somewhat romanticized accounts of coal mining accidents. Both ballads have been recorded in this country only from the coal fields of Pennsylvania. As far as I know these are the only ballads about British land disasters which have been found in America.

Among the remaining ballads worthy of mention are two of considerable age in which the Middle East is used as a setting. "The Valiant London Prentice" and "The Factor's Garland" have no artistic merit, but their stories are remarkable. The first is a ridiculous piece of jingoism in which a young Englishman asserts Queen Elizabeth's superiority over all other rulers and defends his statement in an illogical but effective manner. First he kills the Turkish king's son in a fight, and then he disposes of two lions by thrusting his arms simultaneously down their throats and tearing out their hearts. The king's reaction, which is not analyzed, is to offer the prentice his daughter in marriage. The other ballad, which is a curious mixture of ancient narrative elements and fairly modern phrasing, tells a long and complicated story with the "grateful dead" motif familiar in folklore. After many vicissitudes, the Englishman and the foreign princess are eventually joined in marriage. But this is not the end of the tale. The author covers several more years of their lives before bringing this almost endless ballad to a conclusion.

Finally a word should be said about "The Children in the Wood". This lengthy and pathetic old ballad has attracted considerable attention since Addison praised it.[8] Its style does not rise above the usual broadside level, but the story it tells successfully combines many well worn melodramatic features. The greed and cruelty of the uncle, the battle between the hired slayers, the death of the children—these are story elements of proven appeal. The ballad is cheerless but touching, and its ending is morally satisfying. Probably its unusual length has kept it from achieving greater traditional dispersion.

The foregoing analysis of the broadside types found in America has, I fear, been rather tedious. But it was necessary to demonstrate both the range of ballad subject matter and its limitations. Parallels between certain ballad stories and works of standard literature in various languages will undoubtedly have occurred to the reader. Literature has influenced balladry and vice versa, and both have arisen from the universal fascination of human life. To the ballad maker as to other creators of unsophisticated narratives, the action

---

[8] The *Spectator*, no. 85.

or plot is all important. To the literary artist the plot may be the least significant part of what he is trying to communicate. Each has his own purpose, his own idea of what the final product should be, and his own audience. For reasons which I hope to make clear, the broadside ballad writers have been as successful in their undemanding field as many a greater story teller has in his.

THE APPEAL OF THE BROADSIDE BALLADS

No one, of course, is under any compulsion to remember ballads or to sing them. Many members of the folk, especially those of strict religious training, look upon even the innocuous pieces as sinful songs, and the younger generation leans toward the music of the radio and the record player. Thus balladry is not always available where one expects to find it. But where an educated person will feel an obligation to know something about his native written literature, the folk, whether literate or not, will sing the broadside ballads simply because they like them. Folksongs in general have aesthetic appeal for those who love them, and despite their crudeness, they help to satisfy the universal human need for emotional expression, for art, and for beauty.

Some further evidence about American taste in balladry is gained from studying the traditional broadsides collected in the British Isles. Many of the ballads are widely known on both sides of the Atlantic, but a considerable body of balladry is not known in this country. It is axiomatic that a ballad must be basically understandable and significant to the singer. Ballads which require special knowledge of British social conditions and occupations are not likely to be sung in this country, nor are pieces of primarily local or regional interest.[9]

The British broadside tradition is strong in America primarily because the ballads were composed for the folk and inevitably catered to their demands. The basic appeals of the broadsides are those of all plotted narratives, whatever their literary form or their place of origin. As can be seen from the brief summaries already

---

[9] Many ballads of British rather than American interest may be found in the *Journal of the Folk-Song Society*, in Sharp and Marson's *Folk-Songs from Somerset*, and elsewhere. See for example "The Tythe-Pig", "Parson Hogg", "Widdicome Fair", "The Warson Hunt", and "Green Broom" in Baring-Gould's *Songs of the West*.

given, the ballads deal mainly with subjects of great intrinsic interest to all human beings. War and lesser human conflicts, crime and punishment, violence and death, love and sex, humor and trickery, hatred and revenge, dangerous adventures and calamities —these were among the favorite subjects of the balladists, just as they have been grist for the mill of the scops, the epic poets, the novelists, the newspapermen, the county historians, and the playwrights. Such subjects have universal appeal because as fact or fiction they record the most moving, dramatic, and exciting occurrences of life itself. The ballads offer a wealth of vicarious experience to people whose lives are restricted socially or geographically. The typical folk singer reacts emotionally to his story and firmly believes that it is true. He is likely to weep if the tale is tragic, to grow angry at villainy, and to rejoice when the sympathetic characters are triumphant. The naive sincerity of such reactions is ample proof of the power of balladry over the folk. Nor is it the person of simple tastes alone who finds himself affected by the ballads. Sir Philip Sidney, in a frequently quoted passage,[10] told of the effect of a Chevy Chase ballad upon him, and many later writers have added their confessions to his.

More often, people of literary taste and training have made uncomplimentary remarks about broadside balladry. Their reactions have ranged from polite condescension to scorn. Certainly the broadsides are practically defenseless against literary attack. But neither the literary nor the social historian can afford to ignore a product which has endured over the centuries, which has seen other literary types come and go, and which, like the legitimate theater, is continually about to expire but never does so. It is a mistake to think of the traditional broadsides as mere journalistic scribblings. Had they had nothing to offer but news of momentary interest, they would have long since passed into oblivion. But the ballads, whether or not they were originally based on current happenings, had and have, to quote Coleridge out of context, "a human interest and a semblance of truth sufficient to procure for these shadows of the imagination" not "a willing suspension of disbelief" but belief itself.[11] The broadsides are not so much pure journalism as "pure" literature, that is, they are narratives stripped to their bare dramatic

---

[10] *The Defense of Poesie*, ed. A. S. Cook, p. 29.
[11] *Biographia Literaria*, chapter XIV.

and expository essentials and flourishing without the benefit of genius or even of much artistry.

But it is not only as folk literature that the traditional broadsides merit scholarly attention. Inevitably they reflect the customs, the morals, and the living conditions of the people by whom and for whom they were produced. I can think of no comparable body of living literature which has been so widely published over so long a time and which reveals so much about the past while remaining practically timeless.

Of course a broadside ballad need not become traditional to be of interest as a social document. The expertly edited collections of Professor Hyder Rollins, mainly of non-traditional ballads of the 16th and 17th centuries, are of extraordinary human and historical value. Fortunately some contemporary collectors like Samuel Pepys recognized the value of this throw-away literature and helped to preserve it. Gradually attitudes toward the broadsides changed, and today many great libraries treasure their ballad holdings. Professor H. M. Belden has made the following colorful observations about the later broadsides including those we are studying:

> In the 'large room' of the British Museum, to which faithful students are admitted after a due period of probation, stands a row of solemn, dignified volumes represented in the Museum catalogue by the pressmark Bks. 3. g. 4. Here, amid surroundings never dreamed of by the authors and publishers, the *fliegende blaetter* of the ballad printers of the last century,—Pitts, and Such, and Old Jemmy Catnach, "King of the Picts,"—have found a dim and chilly immortality. Roaring songs of the public house, sentimental ditties of the faithful loves of soldiers, apprentices, political catches, and the last words (in verse) of noted criminals; execrably printed, for the most part, on galley slips of various sizes, with woodcuts of unimaginable rudeness; intended to be hawked about in the streets of the capital and at rural fairs, droned forth by beggars and cripples, or trolled out in the haunts of vulgar mirth,— they have been carefully pasted in the somber folios of Bks. 3. g. 4, and there await the curious student of nineteenth century civilization.[12]

If these fugitive leaves, which include hundreds of pieces eventually or immediately rejected by the folk, are worthy of careful preservation and study, those comparatively few ballads from among them

---

[12] "The Vulgar Ballad", *Sewanee Review* XIX (1911), 214-215. As Appendix I indicates , the printers mentioned by Belden were among the most prolific distributors of the broadsides now traditional in America.

which have found an honored place in the folk memory can hardly be less so. They represent the separation of wheat from chaff and the retention of what, to the folk at least, is of permanent value.

If a stranger wanted to know about the composite character of the common people in the English speaking world, he could hardly do better than to study their traditional ballads. Certainly the sophisticated literature of either England or America would not serve the same purpose because it gives the individual views of its authors, while balladry speaks for the people themselves, even for the illiterate. In the ballads we find reflected the tastes of the people, their level of education, their ethical and moral sense, their religious attitudes, their half-concealed desires, their concept of outsiders, their views on an almost endless variety of subjects, both those touching their own lives and those beyond their realm of experience. Admittedly the ballads are often dull, prosaic, and conventional, but so also is the life of the average man. We may grant, too, that they are frequently ludicrous, but even the distortions and idealizations of reality, which are easy to recognize in many ballads, are indicative of the attitudes of the people. Like the professional writers of higher standing, the balladists produced material both familiar and exotic. The two types seem to merge in the minds of singer and audience until the imaginative ballad world is almost as real as the world of actuality. The scholar comes to know something of both worlds, and as his understanding increases he gains the privilege of seeing into the hearts of the folk. Eventually he realizes that in addition to reflections of national or local customs and character, the broadsides possess, in common with great literature, a more basic ingredient. The ballad stories endure because they are concerned with those fundamental qualities of human nature which remain constant in an otherwise changing world.

Chapter II

The Origin and Distribution
Of the Broadside Ballads

The broadside ballad as a partially new type of popular literature seems to have developed in England in the 16th century. Scholars generally agree that the narrative songs which we call ballads did not appear in considerable numbers until about 1550, although some broadside publications in verse are of earlier date. Since popular ballads of the folk type and the minstrel type had long been in existence, the broadside ballad may be considered more a journalistic adaptation than a completely new invention. Professor Gummere related the broadsides in the Child collection to the minstrel ballads,[1] and other scholars have followed this view, pointing out certain features which the types have in common. The address to the audience, the pious observations, the emphasis upon the veracity of the narrator, and the large amount of specific detail are characteristic of both broadside and minstrel ballads but not of the best examples of Child's folk ballads.[2]

Since practically none of the broadsides now traditional in America are of earlier date than the 17th century, we are not directly concerned with the earliest examples of the type. Thus it seems unnecessary to rehearse here the general history of broadside balladry. The subject has been well surveyed by a number of scholars whose works are easily available, notably by Professor

---

[1] See *The Popular Ballad*, pp. 3-14 and 231ff.

[2] See for example "Minstrel and Broadside Ballads", Chap. 9 in *The Ballad Tree* by Evelyn K. Wells. (To say that broadsides and minstrel ballads are related and are different from folk ballads is not to imply, however, that all the so-called folk ballads are of non-professional origin. The distinguishing features of broadside balladry sometimes wear away in tradition leaving pieces which may exhibit the economical and dramatic folk style. Furthermore, some minstrels and broadside ballad composers may have been successful in producing pieces which did not display the hallmarks of their trade.)

Hyder Rollins in an excellent article entitled "The Black-Letter Broadside Ballad".[3] Since our primary interest is in the pieces which were to become traditional, the emphasis in the following discussion will be upon those aspects of the subject which have some bearing on traditional song.

Except for about three decades, 1550-1580, when the writing of ballads was a novelty indulged in by men of literary talent,[4] the authors of street ballads have generally been people of low literary status. The ballad maker was as a rule neither poet nor musician; he was a practical journalist whose medium of expression happened to be verse. At times he became more than competent in this form of literary endeavor. In fact Professor Rollins speaks by name of a number of notable ballad men of the 16th and 17th centuries.[5] But the later ballad makers it would seem, had no literary ambitions, and even the best of them were never in competition with established authors. The typical ballad maker was often hardly more than a mechanic; he would compose a ballad as readily as another man might mend a kettle or shoe a horse, and his main concern was that he be paid the shilling or so that the printers offered for an acceptable new song. If, as was sometimes the case, the ballad author was also a ballad seller, he put more energy into disposing of his wares than into the composition of new pieces, for the former was the more lucrative occupation, though by no means a certain livelihood.

Most ballad makers were not much concerned with being creative or original. Like many authors of popular material since, they stuck to the formulas which had been found successful. For many of them this was not really a matter of choice, since their knowledge of the printed word probably did not extend much beyond broadsides. Beginnings and endings, moral observations, descriptive passages, and even action and dialogue were all available from earlier pieces. They had only to reshape them, adding whatever new details

---

[3] *PMLA* 34(1919), 258-339. Further discussions of broadside balladry are scattered throughout ballad literature. See especially Wells, *loc. cit.;* "Ballads and Broadsides", Chap. 9 in *The Ballad of Tradition* by Gordon H. Gerould; "Popular Narrative Poetry and the Ballad", Chap. 3 in *English Literature at the Close of the Middle Ages* by E. K. Chambers; and "The Ballad Sheet and Garland" by Frank Kidson in *JFSS* II, 70-78.

[4] Rollins, p. 260.

[5] Rollins, pp. 260-261.

seemed worth recording, and they had what could be sold as new
ballads. The reading of a representative group of the thousands
of ballads extant will offer convincing evidence of the journalistic
methods used in their creation and of the modest talents of the
literary hacks who produced them. And yet the authors of the
ballads now in tradition, obscure and disreputable as they may
have been, have achieved the notable feat of establishing their
works firmly in the memories of succeeding generations.

But traditional broadside balladry in the larger sense is not solely
the product of the commercial city ballad makers. A number of
the ballads treated here differ noticeably from the typical broadsides
and may be the work of folk poets who composed for other motives
than publication in print. Alexander Keith conjectures that some
of the Scottish ballads in the Child collection were the work of
family retainers, possibly unofficial minstrels.[6] Some of our pieces
may well have had the same sort of origin. Wherever there is a
tradition of folk singing, composers will appear, and it is almost
certain that the rural communities had their own authors of "broadside" ballads.

Practically every major poet and song writer has tried his hand
at some sort of balladry, and the evidence indicates that most minor
poets and rhymesters have done the same. Thus we find now and
then that certain of these ballads are credited to authors ranging
from the fairly prominent to the most obscure. For example, "Dark-
Eyed Susan" is the work of John Gay of ballad-opera fame; "High
Barbary" is ascribed to that prolific author of naval songs, Charles
Dibdin; "Patrick Sheehan", according to Padraic Colum, was written
by Charles Kickham; "Robin Tamson's Smiddy", we are told by
Gavin Greig, was composed by a Scottish song writer named Sandy
Rodger; and "Burns and His Highland Mary" is said to be the work
of "a West of Scotland police constable named Thomson". More
or less reliable identifications of other ballad authors turn up from
time to time, enough to indicate the diverse authorship of these
folksongs.

Also to be given credit are those now anonymous composers of
songs for the variety stage whose works have become a part of our
ballad tradition. I suspect that "The Monkey Turned Barber",
"Doran's Ass", "Courting in the Kitchen", and other pieces of

---

[6] *Last Leaves of Traditional Ballads*, p. xxxix.

similar tone were sung by Irish comedians before they became known to the folk. Some of the more sentimental pieces, too, may well have had a stage origin.

First-hand information about the ballad authors' methods of composition is practically non-existent. Considering the final product this absence of information is no great loss to students of the creative imagination, but the ballad student is concerned with the way in which new pieces come into being. The first chapter has shown the great variety of subject matter in the traditional broadsides. An examination of the non-traditional material in any large collection will show that there is almost no limit to ballad topics.

Throughout the history of British street balladry the most dependable ingredient has been news. Local, national, and international events supplied the ballad authors with material for timely and exciting journalism. The *Stationers' Register* is full of ballad titles dealing with current events of the most diverse kinds, and frequently prefixed with such words as "a true relation".[7] Professor Rollins reports that ballad writers were even sent to "cover" events of interest just as the newspaper reporter does today. Obituaries and accounts of battles, treason, murders, storms, executions, and events at court seem to have been especially popular. A second major division of broadside balladry comprised pieces of a more timeless nature including religious, historical, and legendary tales, and romantic or humorous pieces almost without number. While these pieces pretended to no news value, their authors sometimes assumed the role of moralist and emphasized the lessons to be learned from their ballads. Other authors frankly offered their wares for pure entertainment, not infrequently relying upon suggestiveness or indecency for their success. A third class of ballads endeavored to supply dramatic or sensational news even when it was unavailable. Descriptions of people who had not eaten for years, of showers of wheat over large areas, of resurrections from the dead, of sea monsters, and of fantastic monstrous births are included in what we recognize as bait for the gullible. But fictional news ballads are not necessarily incredible. Some of them purport to be straightforward accounts of violent crimes, confessions, catastrophes, and other exciting events. Since these pieces are imitations of news

---

[7] Professor Rollins has indexed the ballad entries in the *Stationers' Register*. See the Bibliography.

ballads in style and substance, they can easily be mistaken for factual reports.[8] Religious disputes and religious history offered further opportunities for ballad making, as did manners, politics, fashions, scandals, rumors, public figures, disputes, fads, and the always fascinating vagaries of human nature.[9]

As might be expected, the purely journalistic and the outrageously incredible ballads have fared the worst in American tradition because they most rapidly became dated and meaningless. Those few news ballads which did survive recount events of enduring interest. Thus we have ballads about horse races, shipwrecks, and battles. Crimes such as highway robbery, larceny, and murder were fruitful sources of traditional balladry as were the trials and executions resulting from them. Apparently fictional ballads disguised as news have remained in considerable numbers, probably because their appeal lay more basically in the subject matter than in its timeliness. But by far the largest percentage of the traditional broadsides are either out and out romantic fiction or have only a remote connection with actual events. The world of balladry is a kind of never-never land where escapism and wishful thinking take precedence over reality. Even the stories which end tragically show a devotion to romantic ideals which is not always conspicuous in actual life. In the love ballads, for example, the world is molded nearer to the heart's desire. The lover overcomes all obstacles or dies in the attempt. Loyalty to the loved one usually endures forever; disloyalty is likely to end in well-deserved death.

A distinction should be made between ballads based directly on actual or supposed events and those on similar themes which sprang up later. If a rich lady once fell in love with her servant in actual life, dozens of such romances would flourish in balladry, and an event of rather rare occurrence, such as a woman's serving in male disguise in the army or navy, might serve the balladists time and again as a story motif. In the later pieces, of course, actual facts would be reflected only dimly if at all. The folk may and usually do believe their ballads, but the perceptive reader will recognize

---

[8] Charles Hindley in *Curiosities of Street Literature,* Division I, describes the methods of the street patterers who sold these 'cocks' or 'catchpennies and gives copious examples of broadsides of this type.

[9] The broadside collections edited by Professor Rollins will illustrate the wide range of subject matter used by the balladists.

many of them as fabrications in which the authors have aided their imaginations by borrowing liberally from the universally available fund of story material.

While it is not always easy to distinguish a factual from a fictional ballad, the following characteristics of the fictional pieces will frequently be observed:

1. The characters have been given conventional names or are nameless.

2. The time and place of the alleged event are not precisely stated.

3. The ballad has a stereotyped or contrived plot.

4. The action is recounted without much circumstantial detail.

If possible, these characteristics should be sought for in the original broadsides, since tradition often alters and abbreviates a ballad drastically.

Stories about conventionalized soldiers and sailors, farmers, and rich men's daughters offered endless possibilities for the balladists. Most of these pieces are fictional, as are ballads of love in general, and the latter are by far the most numerous of all types in American tradition. The humorous pieces display considerable truth to life but have no factual basis, and the supernatural ballads, of course, have no value as reports. In fact, probably not one traditional broadside in ten is a specific report on an actual contemporary occurrence. This is in marked contrast to the native American ballads, about two-thirds of which are founded on fact. A few ballads are factual, others mix fact and fancy, but the greatest number are spun from imaginations aided in no small degree by memories of older pieces. Sometimes the balladists did not even attempt to invent new details for their plots but simply rewrote older ballads in up to date (and usually inferior) English. This was a fruitful source of new texts, and it brought its share of confusion into ballad study. Professor Child more than once expresses the opinion that certain pieces reflect older and better stories, and not a few of the pieces considered here exist in both old and late forms. One is led to believe that ballad makers often felt desperately short of material and supported themselves more by plagiarism than by original composition. And yet the British broadsides do reflect the social conditions of the times in which they were written or rewritten. Not infrequently their authors were inspired by contemporary events which could serve as backgrounds for their stories, or by old or recent news items which could grow into dramatic narratives. But whatever material they used they could not completely disguise the basically fictional quality of their ballad plots.

Ballad Printers

Since the earliest days of the type, broadside ballads have flowed in largest numbers from the presses of London. Most of the ballads treated here were first printed or were reprinted in the capital, and it seems safe to say that the typical broadside is a London product, or at least a city product, for many of the towns and cities throughout Britain had their ballad presses. Professor Rollins reports that "in 1520 John Dorne, a bookseller of Oxford, sold from his shop more than one hundred and ninety unnamed 'ballets' ",[10] and when the 1906 number of the *Journal of the Folk Song Society* was compiled, Henry Such was still printing and selling old ballads in London.[11] Despite occasional attempts to suppress them, notably when the Puritans were in power, ballads were undoubtedly printed during all the decades between these dates and perhaps both earlier and later. The names of several hundred ballad printers are known, and no doubt hundreds of others have been forgotten.[12]

To call a man a ballad printer is not to imply that he confined himself solely to this type of publication. Frequently the printer was also a stationer or the proprietor of a toy shop. He might be in the general printing business, or he might specialize in street literature of diverse types.[13] While it is generally true that the later broadside ballads were miserably printed and were illustrated with

---

[10] Rollins, "The Black-Letter Broadside Ballad", p. 259.
[11] Writing of "The Bonny Bunch of Roses", Cecil Sharp says, "The words are still printed by Such." (*JFSS* II, 278).
[12] A partial list of 19th century ballad printers will be found in Appendix II.
[13] The trade announcement of the London ballad printer W. S. Fortey reads in part as follows: "The cheapest and greatest variety in the trade of large coloured *penny books;* half penny coloured books; farthing books; penny and half penny panoramas; school books; penny and half penny song books; memorandum books; poetry cards; lotteries; ballads (4,000 sorts) and hymns; valentines; scripture sheets; Christmas pieces; Twelfthnight characters; carols; book and sheet almanacks; envelopes, note paper, &c, &c." (Hindley, *The Life and Times of James Catnach*, pp. 410-411).

wildly inappropriate woodcuts left over from other works, many accurate and attractively illustrated examples of earlier ballad printing can be found.

Since there is no space here for a detailed discussion of British ballad printers, some account of one of the most prolific 19th century publishers may be enlightening. *The Life and Times of James Catnach by* Charles Hindley reprints many broadsides and provides much useful and entertaining information about the publication of street literature. In the style of the ballad-spieler, Hindley describes his book in part as follows:

> Now, my friends, you have here just printed . . . the Full, True, and Particular account of the Life . . . of that eccentric individual 'Old Jemmy Catnach', late of the *Seven Dials,* printer, publisher, toy-book manufacturer, dying-speech merchant, and ballad-monger . . .[14]

James Catnach, along with others of his profession, operated his shop in a region of St. Giles's parish, London, known as Seven Dials from a stone monument displaying seven sun dials, which stood in a circular court at the meeting place of seven streets. Catnach remained in business for 25 years, from 1813 to 1838, and at his retirement turned the firm over to his sister, who was the first of his successors (p. 409). At least during his early years, his journalistic ethics were not high, and on two occasions his firm was in trouble with the law. In 1818 he was jailed for libel after distributing completely false prose broadsides announcing that local pork butchers were dealing in human flesh. While he was in jail, his mother, who worked with him in the shop, and two sellers of broadsides were reprimanded by a magistrate for circulating an account of a murder which proved to be a pure fabrication (pp. 84-88). By such means Catnach imposed upon the gullible public when real news was scarce. But his most successful ventures were in the realm of more or less genuine news balladry, which he sometimes composed himself but more frequently bought from the local ballad writers who worked for him and his competitors. It is said that he employed a fiddler who knew the familiar ballad tunes so that any new pieces could be immediately sung to him and to the hawkers who would sell them on the streets (p. 383).

Especially popular at this time was the type of ballad alleged to

---

[14] Facing title page. (Further page references are included in the text).

have been written by a condemned criminal shortly before his execution, "the criminal being unable, in some instances, to read or write being no obstacle to the composition" (pp. 75-76). Political and sporting events, the deaths of prominent people, and crimes almost without number, these and other items of news or commentaries on the news were Catnach's chief stock in trade. His shop normally employed four men and boys, who worked at four presses of two forms each. From each form 200-300 prints an hour could be pulled, and thus his men could turn out more than twenty thousand broadsides a day. It is reported that on the occasion of a particularly sensational murder, his employees worked night and day for a week and printed some 250,000 copies of the broadside describing it. These prints were sold to and resold by "a ragged, dirty crew of newsmen . . . who assembled by hundreds" at his shop. In addition to the local sale, "every night and morning large bundles were dispatched to the principal towns in the three kingdoms" (pp. 143-144). The murder victim in this case was a man named Weare. Some time after the murder, the trial, and the execution, out of which Catnach made about five hundred pounds, he published a broadside headed "WE ARE ALIVE AGAIN!" "He put so little space between the words 'we' and 'are', that it looked at first sight like 'WEARE'. Many thousands were bought . . . , but those who did not like the trick called it a 'catch penny', and this gave rise to this peculiar term, which ever afterwards stuck to the issues of the 'Seven Dials' Press', though they sold as well as ever" (p. 149). In order to profit indirectly from another brutal murder, Catnach sent two hawkers to Brighton, where for four months they received "almost weekly, fresh supplies of street-papers" (p. 235). Such enterprise apparently paid off, for Catnach's business continued to thrive, despite the competition of many other printers, most of whom seem to have had ethics on a par with his own.

Ballad Distribution in Britain

From the early 16th century the work of the city ballad makers was published on single, unfolded sheets of printer's paper, usually of folio size. Proclamations, calls to arms, and public notices in general were more truly broadsides, since the term is most accurately applied to the largest sheet of unfolded paper with which the printer works. Only rarely were these huge sheets used for ballad printing;

thus the term broadside ballad refers to the method of publication rather than to the size of the sheet. The early ballads were usually printed in vertical double columns on one side of the sheet, which was often decorated at the top with a woodcut. The term 'black-letter ballad' refers, of course, to the use of gothic type, which was almost universal in ballad printing before 1700. Later ballads were printed in roman or white-letter type on single sheets sometimes much reduced in size. Many late 18th and early 19th century ballads are to be found on narrow sheets or slips about one-fourth the size of a folio sheet, and still later ballads were printed on square quarto sheets. Some ballad sheets were printed in three or four columns of small type and contained a variety of songs: lyrics, narratives, anonymous folksongs, and songs by known authors. Charles Hindley reproduces a Daguerreotype showing a man described as "long-song seller" offering narrow sheets suspended from a pole higher than his head. The editor's caption reads, " 'Three yards a penny!. . . Beautiful songs! Newest songs! Popular songs!' . . .''[15] The long-song sheet is said by Hindley to have been an innovation of Catnach's. In the series of 18th century prints entitled "The Cries of London", the ballad-seller is shown with a handful of sheets perhaps fifteen inches long draped over her arm. Thus the broadside sheet might vary considerably in physical form.

But whatever the style of type or the size of the sheets, the ballads were designed for wide distribution and cheap sale. According to Rollins, "As far back as the London trade can be traced, ballads sold regularly for a penny",[16] and they were still selling for that amount late in the 19th century, although the smaller sheets usually brought a halfpenny. But many Elizabethan Englishmen, Rollins observes, probably could not afford to spend the penny and hence listened eagerly to the ballad-singers. This may well be true, but to the people who bought ballads they became, once their novelty had worn off, a kind of throw-away literature which was not likely to be preserved except temporarily as wall decorations or by a collector taking special pains.[17]

---

[15] *Curiosities of Street Literature*, facing title page.

[16] "The Black-Letter Broadside Ballad", p. 296.

[17] "The walls of inns, taverns, and dwelling houses, those patronized or owned by the well-to-do no less than by the poor, were commonly lined with broadsheets, which not only helped to supply the absence of wall-

Ballad distribution was effected in a variety of ways, the most popular being by means of the ballad singer, who went about the city or the countryside singing samples of his wares and then selling the broadside sheets.[18] In the country, the ballad singer was a familiar figure at markets and fairs, and was often looked upon as a purveyor of up to the minute news from the outside world. Ballads were also carried by pedlars as part of their regular stock. When country people visited the city, they undoubtedly bought ballads from the street singers and from the proprietors of the numerous small shops and stalls which sold them. Another type of ballad seller was the "pinner-up", who displayed his ballads by the hundreds from twine strung along a wall or fence. Writing about 1870, Hindley says, ". . . We are old enough to remember the day when a good half-mile of wall fluttered with the minstrelsy of war and love under the guardianship of a scattered file of pinners-up, along the south side of Oxford Street alone."[19]

In addition to the ballad sheets and the popular prose broadsides, which contained much the same type of material, chapbooks were widely printed and sold by the publishers of street literature. A chapbook was a small pamphlet usually of from eight to sixteen pages, which was sold by a wandering pedlar or chapman. It contained a series of woodcut illustrations accompanying a text in prose or verse of religious, instructive, or more frequently entertaining matter for children and adults. The narrative chapbooks often contained legendary or romantic stories, pseudo history, and accounts of contemporary events. Practically any subject of potential popular

---

paper and tapestry, but gave to the rooms a picturesque, if bizarre, appearance." (Rollins, p. 336.)

[18] As the outstanding retail ballad salesman, the English ballad singer had a long if not entirely honorable existence in literature and in life from before the days of Shakespeare's Autolycus to well into the 20th century. In 1925, an Irish collector could write as follows: "The Ballad Singer is fast disappearing from our roads and market towns. At one time a familiar figure, with his handful of narrow, ill-printed sheets, or his store of brightly colored song books, he is now only occasionally seen." (Hayward, *Ulster Songs and Ballads,* p. 5). But Patrick Galvin (*Irish Songs of Resistance,* N.Y., [1956] writes as follows: ". . . the tradition of writing ballads, of selling broadsheets and singing ballads at the street-corner or in the market place, has never died out in Ireland; it is still a *living* tradition to this very day." (pp. 1-2).

[19] *The Life and Times of James Catnach,* p. 390.

interest might appear in a chapbook. The appeal of such publications seems to have been for the nearly illiterate, if one may judge by their quality. The modern comic strip is generally superior in workmanship and content. Besides stories in prose and verse and much non-narrative material, chapbooks also contained single long ballads or groups of ballads and songs. Since these pamphlets were sold in great numbers at only a penny or so each, they played an important role in ballad distribution.[20] According to John Ashton, ". . .they formed nearly the sole literature of the poor, until the *Penny Magazine* and Chambers's penny Tracts and Miscellanies gave them their deathblow, and relegated them to the book-shelves of collectors."[21]

Eighteenth century chapbooks of songs are identical with song-books or songsters. The term songster, however, is applied generally to publications which vary greatly in size and scope. Some brief 19th century songsters sold for only a halfpenny or a penny, while others contained hundreds of pages and in some cases ran into several volumes and included thousands of items.[22] Most of the songsters relied heavily on the works of established authors and on songs of the variety stage. Sentimental pieces were usually well represented, and allegedly comic songs in dialect were especially favored. While the typical songster contained few ballads, the total number of broadsides republished by this means was considerable.

Some broadsides, chapbooks, and longer songbooks are referred to in their titles as garlands. The garland was usually a small collection of songs or ballads which a publisher thought worth offering for sale. Sometimes a single ballad in several parts would be published in chapbook form as a garland. Thus the four-part ballad called "The Turkey Factor" was published in the form of a booklet entitled "The Factor's Garland". More often the garland would contain from two to four songs and would derive its title from the first song. Thus "The Exeter Garland" consists of the ballad "The Two Loyal Lovers of Exeter" and another piece entitled "The Ale-wives Forced to Spin". Sometimes when long ballads from garlands

---

[20] For an enlightening discussion of the type, see Harry B. Weiss, *A Book About Chapbooks*.

[21] *Chapbooks of the Eighteenth Century*, pp. ix-x.

[22] See for example *Catalogue of English Song Books Forming a Portion of the Library of Sir John Stainer*, London, Novello, Ewer, and Co., 1891.

were republished on broadside sheets, the garland title would be retained. Many garlands were more ambitious undertakings than the chapbooks or broadsides. For example "Robin Hood's Garland" is an eighteenth century booklet of 87 pages containing "a complete history" of the subject's exploits, and four garlands collected by Joseph Ritson run from about thirty to ninety pages. The songs contained in all the garlands were of many different types and included ballads both old and new.[23]

The publication of broadsides, chapbooks, garlands, and songsters was by no means limited to London but flourished in all the major cities of the British Isles as well as in many smaller communities. With so many established methods of distribution available to them, it is hardly surprising that the ballad printers were able to dispose of their wares in enormous quantities, or that many of their products should have found lasting places in the folk memory.

Ballads composed in rural districts were not likely to be printed for many years, and thus they sooner acquired the qualities of folksong. But the demands of the city presses were insatiable, and the ballad printers sent agents into the country to collect traditional songs from the people and thus to increase their supply of publishable items.[24] Some confusion results when city broadside and country folksong are found side by side in print. When, for example, Child and other editors say that a certain broadside ballad is clearly in the traditional manner, the explanation may be that it was actually collected from the folk. Another method of publication of country ballads suggests itself by analogy with conditions in America, where rural composers have taken their ballads to country printers and

---

[23] For a fuller discussion see Kidson's article (note 3 above). Four late eighteenth century garlands are reprinted in Joseph Ritson's *Northern Garlands*, Edinburgh, E. & C. Goldsmid, 1887. The titles mentioned in my text are listed in the Harvard catalogue.

[24] " 'Seven Dials' is often rightly credited with having turned out feeble stuff of the 'Villikins and his Dinah' type; but, on the other hand, the astute Northumbrian printer, James Catnach, (settled in London 1813), paid men to collect ballads from singers in country taverns; and there exists a serious broadside, 'William and Diana', which is older than his burlesqued version, if hardly of greater literary merit. There is no doubt that other printers followed Catnach's plan, and this offers the only satisfactory explanation of the fluidity of traditional ballads throughout long centuries." Broadwood, *English Traditional Songs*, p. x. (See also note 36 below).

have had a few hundred copies made for local sale.[25] These "ballets", as the printed sheets are called among the folk, have often become the source of traditional song in the United States. Some British ballads may have been similarily published, but evidence on the subject is lacking.

The easiest, most direct, and most widely used method of distributing new ballads in the country was by the author's singing them time and again in public and private. If the ballads had appeal, they would be accepted and learned by a number of other singers and would perhaps be taken down in manuscript ballad books to assist imperfect memories. From this point on, the ballads followed the course of all oral literature and became the property of the folk. The forces of variation worked upon them, they often travelled far from home, the identity of their authors was lost, and these pieces took their places as traditional ballads. While we cannot positively say that any of the ballads treated here had never been printed until they were collected from American tradition, it is highly probable that a few of them have this kind of background.

ORIGINAL BALLAD DISTRIBUTION IN AMERICA

Ballads preserved in the memory of the folk, both broadsides and what were to become Child ballads, were a valued heritage of many of the early immigrants to America. Far from home and lacking even the simplest professional entertainment, the settlers naturally made the most of their own resources and sang the songs learned in earlier years. Collectors have commented on the great age of the traditional songs in the South and on the use of words and phrases long archaic in Standard English. No doubt some of our folksongs have an uninterrupted oral tradition of about 300 years in this country, although most of them came considerably later as did the bulk of the immigrants from the British Isles.

The establishment of British folksong in America parallels the development of the country. In the 17th century the English settlers distributed themselves and their folksongs along the Atlantic seaboard from New England to the Carolinas. As the population grew with the arrival of more colonists in the next century, the people began moving southward and westward to occupy more of the

---

[25] See *Native American Balladry*, Chapter IV.

fertile land east of the Appalachians. When the hardy Scotch-Irish arrived, they pushed on through the rolling countryside of Pennsylvania to establish themselves in the Appalachian Mountains of the upper South. After the Revolution, the migration westward advanced with increasing rapidity, and as one state after another joined the Union in the succeeding decades, British folksong continued to spread and flourish. As the nation expanded further at the time of the Gold Rush and after the Civil War, the dominance of the English language combined with the British heritage of the bulk of the white population assured British folksong of first place. The Irish, who arrived by the tens of thousands from the middle of the 19th century, helped to contribute a huge new supply of songs in English to this body of folk tradition. In fact, every English speaking group of immigrants which has ever come to this country has been a potential source of folksong, and many of them have enriched our store. Great contributions to the British folksong of North America have also been made in the Maritime Provinces of Canada, where the English, Scottish, and Irish settlements have been found full of songs brought from the Old World.

Additions to the body of folksong brought by settlers were made by visitors and travellers and especially by sailors who shipped out of East Coast ports to all parts of the world. These men spent part of their leisure time on shipboard singing songs and ballads. When they returned home or went to the lumber camps to work in the winter, they sang their songs during the evenings in their cottages or in the shanties of the lumber crews.

Besides the large amount of song learned in the traditional manner, there was a considerable body first learned in this country from printed texts. Broadsides of many different kinds, including ballads, were widely printed in America during the 17th, 18th, and 19th centuries. Among the ballads may be found hundreds of native compositions dealing with current events as well as many ballads reprinted or rewritten from British broadsides for the American trade. The printers of the major cities like Boston, New York, and Philadelphia turned out ballads by the thousands.[26] Unfortunate-

---

[26] The names of some American ballad printers are given in Appendix II. Most printers sold both wholesale and retail, and some of the larger establishments advertised several thousand different songs for sale on broadside sheets.

ly the study of American broadside printing is not well advanced, and except for a few specialized works, the field remains largely unexplored.[27] The fact that relatively few collectors seem to have taken an interest in broadsides while they were being published means that by now great numbers of them have disappeared. Such valuable bibliographies as Worthington Ford's *Broadsides, Ballads, etc. Printed in Massachusetts,* 1639-1800, which contains several thousand items, give some idea of the amount of this material that was once available. Miscellaneous broadside collections of various sizes are to be found in libraries throughout the country and especially in the Northeast.[28] Thanks largely to the efforts of Professors Child and Kittredge, the Houghton Library at Harvard University has the greatest ballad collection in North America.

Among the most interesting of the collections made by individuals is that of Isaiah Thomas in the library of the American Antiquarian Society at Worcester, Massachusetts. This consists, in the words of the collector, himself a former ballad printer, of "Songs, Ballads, etc. Purchased from a Ballad Printer and Seller in Boston, 1813. Bound up for Preservation, to show what articles of this kind are in vogue with the Vulgar of this time, 1814." Thomas's collection, which he had bound in three volumes, consists of 302 ballad sheets containing 349 items. Much of the material is non-narrative and much is of American composition, but a good many British broadsides are included, among them such pieces still traditional as "Captain Kidd", "The Bold Soldier", "Will the Weaver", "The Gray Mare", "Rinordine", "Love in the Tub", and "Willie Riley". One regrets that earlier and later social historians did not have Thomas's foresight. Since many old ballads appeared without an imprint, we cannot always say whether a particular print is British or American, but we do know that British ballad prints were imported for sale in America and that native printers made free use

---

[27] A good selection of the older non-traditional ballads will be found in Ola Winslow's *American Broadside Verse*. Robert Neeser's *American Naval Songs and Ballads* is also made up largely of broadside material. Harry B. Weiss's *A Book About Chapbooks* contains much useful information about the publication of broadsides and chapbooks in Britain and America.

[28] Notable ballad holdings are to be found in the public libraries of New York, Boston, and Providence and in Yale and Brown Universities.

of imported material.[29] As late as the end of the 19th century, British ballads were still being sold in broadside form by Wehman and by DeMarsan, New York song publishers, and perhaps by others. That the broadside ballads republished in America for more than 200 years helped to strengthen the American broadside tradition is obvious, although to what extent cannot be precisely determined.

The distribution of printed broadsides in America seems to have followed the general pattern already established in Britain. Ballads were available either wholesale or retail from the city ballad printers. The peddlers and ballad sellers who bought them in quantity would pass them along to eager purchasers throughout the countryside or in the city. And the pinners-up, who were noticed by Hindley in London, were also to be seen in New York.[30]

During the 19th century hundreds or perhaps thousands of different song books were printed and sold throughout America. Most of them contained the word "songster" in the title, sold for about

---

[29] The Thomas Collection, for example, contains half a dozen illustrated ballads with the imprint of J. Evans, 42 Long Lane, West Smithfield. Presumably these were a part of the regular stock of Nathaniel Coverly, Jr., the Boston printer whose name appears on many of the other sheets. Coverly must have been the printer from whom Thomas purchased his collection. Harry Weiss, *A Book About Chapbooks*, p. 125, says, "Andrew Steuart of Philadelphia printed chapbooks in 1763 and 1765, and it is fairly certain that he imported chapbooks from abroad for sale in America." Later (p. 134) he refers to contemporary advertisements of imported street literature and remarks, "There is no doubt that English chapbooks were imported and sold in this country just as were other books." Since British ballad printers usually used narrow sheets of very thin paper, we may assume that 19th century American importers of ballads found them at least as profitable as chapbooks.

[30] Worthington C. Ford writes, "I well remember some street sellers of ballads in New York in the early seventies, who had on twine wound in the iron fences of parks and churchyards or on a light bamboo frame, between strings stretched to keep them down in the wind, the ballads then in vogue." (*The Isaiah Thomas Collection of Ballads*, p. 4). Professor Kittredge reprints the following first stanza from " 'Tony Pastor's Combination Song or A Bunch of Penny Ballads' (sheet music, Boston, cop. 1863; Harvard College Library)":

> As you walk through the town, on a fine summer day,
> The subject of my song you have met on your way,
> On railings and on fences, wherever you may go,
> You will see the Penny Ballads stuck up in a row. (*JAF* 35,358).

a dime, and were of pocket size. Those of the first half of the century were frequently published as bound books about three inches wide by five tall containing two or three hundred pages. The ballads and songs were printed in very small type without music, and many dozens of texts were crowded into each volume. Later songsters were often issued as unbound pamphlets of 60 or 70 pages containing, of course, far less material. The publishers of songsters reprinted their pieces frequently and borrowed freely from one another, so that the same songs and ballads are found time and again in different publications. On the whole the songsters are not especially rewarding to students of traditional song because the great bulk of their material was currently popular and ephemeral. In many of the titles novelty is emphasized, and like those of Britain, the American songsters were largely composed of comic and sentimental stage songs. At the same time, old and modern broadsides are found scattered throughout dozens of American songsters, and these enormously popular books did play a significant part in the distribution of traditional balladry. Furthermore, the songsters are partly responsible for circulating those stage songs which were to become popular ballads. (These, of course, were also widely sold in sheet music form). The range of individual songsters is fairly wide. *The Songster's New Pocket Companion* (Boston, 1821) consists almost entirely of stage songs and contains no traditional material. *The American Songster* (Phila., 1836) purports to be much the same kind of publication but contains a number of the broadside ballads now traditional in America. *The Forget Me Not Songster,* which was published in Philadelphia, New York, and elsewhere about 1840, and was one of the most popular of all, consists mainly of old broadside ballads. Of these three songsters, the second, with its large number of stage songs and its handful of ballads, is the most typical.

Later in the century the steady flow of songsters became a flood, and almost any new song or prominent singer gave the publishers an excuse for a songster with a new title but a largely familiar table of contents. In New York during the 1860's, for example, the firm of Dick and Fitzgerald alone published dozens of songsters with such titles as the following: *Tony Pastor's Irish Comic Songster, Fred May's Comic Irish Songster, The Love and Sentimental Songster, The Heart and Home Songster, The Arkansas Traveler Songster, and The Shamrock; or, Songs of Old Ireland.* The list of late 19th century songsters is practically endless, and since ballads keep turning up in them infrequently but persistently, their influence cannot be ignored.

While the American songster is mainly a 19th century product, the publication of song books of various kinds continues, and, as before, broadsides are sometimes included in them. Music publishers like Schirmer in New York and Boosey, Curwen, or Novello in London have their folksong series and of course offer good tunes along with their texts. Many a scholarly collection has been raided to produce books of folksong for general sale, some with music and some without. Only recently the publishers of the paperbacks have entered the field, so that it is again possible to buy ballads cheaply on the street corner.[31] At first thought, it may seem that the songs in these modern books have lost their connection with oral tradition, but this is not always true. The amateur and professional folk singers keep adding to their repertories as they have always done, and they take advantage of such opportunities to learn new pieces. Matters have been further complicated in the 20th century by the phonograph, the motion pictures, the radio, and television. For several decades the record companies have sold millions of folksong recordings of varying degrees of genuineness, and these have played a part in the dissemination of balladry. Radio and television, and to a lesser degree the movies, have made liberal use of folksongs, and a number of well known singers have reached nationwide audiences through these media. While the believers in the phenomenon of pure oral transmission may deplore the effects of these inventions, they have undoubtedly helped to keep alive a wide interest in and demand for popular balladry.

THE DISTRIBUTION OF TRADITIONAL TEXTS IN AMERICA

A glance at the ballad listings in Appendix I will show that the traditional broadsides are by no means evenly or generally distributed. At one extreme we have ballads which have been reported

---

[31] See for example Sylvia and John Kolb, *A Treasury of Folk Songs*, N. Y., Bantam Books, [1948]; *The Burl Ives Song Book* (paperback edition), N. Y., Ballantine Books, [1953]; Charles O'Brien Kennedy and David Jordan, *American Ballads, Naughty, Ribald, and Classic*, N. Y., Fawcett Publications, Inc., [1952]; and B. A. Botkin, *The Pocket Treasury of American Folklore*, N. Y., Pocket Books, Inc., [1950].

many times from almost every region where collecting has been done; at the other we have a number of ballads which have turned up only once. We can never have more than a hazy idea about the total number of ballad texts in circulation because collecting has been done with uneven skill and intensity. Some regions have been pretty well searched, while others have been largely neglected. But enough has been done to make valid some general statements about the location of traditional texts and the degree to which they are known.

Only about one-fourth of the ballads in Appendix I seem to be generally distributed throughout the United States and the Maritimes. Many of these have been reported from Newfoundland, New Brunswick, and Nova Scotia, and from practically all the states in which major collecting has been done. Such ballads as "Father Grumble", "Willie Riley", "Early, Early in the Spring", "The Boston Burglar", and "The Drowsy Sleeper" seem familiar in all ballad singing communities. But to say that a ballad is well distributed geographically is not necessarily to imply that it is known to many singers. "The Factor's Garland", for example, has been reported in collections from Maine, Vermont, New York, Michigan, North Carolina, and Texas, and yet it is rare in American tradition. The Michigan and Texas texts are from mid-19th and early 20th century ballad manuscripts, while the New York and Vermont texts are only brief fragments of the original. That leaves the North Carolina text of 86 double lines, which was collected in 1906 and the Maine text of 54 double stanzas, which was obtained in 1941. This last text, then, is the only complete one collected from tradition. Still the ballad must be included among those which have traveled widely.

In addition to those generally circulated the ballads are distributed approximately as follows: one-fourth of the total number have been found in the Maritime Provinces alone; fifteen per cent are known both in the Northern United States and in the Maritimes; ten per cent are reported from the North alone, The remaining ten per cent have made two or three scattered appearances.

Since about half the ballads of scattered appearance may be found in the Maritimes and practically all of them in both the North and South, the figures can be rearranged to show the percentage of the total number of ballads from each major area. Combining the 25 per cent of generally circulated ballads with the 15 per cent known in the South alone, and adding the 10 per cent of scattered distribution, we conclude that 50 per cent of all the ballads have been reported from the South. By the same method we find that 60 per cent of the total are known in the northern United States and 70 per cent in the Maritimes. Since 10 per cent are found in the Northern United States alone, no less than 80 per cent of all the ballads have been reported from north of the Mason and Dixon line.

No claim to mathematical accuracy is made for these figures; they are approximations only, but they have definite significance. It will come as a surprise to some to learn that the South is in last place in the total number of broadside ballads found and that the Maritime Provinces rather than the States are the stronghold of imported balladry in North America. It will be recalled that the Southern United States, and particularly the Appalachian mountains, have preserved many fine texts and tunes of old Child ballads and have contributed much to native American balladry. The isolation of the South has properly been credited with preserving much British folklore and folksong. But obviously an isolated South could not benefit greatly from the influx of balladry which came with the imigrants to Northern ports long after the population of the South had been stabilized. Nearly one-third of our broadsides show an Irish heritage, and most of these have been recorded in the North or in Canada. The outstanding strength of British balladry in the Maritimes may be attributed both to ideal conditions for ballad preservation and to strong ties with the British Isles. And there, too, immigration has played its part in bringing new songs to the old communities. Thus it is not so strange, after all, that the number of British ballads increases as the collector moves northward.

THE ORIGIN OF THE TEXTS

Few more baffling literary problems exist than that of determining the history of a large number of ballads. Any analysis which attempts a solution of the problem will be full of question marks, visible or invisible; that which follows is no exception. Yet enough facts emerge from a study of this kind to make it worthwhile, and one can at least produce a general picture of ballad origin.

The British broadside balladry of America has originated primarily in England, Ireland, and Scotland. A few pieces may have come from Australia, and a few of the many of doubtful origin may have been composed on this side of the Atlantic,[32] though they bear evidence of strong British influence. About sixty per cent of our ballads seem to be English, thirty per cent Irish, eight per cent Scottish, and two per cent Australian. These figures are very different from those of the Child collection, which is strong in Scottish texts[33] but contains nothing from Ireland. Irish balladry in English is generally quite late, much of it having been produced in the 19th century, and almost entirely in the broadside manner. Child would hardly have considered it of the same class as most of his pieces. The Australian ballads are of Irish extraction and were written in the same style about transported Irish convicts. These, too, Child would have discarded. The small number of Scottish ballads in our list seems to indicate that the Scots were content with their old balladry or with broadside texts imported from England and Ireland. Apparently they produced little broadside balladry of their own. At any rate, the predominance of English broadsides is not surprising considering that London was always the headquarters of the broadside trade.

In the foregoing paragraphs, as in the title of this work, I have used the term broadside primarily to refer to all imported non-Child ballads in American tradition. A further breakdown is desirable here. Ballad scholars recognize a distinction between the typical broadside and the typical traditional or folk ballad. (This distinction is dealt with in some detail in the next chapter.) Among the ballads treated here are quite a few in which the folk style predominates. Such pieces may have originated with rural composers steeped in the old balladry. In addition, a number of our ballads may have been composed by skilled song writers for conventional publication or for the variety stage. Pieces of both types often found their way into the ballad printer's net. There are, too, many ballads which have not been traced to broadside texts, although they are composed in the usual broadside manner. Of the 290 ballads here treated, 195 or two-thirds have been traced to broadside

---

[32] See for example "The Sons of Liberty", "The *Chesapeake* and the *Shannon* II", "The Butcher Boy", "Kelly the Pirate II", "Devilish Mary", and "The *Flying Cloud*".

[33] E. K. Chambers, *Eng. Lit at the Close of the Middle Ages*, p. 166, says that about 180 of Child's ballads are Scottish.

or songster texts. But since a printed text does not necessarily reveal the origin of a piece we must resort to analyses of style. About ninety precent of all the apparently English ballads seem definitely of the broadside type. Of the rest about three per cent are of the professional type and seven per cent in the folk manner. Again som ninety percent of the Irish pieces are typical broadside ballads, leaving the rest about equally divided between folk type and professional type. Thus of the English and Irish ballads, which constitute nine-tenths of our total, nine ballads out of every ten may be said to have had their start as broadsides.

Subjective considerations must play a part when one attempts to distinguish among ballads of broadside, stage, or folk origin. But to some extent the differences are generally observable, as a close examination of the texts will show. Most of the qualities of typical broadside balladry may be found, for example, in such pieces as "The Female Warrior", "William Hall", "The *Lady Leroy*", and "The Silk Merchant's Daughter".[34] On the other hand, ballads like "Finnegan's Wake", "Doran's Ass", and "Courting in the Kitchen" display none of the hallmarks of street ballads but exhibit smooth professional competence in their use of dialect and in phrasing designed to extract all possible humor from the situations they recount. The same seems true of such Scottish pieces as "The Bonny Wee Window" and "Robin Tamson's Smiddy".[35] These pieces of the music-hall type may in turn be contrasted with ballads like "Sir Neil and Glengyle", "The Lake of Cool Finn", and "A-Growing", each of which in its own way gives evidence of having arisen from an ancient and honorable folk tradition. "Sir Neil and Glengyle", with its vigorous tragic action, its concentration on the dramatic, and its nice combination of folk speech and poetic phrasing might well be the work of some minor Scottish minstrel who had no contact with either the broadside press or the stage. "The Lake of Cool Finn" rises well above the usual broadside level and in its suggestion of the supernatural achieves an air of genuine mystery which seems beyond the power of the commercial ballad makers. And "A-Growing" has the simplicity of phrasing and poign-

---

[34] For texts and analyses of typical broadside ballads, see Chapter IV.

[35] Note also the style of the following pieces: "Jack Sheppard", "Dark-Eyed Susan", "The Kerry Recruit", "Burns and his Highland Mary", and "The Lass of Glenshee".

ancy as well as the antique charm of the better Child ballads. Although all these pieces have appeared in broadside form, one feels that folk origin might be claimed for them.[36]

It would be convenient for ballad students if all ballads of folk type had a history of pure oral tradition behind them, or if all Irish ballads were sung only by the sons of Erin and their descendants. It would be helpful, too, if the first printings of all the professional and stage pieces could be found, and if all the true broadsides were available on the old ballad sheets. But folk ballads were printed from tradition, Irish ballads were reprinted in London and elsewhere, the sources of many stage songs are unknown, and large numbers of the old ballad sheets have vanished. While the names of a few ballad authors are known, and the travels of a handful of pieces can be outlined, the precise facts about the origin and distribution of most ballads must remain tantalizing mysteries.

THE DATING OF THE BROADSIDES

No satisfactory method exists for the precise dating of most traditional ballads of broadside origin. Even where broadside sheets exist, we can rarely tell whether we are dealing with an original printing, a copy of an older work, or a recomposed older work. Furthermore the broadside sheets were almost never dated, and

---

[36] The following pieces may also have originated with the folk: "The Bold Pirate", "The Old Woman of Slapsadam", "Father Grumble", "The Holly Twig", "Will the Weaver", and "Molly Bawn".

Miss Lucy Broadwood suggests some of the difficulties involved in tracing the origin of doubtful texts:

"The words of many country ballads are derived, directly or indirectly, from broadsides. The invention of printing early gave birth to these, which recorded both the orally-traditional and newly-made ballads of the strolling minstrel and tavern-bard. . . . With cheaper printing, there poured forth from the provincial presses an ever-swelling tide of broadsides, still bearing ballads taken from the lips of singers and local rhymesters ignorant of literary conventions. . . . Many ballads were common to most broadside printers, but the versions of these, as given by different publishers, are rarely identical. Indeed the kaleidoscopic shifting of lines or whole verses, the additions, curtailments, borrowings, diversity of metre, and the strange corruptions in these printed versions (ancient or modern), go to prove that, however much the country singer or local bard may be beholden— directly or indirectly—to the broadside, the broadside is equally indebted to the ballad-singer and hedge poet. . . ." (*Eng. Trad. Songs*, p. x).

the fictional stories told in typical ballads preclude our assigning them to particular moments in history. While we can rarely state the year in which any non-factual ballad was composed, we can at least draw some general conclusions about the age of the broadsides in America.

It was customary, though by no means a universal practice, for the ballad printers to include their names on the sheets from their presses. Since something is known of the various printing firms, it is frequently possible to assign a ballad print to a definite decade or quarter century. The size of the ballad sheet, the quality of the paper, the type used, and the printing style may also be significant. The appearance of various ballads in 18th and 19th century chapbooks and songsters is a further aid in guessing their age. Some ballads, of course, deal with factual occurrences of known date, while others treat aspects of life peculiar to a certain era. Stylistic evidence, information provided by folk singers, and the appearance of ballads in old manuscripts are further aids in dating. It may be argued that the typical ballad is simply a conventional imitation of an earlier piece, and hence that the assigning of dates is not especially important. But any information which throws light on this hazy subject is welcome.

Artistic merit may also be considered in dating ballads, though it is unreliable as a test for individual pieces. For example, the skill of the English broadside balladists seemed to reach its height during the 17th century; it declined somewhat in the eighteenth and sank still lower in the nineteenth. Irish broadside balladry, which comes to us mainly from the late 18th and the 19th century, does not seem to have suffered in quality after 1800, possibly because of an inborn Irish talent for verse making and song. The quality of the non-traditional broadsides originally written for and published by James Catnach is markedly inferior to that of the average piece traditional in America. Furthermore, the pieces in John Ashton's *Modern Street Ballads,* which come largely from the Catnach era, lead one to suspect that the 19th century rhymesters of Seven Dials were rarely capable of producing anything of enduring appeal. The non-traditional broadsides of the 17th century, by contrast, display considerable wit and talent. On the basis of quality alone, the most characteristic of our traditional English broadsides might be said to fall between these two extremes and hence be assigned to the

18th century. Supplementary evidence points to the same conclusion. More than a dozen of our English ballads are known to exist in 17th century prints, and a large number are obviously 19th century products. Although the Irish ballads greatly swell the total for the 19th century, we find time and again that the best known and most appealing English broadsides can be traced back to the 18th century but no further.

Among the oldest of the broadsides traditional in America are "The Three Butchers", "Locks and Bolts", and "The Miller's Will", which can all be traced to 17th century broadsides. Since they do not seem to have been reprinted in America, it is possible that they were known to the immigrants of the 17th or 18th century and have remained in tradition to the present. The fact that these ballads are generally distributed and turn up in texts which vary markedly lends credence to this theory, but the possibility that later British prints were available here must not be overlooked. Other 17th century ballads like "The Children in the Wood", "The Dumb Wife", "The Blind Beggar's Daughter", "Kate and Her Horns", and "Captain Glen" are known to have been reprinted in America in the 19th century. The anti-Catholic ballad "The Romish Lady", which probably dates from the 16th century, was republished in 19th century America as a Protestant religious song. Thus despite its age it may have been in tradition for only a century. The same may be true of "The Factor's Garland", late texts of which were widely distributed in England and may have been exported for sale. Thus there is hardly a ballad, no matter what its age, for which we can claim with any certainty an uninterrupted existence in tradition from the time of its first appearance in print.

The occurrence of large numbers of our ballads on the 19th century sheets of such printers as Walker, Cadman, Bebbington, Catnach, and Pitts should not in itself be considered evidence of 19th century origin. Even if their prints are the only ones extant, it should be remembered that they constantly reprinted older material, which cost them nothing and which was known to be saleable. Practically all our known 18th century ballads reappear time and again on the sheets of the following century, and it seems likely that a number of other pieces are of greater age than the printing evidence indicates.

Although a few of them may be older, the following traditional broadsides are representative of those which seem to date from the 18th century: "Will the Weaver", "William Riley", "The Gray Mare", "Rinordine", "The Apprentice Boy", "Love in the Tub", "Captain Kidd", "The Sheffield Apprentice", "The Box upon Her Head", "Nancy of Yarmouth", "Handsome Harry", and "Caroline of Edinburgh Town". Most of these ballads are well plotted, competently phrased, vigorous, and memorable, and most if not all of them were available in American songster and broadside texts.

A number of 19th century ballads can be approximately dated by the events which they recount. This is true of such pieces as "The Heights of Alma", "The *Chesapeake* and the *Shannon*", "Lady Franklin's Lament", "The Plains of Waterloo", "Nelson's Victory at Trafalgar", "The High Blantyre Explosion", and "The Loss of the *Amphitrite*". The quality of these ballads is uneven, and for reasons suggested in Chapter I, they are not well established in tradition. Among the 19th century Irish ballads which can be approximately dated we find "Burke's Dream", "The Bonny Bunch of Roses", "Patrick Sheehan", and "Brennan on the Moor". Many other Irish ballads may be assigned to the last century, including all the comic pieces like "The Irish Wake" and "The Monkey Turned Barber" and the ballads of crime with an Australian setting.

The largest group of undated and perhaps undatable pieces consists of those mainly English ballads of romantic love and adventure which have no factual basis. Stories of disapproving parents, sudden romances, returned sailors, and socially unequal lovers are so common and repetitive that their histories are untraceable. Such pieces as "The Dark-Eyed Sailor", "William and Harriet", "Pretty Fair Maid", "Ellen the Fair", "Cupid the Ploughboy", "MacDonald's Return to Glencoe", and "The Sailor and the Shepherdess" are generally available in 19th century prints but not in older broadsides. And yet in style and substance they are much like various pieces known to be of the preceding century. Since they do not exhibit the original and detailed plots of the most typical 18th century pieces, they may represent a transitional stage in which the fictional ballad became slight in story and largely imitative while retaining a certain smoothness and facility. I would say that most of them belong near the end of the 18th or the beginning of the 19th century. Somewhat later ballads of the same general type are more likely to be Irish than English or Scottish.

While we are unable to date the traditional broadsides with much accuracy, we may safely conclude that the bulk of them originated between 1700 and 1850. Thus in date they fall between the other two bodies of American balladry in English, the Child ballads, most of which were composed before 1700, and the native American ballads, which are largely a product of the last decades of the 19th century.

PRINTED TEXTS AND TRADITIONAL BALLADRY

Those who belong to the romantic school of ballad scholars believe that print is always a contaminating influence and that "pure" folksong is completely traditional. Thus Professor Child, writing about his circularized appeal for traditional ballads from the Scottish people, said, "I received a few copies of the better ballads, half a dozen, from one place or another: but I fear that all of them are recollections of *modern print,* a most undesirable aftergrowth of oral tradition."[37] If by "recollections" Child meant that the contributors had merely given ballads which they had memorized from print some time before, he was clearly justified in denying such texts the status of traditional song. No scholarly collector will knowingly offer as traditional those texts learned directly from print. But if, as seems quite likely on the basis of later findings, the contributors were giving songs which they had learned aurally, without thought of their printed sources, a new tradition was being established.

For several centuries it was a common practice to print old ballad texts on broadsides, either as received from tradition or in rewritten form, for distribution by the ballad sellers. To the extent that badly reshaped texts of fine old ballads were widely circulated, this custom was unfortunate. But when traditional texts were used the results were not entirely negative. Large numbers of people who might otherwise never have learned the old ballads were by this method able to increase their store of folksong and to insure its vigorous continuance. Even the journalistic reshaping of old ballads, disastrous as it may have been aesthetically, is not to be looked upon as entirely evil. The balladist might take a corrupt, incomplete,

---

[37] Letter to Svend Grundtvig, May 8, 1874, printed by Hustvedt, *Ballad Books and Ballad Men,* p. 263.

and archaic text and make an up-to-date and understandable ballad story of it. To the ballad singing public the choice is not between a fine antique and a spurious imitation but rather between something that has little meaning left for them and something they can understand. In short the printing of old ballads in one form or another has done much to save them from oblivion.

The Child ballads which have been received only in fragmentary form from singers in America are usually those which do not have a record of printed texts behind them. On the other hand, ballads like "Lord Bateman" ("Young Beichan", Child no. 53), "Lord Thomas and Fair Annet" (no. 73), and "Bonny Barbara Allan" (no. 84), which have been found widely dispersed and in good condition, are the very ones which appeared frequently in print during the 19th century. No doubt some of the glamor is stripped from popular balladry by the thought that printed texts may have been such a definite aid in survival. But after all, the memories of the people, though often astonishing, are not infallible. What could be more natural than for those who were interested in balladry, if they were literate, to increase their store by so obvious a method? And those who were illiterate could learn from other singers.

Another common belief is that printing a ballad fixes its form and hence prevents the normal variations of folk tradition. This is true to some extent, since a widely distributed printed ballad may tend to crowd out of tradition other versions imperfectly recalled. But once a printed text is established in tradition it is again subject to the same influences toward variation that operate in all oral literature. Many ballads of known broadside origin have been recovered in traditional texts which vary substantially from the original.

With a few exceptions, the most popular traditional broadsides are those which were widely reprinted in America. While many of the broadsides must have been brought from the British Isles as traditional song, many of the same pieces and others could be learned in this country from ballad sheets and songsters. In fact, one of the strongest arguments against the harmful effects of print is the remarkable vitality of the broadside ballad tradition.

While the influence of print is too complex a topic to treat adequately in a survey of this type, we can at least suggest the importance of the subject. By way of example we may take *The Forget Me Not Songster*. Of the various American songbooks of the 19th century, this is the least typical and the most important for the number of ballads it contains. Its subtitle reads, "a choice collection of old ballad songs as sung by our grandmothers." Since the *Songster* was published about 1840, the "ballad songs" must have been sung by the grandmothers near the end of the 18th century. Many of them go further into the past. Of course not all the songs were old; the general statement on a title-page cannot be applied literally to every piece in one of these anthologies. But a large number of these songs now have as long a history as did a number of the pieces which Professor Child selected.

The title indicates that the pieces in the *Songster* were old enough to be traditional when the book was published. Of the 92 titles in the Philadelphia and Baltimore edition of the book, I would classify 43 as British broadsides. Of these no fewer than 30 are included in Appendix I as traditional in North America today. Among them are such pieces as "Willie Riley", "Kate and Her Horns", "Captain Kidd", "Rinordine", "The Apprentice Boy", "The Girl I Left Behind" and "Caroline of Edinburgh Town". Such is the vitality of these "cheap", "vulgar", and "journalistic" pieces produced by hack writers to meet the demands of the ballad press. The extraordinary popularity of *The Forget Me Not Songster* in its many editions implies not only a great interest in old ballads but an actual demand for complete texts to assist flagging memories or to increase singers' repertoires. Because many pieces learned originally from songster texts have now been in tradition for a century or more, their derivation would not be easy to demonstrate. Furthermore many of these pieces must have been learned from sources other than songsters, notably from the ballad sheets, from manuscript "ballet" books, and from other singers. But partial proof of the influence of songsters on the folk is available, as will be shown.

In Nova Scotia one might expect to find folksong in a relatively unspoiled condition, or, as some would have it, uncontaminated by print. The excellent collections of W. Roy Mackenzie and Miss Helen Creighton have demonstrated that the province is a rich source of balladry. A remarkable number of fine texts have been recovered including many not found elsewhere, or found only in fragmentary form. In this connection, the contributions of a singer named Alexander Harrison to Professor Mackenzie's *Ballads and Sea Songs from Nova Scotia* are of unusual interest. A list of Mr.

Harrison's ballads follows, with the number of stanzas given in parentheses: "Lord Bakeman" (25), "Lord Thomas and Fair Ellinor" (21), "Barbara Allan" (18), "The Turkish Lady" (12), "The Prentice Boy" (8 double), "Rinordine" (7 d.), "Ellen the Fair" (6 d.), "The Rocks of Scilly" (19), "The Bonny Bunch of Roses" (6 d.), "Kelly the Pirate" (7 d.), "Bold Dighton" (26 d.), "Captain Glen" (22), "Captain Kidd" (25), and "The Girl Who Was Drowned at Oslow" (7).

The last ballad listed is a Nova Scotian product. All the others, including the three Child ballads, have been learned from the texts of *The Forget Me Not Songster*. I make this statement without qualification for the following reasons: The singer's texts are identical with those in the *Songster* except for the infrequent occurrence of a trifling omission or substitution. The *Songster* texts contain many phrases that are curiously unidiomatic, especially in the long ballad "Bold Dighton". Furthermore in these ballads normal word order is frequently wrenched and the proper names are sometimes unusual. Mr. Harrison has reproduced almost all the difficult passages precisely and has even preserved dialect where it appears, as in "Barbara Allan". With one or two exceptions even archaisms have been retained and properly used. Such accuracy would have been impossible if the singer had not learned these ballads from print. Even if one other singer had intervened, there would have been many more variations.

In "Bold Dighton", for example, Mr. Harrison sang the line "Down by the Umpire the Tiger doth lie". The editor, no doubt thinking *Umpire* a strange name for a ship, checked the old broadsides and appended this footnote: "The broadsides read, 'For 'tis down by yon pier, the Tyger does lay'." Another of Mackenzie's singers gave the line in this form: "Down in yon portway the Tiger she lays." Since the *Umpire* is not mentioned again in the ballad, the editor's footnote seems justified. But the line in the *Songster* reads "Down by the Umpire the Tiger doth lie."

The first four lines of another singer's text of "The Bonny Bunch of Roses" read as follows:

> By the dangers of the ocean,
> In the bonny month of June,
> Those little warbling songsters
> Their notes so cheerfully did tune.

This sounds all right except for the word "dangers". Alexander Harrison's first half stanza reads:

> By the borders of the ocean
> One morning in the month of June,
> For to hear those warlike songsters,
> Their cheerful notes and sweetly tune,

"Warlike songsters" and "and sweetly tune" are obvious corruptions, one would say, caused by oral transmission. But here is the *Songster* text of the same four lines:

> By the borders of the ocean,
> One morning in the month of June,
> For to hear those warlike songsters
> Their cheerful notes and sweetly tune,

If more proof is needed of the source of Mr. Harrison's texts, I might add that with two exceptions all thirteen of his texts are precisely the length of those in the *Songster*—and "Bold Dighton" contains no fewer than 104 long lines, while other texts are also of considerable length. In his rendering of "Lord Bakeman" (Child no. 53), the singer omitted a minor descriptive stanza, and in "Captain Glen" he added a rather meaningless concluding stanza. Here then is a clear case of ballads having been learned from print, although they were accepted by the collector without apparent question. Since the *Songster* does not contain tunes, we must assume that Mr. Harrison appropriated those of other singers. At least he has not contributed any new tunes to Mackenzie's collection.

If a singer like Mr. Harrison taught his texts to his neighbors and they in turn sang them to others, the traditional quality of the pieces would be re-established and their standing as folksongs should be unquestioned. One can hardly doubt that many other singers have learned their ballads from print as Mr. Harrison did long after their original publication and have started them again on the road of traditional song.[38]

---

[38] Herbert Halpert, *JAF* 52, 61, reports that a New Jersey singer of "The Blind Beggar's Daughter" "referred constantly to the text of the song in his copy of the Forget Me Not songster." The editors of *British Ballads from Maine* speak of the Boston edition of the *Forget Me Not Songster*, which was published by J. S. Locke about 1842, as "the songbook most widely known in Maine, with more influence upon our texts than any other printed book." (p. 414). They add, however, that previously learned traditional texts are retained by singers in preference to texts later discovered in songsters.

Chapter III

Broadside Balladry as Traditional Song

During Professor Child's time there was considerable room for doubt about the traditional quality of most of the broadside ballads treated in this book. A number of them were of fairly recent composition and thus too young to be called clearly traditional. Others were widely available in song-books, and it was hard to say whether they had been traditionally learned or merely memorized from print. Still more important, the science of folksong collecting could hardly be said to have developed. Editors were glad enough to print texts which they had received from tradition, but they could rarely resist the temptation to alter and "improve" them, frequently without explanation, Thus Professor Child, throughout his labors, was faced with the necessity of deciding which texts could be called genuine examples of traditional balladry and which had been tampered with by editors or had come from dubious sources. It was only toward the end of the 19th century that a new enthusiasm for genuine folksong took a considerable number of collectors into the field to search for songs among the people who knew them. The founding of the Folk Song Society in London in 1898 helped the cause of balladry immeasurably, and for several decades its journal published hundreds of authentic texts and tunes from British tradition. This type of work has been even more fruitfully pursued in America. Since 1888 the American Folklore Society has constantly been in the forefront of ballad study, and it has been assisted by various regional societies with special interests. The official organ of the Society, The *Journal of American Folklore,* is an outstanding publication in the field of balladry and other branches of folklore. Throughout the United States and the Maritime Provinces of Canada, the collecting of folksongs has flourished for about half a century and shows few signs of diminishing in intensity. Practically all original collections are made with scientific precision, usually

63

with the aid of recording machines. Thus a great wealth of folk balladry has become available to the student.[1]

We rarely worry about the authenticity of our ballad texts because most American editors scrupulously avoid even slight and obvious corrections of texts received from folk singers. Frequently the editors include significant information about their contributors' occupation, age, family background, and way of life, as well as pertinent data on their songs. Thus we are able to judge the value of various texts and to learn something about what happens to songs in tradition. While I have included in Appendix I references to various non-traditional texts from broadsides, songsters, and later anthologies, I have in no known case admitted a ballad which has not been recorded from singers in the 20th century. The singer of "Charming Beauty Bright", or "Molly Bawn" or "The Maid on the Shore" has probably never seen these songs in print, and may in fact be illiterate. He knows the ballads because he learned them, perhaps several decades before, from another singer who had learned them in the same way. Passed as they have been from one singer to another and often imperfectly understood or remembered, these broadside ballads show the inevitable variations characteristic of all folksong. Because most of the pieces are of fairly recent date compared with the Child ballads, and because they circulated widely in print, they have been less affected, for better or worse, by the changes wrought by time, altering social conditions, and a dozen other causes. But the changes that are to be found would show clearly, even without other evidence, that the texts had come from tradition.

The distinction made by scholars between Child ballads and all others is unknown to the folk. An examination of the leading regional collections will show that the contributors of the largest number of pieces have had in their repertories folksongs of many different kinds, old and new, imported and native, humorous and tragic. These singers rarely think in terms of the quality, age, or place of origin of the songs they know; they sing their ballads because they like them. Once accepted by the folk, the broadsides, like the native American ballads, immediately achieved equality with other songs long in tradition. They are sung sincerely, seriously,

---

[1] In the Bibliography I have attempted to list all the important American collections which have been published in book form as well as a representative sampling of British collections.

and without apology. Those collectors who have wondered why some singers will alternate between beautiful old ballads and trite broadsides are applying standards of criticism alien to the folk. Mr. Christie, for example, remarked in a footnote to his text of "A Rich Irish Lady", "The ballad is one of the usual meagre sailor-ballads given to beautiful ballad airs, which thus make trashy ballads favourites with the populace."[2] This statement is based on two generally unjustifiable assumptions, that ballads are preserved because of the airs to which they are sung, and that the populace distinguishes between a so-called trashy ballad and one of greater artistic merit. Undoubtedly a good tune is pleasing to ballad singers, but they would hardly memorize ten or twenty stanzas simply because they found a tune appealing.

Some idea of the comparative strength of the three divisions of American balladry may be gained from examining several representative folksong collections. In the chart given below, I have made use of the following books: Hudson's *Folksongs of Mississippi*, Sharp's *English Folksongs from the Southern Appalachians*, Randolph's *Ozark Folksongs*, Gardner's *Ballads and Songs of Southern Michigan*, Greenleaf's *Ballads and Sea Songs of Newfoundland* and Mackenzie's *Ballads and Sea Songs from Nova Scotia*. The first vertical column shows the total number of folksongs of all types contained in the various collections. The remaining columns are confined to popular ballads as I have defined that term, and the figures, except for the Child ballads, are my own. The columns headed "total number of variants" refer to the collected texts reported by each of the editors. Many of these were obtained as fragments, and others were printed in fragmentary form, if at all. Not all the texts have come from tradition, nor is the exact source of every text given. For these reasons the chart may not be statistically correct, but at least it will give an idea of the relative vigor in America of the native, the broadside, and the Child ballad traditions.[3]

---

[2] *Traditional Ballad Airs* II, 240.

[3] The interests, preferences, and judgments of ballad collectors and editors in some measure determine the contents of ballad anthologies. For instance, Sharp was primarily concerned with folksongs imported from Britain, while Randolph's collection contains practically everything sung by the folk, whatever its style or origin. Thus the printed collections indicate only in a general way the popularity of various ballads and ballad types.

Editor	Total no. of ballads and songs	Native Amer. ballads	Total no. of texts	Child ballads	Total no. of texts	Brit. broad-sides	Total no. of texts
Hudson	157	32	35	27	67	24	25
Sharp	273	8	19	45	365	67	246
Randolph	883	69	196	41	109	67	140
Gardner	201	24	51	28	44	77	125
Greenleaf	185	22	22	19	27	63	69
Mackenzie	162	14	14	16	30	106	122
Totals	1861	169	337	176	642	404	727

Many reasons may be offered to explain the dominant position in America of the British broadside ballads. In the 18th and early 19th centuries, when native American balladry was in its infancy, the British broadsides were being widely distributed throughout this country on ballad sheets both domestic and imported and in hundreds of song books. During the same period relatively few of the Child ballads were generally available in print. In general, the more frequently a ballad was reprinted a century or so ago, the greater the likelihood of its continued vitality in tradition. The broadsides were so well established in American tradition before the Civil War and throughout the period of Westward migration that the native pieces, even if they had been of equal merit and had had equally wide distribution, might have had only partial success in ousting the old favorites. As it was, the native ballads sprang largely from self-contained regions and had only limited diffusion, usually without the aid of print, from their place of origin. Moreover, the native ballads do not, in general, exhibit the competence of the imported pieces in versification and story telling. In addition to having the advantages of early arrival and frequent reprinting, the British broadside tradition was constantly being strengthened by the arrival of immigrants to America. The Irish not only brought with them dozens of new ballads but also helped to create the demand for the great variety of Irish song books which were printed in America late in the 19th century. Immigrants are, in fact, sometimes more successful in cherishing the folklore of the old country than are those who remain at home. Before the American Revolution, of course, there was not even a divided loyalty to separate the British from the colonial ballads. And neither political separation nor the wars that resulted from it could destroy the fondness of some ballad singing Americans for the original homeland. Of course the Canadians, whose ballads are included here, feel much closer to Britain and sing a number of pieces unknown in the States.

While many differences existed between life in the new world and that in the old, the British emigrants brought with them a deeply rooted cultural heritage which has permeated American life. The habits of thought and the social customs reflected in many British broadsides, as well as the characters who appear in them, are so familiar to Americans that singers usually think of them as native or even local pieces. Then, too, many of the broadsides possess a general human interest unrelated to a specific time or place. This is in contrast to some of the Child ballads, which deal with long forgotten occurrences such as the 16th and 17th century conflicts along the Scottish border. The broadsides also have an advantage in this respect over a large percentage of native American ballads, which sprang from unique ways of life in such places as the lumber camp, the Southern prison, or the Western range. Furthermore, the broadsides are generally more modern than the Child ballads by from one to several centuries. Thus they are less likely to contain archaisms of speech or to reflect ways of life and folk beliefs no longer current. The lordly life of bower and hall which gives the older balladry so much of its charm is absent from the broadsides. The decline in belief in the supernatural is also reflected in them. The more fantastic stories of fairy and devil lore or of magic transformations have largely disappeared, although ghost stories occur fairly frequently and are apparently believed in by most singers. While the sophisticated reader will find the average broadsides wretched examples of verse, they are generally quite singable, and if sung to good tunes, as many of them are, they have considerable emotional impact. This statement holds true not only for the people among whom ballads are traditional. Many a city audience in a night club or a concert hall has been held spellbound by broadsides effectively sung. Some of the Child and native American ballads have equal or greater power to hold an audience, but the British broadsides as a class have remained vital and meaningful while many ballads in the other two groups have become obsolete.

Professor Child and the Broadsides

As I am well aware, anyone who attempts to develop a canon of balladry must be constantly assailed, as Professor Child was, by doubts about what to include and exclude. The key phrase in Child's title is "popular ballads". The ballads were the heritage of the people, and the best of them displayed a combination of folk style and folk matter, along with a measure of antiquity. The city ballad rhymester whose products were the ephemeral outpourings of a facile pen held little interest for him. Child once wrote to Professor Grundtvig, the great Danish ballad scholar, as follows:

> The immense collections of broadside ballads, the Roxburghe and Pepys, of which but a small part has been printed, doubtless contain some ballads which we should at once declare to possess the popular character, and yet on the whole they are veritable dung-hills, in which, only after a great deal of sickening grubbing, one finds a very moderate jewel. Some of the later Robin Hood ballads I have scarcely patience or stomach to read: but the declension is so gradual from the freshest and raciest to the thoroughly *vulgar,* (by which I mean always the *essentially* vulgar, the absolutely mean and stupid) that it will be very hard, and to me at this moment looks impossible, to draw a line.[4]

[4] Letter of August 25, 1872, printed by Hustvedt, *Ballad Books and Ballad Men,* p. 254.

A further distinction between the two types of balladry may be found in Child's article "Ballad Poetry" (*Johnson's Universal Cyclopaedia,* 1896, I, 466): ". . . From what has been said, it may be seen or inferred that the popular ballad is not originally the product or the property of the lower orders of the people. Nothing, in fact, is more obvious than that many of the ballads of the now most refined nations had their origin in that class whose acts and fortunes they depict—the upper class —though the growth of civilization has driven them from the memory of the highly polished and instructed, and has left them as an exclusive possession to the uneducated. The genuine popular ballad had its rise in a time when the distinctions since brought by education and other circumstances had practically no existence. The vulgar ballads of our day, the 'broadsides' which were printed in such huge numbers in England and elsewhere in the sixteenth century or later, belong to a different genus; they are products of a low kind of *art,* and most of them are,

This quotation is significant for several reasons. It shows that Child considered "popular character" an indication of genuine worth and that he thought of most broadsides as worthless. Now popular or non-literary character or folk style is not an illusion, but it is easier to recognize than define. It is often concise, suggestive, artless, vigorous, and true, while low literary or broadside style is likely to be artificial, uninspired, detailed, feeble, and false. But unfortunately these sets of qualities are not mutually exclusive, and hence the difficulty in drawing a line between them. The passage indicates also that the Child anthology was to result in part from the necessity of making decisions rather than from an exact system of selection or a feeling of infallibility on the compiler's part. Child would perhaps feel unduly complimented to know that only an additional handful of the clearly traditional ballads have been advanced by his disciples as worthy of a place in his collection.[5] Also worth commenting upon is the implication that the merit of a piece should be considered as a test of genuineness. There is not the slightest reason, however, why there cannot be both good and bad popular ballads, just as there are good and bad examples of every other form of art. Even if we ignore the broadside texts, Child's collection contains ample proof of this assertion. But Child frequently applied aesthetic standards in deciding what to include. Thus he considered not a few of the apparently traditional pieces worthless and included them under protest. He was suspicious for

---

from a literary point of view, thoroughly despicable and worthless." (These remarks do not consider the problems created by those broadside ballads which have become traditional).

[5] For example, M. J. C. Hodgart in *The Ballads* (1950) writes as follows:

"In this short survey of ballad texts, I have discussed only those included in Child's collection. But there are a few others of the same type which Child overlooked or rejected; and since they seem to conform with the ballad aesthetic, and contain much beautiful and unfamiliar verse, they should be mentioned here.

"Only nine of them are worth considering: 'The Bitter Withy', 'Still Growing' [0 35], 'Corpus Christi', 'The Seven Virgins', 'The Blind Beggar of Bethnal Green' [N 27], 'Bruton Town' [M 32], 'The Shooting of his Dear' [0 36], 'The Bold Fisherman' [0 24], and, more doubtfully, 'Six Dukes Went A-Fishing.' 'The Bitter Withy' is the only one of these which has been universally accepted."

Of course everyone is free to propose his own list of candidates for inclusion with the Child ballads, and no two lists will be identical.

example, of certain texts found only in Peter Buchan's collection, such as those which became Child nos. 263-265.[6] Later collecting by Gavin Greig showed that Buchan's ballads were genuine examples of Scottish folk tradition.[7]

Feeling that broadside ballads lacked merit and were not truly popular, he tended to exclude them even when there was evidence of their having entered tradition. Thus in his discussion of "Young Beichan" (no. 53), he refers to "The Turkish Lady" as a broadside ballad but does not reprint it (I, 463). On the other hand he almost always included the available broadside texts of any ballads which he considered popular and which existed in traditional texts. And sometimes he points out that the broadside text has found its way into tradition alongside the older versions. Thus he remarks that the English version of "Lord Thomas and Fair Annet" (no. 73) is a broadside of the time of Charles II which has become traditional in Scotland and Ireland, while his Scottish traditional copy is far superior (II, 180).

Professor Child's rejection of most broadside ballads and his inclusion of a fair number of such pieces cannot be explained on the basis of quality alone. An investigation of the broadside ballads in his collection, aside from those added to traditional texts for the sake of completeness, will show that they appear for several different reasons, some quite unrelated to the merits of the individual pieces. The following discussion will suggest some of the methods which Child used in establishing his canon. Among his reasons for including ballads known only from broadsides or directly traceable to broadsides may be mentioned the following:

    1. The broadside ballad, even though of little worth in itself, is part of an important class of ballads or a major folk tradition. Many of the Robin Hood ballads appear for this reason. Number 137, "Robin Hood and the Pedlars," for example, has not even the dubious authority of a broadside but exists only in a manuscript of uncertain date and may be "a copy of a broadside, or a copy of a copy" (III, 170). "Robin Hood's Golden Prize" (no. 147) exists only in broadside form, as does "A True Tale of Robin Hood" (no. 154), which was written by Martin Parker. In referring to "The King's Disguise and Friendship

---

[6] Francis J. Child, *The English and Scottish Popular Ballads*. See his comments in Vol. IV, pp. 434, 435, and 437.

[7] Alexander Keith convincingly defends Buchan's reputation as a collector and editor in *Last Leaves of Traditional Ballads*, pp. xix-xxxi.

with Robin Hood" (no. 151), as well as to nos. 152 and 153, Child
quotes Ritson's comment that it seems "to have been written by some
miserable retainer to the press . . .; being, in fact, a most contemptible
performance" (III, 220). Once Child had decided to include all the
Robin Hood ballads, he accepted pieces without merit and without
"popular character."

2. The broadside ballad, poor as it is, may contain traces of an
older and better but unknown ballad. Thus of "The Famous Flower
of Serving Men" (no. 106) Child writes, "The English broadside . . .
may reasonably be believed to be formed upon a predecessor in the
popular style" (II, 430).

3. The broadside ballad exhibits folk style and probably comes
from tradition. Child assumes that the text of "Prince Heathen" (no.
104) from Buchan's manuscripts "is no doubt some stall-copy reshaped
from tradition" (II, 424). Child's assumption may or may not be
correct; the point is that he would print a broadside alone if he believed the ballad truly "popular" and if no traditional text was available.

4. The broadside text is apparently the original. This is true of
"King Henry Fifth's Conquest of France" (no. 164), which Child
believed might date from the second quarter of the 18th century. "The
broadside," he writes, "is in a popular manner, but has no mark of
antiquity. It may, however, represent an older ballad, disfigured by
some purveyors for the Aldermary press."[8] He goes on to say, "It
is probable that the recited versions had their ultimate source in
print . . ." (III, 320). These statements are significant in indicating
that Child recognized the existence of the "popular manner" in some
original broadsides and also in pointing out, as he frequently does,
that "recited" or traditional texts are descended from broadsides. "The
Bailiff's Daughter of Islington" (no. 105) is another example of an
original broadside known to have become traditionally popular.

5. The broadside ballad contains elements found elsewhere in European balladry or legend. "The Suffolk Miracle" (no. 272), says Child,
"could not be admitted here on its own merits." But he goes on to add:
"I have printed this ballad because, in a blurred, enfeebled, and disfigured shape, it is the representative in England of one of the most
remarkable tales and one of the most impressive and beautiful ballads
of the European continent" (V, 58-59).

6. The broadside ballad, though it has nothing much to recommend
it, is popular among the folk and serves as a sample of a larger group
of late and inferior ballad imitations. Of "The Crafty Farmer" (no.
283), Child has this to say: "This very ordinary ballad has enjoyed
great popularity, and is given for that reason and as a specimen of

---

[8] A common 18th century imprint reads "Printed and sold in Aldermary
Churchyard".

its class." (V, 283). Child gives references to similar ballads but does not dignify them by individual treatment.

Set up beside Child's ideal ballads, many of the late broadsides must have seemed poor things indeed, and it is not hard to understand why he often apologized for those which he included. He not only knew that the best days of balladry were over, but he felt that they had been over for a long time. The singing of old ballads, he thought, was practically extinct. For example, in his headnote to "The Twa Sisters" (no. 10), Child says, "This is one of the very few old ballads which are not extinct as tradition in the British Isles" (I, 118). Later collectors have dramatically demonstrated how wrong this statement was. Actually it is surprising that Child included as many broadsides as he did, considering how he felt about them and how little was known in his day about the ballads in tradition. He believed that with modern times he had reached the last gasp of balladry, the weak fabrications and imitations of something that was once fine and vigorous. Thus he was not really being so inconsistent when he included "The Crafty Farmer" without adding such related ballads as "The Yorkshire Bite" and "The Highwayman Outwitted". A few examples of the ballad's decline would suffice; it was not necessary to burden an extremely long work with a great deal of trash to illustrate a point. From our point of view, however, it is unfortunate that "The Crafty Farmer" has a Child number while the related pieces do not. All three are still sung, and all merit attention as examples of traditional balladry.

Of the three ballads "The Yorkshire Bite" is the most widely known, having been printed at least twenty times from American tradition. "The Highwayman Outwitted" has been reported only once from North America, though several British texts have appeared. And "The Crafty Farmer", according to Belden and Hudson (Brown, 189) has appeared twice in Britain and once in America. For purposes of comparison I am reprinting a broadside text of each of these pieces.

"THE YORKSHIRE FARMER"

(*The Crafty Farmer*)

Reprinted by Child from Kidson's *Traditional Tunes*.
Kidson's text is from *The Manchester Songster*, 1792.

A song I will sing unto you
A song of merry intent,
It is of a silly old man
That went to pay his rent,
That went to pay his rent.

And as he was riding along,
A riding along the highway,
A gentleman-thief steps before the old man
And thus unto him he did say.

'My friend, how dare you ride alone?
For so many thieves there now be;
If any should but light on you,
They'd rob you of all your money.'

'If that they should light upon me,
I'm sure they'd be very ill-sped,
For, to tell you the truth, my kind sir,
In my saddle my money I've hid.'

So as they were riding along,
And going down a steep hill,
The gentleman-thief slipped before the old man
And quickly he bid him stand still.

The old man, however, being cunning,
As in this world there are many,
He threw his saddle right over the hedge,
Saying,   Fetch it if thou wouldst have any.

The thief being so greedy of money—
He thought that of it there'd been bags—
Whipt out a rusty old sword
And chopped the saddle to rags.

The old man put his foot in the stirrup
And presently he got astride;
He put the thief's horse to the gallop,
You need not bid the old man ride.

'Nay, stay! nay, stay! says the thief,
'And half the money thou shalt have;'
'Nay, by my troth,' says the old man,
'For once I have cheated a knave.'

And so the old man rode along,
And went with a merry devotion,
Saying, If ever I live to get home,
'T will enlarge my daughter's portion.

And having arrived at home,
And got there with merry intent,
Says he, Landlord, show me a room,
And I'll pay you your half-year's rent.

They opened the thief's portmanteau,
And from it they took out so bold
A hundred pounds in silver
And a hundred pounds in gold.

"THE LINCOLNSHIRE FARMER'S DAUGHTER"
(*The Highwayman Outwitted*)

Reprinted from a broadside by Harkness in the Houghton Library
at Harvard University.

In Lincolnshire lived a rich farmer,
And his daughter to market would go;
Thinking that no body would harm her,
As she rode away to and fro.

Till she met with a lusty highwayman,
Her pockets he drew from her sides;
And as she stood shivering and shaking,
He gave her the bridle to hold.

From stirrup to saddle she mounted,
She threw her legs over like a man;
All the way that she gallop'd, she shouted—
Now catch me you rogue, if you can.

This highwayman soon followed after,
A bullet from his pistol let fly;
He ran, but he could not come at her,
His boots they so hampered his knees.

As she rode over her father's green pasters,
It had just struck a eleven by the clock;
Her father was sorely afrighted, to see
Her ride home in her smock.

O daughter what has been the matter, you
Have tarried so long from your home?
O father I have been sorely afrighted,
But still I have come to no harm.

Then he pulled from behind her, a
Port mantell with several articals more;
And ninety score of bright guineas,
He tumbled them out on the floor.

O father this is a grand portion,
It will keep the wild wolf from the door;
O daughter it is a grand portion,
Unto thee I will give as much more.

Then here is a health to the lass,
That the risk of her life she has run;
She tricked the highwayman completely
Out of his horse, money and gun.

"THE CRAFTY PLOUGHBOY, OR HIGHWAYMAN OUTWITTED"
(*The Yorkshire Bite*)

Reprinted from a broadside by Pitts in my possession.

Please draw near and the truth I'll declare,
Of a farmer that lived in Herefordshire,
A fine Yorkshire boy he had for his man,
For to do his business, his name it was John.

One morning right early he sent for his man
And when he came to him all this he resign'd,
He says take this cow this day to the fair,
She is in good order and her I can spare.

Away the boy went with his cow in a band,
He came to the fair as you shall understand,
And in a short time he met with three men,
Sold one of them his cow for six pound ten.

They went to the alehouse in order to drink,
Where farmer paid the boy down the chink,
The boy to the mistress thus he did say,
What mu[s]t I do with my money I pray

I'll sow it within thy coat lining says she,
For fear on the road thou robbed should be,
And there set a highwayman drinking of wine,
Thought he to himself now the money is mine.

The boy took his leave and homeward did go,
The highwayman he follow'd after also
And he soon overtook him upon the highway,
Well overtaken young man he did say.

Will you get up behind me the highwayman said,
How far are you going? replied the lad,
Three or four miles for what I do know,
So he got up behind him and away he did go,

They rode till they came into a dark lane,
Now says the highwayman I will tell you plain,
Deliver your money without fear or strife,
Or else I shall certainly take your sweet life,

The boy found that there was no time to dispute
So he alighted from him without fear or doubt,
Tore his coat lining and the money pulled out
And among the long grass he strew'd it about,

The highwayman he alighted off from his horse,
But little did he dream it was for his loss,
Before he could find all the money they say,
The boy jump'd on horseback and rode away.

The highwayman shouted and bid him to stay,
The boy would not hear him but kept on his way,
And to his old master the boy he did bring,
Horse, saddle and bridal a very fine thing.

The ma[s]ter [h]e came to the door and said thus,
What the pox is my cow turn'd into a horse,
The boy said good master your cow I have sold,
But was robbed on the way by an highwayman bold

My money I strewed it about the ground,
For to take it up then the rogue alighted down,
And while he was putting it into his purse,
To make him amends I came off with his horse.

The master laughed while his side he could hol[d]
And said for a boy thou hast been very bold,
As for the villain thou hast served him right,
And you have put on him a right Yorkshire bite.

They searched his bag and quickly they told,
Two hundred pounds in silver and gold,
And two brace of pistols the boy said I vow,
And I think no[w] good master I sold well your cow

This boy for his courage and valour so rare,
Three parts of the money he got for his share,
And now since the highwayman has lost his store,
He may go a robbing until he gets more.

While the second and third pieces are carelessly printed, "The
Yorkshire Farmer" is certainly not superior to them in style, substance, or folk quality. In fact, "The Lincolnshire Farmer's Daughter" gives evidence, especially in the confused second stanza, of
having been printed from folk tradition. Furthermore, texts of the
latter two ballads which have been collected from the folk show
numerous and sometimes strikingly effective departures from those
printed here.

Here then is the crux of the matter. If pieces of this type are to
be called popular ballads, the term may be applied with equal justice
to dozens or hundreds of traditional broadsides. Professor Gummere
saw this issue with the utmost clarity, although he argued against
broadening the definition of popular balladry. In *The Popular
Ballad* he wrote as follows of the Child canon:

> . . . These three-hundred-odd ballads are either the surviving speci-
> mens of a genre, a literary species, which is called popular because in
> its main qualities it is derived from the 'people', or else they are the
> somewhat arbitrary collection of poems which had in some way be-
> come favorite and even traditional, apart from print, with mainly
> unlettered folk. In the first case they can be treated as a closed literary
> account, as an outcome of conditions which no longer exist and can-
> not be revived. In the second case, while conditions of oral transmission
> may be changed, there is nothing to prevent the daily production of
> ballads which may become in time as popular as any in our collections.[9]

That the Child collection is "somewhat arbitrary" has, I believe,
been demonstrated. That balladry is not a "closed literary account"
the twentieth century collections have proved time and again. Thus
we arrive at the alternative conclusion which Gummere wished to
avoid. The evolution of traditional balladry has continued, and some

---

[9] pp. 15-16.

of the broadsides, as well as some pieces of undetermined origin, have become "as popular as any in our collections".

The foregoing analysis shows that Professor Child made a distinction between ballads displaying the popular character and those which were merely sung by the people. The wealth of material scientifically collected since his time has necessitated a broader view of traditional balladry. We recognize certain distinguishing features of the ballad type, but we do not refuse admittance to a piece because it lacks those qualities which we associate with ballad excellence. This is not an attempt to blur the valid and long-standing distinctions between a fine old ballad like "Sir Patrick Spens" (Child no. 58) and a feeble modern broadside like "The Rocks of Scilly". But as Child said, one type merges with the other, and on the basis of style alone, ballads in a middle position could be placed in either category. While Child found himself unable to exclude all broadsides, he arbitrarily dismissed the bulk of them as worthless. If ballads ranging from excellent to execrable are traditional among the people, it seems more logical today to base our canons of balladry not on abstract theory but on what is actually sung.

Typical Child Ballads and Broadsides

The fact that certain traditional broadsides are indistinguishable in style and content from various Child Ballads does not preclude our making a distinction between the two classes of balladry. A re-examination of the best known Child ballads will show that they appeal to us for the same reasons that they appealed to the literary men of earlier times: they represent the distilled essence of all those qualities which we call romantic. Their stories usually take place in the indefinite past, often in the Middle Ages, among people of high rank or fame. Castles and bowers, gold and silver, minstrels and harpers, kings and queens, high sheriffs and outlaws, fair ladies and wicked step-mothers—all help to transport the reader or listener far from his own prosaic surroundings into a world molded in many ways nearer to the heart's desire. The frequent use of the supernatural and the vestiges of half-forgotten beliefs add further to the charm of the old balladry. Here is freedom from conventions and inhibitions and even freedom from law in a society of personal rewards and punishments, of direct action, and of elemental emotions. Here is romantic love, sometimes triumphant, sometimes ending in death, but usually long-suffering, forthright, and passionate. Here are stories of villainous plotting and cruelty, courageous fighting and dying, and poignant grief. It is not the events alone that move us, or the romantic characters, or the dreamlike setting, but the happy blending of them all in a simple song-story, often crude by artistic standards yet perfect in its lasting power to cast a spell.

Of course there is poetry too in the Child ballads, though not so much as is commonly thought. Those who speak highly of ballad poetry can quote many a memorable couplet or quatrain. But the poetic effect of the ballads is partly the result of the folk tradition which has preserved them. The compression and condensation of narrative and the abrupt transitions which occur in tradition tend to increase the suggestive power of many passages. And the repetitions, simple and incremental, produce a hypnotic effect on the reader or listener which tends to dull his critical perception. The typical Child ballad contains some good poetry, but taken as a whole it is not a good poem. Undoubtedly the old ballad composers possessed considerable poetic skill, but many of their original effects have worn away in tradition, leaving only an approximation of the earlier passages. It should be remembered also that the materials of balladry have always been the common property of all who could use them. The older balladists could draw from a richly colorful storehouse of incidents, characters, and settings, and this unique and effective method of story telling must have been second nature to them. Some of what we call good poetry in the old ballads is the accidental result of the merging of stock materials and the conventional method of narration. But the diction of the old ballads is usually satisfying, whatever its origin, and the real ballad lover resents those editorial attempts at poetic improvement which have been practiced off and on since Bishop Percy's day.

Like their predecessors, the broadside ballad makers also dealt with the world around them, but it was a very different world. The medieval glory had departed, and they were completely out of touch with the life of the Scottish border, the greenwood, or the nobleman's castle. Human passions remained relatively constant, but they now displayed themselves in incidents of everyday life among the common people. In street balladry the nobles are replaced by soldiers, sailors, and tradesmen; the princesses become milkmaids or merchant's daughters. The castles shrink to cottages or taverns, and the great deeds of the past become rather trivial occurrences. Since belief in the supernatural had weakened, the spells and magic transformations disappeared, leaving only some rather prosaic ghosts to walk in the new balladry. A folk hero like Robin Hood gives way to a long succession of obscure criminals who find their way eventually to Botany Bay or the gallows. Romantic love becomes conventionalized and commonplace; its emphasis has shifted from the motivated actions of the characters to unlikely events of the ballad-makers' contriving. To the lovers of literature all these changes represent a marked decline in ballad quality, but the folk have not always reacted in the same way. The broadside ballad-makers' world has been their world, too, and they have accepted some of the new pieces as readily as the old—and sometimes in preference to the old. They respond to the familiar and they are little concerned with aesthetic appeals or with the sophisticated cult of romanticism.

Many of the Child ballads were composed during the 16th and 17th centuries when broadside balladry was flourishing. How then can we account for the general inferiority of the broadsides? Two possible explanations may be offered. The later Child balladry was largely Scottish or border balladry which must have been inspired almost entirely by older balladry of high quality. The later ballads were naturally composed in the same style and in the same dialect, and they made use of the commonplaces of incident and phraseology which are most readily associated with ballad genuineness and merit. In addition the ballads entered tradition under favorable circumstances and had from the start more of the folk character impressed upon them by generations of singers. Thus except for the historical events which they may recount, it would be difficult to distinguish a fairly late ballad from a much older one.

The broadsides, on the other hand, were written largely by city authors out of touch with folk tradition. Their models were earlier broadsides, most of which did not exhibit the techniques of the older popular balladry. These journalistic pieces were then printed and reprinted until a relatively stable form was established. Thus when these broadsides entered tradition, they could not easily or quickly acquire the characteristics of folk balladry. Very few traditional broadsides fail to display evidence of their origin.[10]

---

[10] Professor MacEdward Leach observes, however, that ballads preserved among folk singers with good taste are likely to be improved. It would

Regardless of their many artistic inadequacies, the authors of the traditional broadsides were obviously successful and their success is partly attributable to their mediocrity. The conventional phrasing, the use of stock situations, the uninspired rhymes, and the character types already more than familiar may be condemned by the critics, but they are welcomed by the undiscriminating folk. And conversely many of the best Child ballads with their exotic and archaic qualities which we find most appealing have dropped out of tradition because of their unfamiliarity.

Although their products compare unfavorably with the Child ballads, the British broadside composers are generally superior in technical skill to the authors of native American balladry. Like the verse of many a minor poet, the ballads exhibit a certain fluency of expression which half conceals their lack of substance. The authors manage to get their stories told without doing great violence to rhyme and meter, and not infrequently their phrasing is succinct and appropriate. The American balladists, by contrast, have often labored against the handicap of illiteracy and have had a constant struggle to subdue the language to their purposes. But crude as many of them are, the American ballads share with the Child pieces the ability to move the reader to a sympathetic reaction, while the broadsides are likely to produce a feeling of amused detachment. Perhaps the commercial origin of the broadsides is at fault here. The authors of the Child pieces, like the American authors, may have been inspired by actual events which affected them emotionally, while the broadside writers were merely spinning fanciful yarns for money.

Much has been written about the impersonality of the Child ballads. Their stories are narrated objectively without much intrusion on the part of the authors. The broadside authors, on the other hand, show a fondness for the first person method of narration. Sometimes the use of the first person is merely a means of getting the story under way, as in those ballads in which the narrator acts as an eavesdropper. In other pieces the narrator is the main actor, and the ballads contain many personal expressions of emotion. Where the Child ballad is content with suggestion and implication, the broadside spells out to the listener its advice and its warnings.

---

be interesting to study the fate of standard broadside texts in different communities of folk singers.

Other deficiencies are observable in the balladry which first appears on broadsides. Dialogue, for example, is used less effectively than in the Child ballads. It tends to be expository rather than dramatic, and the speeches are often wordy and stilted. In general the broadsides are dramatically weak. The "leaping and lingering" of the Child ballads, which Professor Gummere spoke about, resulted in brevity where transitional events were concerned and permitted a relatively full development of the most vital action. The broadside writer tells his story at a fairly even rate without distinguishing between major and minor events, and he tends to interrupt the narrative to indicate his own reactions to it. Where the Child ballad moves forward economically and objectively, the broadside is detailed and contrived. The author of the old ballads has receded so far into the background that we are unaware of his existence, while we are conscious of the broadside writer as he manipulates the strings which control his puppets.

The broadside balladist is rarely open-minded, intuitive, or perceptive. His judgments, with which he is rather liberal, are conventional reactions to outward events. He makes no effort to understand or to sympathize with those whose actions fall outside his preconceived notions of what is proper. In telling stories that could be truly poignant or tragic, he relies heavily on sensationalism and sentimentality. The champion of young love, of the law, of female virtue, and of a strict moral code, he is not unaware of the cash value of violence and bloodshed. If he writes of a sordid murder, for example, it is likely to remain just that in his final product. In Child balladry such a story will sometimes achieve the dramatic and passionate quality of great art.

Even the clichés of Child balladry have dramatic impact or connotative power. "Go saddle me my milk-white steed" is more than a trite command; it suggests the outward trappings of an entire way of life. "An ill death may he die" is charged with bitter anger and hatred. "Make my bed soon" clearly foreshadows the death to come. But what can be said of the standard expressions of broadside balladry?

> Come listen to my tragedy
> While I relate the same.
>
> O Willie do not murder me,
> For I'm not prepared to die.

My parents reared me tenderly,
They had no child but me.

Such phrases pulled indiscriminately from the street balladists'
grab-bag of clichés have the power to evoke nothing but disappoint-
ment. The older clichés are compressed expressions essential to the
story, while those of the broadsides are used mainly because the
author could think of nothing better. But triteness in broadside
balladry goes far beyond the use of a few overworked expressions.
The entire ballad is likely to be trite in conception and execution.
Stock characters are put through a series of adventures differing
only in arrangement or in minor details from those of a dozen other
street ballads. The basic situations, the morals drawn from them,
the standard expressions of emotion, and the observations on human
nature, all have been treated time and again. The average or below
average broadside is not so much composed as patched together from
the materials at hand.

The foregoing critical remarks apply more specifically to the
broadsides as printed literature than as folksong. The repetition
of familiar patterns is the essence of traditional art, and the Child
ballads, too, are imitative and repetitious. We cannot condemn the
broadside ballad makers for their conservatism, but we cannot help
wishing that their models had been of higher quality.

Chapter IV

Broadside Ballad Forms and Variants

Most of the broadside ballads have been composed in patterns different from ballad meter, the alternating lines of iambic tetrameter and iambic trimeter rhyming a b c b . Of course, analysis will show that ballad meter has by no means been consistently used in the Child ballads, though many of the better known pieces exist in that form. Ballad meter was well established and widely known long before most of these broadsides appeared; thus we may justly think of it as the basic structure upon which the other ballad forms are built. Since the authors of the now traditional broadsides were not often technically skilful versifiers, they were frequently careless about the number of syllables in a ballad line, and their stresses were often scattered without regard to poetic niceties. On the other hand, they should not be considered mere writers of doggerel. Many of them were able enough in the rather undemanding forms which they chose, and the changes which all ballads undergo in tradition are responsible for some of the apparent irregularities. As used here the metrical terms will refer to the underlying structure of the stanza and will disregard casual variations whether inherent or acquired.[1]

The following stanza will illustrate the broadside composer's use of ballad meter as well as that flatness or lack of color so characteristic of broadside verses:

> In Catherine Street I did resort,
> Where people did me know,
> I fell in love with a pretty girl
> Which proved my overthrow.   (L 17. Eddy, 171)

---

[1] When a ballad is traditionally performed, it is a song rather than a poem, and thus ballad form and accent are best studied in connection with ballad music. The original broadsides, on the other hand, were composed as verses to be printed usually without any indication of a tune. Thus we may be justified in discussing broadside texts as metrical poems. For technical analyses of ballad music and ballad meter see Sharp's *English Folk Song: Some Conclusions* and Hendren's *A Study in Ballad Rhythm*.

This stanza might also have been written as a couplet rhyming a a :

> In Catherine Street I did resort, where people did me know,
> I fell in love with a pretty girl which proved by overthrow.

Not only are stanzas in ballad meter frequently printed as couplets but the music to which they are sung often corresponds more closely to two long lines than to four short ones.

Here is a livelier stanza from another ballad of crime:

> "When once we reach the shore, brave boys,
> We'll shout and sing for joy;
> We'll hiss and stone those horse police
> And sing 'Bold Johnny Troy'." (L 21. Gardner, 330)

The sense of the stanza would lend itself readily to the couplet form, as would that of the next example.

If a final unaccented syllable is added to the trimeter lines, a stanza like the following is produced.

> I went down to her father's house,
> Just like some honest fellow;
> I told her that the plums were ripe,
> And a-getting very mellow. (N 24. Gardner, 393)

If the final syllables of the tetrameter lines are dropped, a stanza in trimeter results:

> It was on one summer's morning
> All in the month of May,
> Down by the flowery garden,
> Miss Betty she did stray,
> Down by the flowery garden,
> Miss Betty she did stray. (N 40. Scarborough, 266)

Here the repetition of the last two lines of a short stanza seems to have been a peculiarity of the singer. The ballad ("The Banks of Claudy") is usually printed in stanzas of eight short lines as in a later example.

Broadside writers have a fondness, too, for the quatrain of regular tetrameter lines. To form one, an iambic foot is added to the trimeter lines of ballad meter:

> She said, "Were I to love inclined
> Perhaps you soon might change your mind
> And court some other damsel fair,
> For men are false, I do declare." (N 22. Mackenzie, 326)

It will be seen that the rhyme scheme here is a a b b. The addition of an unaccented syllable to the first and third lines of the tetrameter quatrain produces this pattern:

> "I dare not go and ask my father,
> For he is on his bed of rest,
> And by his side a shining dagger
> To pierce the one that I love best."   (M 4. Greenleaf, 55)

From the iambic tetrameter lines it is an easy step to the anapestic tetrameter, which is one of the favorite meters of the broadside balladist. A typical line begins with an iambic foot followed by three anapests. A popular old ballad, "The Blind Beggar's Daughter of Bednall Green" is written in this form:

> So Billy and Betsy to church they did go;
> Now Billy and Betsy they cut a fine show;
> The beautifullest creature that ever was seen
> Was the blind beggar's daughter of Bethelan Green.   (N 27. Eddy, 84)

These stanzas, too, are likely to rhyme a a b b. Frequently another unstressed syllable is added to the first and third lines, as in "The Lass of Glenshee". The first stanza of the Gardner text may be seen in Appendix I. If the balladist drops the final foot from each line, the result is again close to ballad meter, except for the anapests. Here is a stanza from "Willie and Mary":

> Three years had pass'd/Without news, when at last,
> As she sat at her cottage door,
> An old beggar came by,/With a patch o'er his eye,
> Quite lame, and did pity implore.[2]

We now come to the double length or "come-all-ye" stanzas, which may be considered a further development of ballad meter and its modifications. It will be seen that the following stanza from "The Banks of Claudy" is equivalent to two stanzas in ballad meter with the final stresses of the tetrameter lines missing. If these eight-line stanzas are written in four lines, the result is the familiar iambic hexameter line with two unstressed syllables in the middle.

> 'This is the banks of Claudy,
> Fair maid on which you stand.
> And do not trust to Johnny,

---

[2] Barry, p. 24. Though the *Songster* text is printed in six-line stanzas, most collectors have printed the ballad in quatrains.

> For he is a false young man.
> For Johnny doth deceive you
> And doth not meet you here.
> Tarry with me in these green woods;
> No dangers need you fear.'   (N 40. Belden, 155).

Combining two full stanzas of ballad meter produces another popular come-all-ye stanza. Here again editors have been uncertain about the proper method of printing these ballads. They appear as separate stanzas in ballad meter, as long couplets, as stanzas of eight short lines, or as stanzas of four long lines. Usually the tune will suggest the preferred form. If not, an original broadside printing might at least indicate the author's intention. This matter is not so important, however, as a realization of the extremely close relationship between ballad meter and the come-all-ye form. The following stanzas illustrate the two common ways of printing the longer stanza.

> She stepped up to her true love
> And she took him by the hand
> She said, "You are my prisoner
> And I will you command;
> You have robbed me of my treasure
> And I will try you for your life."
> "Indeed, my Lord, I never robbed
> A man in all my life."   (N 15. Thomas, 78)

> It's true I am an Irishman, the truth I won't deny;
> Before I'll be put down by you, it's on our deck I'll die;
> And if you're a man of courage bold, it's me you'll stand before;
> I'll fight you here upon the deck of the *City of Baltimore*."
> (K 26. Greenleaf, 354)

Anapestic hexameters appear, too, to create lines of unusual length:

> One morning I careless did ramble where the sweet wind's pure breezes did blow;
> 'Twas down by a clear crystal river where the sweet purling waters doth flow.
> It was there I beheld a fair damsel, some goddess appearing to be,
> As she rose from the reeds by the waters on the green mossy banks of the Lea.   (O 15. Mackenzie, 135).

The writer of such a stanza, whatever his faults as a poet, has at least some knowledge of versification.

These sample stanzas will give an idea of both the sameness and the variety of broadside balladry. In his selection of a stanzaic pattern, the ballad maker has quite a few choices open to him. But he pretty much confines himself to the iambic or the anapestic foot and to some combination of three and four stress lines.

BROADSIDE BALLAD TECHNIQUES

While the broadsides may contain little that the critics find praiseworthy, their narrative method is of considerable interest because it has been used almost without change for several centuries. An analysis of many ballads reveals the recurrent use of certain stock techniques to produce that kind of verse which is instantly recognizable as a broadside ballad.

A glance at the first stanzas in Appendix I will show that many broadside ballads begin with the "come-all-ye" address to the audience. This feature is so widely used that come-all-ye as a substantive means a broadside ballad. Professor Gummere's assumption that the street ballads are descended from the minstrel ballads is recalled in connection with the use of similar stock phrases in the older pieces.[3] Usually the people addressed are those most likely to be interested in or to profit from the story being told. Thus the war ballad "The Heights of Alma" begins, "Ye loyal Britons, I pray draw near/Unto the news I have brought you here."[4] "The Plains of Waterloo III" addresses the veterans of the Napoleonic Wars:

> Come all you sons of Britain,
> And Irish heroes too,
> And all who fought for Wellington
> At the battle of Waterloo.

Love ballads make their appeal to youth, and hence the beginning of "Bessie of Ballington Brae": "Come all you young men and maidens so fair,/Come list to the tale of two lovers so dear." A sea ballad like "The Rocks of Scilly" may use a well-worn formula:

> Come all you jolly sailor boys
> That plough the raging main,
> Come listen to my tragedy
> While I relate the same.

---

[3] See Chapter II, note 1.

[4] This quotation and the eighteen which follow it are repeated in Appendix I where their sources are given.

"Bold McCarthy", a ballad celebrating the fistic prowess of an Irish sailor, begins, "Come all ye true-born Irishmen . . .", while "Captain Kidd" addresses "You captains brave and bold." In "Van Dieman's Land" the balladist limits his audience considerably when he says "Come all you gallant poachers", but like most opening phrases this is only a means of getting the story under way.

Many ballads begin in the first person and set the scene. In ballads of romantic love, the narrator is often taking a walk. The following sample lines are typical:

N 35   As I roved out one evening fair,
       To view the fields and to take the air . . .

N 38   When I was a-roving one morning in Spring . . .

N 40   As I walked out one morning
       In the pleasant month of May . . .

Other familiar opening lines identify one or more of the main characters and suggest what is to follow:

Q 38   'Tis of a wealthy prentice my purpose is to speak . . .

M 7   There was a rich merchant in London did dwell,
       He had an only daughter, the farmer loved her well . . .

M 25   'Twas of a farmer's daughter most beautiful I'm told,
       Her father died and left to her a large amount of gold . . .

In some ballads the narrator identifies himself and tells his own story. This produces the personal and sometimes confessional note largely absent from Child balladry:

J 11   My name is Patrick Sheehan, my years are thirty-four . . .

K 28   My name is Edward Holleran, as you may understand . . .

Other ballads find it convenient to refer at once to the time of the occurrence:

K 1   It happened to be on the first of May . . .

J 18   'Twas on the ninth day of August in the year ninety-eight . . .

This device is typical of ballads based on fact but is not limited to them.

The first stanza may be designed merely to whet the appetite of the listener or it may outline or initiate the basic conflict. Usually it will demonstrate the style of the balladist and give some indication of his skill. The following opening stanzas represent two common types:

O 26   Young virgins all I pray draw near,
        A pretty story you shall hear.
        'Tis of a Turkish lady brave,
        Who fell in love with an English slave.

O 39   I was brought up in Sheffield not of low degree,
        My parents doted on me, having no child but me,
        I rolled about in pleasure just where my fancy led,
        Till I was bound a prentice and all my joys were fled.

The expository opening stanza, which is almost universally used in the broadsides, sets them apart from the Child ballads, which usually employ the more dramatic device of plunging immediately into the story without preliminary explanation. But this more artistic approach may be partly accidental, since it is quite possible that the introductory stanzas of many Child ballads have worn away in tradition. With the opening stanza out of the way, the broadside balladist will continue his story in much the same vein and at the same rate, giving almost equal emphasis to each event in the series as well as to the filler material which he is likely to use to lengthen his narrative. Original broadsides vary greatly in length, but texts of from ten to twelve double length stanzas seem to be the most common. These are almost invariably shortened in tradition, frequently becoming texts of five or six long or twice as many short stanzas.

In most broadsides the characters are designated in the simplest terms without any attempt at analysis. They are given first names only or are described as "a pretty fair maid", "a brisk young farmer", "a butcher boy", "a nobleman's daughter", "Johnny the sailor", "a Wexford girl", "a 'Romish' lady", and so forth. These are usually stereotypes whose actions and reactions are largely determined in the minds of the ballad makers. Thus the motivation for much broadside ballad action is weak or non-existent by literary standards. But this does not disturb the balladist, who is primarily concerned with exciting action and not with artistry.

The following texts of two British ballads exceptionally popular in America are offered to illustrate fairly typical broadside style and content. The first of these, "Caroline of Edinburgh Town" has been found generally distributed in the United States and is known traditionally in Canada and Scotland. "William Taylor", though not so frequently reported by collectors, has been recorded from both England and Scotland and is known throughout North America.

CAROLINE OF EDINBURGH TOWN

Come all you young men and maidens, attend unto my rhyme,
It's of a young maiden who was scarcely in her prime,
She beat the blushing roses, and admired by all round,
Was lovely young Caroline of Edinburgh Town.

Young Henry was a Highland man, a courting to her came,
And when her parents came to know they did not like the same;
Young Henry was offended and unto her did say,
Arise my dearest Caroline, and with me run away.

We will both go to London, love, and there we'll wed with speed,
And then lovely Caroline shall have happiness indeed;
Now enticed by young Henry she put on her other gown,
And away went Caroline of Edinburgh Town.

Over hill and lofty mountains together they did roam,
In time arrived in London far from her happy home,
She said my dearest Henry, pray never on me frown,
Or you'll break the heart of Caroline of Edinburgh Town.

They had not been in London more than half a year,
When hard hearted Henry proved too severe;
Said Henry, I will go to sea, your friends did on me frown,
So beg you way, without delay, to Edinburgh Town.

The fleet is fitting out to Spithead dropping down,
And I will join the fleet to fight for king and crown,
The gallant tars may feel the scars or in the water drown,
Yet I never will return to Edinburgh Town.

Then many a day, she passed away, in sorrow and despair,
Her cheeks, though once like roses, were grown like lilies fair;
She cried, where is my Henry, and often did she swoon,
Crying, sad's the day, I run away, from Edinburgh Town.

Oppress'd with grief, without relief, the damsel she did go,
Into the woods to eat such food as on the bushes did grow,
Some strangers they did pity her, and some did on her frown,
And some did say, what made you stray from Edinburgh Town.

Beneath a lofty spreading oak, this maid sat down to cry,
A watching of the gallant ships as they were passing by,
She gave three shrieks for Henry, then plunged her body down,
And away floated Caroline of Edinburgh Town.

A note, likewise her bonnet, she left upon the shore,
And in the note a lock of hair, with the words "I am no more;"
But fast asleep I'm in the deep, the fish are watching round,
Once comely young Caroline of Edinburgh Town.

Come all you tender parents ne'er try to part true love,
You're sure to see in some degree, the ruin it will prove,
Likewise young men and maidens, ne'er on your lovers frown,
Think of the fate of Caroline of Edinburgh Town.[5]

It will be noticed that this ballad begins not in the fifth act of the play but in the first and proceeds chronologically through half a dozen episodes. The girl's suicide, which is the climax of the story, is not developed any more fully than, for example, Henry's decision to go to sea. Nothing in the conventional opening stanzas prepares us for Henry's perverse reaction to Caroline's devotion. He seems to be looking for an excuse to leave her. Not content with the single moral so often attached to broadsides, this balladist gives two, neither of them especially convincing in terms of the story. Caroline would have been better off if her parents had succeeded in parting the lovers, and since she is the innocent victim, the advice to maidens is hardly appropriate. The ballad displays some technical competence. The a a b b rhymes are accurate throughout, the internal refrain is satisfactorily used, and the meter is adequately maintained. The diction, however, is generally trite and artificial, and the piece jogs along at a level well below that of poetry. On the whole, the ballad is more expository than dramatic, and it falls far short of achieving emotional intensity.

Despite its obvious faults "Caroline" is at least a serious attempt to tell a tragic story. "William Taylor", on the other hand, verges on the ludicrous and invites humorous comment. It exists in two basic forms, that given below, and a slightly different stage form which was apparently intended as a comic piece. The second is probably a parody of the first, although the opposite order of composition is not impossible. The folk have been known to take comic pieces seriously.

---

[5] *The Forget Me Not Songsters* (N.Y., Nafis and Cornish), pp. 175-177.

BOLD WILLIAM TAYLOR

I'll sing you a song about two lovers,
Who from Lichfield town did come;
The young man's name was William Taylor,
The maiden's name was Sarah Dunne.

Now for a sailor William enlisted,
Now for a sailor William's gone,
He's gone and left his charming Sally,
All alone to make me mourn.

She dressed herself in man's apparel,
Man's apparel she put on,
And for to seek her true lover,
For to find him she is gone.

One day as she was exercising,
Exercising among the rest,
A silver locket flew from her jacket,
And exposed her lily-white breast.

O then the captain stepped up to her,
And asked her what brought her there;
'All for my own true lover,
For he has proved to me severe.'

'If you are come to find your lover,
You must tell to me his name.'
'His name is bold William Taylor,
And from Lichfield town he came.'

'If your lover's name is William Taylor,
He has proved to you severe;
He is married to a rich lady,
He was married the other year.

'If you will rise early in the morning,
In the morning by break of day,
There you will see bold William Taylor,
Walking with a lady gay.'

Then she called for a brace of pistols,
'A brace of pistols I command!'
And she shot bold William Taylor
With his bride at his right hand.

O then the captain was well pleased,
Well pleased with what she had done,
And she soon became a bold commander,
On board the ship with all the men.

Then the captain loved her dearly,
Loved her dearly as his life,
Then it was three days after
Sarah became the captain's wife.[6]

The story of the disguised girl seeking her lover is familiar enough in broadside balladry, but the ending of this piece must be unique. As Frank Kidson justly remarked, "The burlesque version could scarcely be more comic than the foregoing." Sarah is obviously a person of forthright action, a quality admired by the captain. Although capable of devotion within limits, she is certainly no sentimentalist; her hasty marriage indicates that she shot William more in anger than sorrow. But we are mainly concerned here with broadside style. "William Taylor" is dramatically presented, impersonal, fast-moving, and full of action. Although these qualities are characteristic of the best English ballads, they are powerless to raise this piece much above the level of farce. The ballad lacks anything approaching high seriousness. Its phrasing is pedestrian in the extreme, its action is badly contrived, and it has no power to touch the deeper emotions. This is the sort of composition which is immediately recognizable as a broadside ballad and which has made some scholars reluctant to accept the broadsides as genuine traditional song.

BALLAD VARIANTS

One sure method of distinguishing traditional songs from those learned directly from print is by the textual variations which inevitably occur in folksong. But variation can reveal much more than the basic fact of traditional existence. From the ways in which ballads vary we can learn something about the mental processes of the singers, their taste in subject matter, and even their attitudes toward the songs they sing. Especially by studying these late broadsides we can draw some conclusions about the influences brought to bear upon older traditional song.

Those who study Child balladry or comparative European bal-

---

[6] Text from a Catnach broadside reprinted by Frank Kidson in *JFSS* I, 255.

ladry are constantly faced with problems of textual priority. Sometimes it is possible to recognize late additions or deletions if an
earlier and better text is available, but if no early texts of an obviously old ballad are known, the scholar must rely heavily on speculation
in tracing its history. The student of broadside balladry has the
distinct advantage of possessing many early printed texts of the
ballads. Not all of these are original printings, but since the printed
broadsides are generally uninfluenced by oral tradition, many of
them are as close to the authors' original texts as one is likely to
get. Thus in studying variations, we are able to relate any number
of modern texts to a common original. Another advantage lies in
the fairly recent origin of most broadsides. The more modern the
ballad, the less it is subject to those corruptions which arise when
singers fail to understand what they have heard.

Occasionally ballad texts will remain in tradition for two or three
hundred years without significant change. This is not necessarily
surprising, because ballads may descend vertically within a small
group. Thus if a piece were learned by successive generations within
a family, it might conceivably be sung by only half a dozen individuals during a couple of centuries and might therefore change
very little. Of course a distinction must be made between the age
of a ballad and the age of a traditional text, since ballads often enter
tradition from print. In general, texts which show considerable
normal variation from their known original have probably had a
long or an active traditional life or both, while the opposite is
true of texts showing little variation. But the number of years a
given text has existed in tradition is usually impossible to determine.

For some time scholars have recognized opposing but not contra-
dictory tendencies in ballad transmission. The more familiar is the
tendency toward degeneration. Degeneration refers to obvious corruptions and omissions from a text which are caused by the singers'
failure to remember or to understand what they have heard. Dozens
of examples of this may be found in any scientifically made ballad
collection. Actually it is far more prevalent than most anthologies
indicate, because editors prefer to print only their better texts.
Extreme verbal degeneration may make an entire text almost un-
intelligible, but more often only a few phrases or stanzas are affected.
Sometimes generations of singers may so wear down a ballad that
the collector obtains only corrupt fragments of the original. Usu-

ally the most important incident is retained and serves as a means of identification. But since many broadsides are lengthy and episodic the effect of the original story will certainly be altered and may even be destroyed. The longest text of "A Gay Spanish Maid", a ballad which is probably not older than the 19th century, contains 13 double-length stanzas. It is printed by Barry from a manuscript of 1870 which is probably close to the author's original. All the traditional texts are shorter, although most of them retain the essentials of the story. In a New Hampshire text of only four double stanzas, however, the story of the youth's shipwreck and the girl's death from grief has been completely forgotten, leaving only a fragment which incompletely describes their final parting. Further degeneration often results in a collector's receiving only a single stanza of a ballad, with or without a tune. Thus in Vance Randolph's B text of "The Foggy Dew" nothing remains but a quatrain telling of the love affair which is the central incident of the story.

The opposing tendency is that toward deleting from the story much of the tiresome detail which burdens many broadsides. If this process, which seems largely accidental, is not carried too far, the result may be a more compact and effective ballad than the original. Thus a distinction must be made between mere fragments and texts which still give the impression of completeness. Forgetfulness may be the cause of shortening in both types; the result will be partly determined by the structure of the ballad. Often both the beginning and the ending of a ballad will show signs of erosion. A more compressed beginning is frequently desirable, but since the balladist often saves important action for the last stanzas, the loss or alteration of these produces major story changes.

As a result of oral variation, some of our broadsides have two or more strikingly different endings. For example, Mackenzie points out that "William Taylor" varies considerably. In the broadside text printed above, the girl marries the captain after shooting her former lover. "An English text contributed to the *Journal of the Folk-Song Society*," says Mackenzie, "ends with a clear visualization —and audition—of Willie's last agonies:

> He rolled over, he rolled over,
> He rolled over on every side.
> 'Adieu, adieu to my true love Sally!
> Once I thought you'd have been my bride.' "

Part of Mackenzie's discussion continues as follows: "The American versions hitherto collected . . . take a very gloomy view of the case. One from North Carolina does not even represent her as shooting her faithless lover, but invites us to believe that she threw herself overboard upon receiving the news of his defection; and a West Virginia text informs us that she was brought to trial after her accomplishment of a good revenge, crying for death to end her sorrows."[7] We might add that in Belden's Missouri text the girl gives Willie fair warning of his fate in the following stanza, with its incomparable third line:

> "O Willie, Willie, long I've loved you,
> For your sake I've risked my life;
> Them that has you shan't enjoy you;
> For your sins I'll end your life."

She does so, but is later overcome by grief and drowns herself. The Brown text from North Carolina also ends with the girl's suicide, but in this the opening stanzas have been changed considerably. On the day of his marriage William is pressed to sea through the plotting of a rival named Samuel, who does not appear in any other known texts. And a Vermont text adds a deterrent to Sarah's marital happiness not recorded elsewhere:

> Now the Captain he has wed her;
> Took her for his lawful wife.
> As she sleeps beside of the Captain,
> She thinks of young William Taylor at night.

We cannot be sure how all these variations have come about, but some speculation is possible. Intentional recomposition as a cause of variation cannot be ruled out and seems likely on the basis of similarities between certain widely scattered texts. But unplanned variation may be responsible for most of the changes. Since the shooting of Willie is the climax of the story, it would be easy enough for singers to forget the rather unpredictable endings of the broadside and stage texts. They would be likely to substitute some reasonable conclusion for the one which had escaped them. The texts reporting Willie's farewell speech, the bringing of the girl to trial, and the suicide after the shooting are explainable on this basis.

---

[7] Mackenzie, pp. xxxii-xxxiii.

The North Carolina texts represent a still further abbreviation of
the original story. Those accustomed to the loyalty of female ballad
lovers perhaps could not bring themselves to accept the shooting;
they may simply have forgotten about it and let the girl kill herself
unstead. The new variants created by such combinations of forgetfulness and invention would then be as acceptable as any to successive singers. Variations of this type seem to have occurred count-
less times in traditional balladry.

Sometimes the causes of ballad variations can be determined by
a collation of several traditional texts, even if the original broadside
is not available. Here for example are parallel quatrains from
"Johnny the Sailor" or "Green Beds". In reply to the sailor's request
for a bed, the tavern hostess speaks as follows:

> 'My beds are full of foreigners,
> And their fortune it is of more;
> My beds are full of foreigners—
> Young Johnie, you are poor.' (Belden)

> "My beds are all full, John,
> Of forty men or more;
> They're valiant young strangers,
> While you are very poor." (Brewster)

An analysis of the longest traditional texts, those of Thompson and
Eddy, shows that the quatrains given above represent the combining of two stanzas. Thompson's stanzas read as follows:

> "For she is very rich, John,
> While you are very poor;
> And if she was at home, John,
> She'd turn you out of door.
>
> . . . .
>
> "My beds are full of strangers
> And have been so this week.
> Now for your lodging, John,
> Somewhere else you must seek."

The more-poor combination in both the combined stanzas suggests
that the telescoped reply is established in tradition, at least in
Middle West. The second line of Stanza 1 is obviously corrupt,
though the singer has made a valiant attempt at consistency. The
use of the word foreigners for strangers in the same stanza is un-

fortunate but understandable. In Stanza 2 the number forty is probably too high, and the valor of the guests need not have been mentioned. These variations are not especially important in themselves, but they suggest the instability of practically any ballad stanza in tradition.

But an imperfect memory for the exact word does not always result in deterioration. The commonest and least drastic type of variation is the substitution of new words and phrases for those in the original text or the received text. These substitutions, which are usually accidental, rarely change either the ballad story or its style significantly. The English language offers many ways of saying approximately the same thing, and ballad singers continually vary their texts in dozens of trivial ways. Few ballad authors had much feeling for language, and the new phrase is usually neither better nor worse than the original. Occasionally a singer might intentionally or unwittingly replace a colorless adjective with a vivid one, or use a direct, idiomatic expression in place of an awkward or stilted phrase. He might recast a line of exposition as dialogue or repeat a striking line where a new one belongs. Substitutions of this kind would tend to improve the received text and could conceivably result in a far better ballad than the original. But the forces of degeneration would be active, too, and the net effect of all substitutions may be either harmful or beneficial. Whether or not oral transmission improves balladry seems to depend partly upon chance and partly upon the poetic and dramatic instincts of the singers.

Since singers are known on occasion to alter or omit gruesome or otherwise unacceptable details, we may say that folk censorship is responsible for variations in certain ballads. This process takes place not only among the folk but in the professional performance of folk songs. Sometimes the result is a more artistic ballad, but frequently there is considerable loss of narrative content. For example in Gardner's text of "The Handsome Cabin Boy" we learn only that the girl is about to have a baby, but in Ord's text and the broadsides, her affair with the captain, whose wife is on board, is the central part of the action. The captain's wife displays both broadmindedness and a sense of humor in the concluding couplet:

> The lady to the captain said, my dear, I wish you joy,
> For it's either you or I betrayed the handsome cabin boy.

The romance recounted in "The Foggy Dew" always results in the birth of a child, but a marriage may or may not take place, and "Blow the Candle Out" may be either a story of seduction and betrayal or one of mutual if illicit love. Other ballads of illicit love like "The Nightingale" and "Home, Dearie, Home" vary considerably in traditional texts, perhaps because of censorship. The singers are not the only ones to censor ballads, however; the dropping out of details considered unpleasant, especially those reflecting upon the character of a young woman, may also occur when a piece is rewritten for the press.

BALLAD IDENTIFICATION

The identification and classification of ballad versions and variants are at best tricky and uncertain matters. Close attention to both the form and the substance of the ballads should prevent major errors and inconsistencies, but some pieces require searching analyses before their variant forms can be properly recognized and described. The following types of texts are most likely to cause confusion:

(a) Single ballads known by widely different titles.
(b) Separate ballads with similar or identical titles.
(c) Ballads somewhat similar in plot but containing significant differences.
(d) Ballads similar or identical in plot but varying in stanzaic form.
(e) Ballad pairs, one member of which is obviously recomposed from the other but differs strikingly from it.
(f) Single ballads partly rewritten in the same stanzaic form with minor variations in details or phrasing.

In Appendix I all the ballads described by types (b), (c), (d), and (e) are identified, numbered, and discussed as separate pieces; those of type (f) as single ballads with variant forms; and those of type (a), of course, as single ballads. Admittedly these distinctions are somewhat vague, and overlapping may occur in various categories. But at least they attempt to standardize classifications in a field in which almost every editor has gone his own way.

Types (a) and (b): Both the broadside authors and the folk singers seem to have taken a rather casual attitude toward ballad titles. Often the title is nothing more than the identification of one or another of the leading characters, as in "Donald Monroe", "Pat-

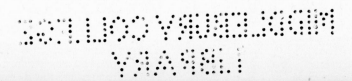

rick Sheehan", and "Captain Kidd", but it may also be taken from the first line, as in "When a Man's in Love" and "In Bruton Town", or from a recurring phrase, as in "Home, Dearie, Home" and "Blow the Candle Out". Other titles refer to the scene of action, as in "Bay of Biscay", "Waterloo", and "Down by the Sea Shore"; to the main plot, as in "Kate and Her Horns" and "The Dog in the Closet"; or to a minor detail of the story, as in "The Half Hitch" and "Green Beds". Ballads are frequently repetitious; the same names and types of characters occur time and again, and one or another feature of the ballad may remain in the singer's mind. Moreover, localization, or the substitution of familiar for unfamiliar place names, occurs constantly in traditional balladry. Furthermore, two or more ballads are often written on the same historical event. Thus the title, which is if anything more unstable than the body of the text, is subject to frequent alteration, and one ballad may be known by several titles or several ballads by one. For example, the ballad listed in Appendix I as "The Undaunted Female" is also known as "The Box Upon Her Head" and "The Staffordshire Maid". The "Bramble Briar" may be received as "In Bruton Town", "In Seaport Town", "The Merchant's Daughter", and so on. Three ballads are known as "The Plains of Waterloo", two as "Young Sailor Bold", and five as "Pretty Polly". The list could be much extended. Thus the experienced editor knows that he must rely on texts rather than titles, which may justly be called the most unreliable of all means of identification.

Type (c): It is surprising how many able students of the ballad make misleading identifications based on superficial similarities of plot. This results partly, I suspect, from the folklorists' thinking in terms of story types or motifs rather than of the final product. This comparative method leads to much confusion because it avoids a precise analysis of the pieces being considered. Take for example "The Love-of-God Shave" and "The Monkey Turned Barber." Both pieces are humorous accounts of an Irishman named Pat who is given a painful shave in a barber shop. But in one piece an escaped monkey gives the shave and in the other the barber deliberately uses a poor razor. The phrasing of the two pieces is different throughout. Obviously they must be considered separate ballads. Other ballads which have been described as if they were identical include "Tarry Sailor" and "Jack the Jolly Tar II"; and "The Boatsman and the

Chest" and "The Old Dyer". An examination will show that each member of these pairs is clearly distinguishable from the other.

At times this problem carries over into the realm of Child balladry. A certain amount of confusion has resulted from a tendency of editors to identify all possible pieces with those of the Child collection. This habit can, I suppose, be traced to the belief that Child was almost infallible and that a ballad which does not appear in his book is somehow suspect. In *British Ballads from Maine,* for example, Barry, Eckstorm, and Smyth print "The Yorkshire Bite", "The Half Hitch", "The Bold Soldier", "Gallows", and "High Barbary" as secondary forms of various Child ballads (see Appendix I). Even a hasty comparison of texts will show that each of these pieces is entitled to separate identity.

Type (d) : According to Professor Belden, "Form is a more trustworthy mark of identity than particulars of plot."[8] This is especially true of the broadsides because in them the same plot devices are used in completely unrelated ballads. Sometimes, as in the ballads of returned lovers, identical plots occur in a number of pieces. Their identity as separate ballads can be determined only on the basis of form. The answer to the following question should determine whether one is dealing with versions of a single ballad or with two different pieces: *Do the two texts not only tell the same story but tell it in the same stanzaic pattern with essentially the same phraseology?* If not they should be separately listed. The stanzic pattern is particularly important in ballad identification because it is least subject to change in oral transmission. In discussing these crudely composed pieces we hesitate to use the standard metrical designations without apology. But we may say, for example, that a quatrain in what may roughly be called iambic heptameter cannot by a simple process of oral variation become an iambic pentameter quatrain. To substitute one title or place name or phrase for another is an easy matter, but to make a basic structural change that will carry through all stanzas is impossible without complete rewriting. And a rewritten piece will usually contain various other significant changes.

Type (e) : We now come to a type of classification about which

---

[8] Belden, p. 87.

editors may always disagree. If one ballad has been recomposed and exists in two or more strikingly different forms, should these forms be listed as variants of a single piece or as separate ballads? If in rewriting the ballad the new author has changed the stanzaic pattern or major details of the plot, there is little likelihood of being unable to distinguish one from the other. Thus "Johnny Sands" is rewritten from "The Old Woman of Slapsadam" with considerable variation. In such cases it seems best to treat the variant forms as separate ballads with appropriate cross references, as I have done in Appendix I.

The listing of "A Rich Irish Lady" as "The Brown Girl" (Child no. 295) further illustrates the tendency to use Child's numbering wherever possible. Editors have disagreed about whether to call "A Rich Irish Lady" a derivative of Child no. 295, Child no. 295 itself in modern dress, or a separate ballad of the broadside type. This is more a problem in semantics than anything else. Obviously the ballad is related to "The Brown Girl" because it contains too many of the same details to be explained away by coincidence. But just as obviously the piece has been recomposed, presumably for the broadside press. The meter has been changed along with many of the narrative details. Even a casual comparison will show that these changes cannot be explained by oral transmission alone. Arguments about whether or not this is Child 295 become futile once these statements are agreed upon, and the method of listing will depend upon the individual editor. I have chosen to list "A Brave Irish Lady" separately, as I have done with other examples of major rewriting.

Type (f): Finally we come to examples of recomposition which do not involve major changes. The main difference between "Captain Glen" and "The New York Trader", for example, is in the opening stanza. Despite the variation in names and a few other details, the two texts pass the test of identity mentioned under (d) above. Pieces of this type will be listed and discussed as variants of a single ballad. The intentional revision of ballads which have been popular over the years is likely to produce this type of variation, as will be seen from the following discussion of "The Wexford Girl".

BALLAD RECOMPOSITION

Although the rewriting of ballads has received little attention from scholars, it is a significant cause of variation among traditional texts. Since the folk singer will usually try to repeat a ballad exactly as he has learned it, students should pay close attention to any texts which depart significantly and consistently from those generally received. The possibility that the variant descends from a rewritten text should always be considered, since the normal changes which occur in oral transmission are usually the result of casual omissions, substitutions, and misunderstandings. Ballads change constantly, sometimes in predictable ways, but if a given text is of reasonable length, it always preserves the essential character of the text from which it developed.

To illustrate both the rewriting of a ballad in the same stanzaic form and more of the normal variations which occur in tradition, I have chosen "The Wexford Girl", one of the most widely known ballads in America. This is the sordid story of a love affair which ends in the girl's murder. About fifty texts of this ballad have been printed from American tradition. They vary from brief and all but forgotten fragments to texts of from 12 to 18 stanzas. Three different broadside variants are available for study. The oldest of these and presumably the original is "The Berkshire Tragedy; or, the Wittam Miller" an 18th century broadside included in the Roxburghe collection. The text from another broadside copy is printed below. The second version, which is much shortened, comes from a Boston broadside of the early 19th century and is entitled "The Lexington Miller". Finally we have "The Cruel Miller", a retelling of the story as found on a late English broadside. These two pieces are also reprinted and discussed below.

THE BERKSHIRE TRAGEDY, OR THE WITTAM MILLER
With an Account of his Murdering his Sweetheart

(From an 18th century broadside in Harvard College Library. The imprint reads: "London: Printed and Sold in Stonecutter-street, Fleet-Market." The stanzas are not divided or numbered in the broadside.)

> 1. Young men and maidens all give ear,
>   Unto what I shall now relate;
>   O mark you well, and you shall hear,
>   Of my unhappy fate.

2. Near famous Oxford Town,
   I first did draw my Breath,
   Oh! that I had been cast away
   In an untimely Birth.

3. My tender parents brought me up,
   Provided for me well.
   And in the town of Wittam then,
   They plac'd me in a Mill.

4. By chance upon an Oxford Lass,
   I cast a wanton Eye,
   And promised I would Marry her,
   If she would with me lie.

5. But to the World I do declare,
   With sorrow, grief and woe:
   This folly brought us in a snare,
   And wrought our overthrow.

6. For the damsel came to me and said
   By you I am with Child:
   I hope dear John, you'll marry me,
   For you have me defil'd.

7. Soon after that, her mother came,
   As you shall understand,
   And oftentimes did me persuade
   To wed her out of hand.

8. And thus perplex'd on every side,
   I could not comfort find:
   So to make .... Creature,
   A thought came in ....

9. About a month before Christmas last,
   Oh! cursed be the Day,
   The Devil then did me persuade,
   To take her Life away.

10. I call'd her from her Sister's Door,
    At eight o'Clock at Night:
    Poor Creature she did little dream,
    I ow'd her any spight.

11. I told her, if she'd walk with me,
     A side a little way:
     We both together would agree,
     About our Wedding-day.

12. Thus I deluded her again,
     Into a private Place:
     Then took a Stick out of the Hedge,
     And struck her in the Face.

13. But she fell on her bended Knee,
     And did for Mercy cry,
     For Heaven's sake don't murder me,
     I am not fit to die.

14. But I on her no pity took,
     But wounded her full sore,
     Until her Life away I took,
     Which I can never restore.

15. With many grievous Shrieks and Cries,
     She did resign her Breath,
     And in inhuman and barbarous sort,
     I put my Love to death.

16. And then I took her by the hair,
     To cover this foul sin:
     And drag'd her to the River side,
     Then Threw her body in.

17. Thus in the blood of innocence,
     My hands were deeply dy'd,
     And shined in her purple gore,
     That should have been my Bride.

18. Then home unto my Mill I ran,
     But sorely was amaz'd,
     My man he thought I had mischief done,
     And strangely on me gaz'd.

19. Oh! what's the matter then said he?
     You look as pale as death:
     What makes you shake and tremble so,
     As though you had lost your Breath.

20. How came you by that Blood upon
    Your trembling Hands and Cloaths?
    I presently to him reply'd,
    By bleeding at the Nose.

21. I wishfully upon him look'd,
    But little to him said,
    But snatched the Candle from his Hand,
    And went unto my Bed.

22. Where I lay trembling all the Night,
    For I could take no rest,
    And perfect Flames of Hell did Flash,
    Within my guilty Face.

23. Next day the Damsel being miss'd,
    And no where to be found,
    Then I was apprehended soon,
    And to the Assizes bound.

24. Her Sister did against me swear,
    She reason had no doubt,
    That I had made away with her,
    Because I call'd her out.

25. But Satan did me still persuade,
    I stifly should deny:
    Quoth he, there is no witness can,
    Against thee Testify.

26. Now when her Mother did her cry,
    I scoffingly did say,
    On purpose then to frighten me,
    She sent her Child away.

27. I publish'd in the Post-boy then,
    My Wickedness to blind,
    Five Guineas any one should have,
    That could her Body find.

28. But Heaven had a watchful eye,
    And brought it so about:
    That though I stifly did deny,
    This Murder would come out,

29.   The very day before, the Assize,
      Her Body is was found,
      Floating before her Father's door,
      At *Hendly* Ferry Town,

30.   So the second Time I was seiz'd,
      To *Oxford* brought with speed,
      And there examined again,
      About the bloody deed.

31.   Now the Coroner and Jury both
      Together did agree,
      That this Damsel was made away,
      And murdered by me.

32.   The Justice too perceiv'd the guilt,
      Nor longer would take bail:
      But the next Morning I was sent
      Away to *Reading* Goal.

33.   When I was brought before the Judge,
      My Man did testify,
      That Blood upon my Hands and Cloaths,
      That Night he did espy.

34.   The Judge he told the Jury then,
      The Circumstance is plain,
      Look on the Prisoner at the Bar,
      He hath this Creature slain.

35.   About the Murder at the first,
      The Jury did divide:
      But when they brought their Verdict in,
      All of them Guilty cry'd.

36.   The Jailor took and bound me straight,
      As soon as I was cast:
      And then within the Prison strong
      He there did lay me fast:

37.   With Fetters strong then I was bound,
      And shin-bolted was I,
      Yet I the Murder would not own,
      But still did it deny.

38. My father did on me Pervail,
    My kindred all likewise,
    To own the Murder, which I did
    To them with watery Eyes.

39. My Father he then did me blame,
    Saying, my Son, oh! why
    Have you thus brought yourself to shame,
    And all you Family

40. Father, I own the Crime I did,
    I guilty am indeed,
    Which cruel fact I must confess,
    Doth make my heart to bleed.

41. The worst of Deaths I do deserve,
    My crime it is so base:
    For I no mercy shew'd to her,
    Most wretched is my case.

42. Lord grant me grace while I do stay:
    That I may now repent:
    Before I from this wicked world,
    Most shamefully am sent.

43. Young men take warning by my fall:
    All filthy lusts defy;
    By giving way to wickedness,
    Alas! This Day I die.

44. Lord, wash my hateful Sins away,
    Which have been manifold,
    Have mercy on me I thee pray,
    And Christ receive my Soul.

* * *

THE LEXINGTON MILLER

(This text is from an early 19th century broadside in the Harvard College Library. The imprint reads: "Boston, Corner of Cross and Fulton Streets." It is here reprinted from *JAF* 42, 249-250.)

1. Come all you men and maidens dear, to you I will relate,
   Pray lend an ear and you shall hear concerning my sad fate,
   My parents brought me up with care, provided for me well,
   And in the town of Lexington employ'd me in a mill.

2. 'Twas there I spied a comely lass, she cast a winning eye,
   I promis'd I would marry her if she would but comply:
   I courted her about six months, which caused us pain and woe;
   'Twas folly brought us into a snare, and it prov'd our overthrow.

3. Her mother came to me one day as you shall understand,
   Begging that I would appoint a day, and marry her at hand;
   It was about one month from Christmas, O, cursed be that day,
   The devil put it in my heart to take her life away.

4. I was perplex'd on every side, no comfort could I find
   Then for to take her life away, my wicked heart inclin'd;
   I went unto her sister's house at eight o'clock that night,
   And she, poor soul, little thought or knew I ow'd her any spite.

5. I said, come go along with me, out door a little way,
   That you and I may both agree upon our wedding day,
   Then hand in hand I led her on, down to some silent place;
   I took a stake out of the fence, and struck her on the face.

6. Now she upon her knees did fall, and most heartily did cry,
   Saying, kind sir, don't murder me for I am not fit to die;
   I would not hearken unto her cries, but laid it on the more,
   Till I had taken her life away, which I could not restore.

7. All in the blood of innocence, my trembling hand have dy'd,
   All in the blood of her who should have been my lawful bride;
   She gave a sigh and bitter groan, and cast a wistful look,
   I took her by the hair of the head and flung her in the brook.

8. Now straight unto the Mill I went, like one that's in a maze,
   And first I met was my servant boy, who deeply on me gaz'd;
   How came that blood upon your hands, likewise on your clothes?
   I instantly made reply, 'twas bleeding of the nose.

9. I called for a candle, the same was brought to me.
   And when the candle I had light, an awful sight I see;
   Now straightway unto bed I went, thinking relief to find,
   It seemed as if the plagues of hell, were lodged within my mind.

10. Next day her body was search'd for, but it could not be found,
   Then I was in my chamber seized, and in my chains were bound.
   In two or three days after, this fair maid she was found,
   Came floating by her mother's house, that was near Wentontown.

11. Her sister swore against me, she said she had no doubt,
   'Twas I that took her life away, as 'twas I that led her out.
   It's now my end comes hastening on, and death approaches nigh,
   And by my own confession I am condemned to die.

12. Now fare you well to Lexington, where my first breath I drew,
    I warn all men and maidens, to all their vows prove true.

*   *   *

THE CRUEL MILLER

(From an undated broadside without imprint in the Harvard College
Library).

1. My parents educated me good learning gave to me
   They bound me apprentice to a miller with whom I did agree,
   Till I fell courting a pretty lass with a black and rolling eye,
   I promised to marry her if she with me would lie.

2. I courted her for six long months a little now and then
   I was ashamed to marry her being so young a man
   Till at length she proved with child by me and thus to me did say,
   O Johnny do but marry me or else for love I die.

3. I went unto her sisters house at 8 oclock at night
   And little did this fair one know I owed her spite,
   I asked her if she would take a walk into the meadows gay,
   And there we'd sit and talk awhile about our wedding day,

4. I took a stick out of the hedge and I hit her on the crown
   The blood from this young innocent came trickling on the ground
   She on her bended knees did fall and loud for mercy cried
   Saying Johnny dear dont murder me for I am big with child

5. I took her by the yellow locks and dragged her to the ground
   And we came to the river side where I threw her body down
   With blood from this young innocent my hands and feet were dyed
   And if you d seen her in her bloom she might have been my bride

6. I went unto my masters house at 10 oclock at night
   My master getting out of bed and striking a light
   He asked me and questioned me what dyed my hands and clothes
   I made a fit answer I'd been bleeding at the nose

7. I then took up a candle to light myself to bed
   And all that blessed long night my own true love lay dead
   And all that blessed long night no sleep could find
   For the burning flames of torment all round my ey's did shine.

8. In two or three days after this fair maid was missed
   I was taken on suspicion and into prison cast
   Her sister prosecuted me for my own awful doubt
   Her sister prosecuted me for taking of her out.

9. In two or three days after this fair maid was found
Came floating by her mothers door that was near to Wexford town
The judge and jury quickly did agree
For the murder of my true love that hanged I should be.

*   *   *

"The Lexington Miller" is obviously nothing more than a drastically condensed text of "The Berkshire Tragedy". Twenty-one stanzas of the latter have been omitted, most of them dealing with the inquest, the murderer's trial, and his belated confession. The original has a certain journalistic merit in its precise and circumstantial telling of a lengthy and realistic story with a large cast of characters. The legal procedure is accurately reported, and the reactions of the murderer to each new development seem psychologically sound. Furthermore the presentation is more dramatic than expository. The condensed version, which lacks these features, shows no signs of having come from tradition; it may have been produced for the Boston ballad printer who issued the broadside. The failure to mention specifically either the illicit relationship or the girl's pregnancy is typical of murder ballads known in America.

The third broadside text is the shortest of the printed versions, containing only nine double stanzas. While it covers approximately the same material as "The Lexington Miller", it varies from that piece in several ways and conforms to "The Berkshire Tragedy" in others. Stanza 4 of the latter is much like the second half of stanza 1 in "The Cruel Miller", and the unborn child is mentioned in both pieces. While many of the rhyming words are identical in the two texts, "The Cruel Miller" contains several new rhymes and rewritten lines. The girl's mother, who appears twice in "The Berkshire Tragedy" and once in "The Lexington Miller", does not come on the scene in this version. The youth is questioned in "The Cruel Miller" by his master, a logical alteration, since the boy is now an apprentice, and apprentices are not likely to have servants.

"The Cruel Miller" has had less direct influence on American tradition than "The Lexington Miller", although it is known both here and abroad. The *Journal of the Folk-Song Society* prints two texts under the titles "Hanged I Shall Be" and "The Prentice Boy". This form of the ballad is, in fact, the only one reported from traditional singing in England. Three American texts seem almost wholly derived from this variant. Belden's A text, from a manuscript of the 1870's, is closest to the broadside. Randolph's G version from Missouri, a text of 14 stanzas, begins as follows:

> My father bound me a printer's boy
> 'Bout eighteen years of age,
> He bound me to a miller
> That I might learn some trade.[9]

("A printer's boy" is clearly a corruption of "a prentice boy.) Randolph's text continues with many variations from its original but with the same general substance. The boy is called John or Johnny in both and is questioned by the miller. And Brewster (*SFQ* III, 208) prints a similar but less coherent text called "The Printer's Boy", in which the word "miller" has been altered to "millionaire".

Several traditional texts related to "The Lexington Miller" may be found in American folksong collections. In *Our Singing Country* Lomax prints a good text from Virginia under the title "The Lexington Murder", a title found also in North Carolina. Randolph's A text is strikingly similar, as are several others. Some of these versions contain a reference to the murderer's wiping his hands in the girl's hair, a detail not found in the known broadsides. Randolph's stanza reads:

> I run my fingers through her coal black hair,
> To cover up my sin,
> I drug her to the river side
> An' there I plunged her in.

This is reminiscent of stanza 16 in "The Berkshire Tragedy", although the revision is more graphic. In most of these traditional versions the miller is questioned by his servant John, and all of them omit references to finding the girl's body. Immediately after the murderer has spoken of a nosebleed, another stanza closer to "The Berkshire Tragedy" than to the other broadsides occurs:

> I lit my candle an' went to bed
> Expectin' to take some rest,
> But it seemed to me the fires of hell
> Was a-burnin' in my breast.

---

[9] Page references for this and the following quotations will be found under "The Wexford Girl" in Appendix I.

The narrative ends at this point in most texts of "The Lexington Murder", and the ballad is concluded with a single moralizing stanza:

> Come all young men an' warnin' take,
> That to your lovers prove true,
> An' never let the devil get
> The upper hand of you.

The phraseology of these pieces is so similar that they must be based upon a common original of 13 stanzas different from the available broadsides but closely akin to them. It seems probable that the reviser who produced "The Lexington Murder" worked from both "The Berkshire Tragedy" and "The Lexington Miller". His use of the latter piece suggests that he was an American.

Mellinger Henry's longest text of "The Lexington Girl" is especially interesting. It contains roughly 18 stanzas, and although it is in many places corrupt it preserves the most striking details of the story. This text is based directly upon "The Berkshire Tragedy" rather than upon any of the shorter broadsides. A few examples will demonstrate this fact. "In the town of Wittam then" becomes "in a town of wickedness" in Henry's text; "a wanton eye" becomes "a wanting eye"; "Hendly Ferry Town" becomes "Harry Fairy Town"; and the reward offered by the youth for finding the girl's body is also mentioned. None of these elements appear in the shorter broadside versions. But oddly enough the local title of the piece and the fact that the youth is questioned by his master seem to relate it to both the other broadsides.

"The Berkshire Tragedy" is obviously too long a ballad for convenient memorizing and singing, while the other broadsides are of more reasonable length. The following stanzas of the original are omitted entirely from Henry's text: 1, 2, 5, 7, 9, 14, 17, 23, 25, 26, 28, and 30-43. Most of the early omitted stanzas are either reflective or repetitious; they add nothing essential to the story. Thus the folk lean toward that economy which is the hallmark of traditional balladry. On the other hand, only two stanzas are omitted between the youth's setting out to kill the girl and his going to bed at home. The stanzas which are preserved contain the largest amount of pertinent dialogue and dramatic action, two more features of the traditional ballad. Following the murder in "The Berkshire Tragedy", we have a complicated series of scenes recounting the accusations, the youth's arrest, the finding of the girl's body, his rearrest, the coroner's inquest, the murderer's trial and conviction, his imprisonment for the second time, and finally his confession and repentance. All this makes vivid reading, but it is not the kind of material which folk singers are likely to keep clearly in mind. Henry's version solves this problem by following the example of the other two broadsides and cutting out the second half of the original ballad. As soon as the girl's body is found, her sister accuses the youth, and the ballad ends with the penitent sinner's prayer. Thus the ending of this text suggests more than it relates, as the Child ballads often do, and gains the unity and simplicity of plot which are more typical of folk ballads than of printed broadsides.

Yet we find generally distributed throughout the United States still another form of the ballad, which varies so strikingly and so consistently from those discussed that we must assume the existence of a fifth basic text. This may well have been called "The Oxford Girl"; at least that is the title by which the ballad is frequently known. This piece, which seems to have descended from "The Cruel Miller", has been recorded only in America and only from tradition. Here are the opening six lines from a Texas version:

> 'Twas in the town of Oxford
> That I did live and dwell;
> 'Twas in the town of Oxford
> I owned a flour mill.
>
> I fell in love with an Oxford girl
> With dark and rolling eyes . . .

The term "flour mill" commonly appears in this variant, and the name "Oxford" or the phrase "Oxford girl" is organic in many stanzas. No motive is given for the murder, and the youth, who is called Willie, lures the girl away from home as usual and hits her with a stick. Hudson has a good text from Mississippi which proceeds as follows:

> I listened not to a word she said,
> But I beat her more and more,
> Until the ground where she lay
> Was in a bloody gore.
>
> I picked her up by the lily white hands,
> I threw her round and round,
> I threw her in the river stream
> That flows through Oxford town.

"Lay there, lay there, you Oxford girl;
Lay there, lay there, I say;
Lay there, lay there, you Oxford girl;
My bride you never will be."

The equivalent stanzas from the Texas version, along with several others which I might include, show that these variations are not accidental:

I did not listen to her cry
But beat her more and more;
I beat her until her body lay
A-bleeding in the gore.

I picked her up by the long yellow hair
And slung her round and round;
I took her to the Oxford stream
And plunged her in to drown.

"Lie there, lie there, you Oxford girl,
You never will be my bride;
Lie there, lie there, you Oxford girl,
You never will be my bride."

In "The Oxford Girl", the youth's arrival home wakes his mother "in a fright", she questions him about the blood, and he gives the established answer. He now has two requests:

I asked her for a candle
To light my way to bed;
I asked her for a handkerchief
To bind my aching head.

Eventually the girl's body is found, and we learn that the youth has been sentenced to death:

"Oh, mother, they're going to hang me
Between the earth and sky;
Oh, mother, they're going to hang me,
And I'm not prepared to die."

Some of these lines and stanzas have genuine folk ballad quality and represent a dramatic improvement over the other forms of the ballad. Yet we cannot say that they have evolved among the folk entirely through oral transmission because they recur time and again from widely separated parts of the country. Despite frequent variations in the different versions, the singers are clearly harking back to a basic text containing all the unique features just referred to. The typical folk singer is the transmitter of a received text. He rarely makes an effort to improve upon what he has learned or to invent anything new. What then can be said of the origin of the Oxford Girl variant? Here a new complication presents itself.

The occurrence of the name Wexford not only near the end of the print of "The Cruel Miller" but also in several traditional texts of the Oxford Girl type indicates that an Irish variant must also be considered. Both Waterford and Wexford are mentioned in the first stanza of Mackenzie's text from Nova Scotia, and Wexford appears again later. Wexford occurs also in Cox's texts from West Virginia, in one of Gardner's Michigan texts, and in a text collected in New York but apparently learned in Ireland. These texts depart consistently from "The Oxford Girl" in the final stanzas, showing that they represent a separate form of the ballad. The last four stanzas of Mackenzie's text read as follows:

> 12. And all that saw her said she was
>   A beauteous handsome bride,
>   That she was fit for any lord, duke, or king,
>   Or any squire's bride.
>
> 13. I was taken on suspicion,
>   And placed in Wexford gaol,
>   Where there was none to pity me,
>   Or none to go my bail.
>
> 14. Come all ye royal true lovers,
>   A warning take by me,
>   And never treat your own true love
>   To any cruelty.
>
> 15. For if you do, you'll rue like me
>   Until the day you die;
>   You'll hang like me, a murderer,
>   All on the gallows high.

The awkward and feeble lines of stanza 12 could have been added by any British folk singer, although the use of the word "squire" to indicate high rank is typical of Irish ballads. The last two stanzas could belong as well to one murder ballad as another, but they appear also, with variations, in the other Wexford texts.

Since the Oxford and Wexford texts are so similar, it would seem difficult to establish priority for either of them. A clue to the line of descent is provided, however, by a twelve stanza text from Scotland printed by Greig under the title "The Butcher Boy". The collector remarks that the piece is well known in his part of the country. Since this seems to be a rewriting of "The Cruel Miller" and since it contains some features found also in "The Oxford Girl" and "The Wexford Girl", it may represent the variant on which the other pieces were partially based. As in the Oxford-Wexford texts, the youth is called Willie and he is questioned by his mother, but he is a butcher's boy and he stabs the girl to death instead of hitting her with a stick. Two of Greig's stanzas have risen above the usual broadside level and display something of the old ballad quality:

> 5. They've walked up, and they've walked down,
> And they've walked all along,
> Till from his breast he drew a knife,
> And stabbed her to the bone.

> 7. He's ta'en her by the lily white hand,
> And dragged her all along,
> Until he came to yon running stream,
> And he plunged her body in.

It will be noticed that stanza 7 is much like the second stanza quoted from Hudson's text of "The Oxford Girl." Interestingly enough the youth is described as a butcher's boy in the last line of the New York text mentioned above. Since this is a text of the Wexford Girl type, it seems probable that "The Wexford Girl" was derived both from the broadside "The Cruel Miller" (which contains the word Wexford) and from the British variant "The Butcher Boy", which is known in Scotland and perhaps in Ireland. The recurring references to Wexford, however, do not appear in either "The Cruel Miller" or "The Butcher Boy". Since they could not easily drop out of the ballad once it had entered tradition, they must have been added when the Wexford variant was composed. The author of "The Wexford Girl" presumably dropped the reference to the butcher boy, since the murderer was again a miller's apprentice. But the butcher boy may have lingered in the memory of someone who knew both forms of the song to appear across the Atlantic in the much confused New York text.

This leaves "The Oxford Girl" as the only variant unaccounted for. Since this piece has been reported only from the United States, where it is the most popular of all the variants, it may well have been recomposed here. The substitution of Oxford, the original place name of "The Berkshire Tragedy", for the Irish Wexford may have been made simply because Oxford was the more familiar place name. Of course it is also possible that the author knew "The Berkshire Tragedy". Either explanation involves a coincidence, but neither is highly improbable.

Admittedly this long and complicated analysis has been based on incomplete evidence and is full of speculation, but it seems to explain fairly satisfactorily the development of the variants of this ballad. By way of summary we may tentatively suggest the following genealogy for the descendants of "The Berkshire Tragedy":

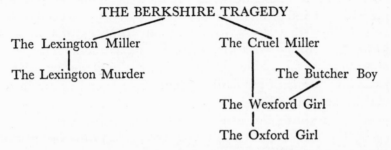

THE BERKSHIRE TRAGEDY

The Lexington Miller   The Cruel Miller

The Lexington Murder   The Butcher Boy

The Wexford Girl

The Oxford Girl

Although only two of these revisions are available in broadside form, the evidence indicates that all six have resulted from deliberate recomposition rather than from casual variation in tradition. Since "The Lexington Murder", "The Oxford Girl", and "The Wexford Girl" are so widely distributed, the probability is that they too existed as printed broadsides.

Most students will agree that "the Oxford Girl", which seems at present to be the final basic form of the ballad, is the most effective in its economy, its use of the folk idiom, and its dramatic impact. But the credit for these qualities belongs more to the individual recomposers than to the folk singers who have preserved the piece in tradition.

Ballad scholars have been inclined to speculate freely in dealing with phases of the subject about which they lacked precise knowledge. Thus the theory of communal origin flourished more because the origin of ballads was ancient and obscure than through any intrinsic merit. What Sir Edmund Chambers calls "Teutonic mysticism"[10] in ballad study has been applied to the problems of ballad variation. It has been tacitly assumed that a ballad may vary almost without limitation once it is subjected to the mysterious processes of folk transmission. This romantic concept seems to have influenced the study of the Child ballads. While much of the variation in the Child pieces undoubtedly occurred in the rather distant past, there is no good reason to assume that the basic causes and results of variation have altered significantly over the centuries.

Scholars accustomed to the stability of standard works by known authors are somewhat baffled by a ballad like "The Oxford Girl", which may seem to exist in an almost unlimited variety of forms. Thus they have concluded somewhat hastily that a ballad has no established form or content and that we can do little more than analyze the available texts as separate phenomena. But once the principle of individual authorship of ballads is accepted, it inevitably follows that every ballad at one time existed in a definite form. Any future variation, whatever its aesthetic value, must represent either an accidental or an intentional departure from the basic text. Many of the Child ballads have been so long in tradition that we have no dependable way of reconstructing the original texts or of determining the extent to which variation has operated upon them. But with the broadsides we are more fortunate, because they are generally of later date and the basic texts often exist in print. Thus we are able at least partially to trace the devious courses of variation and to draw some conclusions which may be applicable to all folk balladry.

The foregoing discussion of "The Oxford Girl" would seem to have significance beyond the ballad itself and even beyond traditional broadside balladry. I have tried to show how one ballad, in this case "The Berkshire Tragedy", has been consciously recomposed at least six times and that six of the seven forms of the ballad have entered tradition. Thus the most noticeable differences between one text and another seem primarily to result from intentional re-

---

[10] *English Literature at the Close of the Middle Ages*, p. 179. Sir Edmund is referring to statements by Cecil Sharp, Gordon H. Gerould, and William J. Entwistle, all of whom have considered folk tradition and oral transmission extremely important in determining what a ballad was to become.

composition rather than from simple variation. Yet the ballad in all its forms preserves the same stanzic pattern, the same basic sequence of events, many of the same descriptive and narrative details, and even the same phrases and rhyming words. If so much intentional variation can occur in a ballad which everyone will immediately recognize as basically a single piece, how much more readily should we be willing to recognize the probability of recomposition in cases where a new stanzaic pattern has been created or strikingly different phraseology is present in one of two or more texts which tell much the same story. To attribute such drastic variation to the vagaries of folk transmission is to misunderstand the function of the average folk singer, which is simply to repeat what he has learned.[11]

Scattered references have already been made to some of the possible reasons for ballad recomposition, but some further remarks may be added. Unlike the work of standard authors, popular literature is generally regarded as common property. In their attempt to keep their customers well supplied, the ballad printers of Britain and America apparently ransacked the old broadside sheets for anything that was usable. Frequently an archaic ballad could be given local application, or could be redesigned to fit a predetermined amount of space. The techniques of broadside ballad making were generally familiar, and it was an easy matter to retouch almost any old piece. The ballad audiences never demanded much originality and would probably have been bewildered by serious departures from the familiar pattern. Since ballads of moderate length were more satisfactory to seller and buyer in the latter days of balladry, much of the revision was in the direction of deleting unnecessary

---

[11] The communal theory of ballad origins has been so convincingly discredited, notably by Professor Louise Pound, that I shall not dwell upon it here. But some modifications of it persist, especially that of communal recreation, the theory that the folk keep molding ballads to suit their traditional tastes. While the theory is basically sound it is often carried too far. As Sir Edmund Chambers wisely but cautiously remarks, "I am not sure that, at its best, oral transmission is quite sufficient to account for all the wider differences between the extant 'versions' of a ballad, as distinct from the 'variants' in texts of what is recognizably the same ballad. One may suspect that sometimes a more wholesale rehandling may have taken place." (*English Literature at the Close of the Middle Ages*, p. 180).

details. No doubt some of the revisers took an interest in their work and found room for improvement in the efforts of others. Thus one ballad might be rewritten several times if a number of printers used it over a period of years.

Some readers may wonder why I give the credit for recomposition to ballad printers and their employees rather than to members of the folk. It is certainly true that folk composers have altered traditional pieces to suit new situations. Not a few of what I have called native American ballads are revisions of British pieces and are known to be the work of cowboys and lumberjacks. I do not deny the possibility that one or more revisions of such a ballad as "The Oxford Girl" may have first come to the printer by way of a folk composer or even directly from tradition. But it seems unlikely that the revised text of, let us say, "The Lexington Murder" could have become well established without the aid of print or perhaps of a phonograph recording. When we find widely distributed texts of a variant which is everywhere sung almost identically, we logically assume that the text was once available in a number of places and not merely in the mind of a single singer. (Of course the revision would not have to be published by an established ballad printer in a large city; a rural or itinerant printer could do the job.) The belief that such a revision as "The Lexington Murder" is the evolutionary result of many contributions from folk singers can be more easily disproved. If the evolutionary theory were correct, we should expect to find the variant in tradition in all its stages and not in the final one alone.

In conclusion we may say that the folk are responsible for endless verbal variations, occasional minor additions and substitutions, and frequent and sometimes drastic deletions and corruptions in balladry. But the tendency toward improvement of the folk texts over the original broadsides, which is often observable, results largely from the unconscious selection of idiomatic phrases and dramatic details. Major alterations are usually to be attributed to conscious recomposition by individual ballad makers.

Appendix I

British Broadside Ballads
Current in American Tradition

A BIBLIOGRAPHICAL SYLLABUS

Contents

Appendix I

EXPLANATORY NOTES

The following bibliographical syllabus is designed to classify, to describe, and to indicate the origin and distribution of the British broadside ballads in America. The emphasis throughout is upon texts recorded from tradition in the United States and Canada and printed within the last generation or so by students of folksong. Texts which have appeared without indication of source in purely popular anthologies are largely ignored as of little scholarly value. References to published and unpublished check-lists, syllabi, and indexes are generally excluded, as are the frequent listings of unpublished texts contained in the various regional collections. Ballad texts which have appeared only in newspapers and magazines are also omitted. This syllabus is not concerned with ballads no longer traditionally sung, with pieces recovered only as brief fragments, or with ballads printed from manuscripts or from other non-traditional sources. The syllabus concentrates upon texts which are both reliable and reasonably accessible.

The general plan is to provide the following items of information about each ballad:

1. *An identifying letter and number* for each piece designated as a separate ballad. The letters begin with J because the letters A through I are used in *Native American Balladry*. Clearly distinguishable variants of a single piece are indicated by additional capital letters. (Thus we have K 22 A and K 22 B).

2. *The title,* followed by any alternate titles which seem significant or which are commonly used. No attempt has been made to list the multitude of titles by which some of the more popular pieces are known to singers.

3. *A summary of the ballad story.* The summary rarely considers variation but concentrates on those features of the story found in good traditional texts and in the broadsides.

4. *A sample stanza,* usually from a traditional American text. The first stanza is used unless otherwise indicated, and the source of the stanza is shown by the first reference given below it.

5. *A list of printed texts* in the following order: American and Canadian

texts from tradition, sample British texts from tradition, sample texts on British and American broadsides and in chapbooks (or reprinted from any of these), and sample texts in American and British songsters. No attempt at an exhaustive listing has been made except for American traditional texts. The lists of traditional texts from Britain could frequently be much extended, but they are given only by way of example. Likewise the listings of broadside and songster texts are intended not to be complete in themselves but to indicate the sources and origins of the traditional texts.

To save space I usually identify collections by the last names of the editors. The full title of each book will be found in the Bibliography, which immediately precedes the Index of Ballads. Abbreviated titles follow the editors' names where necessary. Editors' names are not used in connection with ballads which have appeared in scholarly journals. The journals are indicated by abbreviations and are listed in the Bibliography. (If a ballad text has been published in the *Journal of American Folklore* and then in a separate collection, usualy the later reference alone is given.) Only the last names of broadside ballad printers are normally given in this appendix. Their names and addresses will be found in Appendix II.

A typical bibliographical entry (from "The Sheffield Apprentice") reads as follows: "Creighton and Senior, 203, 10d, m.; 5d; 9d (N.S.)." This indicates that three Nova Scotian texts of the ballad are printed in *Traditional Songs from Nova Scotia* beginning on page 203. The texts are of ten, five, and nine double length stanzas, and the first text is provided with a melody (m.). Nova Scotia is indicated only once because all three texts are from the same province. (The place designation refers to all texts previously listed). Stanzas in ballad meter or something near it would be indicated by the numeral alone; thus "6" means "six short stanzas". A text described as "4 8-line d. sts." means one of 32 long lines printed as four stanzas of eight lines each, and a text of "6d couplets" would be about as long as one of "6" [stanzas] since two come-all-ye lines equal four lines of ballad meter.

Unless otherwise indicated, the broadsides referred to are among the thousands, largely uncatalogued, in the Houghton Library at Harvard University. Fortunately a great many of the ballads listed here may be found in the fourteen volume bound collection of 19th century broadsides which has the library number 25242.17. Wherever possible I have referred to this collection, as Professor Kittredge frequently did in the *Journal of American Folklore* and as Professor Mackenzie does in the remarkably detailed headnotes of his *Ballads and Sea Songs from Nova Scotia*. Thus "(Harvard V, 176)" means that the ballad is to be found on page 176 of volume five of the bound collection. The designation "(L of C)" following a broadside reference means that the ballad sheet is located in the Rare Books Division of the Library of Congress.

Any reference followed by "(K)" or "(M)" indicates that I have not personally examined the text referred to but am relying on the notes of

Kittredge or Mackenzie, or in a few cases of Professor Cox "(C)" or Professor Belden "(B)".

Since most of the ballads considered in this work were either originally printed or reprinted during the last century, I have referred mainly to 19th century broadsides. Furthermore many of the older ballads were rewritten for the 19th century press, and it is largely in their recomposed form that they are known in tradition. The letter "(A)" before a list of broadsides, chapbooks, or songsters refers to American texts, while "(B)" refers to British.

WAR BALLADS

J   1   The Drummer Boy of Waterloo
J   2   Waterloo I
J   3   The Plains of Waterloo II
J   4   The Plains of Waterloo III
J   5   The Bonny Bunch of Roses
J   6   Erin Far Away I
J   7   The Dying Soldier (Erin Far Away II)
J   8   The True Paddy's Song (The Kerry Recruit)
J   9   The Crimean War
J 10   The Heights of Alma
J 11   Patrick Sheehan
J 12   Donald Monroe
J 13   The Sons of Liberty
J 14   The Croppy Boy
J 15   James Ervin
J 16   Burke's Dream
J 17   Nelson's Victory at Trafalgar
J 18   The Battle of the Nile
J 19   The *Little Fighting Chance*
J 20 - J 22 The *Chesapeake* and the *Shannon* I, II, & III.
J 23   When the Battle it was Won
         (Young Jimmy and the Officer)

J 1

THE DRUMMER BOY OF WATERLOO

His mother grieves to see her son leave for Waterloo, but he is confident that he will return. He is fatally wounded, however, and dies after sending his mother a message. His grave is dug at Waterloo by moonlight.

> When battle roused each warlike charm,
> And carnage loud her trumpet blew,
> Young Edwin left his native land,
> A drummer boy for Waterloo.

Eddy, 163, 6, m.; frags. with tunes (0.). Brown, 358, 5 (N.C.). Cox, 293, 6 (0. via W. Va.). Creighton, 145, 6, m. (N.S.). Owens, 77, 6, m. (Tex.). Randolph I, 338, 5, m. (Mo.) Refs. *JAF* 60, 217, 6 (Ill. from ms.).
Broadsides: (B) Such, 3d (Harvard XII, 14). (A) DeMarsan (C). Johnson, Phila., 3d (L of C). Bonsal, Baltimore, 6 (L of C). Songsters: (A) *The Forget Me Not Songster*, Phila., 235, 3d. The same, N.Y., 202, 3d.

J 2

WATERLOO I

The speaker unwillingly leaves his true-love, becomes a redcoat, goes to Belfast, and eventually loses a leg and an arm at Waterloo. The wounded are evacuated on horseback. Now he is entitled to a pension of thirty pounds a year.

> It happened on a Wednesday in the lovely month of June
> I went for to convince my love, all in her youthful bloom,
> Where the press gang lay in ambush and up to me they drew.
> And the very next day we marched away to fight at Waterloo.

Greenleaf, 165, 8d with 5 lines missing, m. (Nfld.).

J 3

THE PLAINS OF WATERLOO II

The narrator tells of Napoleon's pitching his tents at Waterloo, being victorious during the first two days of battle, and losing to Wellington on the third. The soldier is grateful to Providence for emerging alive.

Come all you brisk and lively lads, come listen unto me,
While I relate how I have fought through the wars of Germany.
I have fought through Spain, through Portugal, through France
    and Flanders too;
But it's little I thought I'd be reserved for the plains of
    Waterloo.

Mackenzie, 192, 5d (N.S.) Notes and refs. Dean, 118, 6d (Minn.).

"This song is plainly derived from the English song 'The Plains of Waterloo', which begins:

On the sixteenth day of June, my boys, in Flanders where we lay,
Our bugles the alarm did sound before the break of day.
The British, Belgians, Brunswickers, and Hanoverians too,
All Brussels left that morning for the plains of Waterloo."

(Note from Mackenzie, p. 192, who lists appearances of the latter piece in Ford I, 59, [13d, m.]; Logan, 106, [12d]; Christie I, 266, [7 8-line d. sts.]; Greig, lxxix, [15d]; Kidson, 120, [3d]; and elsewhere. These texts are much more detailed and circumstantial than the traditional variants. A lengthier related ballad with the same title is reprinted from a broadside in Kidson, p. 121, 19 d. sts. A fourth piece is reprinted by Mackenzie from a Nova Scotia broadside, p. 193, 5 d. sts. and chorus. One double stanza and the chorus of this piece are also printed by Kidson, p. 162, under the title "Battle of Waterloo". Most of the stanzas in all these ballads end with the phrase "on the plains of Waterloo." See also the following piece (J 4).

J 4
THE PLAINS OF WATERLOO III

The balladist speaks of Mooney, who led his troops in the bloody battle on a milk-white steed, and of General Hill, who died with thousands of others.

Come all you sons of Britain,
And Irish heroes too,
And all who fought for Wellington
At the battle of Waterloo

.   .   .   .

But let us fight with all our might,
And I will promise you,
We'll spread victorious banners
O'er the plains of Waterloo.

Sharp II, 176, 6, m. (Va.).
For a discussion of related Waterloo ballads see the preceding piece.

J 5

THE BONNY BUNCH OF ROSES

Napoleon's son offers to gain England, Ireland, and Scotland (i.e., the bonny bunch of roses) for his mother. She tells him of his father's disastrous Russian campaign, speaks of the valor of the British, and reminds him that Napoleon's body lies at St. Helena. She adds that he is about to join his father, and the youth mournfully awaits the coming of death.

> By the borders of the ocean
> One morning in the month of June,
> For to hear those warlike songsters,
> Their cheerful notes and sweetly tune,
> I overheard a female talking
> Who seemed to be in grief and woe,
> Conversing with young Bonaparte
> Concerning the bonny bunch of roses, O.

Greenleaf, 170, 6d, m. (Nfld.) Text from *Wehman Bros. Irish Song Book No.* 1, 1887, pp. 49-50. Mackenzie, 188, 5½d; 6d (N.S.) Notes and refs. Creighton, 140, 6d, m. (N.S.).

Christie II, 232, 5d, m. (Scot.). Greig, xciv, 5d (Scot.). Hayward 17, 6d (Tyrone). Ord, 301, 6d, (Scot.). Baring-Gould, 56, 5d, m. (W. of Eng.). *JFSS* II, 276, 1d, m. (Yorks.).

Broadsides (B) W. S. Fortey, 6d. Reprinted in *JFSS* II, 277. Walker, Durham (Harvard II, 98). W. R. Walker, Newcastle (Harvard IV, 163). (A) DeMarsan (M); Wehman, no. 411 (M). Songsters: (A) *The Forget Me Not Songster*, Phila., 136, 6d. The same, N.Y., 222.

J 6

ERIN FAR AWAY I

The dying soldier is comforted by his brother, who asks what messages he wishes to send home. He says to tell his parents that he fell nobly facing the rebels, and he asks his brother to mark his grave and to bring his love to plant a shamrock on it. He dies and is buried, and the soldiers return to Erin.

> The sun was fast declining on India's fatal shore
> There laid the dead and dying at the close of that sad war,
> But the saddest sight that I did see upon that field of gore
> Was a young and handsome Irishman who sailed from Erin's shore.

Creighton, 146, 7d, m. (N.S.).

J 7

THE DYING SOLDIER
(*Erin Far Away II*)

The soldier dying in India asks his comrades to send a lock of his hair to his mother in Ireland. He sends a message to his sister and asks that his brothers be told of the brave fight against the Sepoys. Then he dies and is buried by the other soldiers.

> The sun went down on Asia's shores when the deadly fight was o'er,
> And thousands lay on the battlefield till it could hold no more.
> The pale moon shone on the battlefield where the dying soldier lay,
> And the shadows of death around him crept while his life's blood
>   ebbed away.

Rickaby, 182, 7d, m. (Mich.). Dean 5, 7d (Minn.).

J 8

THE TRUE PADDY'S SONG
(*The Kerry Recruit*)

The country boy goes to the sergeant and says he wants to enlist. He is sent to headquarters where he is fitted out with an overcoat, a sword, a pistol, a gray horse, and a gun. After nine years in the service, during which he is afraid to shoot because he may be shot, he returns to the Old Sod.

> Nine years ago I was diggin' up the land,
> With me brogues on me feet and me shovel in me hand;
> Says I to myself, "What a pity for to see
> Such a tall handsome laddie diggin' turf on the Dee!"

Lomax, *Our Singing Country*, 200, 11d and ref., m. (Mich.). Sharp II, 228, 4d couplets, m. (Ky. "The Boy on the Land").
Broadsides: (B) Ryle, 10d ("The Irish Recruit". Harvard V, 171). Jennings, 7d ("The Frolicsome Irishman"). Songster: (A) *617 Irish Songs*, 123, 11d ("The Kerry Recruit").

J 9

THE CRIMEAN WAR

This sentimental ballad is spoken partly by the mother, partly by Johnny, who has landed on the Russian shore and has fought at Balaklava, on the heights of Alma, and at Sebastopol. Now Johnny is safely home again.

As I roved out through Irish town one evening last July,
The mother of a soldier in tears I did espy,
Saying: "God be with you, Johnny dear, though you are far
　　from me;
For you my heart is breaking, since you went to the Crimee.

Gardner, 231, 6d, m. (Mich.). Dean, 49, 8d (Minn. "As I Rode Down
through Irishtown").
Broadside: (B) Midgley, 28d lines (Harvard I, 63).

J 10

THE HEIGHTS OF ALMA

The ballad tells of the British soldiers landing on the Crimea, fighting
the Russians, and making them flee back to Sebastopol. Both sides lose
thousands of men in the bloody battle.

Ye loyal Britons, I pray draw near
Unto the news I have brought you here;
I'm sure it will make your hearts to cheer,
For the vict'ry is gained at Alma.

Gardner, 229, 7 and chor., m. (Can. via Mich.). Dean, 40, 8 (Minn.).
Creighton, 138, 10 and chor., m. (N.S.). Mackenzie, 195, 8 and chor.
(N.S.). *JAF* 31, 163, 2, m. (Belfast via Can.).
Ford, II, 73, 9, m. (Scot.).
A different ballad (in hexameter lines) with the same title is found on
broadsides by Bebbington, 6d and chor. (Harvard X, 44) and Beaumont,
5d and chor. (Harvard XIV, 4).

J 11

PATRICK SHEEHAN

Patrick's family is evicted from home by the landlord and the sheriff.
His mother dies in the poor house, and he joins the English army and is
badly treated. He is blinded at Sebastopol, and when his nine months'
pension expires, he becomes a wandering beggar.

My name is Patrick Sheehan, my years are thirty-four,
I was born in Tipperary, not far from Galtimore;
I came of honest parents, but now they are lying low,
And it's many the happy days I spent in the glens of Aherloe.

Dean, 3, 9d (Minn.). Barry, 33, 8d, m. (Me.) Reprinted from *Bulletin*
no. 11, p. 11.
Broadsides: (B) No imprint, no. 1012, 7d ("Patrick Shean and the
Glens of Arloe"). Colum, 65, 9d. Barry, *Bulletin* no. 11, p. 12, says that

an Irish broadside of this ballad is no. 278 in the Williams Coll. in the Providence, R. I., Public Library. Songsters: (A) *617 Irish Songs*, 71, 9d. O'Connor, 72, 9d. *Delaney's Irish Song Book No. 1*, p. 25.

Patrick Sheehan was written by Charles J. Kickham (1826-1882), author of *Knock-na-Gow*. (Note from Barry, p. 98).

J 12

DONALD MONROE

Monroe emigrates to America, leaving his two sons with their uncle in Scotland because he is unable to pay their passage. Seven years later the two boys enlist in the British army and sail to America to see their parents. Soon after landing, the younger is killed by rebels and the elder is fatally wounded. One of the rebels proves to be their father. His son forgives him, but the older man is overwhelmed with grief and remorse.

> Ye sons of North Britain, you that used to range
> In search of foreign countries and lands that was strange,
> Amongst this great number was Donald Munro.
> Away to America he likewise did go.

Mackenzie, 323, 8d (N.S.) Refs. Creighton, 124, 9d, m. (N.S.). Greenleaf, 318, 5-line frag. (Nfld.). *JAF* 26, 183, 28d lines, m. (N.S. via Mass. "The Sons of North Britain").

Broadsides: (B) "A broadside containing this song (together with 'Napoleon's Farewell') was printed by James Wright, Edinburgh." (Note from Mackenzie). Logan, 413, 19d, from a chapbook of ca. 1778.

This interesting by-product of the American Revolution is violent in its denunciation of the "rebels".

J 13

THE SONS OF LIBERTY

The narrator tells of anchoring in New York Bay, landing, and engaging in a fierce fight against the powerful Sons of Liberty. He speaks of the grief of those who lost husbands and fathers in the battle. The ballad ends with a stanza praising George Washington and his brave soldiers.

> O fare you well, sweet Ireland, whom I shall see no more,
> My heart is almost bleeding to leave this native shore.
> The king he has commanded that we shall sail away
> To fight the boys of liberty in North Amerikee.

Sharp II, 225, 6d, m.; 4d. m. (Ky.).

J 14

THE CROPPY BOY

After being arrested as a suspected rebel against England, the Irish youth is betrayed by a vindictive girl, sometimes his sister. He is sentenced to die, and he and his family grieve. At his hanging his father denies him and gives him the name "The Croppy Boy".

> It was early in the spring;
> The small birds whistling sweet did sing,
> Changing their notes from tree to tree;
> The song they sang was 'Old Ireland free'.
>
> It was early last Thursday night
> The yeoman cavalry gave me a fright;
> The yeoman cavalry was my downfall
> When I was taken before Lord Cornwall.

Belden, 283, 12 (Mo.). Creighton, 183, 8, m. (N.S.). Dean, 45, 10 (Minn.). Randolph I, 436, 8 (Mo. from ms.).

Colum, 52, 10 (Ireland). Joyce, 192, 6, m. (Ireland).

Broadsides: (B) Forth, 11 (Harvard III, 191). Bebbington, 10 (Harvard VI, 67). No imprint, 10. (A) Partridge (B). W. Auner, Phila., 12 sts. DeMarsan, 12 sts. Songsters: (A) *617 Irish Songs,* p. 40, 11 sts.; p. 115, 12 sts. O'Conor, 11, 11 sts.

See Patrick Galvin, *Irish Songs of Resistance,* N. Y.: The Folklore Press, [1956], pp. 22-23, for various possible derivations of the word "croppy".

J 15

JAMES ERVIN

James Ervin tells of enlisting and then deserting. His sweetheart, Jane Wilson, helps him escape, but he is pursued. He fights with five of the train and defeats them, works at shoemaking for a year and a half, is captured, and escapes again. The ballad ends with a boast that he can defeat any Kingsman or Orangeman.

> I am a bold Republican, James Ervin is my name;
> I enlisted in the train,
> And for to exercise on Sunday did not with me agree,
> And that's the time, my brave boys, I took my liberty.

Gardner, 233, 6½d (Mich.).

J 16

BURKE'S DREAM

Burke dreams that he is among his comrades fighting with the other Fenians against the British. After a decisive victory he returns home. His mother screams and faints when she sees him, and he awakens in his cell.

> Sadly but slowly one night in November
> I laid down my weary head for to repose
> On my pillow of straw which I long shall remember;
> I been weary for sleep, I fell into a doze.

Greenleaf, 146, 9d, m. (Nfld.) Notes and refs.

Broadside: (A) Wehman no. 775 (Greenleaf). Songsters: (A) *Delaney's Irish Song Book No. 1,* p. 20. O'Conor, 70, 5 8-line d. sts. *617 Irish Songs,* 46, 5 8-line d. sts.

"General Thomas F. Burke was one of the leaders in the Fenian insurrection of 1867. He was convicted of high treason and sentenced to death at Dublin on May 1, 1867, but the sentence was commuted and he was released." (Note from Greenleaf, p. 148).

J 17

NELSON'S VICTORY AT TRAFALGAR
(*Brave Nelson*)

Nelson leads his ships against the enemy, is fatally wounded, and dies sure of victory.

> We got ready for the battle
> To face the daring foe.
> Our ships were numbered twenty-seven
> To shake the Spanish shore.
> Lord Nelson on the poop stood high,
> And to his men he then did cry,
> "My lads we'll conquer them or die!"
> Said brave Nelson.

Mackenzie, 203, 4d (N.S.) Refs.

Broadsides: (B) Ashton, 298, 6d. Logan, 67, 7d. Harkness, 6d. H. Andrews, 6d (Harvard XIV, 26). In a chapbook by R. Hutchison, Glasgow, 7d "Brave Nelson's Last Victory and Death" (Bell Coll. no. 12. Item 1471 in the Harvard Catalogue).

Ashton, *Real Sailor Songs,* p. 18, prints a different ballad on the same subject. His index contains the following note: "On October 21st, 1805, Admiral Lord Viscount Nelson, with twenty-seven sail of the line, attacked the united French and Spanish fleets, consisting of thirty-three sail of the line. . . . The action began at twelve o'clock, off Cape Trafalgar, and, after a conflict of upwards of four hours, nineteen sail of the line struck their colours. About the middle of the action Lord Nelson was struck by a musket ball, and soon afterwards died, and the total loss on board the British fleet was 1,587."

J 18

THE BATTLE OF THE NILE

Nelson's fleet comes upon Napoleon's near the Egyptian shore. In the ensuing battle, the narrator's ship, the *Majestic,* suffers heavy losses, but the French are soundly beaten. Four of their ships are burned, nine are captured, and the rest flee.

'Twas on the ninth day of August in the year ninety-eight,
We'll sing the praise of Nelson and the bold British fleet,
For the victory we've gained o'er the rebellious crew,
And to the Mediterranean Sea, brave boys, we'll bid adieu.

Mackenzie, 201, 7d (N.S.).

Ashton, *Real Sailor Songs,* p. 11, prints a different ballad on the same battle. His index contains the following note: "On 1st August, 1798, Rear-Admiral Sir Horatio Nelson, K. C. B., with the squadron under his command, consisting of fourteen ships of the line, attacked the French fleet of thirteen ships of the line and four frigates, at anchor across the bay of Aboukir, near the Mouth of the Nile; . . . nine ships of the line were taken, two burnt, and one frigate sunk . . . . For this Nelson was loaded with honours and made Baron Nelson of the Nile."

J 19

THE LITTLE FIGHTING CHANCE

The British ship fights for four hours and is victorious over the French vessel. Four men are killed and sixteen wounded. The British sail back to England with their prize.

On the fourteenth of July once so clear was the sky,
. . . . . . came bearing down so nigh,
Came bearing down upon us as we sailed out of France.
The name that she was called was the *Little Fighting Chance.*

Mackenzie, 215, 5 d. sts. and chorus. (N.S.)
Reynardson, *Sussex Songs,* 18 (M).

J 20

THE *CHESAPEAKE* AND THE *SHANNON* I

The American sailors are confident of an easy victory over the British and plan to tow the enemy ship to Boston. The British "hearts of oak", however, fight furiously, board the American ship, and capture it.

> The Chesapeake so bold
> Out of Boston as we're told,
> Came to take the British frigate neat and handy O.
> The people all in port
> They came out to see the sport
> And their music played up Yankee Doodle Dandy O.

Mackenzie, 208, 6 6-line sts. (N.S.) Refs. Finger, 159, 5 6-line sts., m. Sharp and Marson V, 56, 6d, m. (Somerest) Notes.

Broadside texts: (B) Logan, 71, 5 6-line sts. Detailed historical notes. Hale, *New England History in Ballads*, 135, 5 8-line sts. Firth, *Naval Sonsg*, 311, 6 sts. (Reprinted by Neeser, 169).

On June 1, 1813, the American frigate *Chesapeake*, Captain Lawrence, was challenged to single combat by the British frigate *Shannon*, Captain Broke. A large crowd gathered in Boston harbor to watch the engagement. Within a short time the *Chesapeake* was boarded and captured. (Note condensed from Logan). Nearly 140 years later, the United States Government posthumously restored the commission of Third Lieutenant William S. Cox, second in command of the *Chesapeake*. "It was Cox, during the War of 1812, who was blamed for the loss of the American vessel *Chesapeake*. . . . Cox left his post to carry below his mortally wounded commander, James Lawrence, who uttered the famous words 'Don't give up the ship,' before he died . . . Cox . . . was court-martialed and cashiered out of the Navy for 'neglect of duty and conduct unbecoming an officer. . . .' The 82nd Congress passed a bill restoring Cox's honor and nullifying the 1814 court-martial decision." (The Phila. *Inquirer*, Tues., Sept. 9, 1952).

J 21

THE *CHESAPEAKE* AND THE *SHANNON* II

After only ten minutes of fighting the outnumbered British crew boards the American ship and hauls down her colors.

> 'Twas on the glorious fourth of June
> At ten o'clock in the forenoon
> That we sailed out of Boston Bay,
> That we sailed out of Boston Bay,
> For to fight the *Chesapeake* boys.

Creighton and Senior, 266, 7 5-line sts., m. (N.S.) Notes.

"On Sunday morning, June 6th, Halifax was agog with excitement when the shabby and war-worn Shannon, towing the beautiful new vessel she had captured, sailed up the harbour. There were horrible scenes upon the decks of both vessels. People living along the coast tell me that their fathers seldom sang or talked of this engagement because of the sights they had witnessed." (Note from Creighton and Senior, p. 266).

J 22

THE *CHESAPEAKE* AND THE *SHANNON* III

Captain Broke of the *Shannon* challenges Captain Lawrence to fight. The *Chesapeake* sails to meet the enemy, and after a quarter of an hour the two frigates are locked together.

> 'Twas of the *Shannon* frigate in the merry month of May;
> To watch those bold Americans off Boston light she lay.
> The *Chesapeake* lying in harbor, a frigate stout and fine,
> She had four hundred and sixty men on board and her guns
> were forty-nine.

Mackenzie, 210, 3d (N.S. A fragment) Refs.

Such. no. 154, 9d. (Harvard XII, 1), reprinted by Firth, *Naval Songs*, 312; (reprinted by Neeser, 171). Pitts. Catnach, 9d (Harvard V, 206).

A fourth ballad celebrating the British victory is found on the Such and Catnach sheets listed above and in Ashton's *Real Sailor Songs*, p. 40, 5 8-line sts. Various American songs on this engagement are reprinted by Neeser.

J 23

WHEN THE BATTLE IT WAS WON
(*Young Jimmy and the Officer*)

A young man deserts from a battle when he receives a letter from his dying mother begging him to come home. He is pursued by an officer and some men, is dragged away from his mother's bedside, and is told he will be shot. In Greenleaf's text, the officer shoots Jimmy in the hope of winning the youth's fiancée, but when the girl hears what he has done, she shoots the officer.

> Come all you aged people, I pray you lend an ear,
> You'll hear my feeling story, you can't but shed a tear.
> 'T was of an aged couple that had one only son;
> He was shot as a deserter when the battle it was won.

Mackenzie, 297, 8d (N.S.). Greenleaf, 361, 10½d (Nfld.).

BALLADS OF SAILORS AND THE SEA (K)

K   1   The Loss of the *Ramillies*
K   2   Ye Gentlemen of England I
K   3   Bay of Biscay (Ye Gentlemen of England II)
K   4   The Loss of the *Amphitrite*
K   5   Captain Burke
K   6   By the Lightning We Lost Our Sight
K   7   The Isle of Man Shore
K   8   The Rocks of Scilly
K   9   Lady Franklin's Lament (The Sailor's Dream)
K 10   The Sailor and His Bride
K 11   Sally Monroe
K 12   The Sailor Boy I
K 13   The Faithful Sailor Boy
K 14   Farewell, Charming Nancy
K 15   Thomas and Nancy
K 16   A Gay Spanish Maid
K 17   Down by the Sea Shore
K 18   Scarboro Sand
K 19   Susan Strayed the Briny Beach
K 20   Mary's Dream
K 21   The Greenland Whale Fishery
K 22   A & B Captain Glen (The Guilty Sea Captain A) and The New York Trader (The Guilty Sea Captain B).

K 23   The *Flying Dutchman*
K 24   The Merman (Pretty Fair Maid with a Tail)
K 25   The Banks of Newfoundland
K 26   Bold McCarthy (The *City of Baltimore*)
K 27   The Maid on the Shore
K 28   The *Flying Cloud*
K 29   The Bold *Princess Royal*
K 30   The Bold Pirate
K 31   Kelly the Pirate I
K 32   Kelly the Pirate II
K 33   High Barbary
K 34   Bold Daniels (The *Roving Lizzie*)
K 35   Captain Kidd
K 36   Johnny the Sailor (Green Beds)
K 37   Will You Wed with a Tarry Sailor?
K 38   The Saucy Sailor (Jack the Jolly Tar II)
K 39   Jack Tar
K 40   Jack the Jolly Tar I (Tarry Sailor)
K 41   Gold Watch
K 42   The Shirt and the Apron
K 43   Home, Dearie, Home (Bell-Bottom Trousers)

K 1

THE LOSS OF THE *RAMILLIES*

When the storm becomes so fierce that H. M. S. *Ramillies* is doomed, the boatswain orders the crew to the lifeboats. Five hundred are lost; only four men escape. The news of the disaster causes great distress in Plymouth.

> It happened to be on the first of May
> While the *Ramillies* to her anchor lay.
> At twelve o'clock a gale came on,
> And she from her anchor cut and run.

Mackenzie, 225, 7 (N.S. "The Old *Ramillies*"). Refs. Doerflinger, 144, 3, m. (N.S.).

JFSS III, 286, 6, m. (Hampshire) Notes.

Note: Only 26 men were saved when H. M. S. *Ramillies* went to pieces on the coast of Devonshire on February 15, 1760. (Note from Doerflinger and Williams).

See Williams, 144, 5d sts., for a different piece on the same disaster and broadsides by Pitts, Catnach, and Keys, 6d sts. "The Fatal Ramillies".

K 2

YE GENTLEMEN OF ENGLAND I

Nine English ships are wrecked when they run aground in a storm off Ram's Head. All the crew of the *Coronation*, the largest ship, are lost, except for nineteen who reach shore in a long boat. The other ships mentioned (in Ashton's broadside) are the *Lyon, Lynx, Antelope, Loyalty, Eagle, Elizabeth,* and *Hardwick*.

> Ye gentlemen of England fair,
> Who live at home free from all care,
> It's little do you think or know
> What we poor seamen undergo,
> It's mild we toil along our way
> Worked like Turks or galley slaves.

Creighton, 136, 6 6-line sts. m. (N.S.) Flanders and Olney, 193, 8 6-line sts. (Vt. from ms.)

Ashton, *Real Sailor Songs,* after p. 40, 7 6-line sts. "England's Great Loss by a Storm of Wind").

K 3

BAY OF BISCAY, OH
(*Ye Gentlemen of England* II)
(*The Stormy Winds Did Blow*)

The *Rameley* leaves the narrator's ship in a storm and arriving at Gibraltar reports it probably lost. The ship does lose its masts and ten men, and the captain is killed in the forecastle. The storm abates, however, and after rigging a jury mast, the crew takes the ship to Gibraltar, "a dismal sight".

> Ye gentlemen of England who live home at your ease,
> It's little do you think of the dangers of the seas,
> When we receive our orders we are obliged to go
> On the main to proud Spain where the stormy winds do blow.
>
> Was on the fourth of August from Spithead we set sail
> With *Rameley* and Company blest with a pleasant gale,
> We sailed along together in the Bay of Biscay Oh,
> Where a dreadful storm it did arise and the stormy winds did blow.

Creighton, 105, 7d, m. (N.S.)
Broadside: (B) Harkness, Preston, 14 sts. ("New Version of The Bay of Biscay, or The Stormy Winds did Blow").

K 4

THE LOSS OF THE *AMPHITRITE*

Two days after leaving the home port, the ship runs aground. It soon sinks, carrying to death all its passengers and most of the crew. Three crewmen reach shore on a spar, one dies, and only the narrator and a companion remain alive.

> Come all ye jolly sailors brave that wear the jackets blue,
> While I relate the dangers great and hardships of the sea;
> It's of a ship called the Anford-Wright, with a hundred and
>   eight females,
> With cargo and crew and passengers too, bound out for
>   New South Wales.

Cox, 303, 6 d (W. Va.)
Broadside: (B) J. Livsey, Manchester, 9 d (Harvard II, 86).
Cox reprints an article from the *Gentleman's Magazine* for Sept., 1833 which gives a report of this disaster. In a violent storm . . . "the Amphitrite, with female convicts bound to Botany Bay, went on shore near Boulogne, and out of 130 persons only three were saved." See Cox for further details.

K 5

CAPTAIN BURKE

During a voyage with a cargo of slaves, the narrator is sent aloft to reef sail in a violent storm. He and three others are struck by lightning and hurled to the deck. They arrive in port lame and blind. The doctors are unable to restore their sight.

> I sailed on a ship called the Caroline,
> Burke was the captain's name,
> Bound out on the coast of Africa
> On a sweet and pleasant gale.

Creighton, 109, 9, m. (N.S.)
Cf. "By the Lightning We Lost Our Sight".

K 6

BY THE LIGHTNING WE LOST OUR SIGHT

While reefing sail in a hurricane between Gibraltar and England, the narrator and four other sailors are struck blind when the topgallant mast is shattered by lightning. Five others of the crew are washed overboard in the storm.

> Come all young lads bound over the deep, I hope you will attend,
> And listen unto those few lines which I have lately penned.
> I was once as hardy a sailor lad as ever furled a sail,
> Till by the lightning I lost my sight in that tremendous gale.

Mackenzie, 226, 6 d (N.S.).
Cf. "Captain Burke".

K 7

THE ISLE OF MAN SHORE
(The Quay of Dundocken; The Desolate Widow)

The widow tells of leaving the quay of Dundocken on board a ship bound for Liverpool. The ship is caught in a heavy gale, and the passengers are terrified. Two longboats are launched, one of which contains the narrator and her husband. Both boats are swamped, with the loss of forty persons, but Willie sees his wife safely to the Isle of Man shore. He, too, is lost after returning to the ship to rescue his father. The widow tells of having to beg bread for herself and her children.

One dark stormy night in the month of November
I heard a poor widow sit down to deplore,
And many another got cause to remember
That dark stormy night upon Galloway shore.

Greenleaf, 208, 7d, m. (Nfld.). *Bulletin* I, 10d, m. (Me.).

K 8
THE ROCKS OF SCILLY

The narrator leaves his beloved wife and goes to sea. He is lonely and unhappy thinking of her and fearing a disaster. After a violent storm the ship crashes on the Rocks of Scilly. Only four of the sailors survive, the narrator, oddly enough, being one of those lost. His wife dies of a broken heart.

Come all you jolly sailor boys
That plough the raging main,
Come listen to my tragedy
While I relate the same.
O I left my newly wedded bride
So well I did adore
To the seas we were commanded
Where the lofty billows roar.

Creighton and Senior, 200, 8d, m. (N.S.). Mackenzie, 140, 19 (N.S.) Refs.

Baring-Gould, 112, 5d, m. (W. of Eng.). *JFSS* V, 173, 11d couplets, m. (Dorset).

Broadsides: (B) W. Dickinson (Harvard II, 196) (M.) Spencer, 7d (Harvard I, 140). George Walker, 7d (Harvard II, 114). Songsters: (A) *The Uncle True Songster*, Phila., p. 75 (M). *The Forget Me Not Songster*, Phila., 75, 19 sts. The same, N.Y., 51.

K 9
LADY FRANKLIN'S LAMENT
(*The Sailor's Dream*)

The sailor dreams that he hears Lady Franklin sorrowfully recounting the events which led to the disappearance of her husband, his ships, and their crews in an Arctic expedition. She supposes that his ships were crushed in the ice of Baffin's Bay and she fears that her husband is dead, but she would give ten thousand pounds to know that he still lives.

Being homeward bound on the mighty deep,
Lying in a hammock, I fell asleep.
I dreamed a dream that I thought was true,
Concerning Franklin and his bold crew.

Doerflinger, 145, 7, m. (N.S. A composite text. Tune from Greenleaf) Notes; 146, 9 sts. from Jos. Faulkner's *Eighteen Months on a Greenland Whaler* (1878), p. 73. Colcord, 158, 7, m. ("Franklin's Crew") Notes. Greenleaf, 308, 4, m.; 309, equiv. of 5½ sts. (Nfld.) Notes.

Greig, lxxxvi, 12 (Scot.).

Broadsides: (B) John Gilbert, 12 sts. (Harvard IV, 26). Such no. 664, 13 sts. and chor. Songsters (A) (The following refs. from Doerflinger) *Delaney's Songbook* No. 23, p. 26. *Wehman's Collection of Songs* No. 10, p. 24.

"One of the most famous mysteries of the sea was the fate of Sir John Franklin, the Arctic explorer, and his more than two hundred men. They had sailed from England in 1845 in two ships, H.M.S. *Erebus* and *Terror*— portentous names!—and after an early report from a whaling skipper who fell in with them near Baffin Land, vanished without a trace in the wastes of the Arctic." (Note from Doerflinger, p. 145). (Searching parties eventually found remains of the doomed expedition.)

K 10

THE SAILOR AND HIS BRIDE

In this lament the widow says that her husband went to sea three years before, after only three months of marriage. His ship was lost in a storm, and she wishes that she, too, were sleeping beneath the waves.

> 'Twas in the spring when I was young,
> The flowers they bloomed, the birds they sung,
> But not a bird was as happy as I
> When the lovely sailor lad was nigh.

Flanders-Barry, 231, 5 and ref., m. (Vt.) Brown, 344, 7; 5 (N.C.). Cox, 364, 4 and ref.; 4½ (W. Va.). Eddy, 104, 7, m. (0); 7 (0. from ms.). Randolph IV, 268, 3½, m.; 5 and ref. (Mo.). Thompson, 218, 7 (N.Y. A composite text). *JAF* 35, 411, 7 (0. from ms. This text later printed by Eddy); 412, 2 (0.).

Broadside: (A) DeMarsan.

" 'The Sailor's Bride' was first printed, without music, by H. DeMarsan, on a broadside at some time between 1860 and 1878." (Note from Flanders-Barry.) The editors fail to offer proof that DeMarsan's text was a first printing, but I have come across no other broadside.

K 11

SALLY MONROE

Jim Dixon, a blacksmith, sends a letter to Sally by a comrade, who retains the letter and tells her mother that the youth is already married.

Two years later the lovers meet by chance, elope, and marry. Soon after sailing with five hundred other passengers for Quebec, their ship strikes a rock off the Welsh coast. Sally is lost, along with most of the others. Her husband grieves for her and feels conscience-stricken because her aged parents are now left alone.

> Come, all you lads and lassies, I pray you will attend,
> And listen to these few lines that I have lately penned;
> And I'll tell you of the hardships that I did undergo,
> 'Twas all for a lassie called Sally Munroe.

Dean, 35, 10½d (Minn. "Young Sally Munroe"). Doerflinger, 303, 4d, m. (Scott. via Mass.). Greenleaf, 120, 7-line frag. mixed with "The Gosport Tragedy" (Nfld.).

Greif, lxxiv, 15d (Scot.). Greig writes: "In none of our ballads is the note of sincerity more strong and convincing". Ord, 115, 14d (Scot.). *JFSS* III, 291, 4d, m. (Hampshire).

K 12

THE SAILOR BOY I

A girl has her father build her a boat and sets out in it to find her sailor boy. She describes the boy to a ship's captain, who tells her that her lover was drowned at Rocky Isle. Grief-stricken, she commits suicide by dashing her boat against the rocks. The ballad ends with her written directions for her funeral.

> "O Father, O Father, come build me a boat
> That over the ocean I may float,
> And every ship that I pass by
> There I'll inquire for my sweet sailor boy."

Belden, 186, 7, m. (Mo.) Stanza two is given above. 187, 5½ (Mo. from ms.); 8; 4 (Mo.); 6 (Kan.); 3 (Mo.). Barry, 58, 9, m. (Me. A composite text). Brewster, 269, 9 (Ind.). Brown, 324, 3½; 8 frags.; 6½d, mixed with another ballad (N.C.). Cox, 353, 10; 9; 7½ (W. Va.). Creighton, 89, 6, m.; 4½, m. (N.S.). Gardner, 94, 4½ (Va. via Mich.). Henry, *Songs Sung*, 177, 8 (N.C.). Owens, 135, 5, m. (Tex.). Randolph I, 297, 7, m.; 2½, m.; 3d, m.; 4, m. (Mo.); frag. with tune (Ark.) Refs. Rickaby, 85, 8, m. (Wis. "The Pinery Boy"—a lumberjacks' version). Sharp II, 84, 7, m.; 4, m. (N.C.); 10 frags. with tunes from N.C., Va., Ky., and Tenn. *JAF* 29, 45, 4½ (Ga.). *JAF* 31, 162, 5d, m. (Belfast via Can.); 170, 6d, m. (Quebec). *JAF* 35, 410, 9, m. (O.) *JAF* 60, 235, 8 (Ill. from ms.). *SFQ* V, 145, 6, m. (N.C.); 186, 3½ (Ind.).

Greig, lxiv, 10 sts. (Scot.). Sharp, *One Hundred*, 162, 6, m. *JFSS* I, 99, 7, m. (Sussex). *JFSS* II, 293, 10, m. (Lincs.). *JFSS* VIII, 212, 2 frags. with tunes from Dorset and Co. Down.

Broadsides: (B) Belden refers to broadsides by Catnach and Such. Brereton, 8 sts., "A New Song Call'd The Young Lady's Lamanetation for the Loss of Her True Love".

Note: For ballads in which the same last requests are made in the same phraseology see "The Butcher Boy" and "Love Has Brought Me to Despair."

K 13

THE FAITHFUL SAILOR BOY

The sailor dies at sea, and his comrades take his girl a farewell note in which he has said that they will meet in heaven.

> 'Twas on a dark and stormy night,
> The snow lay on the ground,
> A sailor boy stood on the deck;
> The ship was outward bound.
> His sweetheart standing by his side,
> Shed many a bitter tear.
> At last he pressed her to his heart
> And whispered in her ear:

Brown, 342, 5d (N.C.). Chappell, 59, 6 (N.C.).

K 14

FAREWELL, CHARMING NANCY

Nancy begs to accompany Johnny while he's plowing the main, but he says that her fingers couldn't manage the cables and her feet couldn't take her to the topmast. She bids him a sad farewell.

> "Farewell, charming Nancy, since I must go and leave you,
> It's to the East Indies my course I must steer.
> If you will prove roal, love, I will prove stonance,
> And we will be married if there's nothing to fear."

Brown, 320, 5d; 319, 3d (N.C.) In these texts Nancy sees the youth swept into the sea and dies at the sight. Chappell, 68, 4d, m. (N.C.) Scarborough, 372, 4d (Ky.) Thomas, *Devil's Ditties,* 87, 4d (Ky. Same singer as Scarborough's?).

Sharp, *One Hundred,* 70, 4d, m. *JFSS* I, 130, 3d, m. (Sussex); III, 298, 6d, m. (Hampshire).

Broadsides: (B) Bebbington, 5d (Harvard IX, 4). 60 Old St., 4d ("Sailor and his Truelove").

K 15

THOMAS AND NANCY

Nancy sadly watches Thomas's ship sail away and calls to him to remember his true love, his parents, and his home. The ship soon crashes into the rocks and is destroyed. Nancy finds her lover's corpse floating near the shore, kisses its pale lips, and dies of grief.

> When the bo's'n's loud whistle keeps sounding,
> Causing Nancy and Thomas to part,
> As she stood on the beach broken-hearted,
> The tears from her blue eyes did start.

Greenleaf, 114, 7, n. (Nfld.).
Broadsides: (B) Paul, 22 Brick Lane, Spitalfields, 6 sts. Catnach. George Walker, Jr., Durham, 6 sts. (Harvard II, 19).

K 16

A GAY SPANISH MAID

The maid, Linnete, meets her lover on the shore the night he is to sail and bids him a sad farewell. A violent storm comes up soon after he leaves, the ship sinks, and all but her lover are lost. He saves himself by clinging to a plank and is later picked up. The girl, however, hears that the ship is lost, and dies of grief before her lover reaches home.

> A gay Spanish maid at the age of sixteen
> Through a meadow strayed far and wide;
> Down by a beech tree she sat down to rest,
> With a gay handsome youth by her side.

Barry, 84, 13, m. (Me. from ms.). Combs, 153, 10, (W. Va.). Cox, 371, 7 (W. Va.). Creighton, 71, 7, m. (N.S.). Flanders-Barry, 84, 4, m. (N.H.); 7 (N.Y. via Mass.). Gardner, 123, 12, m.; 1, m. (Mich.). Mackenzie, 104, 11 (N.S.). Randolph I, 434, 7 (Mo.).

K 17

DOWN BY THE SEA SHORE

The narrator learns from the damsel that her lover has died at sea. He proposes marriage but the girl rejects him, saying she will never marry, and then commits suicide by plunging into the ocean.

> One mornin' as I rambled down by th' sea shore,
> Th' wind it did whistle, th' waters did roar,
> I spied a fair damsel a-kneelin' in the sand,
> A-readin' a letter she held in her hand . . .

Randolph I, 341, 2½d and chor., m. (Mo.) ; 6, 1; 3 and chor., m. (Ark.).
Belden, 167, 7d, couplets and chor.; 16d lines and chor. (Mo.). Henry,
Folk-Songs, 204, 5 and chor. (Tenn. via Ga.).

Broadsides: (B) According to Belden, the Harvard Library owns four
stall prints of this ballad.

K 18

SCARBORO SAND
(*The Drowned Sailor*)

When the girl hears that her fiancé has been lost in a storm at sea, she
asks that the waves wash her true love's body ashore. She finds the body,
hugs and kisses it, and dies. The lovers are buried in Robin Hood's churchyard.

> There was a fair lady in Scarboro did dwell,
> She was courted by a sailor, whom she loved him full well.
> They were promised to be married when he did return;
> But mark, a misfortune upon him did frown.

Brown, 329, 7d (N.C.). Chappell, 70, 7d, m. (N.C. Same text as
Brown's).

Greig, lxxxiii, 7d (Scot. "Scarborough Banks"). Kidson, 112, 6d, m.
(Yorks. "The Drowned Sailor"). Ord, 332, 7d (Scot.).*JFSS* III, 258, 6d,
m. (Hants.) ; 7½d (Southampton) Notes.

Cf. "The Drowned Lover", Sharp and Marson II, 12, 4d, m. (Somerset) and Baring-Gould, 66, 3d, m. This lament is apparently the ancestor
of "Scarboro Sand". According to Baring-Gould (Part IV, p. xxxii), the
earlier piece dates from a broadside of 1671, and the later, if I understand
his rather involved note correctly, was printed as a broadside by Catnach,
Harkness, and others.

K 19

SUSAN STRAYED THE BRINY BEACH

The nobleman's daughter would not exchange her Willy for any lover
of high degree. She worries about him as she strolls along the beach.
Seeing a floating body, she drags it ashore and finds that it is Willy. She
dies of grief, and the lovers are buried in one tomb.

> Susan strayed the briny beach along the Sligo shore;
> She oftentimes thought on a boy her fond heart did adore,
> And often in sad accident her tongue pronounced his name;
> To love a simple sailor she thought it was no shame.

Greenleaf, 206, 9d; 2d (Nfld.).

K 20

MARY'S DREAM
(*Mary o' the Dee*)

Sandy's ghost appears and tells Mary that he was drowned in a shipwreck. He asks his love to prepare to go with him "where love is free from grief and care". The cock crows and the ghost vanishes.

> The moon had climbed the highest hill
> That rises o'er the source of Dee,
> And from its eastern summit shed
> A silver light o'er town and tree.
> Mary had lain her down to sleep,
> Her thoughts on Sandy, far at sea,
> When soft and low a voice she heard,
> Saying, "Mary, weep no more for me."

Cox, 435, 4d (W. Va.). Eddy, 201, 8 (O. from 18th cent. ms.). Shoemaker, 214, 5d (in Scots dialect) ; 4d (Pa.). *JAF* 28, 157, 6 (Ky.).

Broadside: (A) DeMarsan (C). Songsters: (A) *The New American Songster*, Phila., 1817, p. 71 (C). *The American Songster*, Phila., 1836, p. 15, 4d.

According to Cox, the version in Scots dialect is not the original. The ballad was written by John Lowe (1750-1798), a clergyman who emigrated from Scotland to America in 1773. (See DNB).

K 21

THE GREENLAND WHALE FISHERY

In need of money, the narrator and his comrades ship on board a whaler from Liverpool. A whale is sighted and harpooned, but it capsizes the boat, killing five of the crew. The captain is grieved at the loss of the whale and his men. Soon the ship starts home from barren Greenland.

> In eighteen hundred and forty-five,
> Being March on the twentieth day,
> Oh, we hoisted our colors to our topmast high
> And for Greenland forged away, brave boys,
> And for Greenland forged away.

Lomax, *Our Singing Country*, 214, 6, m. (Mich.). Belden, 104, 8 (Vt. from ms.). Eckstorm, 226, 8 (Me.). Refs. Colcord, 151, 8, m.

Greig, lxxxv, 10 sts. Sharp and Marson III, 54, 7 m. (Somerset).

Broadsides: (B) Ashton, 265, 12 sts. Ashton, *Real Sailor Songs*, 83, 12 sts. Such, no. 292, 12 sts., reprinted by Johnson, *Pop. Brit. Ballads* II, 269. Catnach (Harvard V, 168). Pitts, 12 sts, reprinted by Eckstorm, 227 and by Leach, 707. Spencer, 12 sts (Harvard I, 119).

Notes: "The Greenland Voyage: or, the Whale-Fisher's Delight", *Coll. of Old Ballads* III, 175, is an entirely different ballad which describes the old method of whaling from small boats launched from shore. A lyrical song called "The Greenland Whale Fishery" may be found in *JFSS* I, 101 and II, 243.

K 22 A
CAPTAIN GLEN
(*The Guilty Sea Captain* A)

Soon after the ship leaves England many of the crew become ill. After the captain has a dream warning him that he and the ship are doomed, he confesses to the boatswain that he has led a sinful life ashore and has killed a squire. When a violent storm threatens to destroy the ship, the boatswain reveals the captain's secret, and the crew members toss the captain overboard. The storm immediately subsides, and the ship is able to proceed to a port for repairs. She eventually returns to London with only 73 of her original 150 men alive. The ballad ends with a warning against sailing with a murderer.

> There was a ship and a ship of fame
> Launch'd off the stocks, bound to the main,
> With a hundred and fifty brisk young men
> Was picked and chosen every one.

> William Glen was our captain's name.
> He was a tall and brisk young man,
> As bold a sailor as ever went to sea,
> And he was bound to New Barbary.

Mackenzie, 238, 22 (N.S.) Notes and refs. Creighton, 111, 12, m. (N.S.).

Christie, I, 240, 6d, m. (Scot.) (Reprinted by Leach, 697). Greig, cxxx, 21 (Scot.). *JFSS* V, 263, 9, m.; 8, m. (Somerset. "Sir William Gower").

Broadsides: (B) Logan, 47, 21 ("Captain Glen's Unhappy Voyage to New Barbary"). *Roxburghe Ballads* VIII, 141, 11d (Ca. 1770. "An Excellent New Song, entitled Captain Glen"). (A) Mackenzie refers to an early 19th century broadside with the same title as Logan's (Ford, *Mass. Broadsides,* no. 3003). Songsters: (A) *The Forget Me Not Songster,* Phila., 43, 21 sts.; The same, N.Y., 76, 22 sts.

K 22 B
THE NEW YORK TRADER
(*The Guilty Sea Captain* B)

The story is essentially the same as the preceding, except that the ship is bound for New York, the captain's name is not given, he confesses that

he has murdered his master and his own wife and children, and the ship
proceeds home as soon as the captain is removed from it.

> To a New York trader I did belong.
> She was well built, both stout and strong,
> Well rigged, well manned, well fit for sea,
> Bound for New York in America.

Mackenzie, 241, 11 (N.S.) Refs.
Williams, 265, 10 (Wilts.) *JFSS* VII, 2, 14, m. (Norfolk) Refs.
Broadsides: (B) Ashton, 268, 14. G. Walker, Jr., 14 (Harvard, II, 31).
Spencer, Broadstones, 7d (Harvard I, 118). Batchelar, 14 sts. Catnach.
Songsters: (A) *The Forget Me Not Songster,* N. Y., Nafis and Cornish,
p. 100 (M). *The Washington Songster,* N. Y., Turner and Fisher, p.
123 (M).

Note: These pieces are listed as variants of one ballad because many
of the stanzas are almost identical. "The New York Trader" is almost certainly a rewriting of "Captain Glen".
Mackenzie points out the similarity between this piece and "Brown
Robin's Confession" (Child no. 57).

K 23

THE FLYING DUTCHMAN
(*Vanderdecken*)

When the *Flying Dutchman* appears, the captain orders his men to take
in sail, for he feels that his ship is in danger. The ghost ship tries to enter
Table Bay but sails past it. The sailors on the other ship pity Captain
Vanderdecken, who is doomed to sail forever.

> At length our helmman gave a shout of terror and of fear,
> As if he had just gazed upon some sudden danger near,
> The sea all round was clad in foam and just upon our lee,
> We saw the Flying Dutchman come bounding o'er the sea,

Doerflinger, 148, 5d, m. (N.Y.) Stanza two is given above. Refs.
Broadsides: (B) Cadman, 3 8-line d. sts. (Harvard VI, 180). Bebbington, 3 8-line d. sts. (Harvard X, 110). Songsters: (A) Doerflinger refers
to texts in several songsters including *Delaney's Song Book No. 71,* p. 23
and *Leonard and Jones Telegraph Lads Songsters,* N. Y., 1881, p. 34.
See "The Flying Dutchman of the Western World" by W. H. Bonner,
JAF 59, 282-288. The author relates the legends of Vanderdecken to those
of Captain Kidd and mentions a ballad sung in the melodrama "The Flying Dutchman," which was performed in New York from 1827 to the
1850's.

K 24

THE MERMAN
(*Pretty Fair Maid with a Tail*)

The sailors hear a splash and a shout, and a merman appears. He complains to the captain that the ship's anchor has stopped up his front door. When questioned the merman says he was once a sailor, was washed overboard in a gale, married a mermaid, and grew a tail.

> It been in the month of January,
> Bound away for the Southern seas,
> We dropped our anchor beneath the carriage,
> A-waiting for a breeze.

Greenleaf, 130, 11, m. (Nfld. "The Pretty Fair Maid with a Tail"). Flanders and Brown, 176, 8 (Nfld. via Vt. "The Merman").

Greenleaf, p. 131, contains the following note on this piece: "It has some resemblance to the well-known 'Married to a Mermaid' (L. A. Smith, *The Music of the Waters*, pp. 90-91 . . .."

In "The Mermaid" (Child no. 289), the tragic story of a shipwreck, the appearance of the mermaid is taken as an omen of disaster.

K 25

THE BANKS OF NEWFOUNDLAND

Having pawned their clothes in Liverpool, the sailors are bitterly cold on the Newfoundland Banks. An Irish girl passenger, who has become engaged to the narrator, tears up her flannel petticoat to make mittens for him. Eventually the ship arrives in New York.

> Ye rambling boys of pleasure, I have you to beware,
> If ever you sail in a Yankee ship, no dungaree jumpers wear,
> But have your monkey jacket always at your command,
> For beware of the cold nor'westers on the Banks of Newfoundland.

Greenleaf, 230, 7d and ref. (Nfld.) Refs. Colcord, 173, 5d and ref., m. Creighton, 221, 6d, m. (N.S.). Doerflinger, 123, 6d, m. (N.Y. A composite text). Eckstorm, 220, frag. of 3d and ref. from print; 221, 2 (Me.). Mackenzie, 385, 6d (N.S.).

JFSS V, 300, 4d, m. (recorded at sea). *JFSS* VIII, 99, 5d, m. (Cornwall).

Broadsides: (B) Hodges, 9d. Ross, Newcastle, 10d (Harvard IV, 82).

K 26

BOLD McCARTHY
(*The City of Baltimore*)

McCarthy sails from Liverpool on the *City of Baltimore*, bound for New York. The mate taunts the Irishman, and a fierce fight follows, in which the mate is soundly beaten. The Scottish captain then makes McCarthy an officer.

> Come all ye true-born Irishmen, come listen to what I'll tell,
> Concerning Bold McCarthy at Liverpool did dwell.
> Down by a western dock one day McCarthy chanced to stroll
> On board of a western ocean boat, the *City of Baltimore*.

Greenleaf, 354, 7d (Nfld.). Creighton, 117, 9d, m. (N.S.). Doerflinger, 128, 4d; 1d (N.S. Tune from N.B.).

K 27

THE MAID ON THE SHORE
(*The Fair Maid by the Sea Shore; The Sea Captain*)

Attracted by the young lady, the sea captain, after much persuasion, succeeds in having her come aboard. He invites her to his cabin where she sings him and the sailors to sleep. She then robs him of silver, gold, and costly ware and paddles her boat to shore, using his broadsword as an oar.

> There was a fair lady far crossed in love,
> Far crossed in love, as it were, O;
> Nothing could she find,
> To ease her fair mind,
> Than to stray all along the sea shore, O,
> Than to stray all along the sea shore!

Barry, 40, 9, m. (Me.) Reprinted from *Bulletin* no. 7, p. 12. (Reprinted by Leach, 731). Belden, 107, 8, m. (Mo.). Greenleaf, 63, 8, m. (Nfld.). Korson, *Penna. Songs,* 54, 6, m. (Pa.). Mackenzie, 74, 6; 5 (N.S.). *Western Folklore* XI, 177, 5, m. (Ore.). *JAF* 60, 230, 10d (Ill. from ms.).

K 28

THE FLYING CLOUD

The narrator becomes an apprentice to a cooper in Waterford but leaves him to ship on board the *Ocean Queen,* bound (usually) for Valparaiso. There he falls in with Captain Moore, commander of the *Flying Cloud,* which goes to Africa for a cargo of slaves, many of whom die on the return trip to Cuba. Moore decides to turn pirate and all the crew but five join him. The pirates rob and plunder many ships on the Spanish Main. Often pursued by warships, they outrun them all until finally a ship shoots away their mizzenmast. In the fight that follows, Captain Moore and many of his men are killed and the rest are captured. The narrator and his fellows next appear in Newgate under sentence of death.

> My name is Edward Holleran, as you may understand,
> I was born in County Waterford, in Erin's lovely land;
> I being young and in my prime, my age scarce twenty-one,
> My parents doted on me, I being their only son.

Eckstorm, 214, 16d (N.S. via Me.). Belden, 128, 15d (Mich. via Wis.). Colcord, 145, 15d, m. Creighton, 126, 17d, m. (N.S.) Creighton and Senior, 223, 15d; 2d (N.S.). Dean, 1, 16d (Minn.). Doerflinger, 135, 17d, m. (N.S.); 3d, m. (N.Y.) Notes and refs. Finger, 84, 12d, m. Gray, 116, 24 sts. (from a Boston newspaper); 12d sts. (reprinted from *JAF* 35, 370) Greenleaf, 349, 30, m. (Nfld.). Leach, 778, 30 (Me.). Lomax, *Amer. Ballads,* 504, 13d. m. (Mo.). Mackenzie, 283, 16d (N.S.) Refs. Rickaby, 145, 15d, m. (N.D.). Thompson, 39, 15d (N.Y. a composite text). Shay, 183, 15d, m. *JAF* 35, 370, 12d (Minn. A composite text).

Greig, cxviii, 12d ("William Hollander").

Doerflinger, 334-335, feels that the author of this ballad was influenced by a prose temperance pamphlet of 1830 entitled "Dying Declaration of Nicholas Fernandez, Who with Nine Others were Executed . . . for Piracy and Murder on the High Seas". Most of the parallels he cites, however, are commonplaces in crime literature of this type.

For an enlightening analysis of the ballad see Horace P. Beck, "The Riddle of 'The *Flying Cloud*' ", *JAF* 66, 123-133.

K 29

THE BOLD *PRINCESS ROYAL*

A pirate ship overtakes the *Princess Royal*, which is on her way from England to Newfoundland. The captain ignores a request to heave to, supposedly for the delivery of mail, and safely outraces the pirate ship.

> Bright Monday morning
> We had sailed from the Strand,
> In the bold *Prince of Royal*
> Bound to Newfoundland;
> Sixteen jolly seamen
> Was our ship's company,
> And the wind from the eastward,
> To the westward steered we.

Greenleaf, 78, 7d, m. (Nfld.). Chappell, 52, 12, m. (N.C. "Buxter's Bold Crew"). Brown, 353, frag. of 3 sts. (N.C. "Lorena Bold Crew"). Colcord, 148, 8d, m. (Tune from Greenleaf). Creighton, 107, 8d, m. (N.S.) Refs. Doerflinger, 142, 6d, m. (N.S.); 1d, m. (Scotland via Mass.). Eckstorm, 256, 5d (Me. from ms.).

Kidson, *A Garland,* 34, 7d, m. *JFSS* I, 62, 6d, m. (Yorks.); I, 103, 5d, m. (Sussex). *JFSS* II, 145, 2d, m. (Essex); II, 170, 1d, m. (Norfolk); *JEFDSS* IV, 184, 6d, m. (Kent).

Broadsides: (B) Catnach, 8d. Ryle, 8d (Harvard VII, 218).

K 30
THE BOLD PIRATE

The British sailors fight valiantly and slaughter the pirates who have intercepted and boarded their ship. When the pirate ship tries to escape, a broadside halts it. The commander of the pirates, who loses both legs in the action, commends the sailors and tells them that his ship contains five hundred chests of gold. The British ships tows its prize back to Bristol, and the newly rich crew retire to a life of ease on shore.

> 'Twas on the eighteenth day of March
> We sailed from Bristol town,
> And we sailed all that livelong day
> Till the night came rolling on.
>
> And then we saw a bold pirate
> Sailing three foot to our one;
> He hail-ed us in English,
> And asked us whence we come.

Eckstorm, 254, 15 (Me. A composite text). Creighton and Senior, 229, 8d, m. (N.S. "Pirate Song").
JFSS VII, 7½d, m. (Dorset).

K 31
KELLY THE PIRATE I

The frigate *Stag* encounters a large cutter commanded by Kelly the pirate. Kelly warns his men that defeat means the gallows for them and encourages them to fight. The British ship shoots away their mainmast, peppers them with shot, and sinks them. The ballad ends with praise for Captain Cooper.

> Come all ye jolly tarsmen, come listen to my song;
> If you pay good attention I'll not keep you long.
> 'Twas of the *Stag* frigate, that ship of great fame,
> That fought the arch-pirate, bold Kelly by name.

Mackenzie, 211, 9d (N.S.) Notes and refs. Greenleaf, 95, 5d (Nfld.). *JFSS* VI, 34, 7d, m. (Sussex. "George Keary").

Broadsides: (B) Pitts (reprinted by Shoemaker, 178, 5d). C. Croshaw, York, 10d ('The Bold Pirate"). Paul, 5d (Harvard VII, 129). In a chapbook by R. Hutchinson, Glasgow (items 912 and 1403 in the Harvard Catalogue). (A?) No imprint, Phila.? (item 2461 in the Harvard Catalogue).

K 32

KELLY THE PIRATE II

A British naval frigate intercepts the pirate ship commanded by bold Kelly, who refuses to surrender. In the ensuing battle, the soundly beaten pirates strike their colors, the ship is taken, and Kelly is sent to prison.

> Our Admiral gave orders on the same day .
> To cruise in the Channel for our enemy,
> To protect all our merchants from the brave foe,
> And all interlopers, as you may suppose.

Mackenzie, 213, 7d; 7d (N.S.). Notes and refs. Shoemaker, 177, 6d and ref. (Pa.)

Songsters: (A) *The Forget Me Not Songster,* N.Y., 75, 7d. The same, Phila., 48, 7d. *Uncle Sam's Naval and Patriotic Songster,* N.Y., 29 (M).

Mackenzie suggests that this ballad is an American composition which is derived from the preceding piece.

K 33

HIGH BARBARY

(*The Coast of Barbary*)

The two British ships sight a strange vessel, ask its identity, and learn that it is a pirate ship. A battle follows in which the *Prince of Luther* shoots away the pirate's masts. The pirates call for quarter, but the British ships sink them.

> There were two lofty ships from old England came,
> Blow high, blow low, and so sailed we;
> One was the *Prince of Luther,* and the other *Prince of Wales,*
> Cruising down along the coast of the High Barbaree.

Lomax, *Our Singing Country,* 212, 7d, m. (Bermuda). Barry, Eckstorm, and Smyth, 413, 7d (Me.) (Reprinted by Leach, 777). Brown, 352, 3d (N.C.) Refs. Chappell, 50, 8d, m. (N.C.). Colcord, 153, 8d. Morris, 53, 4d, m.; 3d. m. (Fla.). Shay, 91, 8d, m. Thompson, 38, 8d (N.Y. from ms.).

Baring-Gould and Sharp, 18, 7d, m. Sharp and Marson, IV, 18, 9d, m.

(Somerset. A composite text). *JFSS* V, 262, 8d, m. (Exmoor. "The Coasts of Barbary").

Broadsides: (B) Quick, Clerkenwell, 7d ("Coast of Barbary"). (A) Deming, Boston, 7d (L of C). (A?) Barry, Eckstorm, and Smyth, 415, reprint a text of 6 d. sts. from a photostat of "a very old broadside" in the Mass. Historical Society. Neeser, 303, 8d. Songsters: (A) Barry, Eckstorm, and Smyth reprint a text of 6 d. sts. from *The American Songster,* Philip J. Cozzens, N.Y., n. d., and another of 7 d. sts. from *The Forget Me Not Songster,* Phila. and N.Y., Turner and Fisher.

A relationship between this ballad and "The George Aloe and the Sweepstake" (Child, no. 285) has been observed by Cecil Sharp and others. In fact, Barry, Eckstorm, and Smyth consider 'High Barbary" a secondary form of the Child ballad. Though the two pieces have points of similarity, they are quite different in phraseology and content. According to Frank Shay, "High Barbary" was written by Charles Dibdin (1745-1814), that prolific song-writer for the Royal Navy. The author was probably inspired by the older ballad.

K 34

BOLD DANIELS
(The Roving Lizzie)

Sailing from La Guayra to Rio, the *Roving Lizzie* encounters a pirate ship, which calls on the *Lizzie* to surrender. Instead, Bold Daniels and his outnumbered crew fight bravely, capture the pirate ship, and take it to Baltimore.

> It was on the fourteenth day of January
> From England we set sail,
> With the favoring Heavens to guard us
> And a sweet and pleasant gale;
> The Roving Lizzie we are called,
> Bold Daniels is my name,
> And we sailed away to La Guayra
> All out on the Spanish Main.

Colcord, 149, 7d. Dean, 39, 7d (Minn. "Bold Daniel"). Eckstorm, 257, 7d (Me. "The Rovin' Lizzie"). Rickaby, 135, 7d, m. (Minn. Sung by M. C. Dean).

K 35

CAPTAIN KIDD

Captain Kidd elaborates on his own wickedness as he tells of cursing his father, vowing not to pray, burying the Bible, and murdering William Moore and his own gunner. He repented for a while, after a warning from his dying mate and an attack of illness, but the repentance did not last.

His career continued with the robbing and burning of ships from France and Spain. Finally he was captured by fourteen ships, taken to Newgate, and sentenced to death. He warns others against a life that leads to hell.

> You captains brave and bold, hear our cries, hear our cries,
> You captains brave and bold, hear our cries.
> You captains brave and bold, though you seem uncontrolled,
> Don't for the sake of gold lose your souls, lose your souls,
> Don't for the sake of gold lose your souls.

Mackenzie, 279, 25 (N.S.) Detailed refs. Brown, 350, 5 (N.C.). Colcord, 141, 25, m. Eckstorm, 246, frags. and discussion. Gardner, 318, 5, m. (Mich.). Hudson, 238, 4 (Miss.). Linscott, 131, 13, m. (Mass.). Lomax, *Amer. Ballads*, 501, 25. Morris, 51, 5, m. (Fla.). Pound, 160, 4 (Kan.). Shay, 187, 15. Thompson, 23, 18 from *The Forget Me Not Songster;* discussion.

Broadsides: (A) Hale, *New England History in Ballads*, 40, 25 sts.; discussion, pp. 37-39. Hunt, Boston, 25 sts. Hunts and Shaw, Boston. No imprint, 25 sts. (Thomas Coll, I, 65). Songsters: (A) *The Forget Me Not Songster*, Phila., 53, 25 sts. The same, N.Y., 28, 25 sts.

Captain William Kidd was arrested in Boston in 1699, was returned to England for trial at the Old Bailey for murder and piracy on the high seas, and was hanged at Execution Dock, London, on May 23, 1701. "The original broadside of 1701 [22 sts.] . . . is reprinted in Firth's *Naval Songs and Ballads*, pp. 134-137." (notes from Mackenzie, p. 278).

K 36

JOHNNY THE SAILOR
(*Green Beds*)

Johnny returns from sea pretending he has lost everything and goes calling on the innkeeper's daughter. Her mother treats him scornfully until he produces handfuls of gold. Then Polly appears, embraces him, and suggests (or her mother does) that he go to bed with her. Johnny declines, saying that he will "make the taverns whirl,/With a bottle of good whiskey,/And on each knee a girl."

> Oh Johnny been on sea,
> An' Johnny been on shore,
> And Johnny come to London,
> To where he's been before,
> Welcome home on shore, Johnny,
> Welcome home from sea,
> Last night my daughter Polly
> Lay a-dreaming of thee.

Randolph I, 250, 6d, m.; add. sts. (Mo.). Belden, 160, 16 (Mo.); 14 (Mo. from ms.). Brown, 335, 11½; add. sts.; 14 (N.C.). Brewster, 188, 10, m.; 15 (Ind.). Cox, 390, 8 (W. Va.) Refs. Eddy, 95, 17 (O.). Gardner, 91, 9d, m.; 5d (Mich.). Henry, *Folk-Songs*, 168, 15 (Tenn.); 15 (Ky.). Hudson, 156, 12 (Miss.). Mackenzie, 246, 10d; 16; 8d (N.S.) Notes and refs. Owens, 85, 13, m. (Tex.). Sandburg, 430, 8d, m. ("Jackson"). Sharp I, 365, 12, m. (N.C.); 5d, m.; 1d, m. (Ky.); 1d, m. (Va.) Thompson, 211, 17½; 2 (N.Y.). *JAF* 28, 156, 14d couplets (N.C.). *JAF* 35, 373, refs. *JAF* 52, 45, 4½d, m. (Ky. via Wis.)

Greig, cxv, 8d (Scot.). *JFSS* I, 48, 8d, m. (Stratford). *JFSS* III, 281, 8d, m. (Winchester). *JFSS* V, 68, 1d, m. (Somerset).

Broadsides: (B) Bebbington, 10d ("Jack Tar; or, The Green Bed Empty." Harvard X, 155). George Walker, Jr., Durham, (Harvard II, 46). Ashton, *Real Sailor Songs*, 47, 38d lines, ("A Comical Dialogue between an Honest Sailor and a Deluding Landlady, etc.")

K 37

WILL YOU WED WITH A TARRY SAILOR?
(*Poor Jack*)

Nancy spurns the sailor's love until she sees his gold. Then she wants to marry him, but he in turn refuses her.

> I come on shore to see my love,
> To see if she would marry me.
> "Say, pretty pretty Nancy, will you, yes or no,
> Will you wed with a tarry sailor?"

Brown, 339, 7 (N.C.) Stanza 2 is given above.

Broadsides: (B) Ashton, *Real Sailor-Songs*, after p. 48, 9 ("The Tarry Sailor"). Catnach, 9 sts.

K 38

THE SAUCY SAILOR
(*Jack and Jolly Tar II*)

Jack announces that he is a poor sailor and is treated scornfully by his girl, who refuses to marry him. He then reveals that he is wealthy, and the girl suddenly finds herself deeply in love with him and eager to be married. Jack haughtily refuses to marry a country girl with no fortune.

> "You are ragged, you are dirty
> And your clothes smell strong of tar.
> Go way you dirty sailor boy!
> Go away, you Jack of Tar."

Flanders and Brown, 151, 6 (Vt.) Stanza two is given above. Cox, 389,
6 (W. Va.) Refs. Creighton and Senior, 6, m.; 6, m. (N.S.). Doerflinger,
294, 5, m. (N.S.). Morris, 374, 6, m. (Fla.). Sharp II, 235, 5, m. (Ky.).

Baring-Gould, 44, 4d, m. (W. of Eng.). Sharp, *One Hundred,* 102, 8, m.
Sharp and Marson, IV, 42, 8, m. (Somerset. A composite text).

Broadsides: (B) Kittredge, *JAF* 35, 373, gives the following references:.
Ryle (Harvard VII, 113); Bebbington, no. 350 (Harvard X, 96); Such,
no. 260 (Harvard XII, 105).

K 39
JACK TAR

When Jack comes ashore with his pay, he demands a fiddler, liquor,
a parlor, and a girl. The landlady treats him well until his money is gone
and then tells him to leave. Furious, Jack begins to throw things, and the
landlady calls the watchman. Jack is persuaded to return to sea.

> When Jack he came on shore with his gold and silver store,
> No one could get rid of it quicker,
> The first thing Jack demand was a fiddler at his hand,
> Good ale and all sorts of liquor.

Creighton and Senior, 168, 8d, m.; 6d (N.S.).

K 40
JACK THE JOLLY TAR I
(*Tarry Sailor*)

Jack overhears a squire and a farmer's daughter making an assignation.
The girl will tie a string to her finger and let the other end hang out the
window for the squire. Jack arrives first and spends a pleasant night with
the girl, who doesn't discover the situation until morning. Jack returns
happy and boastful to his ship.

> As I roved out in fair London city,
> To view those girls they were so pretty,
> O, I thought I heard the people say
> " 'Twas in the street where Jack do lay."

Greenleaf, 106, 9 and ref., m. (Nfld.) Refs. Finger, 16, 5, m. ("Doo Me
Ama"). *Bulletin* no. 3, p. 10, 7, m.; (Me.).
JFSS II, 38, 8, m. (Somerset. "Jack the Jolly Tar").

K 41
GOLD WATCH

A sailor accosts a girl and gives her kisses. At first she refuses to go with
him but then says he must pay her five guineas. He does so, and they go

to supper and then to bed. He awakes to find the girl gone, along with his gold watch and his money.

> As I was a-walking one fair summer evening,
> In London fair city, I chanced for to spy,
> I spied in the city a handsome young ducksie,
> With her cheeks like two roses and her clothing was gay.

Greenleaf, 110, 7d. m. (Nfld.).

K   42

THE SHIRT AND THE APRON

The sailor incautiously tells a girl that he has come from sea with fifty pounds. She invites him to a dance in a barroom and then suggests that they go to a room upstairs. When he awakens later, he finds that she has stolen his money and all his clothes. He returns to his ship in a woman's shirt and apron, to the amusement of his shipmates and captain.

> O ye landsmen and ye seamen bold, come listen to my song;
> I'll tell you of a trick was played once on me before it's long.
> The other day I came from sea, a fair one I did meet;
> She kindly asked me to a dance; 'twas up on Peter Street.

Greenleaf, 222, 11d (Nfld.).
For a ballad in which the tables are turned see "London Town", *JFSS* VIII, 272, 7 sts., m. (Norfolk).

K 43

HOME, DEARIE, HOME
(*Bell-Bottom Trousers*)

The girl lights the sailor to bed and at his request jumps in with him. He gives her gold and says she can pay the nurse's fee with it, if she has a baby. If it's a boy, he'll fight for the king; if it's a girl, she'll wear a gold ring.

> There came a jolly sailor
> To my house to lodge.
> He called for a candle
> To light him to bed.
> He called for a candle
> To light him to bed.
> And likewise a napkin
> To bind up his head.

Henry, *Folk -Songs*, 158, 8d, m. (Tenn. "Home, Dearie, Home") Stanza two is given above; 160, 5 (N.C.). Chappell, 60, 4 (N.C. A ribald fragment). Colcord, 167, 3d and ref., m. ("Home, Dearie, Home". This text, which is primarily lyrical, says nothing of the first meeting between the sailor and the girl). Gardner, 403, 6d (Que. via. Mich. "Jack, the Sailor Boy"). Randolph IV, 328, 3d (Ark. A related song entitled "Don't Never Trust a Sailor"). Shay, 146, 4d and ref. ("Bell-Bottom Trousers"). *JAF* 66, 53, 5d and ref. (N.Y. "The Sailor Boy").

JFSS VI, 1, 5d, m. (Surrey) ; add. tunes ("Rosemary Lane").

Although Miss Broadwood in *JFSS* VI writes, "This is a stock broadside", I have not come across a ballad print of it. As "Bell-Bottom Trousers" the piece is widely sung by American students.

BALLADS OF CRIME AND CRIMINALS (L)

L 1   The Yorkshire Bite
L 2   The Highwayman Outwitted
L 3   The Undaunted Female (The Box upon Her Head)
L 4   The Three Butchers
L 5   Sam Hall (Jack Hall)
L 6   Jack Sheppard
L 7   Brennan on the Moor
L 8   My Bonny Black Bess I
L 9   My Bonny Black Bess II
L 10   Dick Turpin and the Lawyer
L 11   Gallows
L 12   The Rambling Boy
L 13 A & B   Whiskey in the Jar (The Irish Robber A) and The Irish
             Robber B (McCollister)
L 14   The Poacher's Fate
L 15   The Irish Mail Robber
L 16   A & B   Botany Bay A and The Boston Burglar (Botany Bay B)
L 17   Jack Williams
L 18   Van Diemans' Land
L 19   I Am a Wild Young Irish Boy
L 20   The Wild Colonial Boy
L 21   Johnny Troy
L 22   Jack Donahue

L 1

THE YORKSHIRE BITE

His master sends young John to the fair to sell a cow. When, later, the boy stops in a tavern for a drink, a highwayman overhears his discussing his money. He offers to let the boy ride with him and attempts to rob him. But while he is retrieving the money which the boy has scattered on the ground, John rides away on the robber's horse and returns to his master with saddle-bags full of money.

> In London there lived a mason by trade,
> He kept two servants, a man and a maid;
> A Yorkshire boy by the name of John
> Was the one that he kept to be his man.
> *Refrain:*
> Lol-de-dum, lol-de-do, lol-de-daddy, del-do-dum.

Flanders-Barry, 97, 13d, m. (Vt.); 99-102, notes and comment. Barry, Eckstorm, and Smyth, 406, 15d; 6d; 14 d (Me.). Combs, 149, 20 (W. Va. "Selling the Cow"). Creighton, 29, 12d and chor., m. (N.S.). Creighton and Senior, 237, 12d, m. (N.S.). Flanders and Brown, 234, 3 m. (Vt.). Flanders and Olney, 51, 13d and chor., m. (Vt.). Gardner, 382, 15d (Can. via Mich.). Greenleaf, 44, 14d, m. (Nfld.). Henry, *Folk-Songs,* 135, 9d (N.C.); 15, (Tenn.); 1 (Ga.). Gardner, 382, 15d (Can. via Mich.). Sandburg, 118, 13d, m. (Ill.). Thompson, 163, 14d (N.Y. from ms.). *JAF* 23, 451, frag. of 22 lines, m. (Mass.). *JAF* 30, 367, 14d, with some lines missing (Mass. from ms.) Refs.

Greig, xxxv, 15d (Scot.). *JFSS* VIII, 180, 10d, m. (Corfe).

Broadsides: (B) Logan, 131, 16d. Bebbington, 13d (Harvard IX, 113). No imprint, 16d ("The Crafty Plough Boy").

A complete text of this ballad is given in Chapter III.

L 2

THE HIGHWAYMAN OUTWITTED

Returning home on her horse from market, the merchant's daughter is stopped by a highwayman who threatens her with death. She dismounts and her horse starts home with her father's money in the saddle-bags. The robber strips the girl and forces her to hold his horse. Suddenly gaining courage, she jumps astride his horse and races away. His saddle-bags contain diamonds or gold worth thousands of pounds which she shares with her father.

'Tis of a rich merchant of London,
Who had lots of land that he sold,
Who sent out his daughter to market
To receive every penny in gold.

Greenleaf, 47, 14 (Nfld.).

Sharp and Marson II, 50, 12, m. (Somerset. "The Farmer's Daughter").
JFSS I, 236, 7, m. (Knaresborough); tune only, (Herts.). *JFSS* II, 21,
5½d, m. (Somerset).

Broadsides: (B) Logan, 134, 18 ("The Maid of Rygate"). G. Jacques,
Manchester, 15 (Harvard I, 86). J. Kendrew, York, 15½ (Harvard III,
49). Such, no. 217, 16. W. R. Walker, 16 (Harvard IV, 153).

A complete text of this ballad is given in Chapter III.

L 3

THE UNDAUNTED FEMALE
*(The Box upon her Head; The Staffordshire Maid;
The Maid and the Robber)*

Having dreamed that her father needs her, the servant girl sets out for
home. A man who offers to show her a short cut proves to be a robber and
demands her money or her life. She kills him with his staff and walks on.
She encounters another stranger, who returns with her to the robber's
body. They search his bundle and find a whistle which, when blown, calls
four more robbers from the woods. After the man has killed one of them
and the girl has disposed of the other three, he offers to marry her.

With her box upon her head she marched it along
Until that she met with a noble gentleman.
He says, "My pretty fair maid, if you'll come along with me,
I'll show you a nigh way across the country."

Mackenzie, 321, 10½d (N.S.) Detailed refs. Stanza three is given above.

Broadwood, 60, 12d, m. (Northamptonshire). Greig, xxxv, 9d (Scot.
"The Maid and the Robber"). *JFSS* VIII, 129, 10d, m. (Essex); tune
from Lancs.

Broadsides: (B) Ryle, 11d ("The Undaunted Female". Harvard VII,
163). No imprint, 11d. Keys, 11d ("The Fair Maid and the Robber").

L 4

THE THREE BUTCHERS
(Dixon and Johnson)

Riding along with large sums of money to pay their creditors, the butchers
hear cries for help and come upon a naked woman, bound with cords, who

says she has been robbed. Johnson frees her, and the four ride on together. The woman whistles a signal and ten thieves spring from hiding. Two of the butchers yield and are bound. Johnson fights gallantly and kills eight of the robbers, but the woman gives him his death blow from behind. The remaining thieves then murder the other two butchers and escape from England. (This is a summary of the old broadside text. The late broadsides are rewritten and much condensed but preserve the main details of the story. In them the woman is arrested and bound down in irons).

> There is three jolly boochers,
> Three jolly boochers, three;
> 'Twas Wilson and 'twas Jilson
> And Jonathan, it might be.
> As they were riding through dark fields
> As fast as they could ride,
> "O hush!" says Wilson unto Jilson,
> "I hear a woman's cry."

Flanders-Barry, 238, 9d, m. (Vt.) Notes and refs. Brown, 270, 10d couplets; 6d couplets (N.C.). Cox, 302, 3½d (W. Va.). Creighton, 208, 8d, m. (N.S.). Creighton and Senior, 120, 7d, m.; 5d, m. (N.S.) In the first of these versions, "The Three Jovial Huntsmen", the men all bravely resist the assault, and Johnson pursues the woman and shoots her dead. Greenleaf, 82, 12, m.; 15, m. (Nfld.). Morris, 385, 8d couplets, m. (Ga. via Fla.). Randolph I, 375, 7d, m. (Ark.) A confused text. Sharp I, 370, 10, m. (Tenn.); 13d couplets, m. (Ky.); frag. with m. (N.C.).

Broadwood, *Eng. Trad, Songs,* 42, 10d, m. (Sussex. Reprinted from *JFSS* I, 174). Greig, xxxvi, 9d (Scot.). Williams, 275, 7d; 1d (Wilts.). *JFSS* I, 174, 10d, m. (Sussex). *JFSS* VIII, 2, 1d, m. (Somerset).

Broadsides: (B) The original 17th century broadside, "The Three Worthy Butchers of the North", from *Roxburghe Ballads* VII, 59-63, is reprinted by Flanders-Barry, pp. 241-244. Robert Marchbank, Newcastle, "A New Ballad of the Three Merry Butchers, and the Ten Highwaymen"; no imprint, same title (items 1123 and 1124 in the Harvard Catalogue). Ashton, 403, 8d (This text begins "It was Ips, Gips, and Johnson . . ."). Walker, 9d (Harvard II, 51). Forth, 8d (Harvard III, 40). Wheeler, 8d. Such, no. 463, 9d ("Ips, Gips, and Johnson; or, The Three Butchers").

L 5

SAM HALL

(*Jack Hall*)

About to be hanged, Sam curses everyone in sight, tells of killing a man, refers scornfully to the parson, the sheriff, and his girl, and ends his farewell with another bitter curse.

Oh, my name it is Sam Hall, it is Sam Hall.
Yes, my name it is Sam Hall, it is Sam Hall;
Yes, my name it is Sam Hall, and I hate you one and all,
Yes, I hate you one and all, God damn your eyes.

Lomax, *American Ballads*, 133, 7, m. ("Tune and words from Professor Arthur D. Brodeur, as developed by that unique organization 'The Adventure Campfire Club', Berkeley, California."). Lomax, *Cowboy Songs*, 422, same text as above. Davis, *Folk-Songs of Virginia*, p. 278, refers to two texts of "Samuel Hall" collected in Virginia. Flanders and Brown, 96, 4 brief stanzas (Vt. Although entitled "Jack Hall", this fragment seems more closely related to the "Sam Hall" variant. See below).

Sharp, *One Hundred*, 182, 5, m. ("Jack Hall"). Sharp and Marson, IV, 20, 5, m. (Somerset. "Jack Hall") Notes.

Sharp, (*Folk Songs from Somerset* IV, 77) quotes Frank Kidson as follows: ". . . Jack Hall was a chimney sweeper, who was executed for burglary in 1701. He had been sold when a child to a chimney sweeper for a guinea and was quite a young man when Tyburn claimed him. . . . About 1845-50 a comic singer named G. W. Ross revived the song under the name 'Sam Hall', with an added coarseness not in the original. He sang it, according to a small song-book, 'The Sam Hall Songster', 'for upwards of 400 nights' . . . " Sharp remarks, "I have never heard Somserset singers sing the modernized version 'Sam Hall', to which Mr. Kidson refers in his interesting note."

See Bertrand H. Bronson, "Samuel Hall's Family Tree", *California Folklore Quarterly*, I (1942), 47-64.

L 6

JACK SHEPPARD

Jack Sheppard was apprenticed to a carpenter named William Woods, courted his daughter, who jilted him, and married Emma Maggot and Edgeworth Bess. In attempting to rob Woods, he is captured by Woods' wife but freed by Mr. Blueskin, his accomplice. Later he escapes from prison with the help of his wife, and at last, "He being tired of escaping,/They hung him up on a summer's day".

Some years ago, perhaps a hundred,
Jack Sheppard lived, the bold and free.
A smarter chap ne'er cracked a crib, sir,
Nor swung upon old Tyburn tree.

Mackenzie, 315, 9 (N.S.).

L 7

BRENNAN ON THE MOOR

Brennan, who "never robbed a poor man/Upon the king's highway" robs a pedlar and in turn is robbed by him. The two become lifelong comrades. Captured by the mayor, Brennan escapes with the aid of a blunderbuss supplied by his wife and robs the mayor. He becomes a mountain outlaw, is betrayed by a woman, and is captured after being shot a dozen times. He dies on the scaffold thinking sadly of his family.

> 'Tis of a fearless Irishman
> The story I will tell
> His name was Willie Brennan,
> In Ireland he did dwell.
> 'Twas in the Cumberland Mountains
> He commenced his wild career,
> And many a wealthy nobleman
> Before him shook with fear.

> *Chorus:*
> And it's Brennan on the moor,
> Brennan on the moor,
> Bold, gay, undaunted stood young
> Brennan on the moor.

Belden, 284, 11d (Kan.). (Reprinted by Leach, 745). Creighton and Senior, 236, 9d, m. (N.S.). Flanders and Brown, 98, a confused frag. of 18 lines (Vt.). Lomax, *Our Singing Country*, 317, 11d and chor., m. (Ore. via Wash., D.C.). Mackenzie, 309, 6d and chor. (N.S.). Detailed refs. Randolph II, 168, 4d and chor. (Ark.). Sharp II, 170, 6d and chor., m. (Va.). Shoemaker, 242, 11d and chor. (Pa.).

Ford II, 56, 6d, m.; 11d (Scot.). Joyce, 186, 11d, m. (Ireland). Kidson, 123, 12d, m. (from a broadside?). Sharp and Marson I, 70, 8d and chor., m. (Somerset).

Broadsides: (B) Such, no. 68, 12d (Harvard XI, 68). Bebbington, 12d (Harvard X, 144). (A) DeMarsan (M). Partridge, 11d (L of C). Wehman, no. 133 (M). Songsters: (A) O'Connor, 59, 11d. *617 Irish Songs*, 107, 11d.

"This Brennan was a noted highwayman, who, in the eighteenth century, ran his career in the Kilworth mountains near Fermoy in Cork, and in the neighborhood." (Note from Joyce, p. 186).

L 8

MY BONNY BLACK BESS I

Turpin praises Bess's swiftness, describes her beauty in detail, and speaks of the life they have shared. He then tells of robbing a horseman in

Cheshire and of being recognized by his victim and threatened with hanging. Turpin speeds away, takes a direct route across the countryside, and arrives in a town within a few minutes. He lounges around, observes that it is four o'clock, and calmly plays bowls. Thus he has a well-established alibi when the horseman arrives much later claiming that Turpin robbed him at four o'clock.

> Let the lover his mistress's beauty rehearse,
> And laud her attractions in languishing verse;
> Be it mine in rude strain but with truth to express
> The love that I bear to my Bonny Black Bess.
>
> .   .   .   .
>
> Once it happened in Cheshire, near Durham, I popped
> On a horseman alone whom I suddenly stopped;
> That I lightened his pockets you'll readily guess—
> Quick work makes Dick Turpin when mounted on Bess.

Pound, 155, 13d (Mont.) Stanzas 1 and 7 are given above. Randolph II, 154, 10d (Ark. from ms.).

Broadside: (B) Such no. 176, 14d sts.

See also the following two pieces.

L 9

MY BONNY BLACK BESS II
(Poor Black Bess; Dick Turpin's Ride)

Dick Turpin speaks affectionately to the horse which has served him so well. Together they have robbed the wealthy, but they never harmed a poor man. As he speaks he has ridden from London to York in twelve hours, pursued by the justice's bloodhounds. To prevent the dogs from having his faithful horse, he shoots her and says he, too, will die.

> The gods of misfortune have led me abroad,
> Kind friends proved ungrateful, I took to the road,
> To plunder the wealthy and leave my distress
> I brought you to aid me, my bonnie black Bess.

Randolph II, 153, 6½d; 2, m. (Ark.) Notes. Brown, 356, 9d (N.C.). Gardner, 320, equiv. of 7d, m.; 3d; 1d, m. (Mich.). Lomax, *Cowboy Songs*, 217, 9d. Mackenzie, 313, 8d (N.S.) Refs.

Broadsides: (B) Henderson, 32, 8d "Poor Black Bess". Such, no. 450, 9d (Harvard XIII, 143). Ryle, 9d (Harvard VII, 78). (A) DeMarsan (M).

Dick Turpin, the English highwayman, was hanged for horse-stealing at York, April 7, 1739 (Note condensed from Randolph II, 152).

L 10

DICK TURPIN AND THE LAWYER

Turpin asks the lawyer if he is not afraid of meeting Turpin and tells him that he has hidden his money in his boot. The lawyer reveals that his is in the cape of his coat. A short time later Turpin robs him and discloses his identity.

> As Turpin was riding across the moor
> There he saw a lawyer riding on before.
> Turpin, riding up to him, said, "Are you not afraid
> To meet Dick Turpin, that mischievous blade?"
>
> *Chorus*
> Singing Eh ro, Turpin I ro.

Mackenzie, 311, 4 and ref. (N.S.) Notes and refs. Pound, 157, 4 and ref. (from Mackenzie).

Williams, 99, 4 and ref.; 4½ and ref. (Eng.). *JFSS* II, 279, 3, m. (Somerset); 2, m. (Yorks.).

Broadsides: (B) No imprint, 5d and ref. (Harvard V, 176). Such, no. 548, 5d ("O Rare Turpin"). *JFSS* II, 280, 7 ("Turpin Hero") from a broadside without imprint. The short broadsides are apparently condensed from a longer piece in which Turpin meets a series of victims. See Logan, 118, 18 sts. and ref. ("Turpin's Valour") and "The Dunghill-Cock; or, Turnpin's Valiant Exploits", in a chapbook by J. & M. Robertson, Glasgow, 1809 (Item 1265 in the Harvard Catalogue).

An entertaining account of Turpin's career is given by Logan, pp. 115-118.

L 11

GALLOWS

A young man is about to be hanged. His father, his mother, and his sister ask for a few words with him to delay the hanging. The clergyman, too, staves off the fatal moment by demanding to hear the youth's confession. Just as the boy reaches the top step, his true-love rides up with his pardon signed by the queen (or by King George).

> My love is one of the nicest young men
> That ever nature or the sun shone on,
> And how to gain him I do not know,
> He has his sentence for to be hung.
>
> .   .   .   .
>
> As he was going up the first step of the gallows
> His own dear father he chanced to see,
> "Come down, come down from that hateful gallows,
> I have one word to exchange with thee."

Creighton and Senior, 110, 10d, m.; 8d (the first stanzas of each are given above); 6d (N.S.). Barry, Eckstorm, and Smyth, 389, 8d (Me.); 4½d, m. (N.B.); frags. (Me.). Flanders-Barry, 117, 1d, m. (N.H.). *JAF* 26, 175, 2 lines from this piece?.

"This ballad is Irish. The references to King George and the streets of Derry convey the suggestion that it has something to do with an incident of the rising of 1798." (note from Barry, Eckstorm, and Smyth, p. 392).

While this piece is related in content and structure to "The Maid Freed from the Gallows", Child no. 95, it is clearly a separate ballad.

L 12

THE RAMBLING BOY
(*Wild and Wicked Youth*)

The speaker lists some of his achievements in highway robbery, reflects that he is leaving his family in sorrow, now that he has been condemned to the gallows, and gives directions for his funeral.

> I was a rich and rambling boy;
> In many a city I have been;
> In London city going to pay my way,
> Going to spend my money at the ball and play.
>
> There I married me a lovely wife;
> I loved her as I loved my life;
> Her deep blue eyes and manner gay
> Caused me to rob on the King's highway.

Fuson, 63, 7 (Ky. "The Rich Rambler"). Belden, 136, 5 (Mo.). Brown, 355, 7 (N.C.). Cambiaire, 43, 8 sts. Combs, 215, 6 (Ky.). Henry, *Folk-Songs*, 327, 8 (Tenn.). Randolph II, 84, 8, m. (Mo.); 7 (Ark.); Refs.

Sharp and Marson V, 53, 6, m. (Somerset. "The Robber"). *JFSS* I, 114, 9, m. (Sussex. "In Newry Town"). *JFSS* VIII, 190, 4, m. (Dorset).

Broadsides: (B) Cadman, 8 sts. (Harvard V, 29. "Wild and Wicked Youth") (A) No imprint, 10 sts. ("The Irish Robber") (Thomas Coll., II, 120). Deming, Boston, 10 sts. (L of C).

Note: Traditional variants differ widely, probably because the narrative element is weak in the original broadsides. In the broadside texts the narrator robs lords, dukes, and earls, including Lord Mansfield, and is captured by "Fielding's gang". Sir John Fielding (*d*. 1780). the blind half-brother of the novelist, "carried on Henry Fielding's plan for breaking up robber-gangs" (*Concise DNB*).

L 13 A

WHISKEY IN THE JAR
(*The Irish Robber* A)

The highwayman robs a captain and returns to his girl with the loot. During the night he is awakened by a press-gang led by the man he has robbed. Because Molly has discharged his pistols and filled them with water, he is unable to fight and is taken prisoner. He wishes that his two brothers, who are in the army, were there to help him.

> As I was going over the far fam'd Kerry mountain
> I met with Captain Farrell and his money he was counting,
> I first produced my pistol and I then produced my rapier
> Sayin', "Stand and deliver for you are my bold deceiver, O,
> Whack fol the diddle, O, Whack fol the diddle, O,
> There's whiskey in the jar.

Creighton, 192, 7d and ref., m. (N.S.). The stanza above is from O'Lochlainn's text. *JAF* 25, 152, 1½ d and ref. (W. Va. "Captain Kelly").

O'Lochlainn, 24, 5d and ref., m. (Ireland). Joyce, 345, tune only ("There's Whiskey in the Jar").

Broadsides: (B) Cadman, 8d ("Sporting Hero, or Whiskey in the Bar". Harvard V, 98). Pratt, 8d ("Whiskey in a Jar"). Forth, 7d and ref. (A) Andrews, 6d (L of C). Wrigley, 6d (L of C).

L 13 B

THE IRISH ROBBER B (*McCollister*)

The light-hearted Irish robber relieves two peddlers of their money. When the sheriff appears, the robber blames Polly for having betrayed him by filling his pistols with water. After he is sentenced to be hanged, he complains that it is hard to die for taking a little money.

> Oh, Allen McCollister, he was a valiant soldier.
> He carried his musket all on his right shoulder,
> His pistol being loaded and ready for a fire.
> "Deliver up your money, boys, for this is my desire."
> Teedle toddle teedle tum ul teedle teedle teedle
> Ludly tum tee tum.

Flanders and Brown, 139, 4d and ref., m. (Vt. via Mass. "McCollister"). Flanders-Barry, 245, 6d and ref., m. (Vt. "Lovel the Robber") Notes and refs.

L 14

THE POACHER'S FATE

Six young men on a poaching expedition are discovered by the keeper, who swears to shoot one of them and then gives "the bravest lad in all the lot" a mortal wound.

> Come all ye lads of high renown
> Who love to drink strong ale that's brown,
> And pull the lofty pheasant down
> With powder, shot and gun.

Scarborough, 351, 5 (Yorks. via N.Y.).
Broadsides: (B) Walker. Forth, 6 sts. (Harvard III, 135).

L 15

THE IRISH MAIL ROBBER

Despite his father's warnings, the youth persists in drinking, gambling, and maintaining "rude women". Convicted of mail robbery, he is sentenced to be transported for nine years and must leave his grieving father and the girl he loves.

> It's adieu to old Ireland, the place where I was born,
> Near the county of Limerick, near the state of Glengall;
> Far away to some island, bound down like a slave,
> It was in my own country I did misbehave.
>
> .   .   .   .
>
> I had not been long in this wicked career
> Before I was taken by the laws of the land;
> Was tried and found guilty of a mail robbery,
> And for ages transported across the salt sea.

Flanders-Barry, 140, 6d, m. (N.H.). Randolph II, 147, 6d, m. (Mo.) Printed as version A of a different piece entitled "A Prisoner for Life".

"'The Irish Mail Robber' is an Irish street ballad of the 1840's. It is found on English broadsides of that period, issued by various printers in London and in the large industrial centers. We suspect it entered the Northeastern woods tradition during the Civil War, when Canadians and recent comers from Ireland were filling the places of native woodsmen who had gone into military service." (Note from Flanders-Barry, p. 146).

L 16 A

BOTANY BAY A

The well-reared boy becomes a rover, is involved in unnamed difficulties, and is sentenced to be transported to Botany Bay. He thinks sadly of his aged father and mother, tells of sailing away from England with the other convicts, and looks forward to a decent life with the girl he loves after his release.

> I was brought up in London town, a place you all know well;
> Brought up by honest parents, the truth to you I'll tell;
> Brought up by honest parents and reared most carefully,
> Till I a roving lad became, which proved my destiny.

Flanders-Barry, 253, 5d, m. (Vt.). Gardner, 323, 4d (Mich.). Cox, 296, refs. Sturgis, 32, 6d, m. (Vt.).

Sharp, *One Hundred*, 198, 4d, m. Barrett, 90, 6d, m. (Eng.). *JFSS* V, 85, 3d, m. (Cirencester).

Broadsides: (B) Ashton, 359, 6d. Such, no. 499, 6d. No imprint, 6d. Catnach, 6d ("The Transport". Harvard V, 124).

L 16 B

THE BOSTON BURGLAR
(*Botany Bay B*)

The youth says that his friends were unable to help him because of his bad character; he was found guilty and sentenced to Charlestown. At every railroad station, as his train went by, he heard people speak of him as the Boston burglar. He remembers his aged parents grieving for him in court and thinks of his girl in Boston. He plans to give up drinking, gambling, and night-walking when he is free to return to her.

> I was born and brought up in Boston, boys,
> A place you all know well;
> Brought up by honest parents—
> The truth to you I'll tell,
> Brought up by honest parents
> And raised most tenderly,
> Til I became a roving lad
> At the age of twenty-three.

Flanders and Brown, 53, 6d (Vt.). Brown, 555, 5d; add. sts. (N.C.). Arnold, 52, 11, m. (Ala.). Cambiaire, 69, 14 sts. Chappell, 100, 11½ (N.C.). Cox, 296, 6d; 6d; 6d (W. Va.). Eddy, 204, 11, m. (O.). Finger, 88, 6d, m. (Ark.). Gardner, 335, 5d, m.; 1d (Mich.). Lomax, *Cowboy Songs*, 203, 6d, m. Morris, 387, 12 (Kan. via Fla.). Owens, 104, 6d, m. (Tex.). Pound, 57, 6d (Ia.); 6d (Wyo.). Randolph II, 37, 10, m. (Ark.); 10 (Mo.). Scarborough, 289, 6d (Va. from ms.); 12; 15 (Va.); 6; 10; 2 (N.C.). Spaeth, *Read*, 178, 6d, m. Spaeth says that M. J. Fitzpatrick is credited with the authorship of this piece.

Greig, cxxxii, 7d (Scot. "The Boston Smuggler").

Broadside: (B) O'Lochlainn, 88, 5d ("Boston City". From a ballad sheet).

L 17

JACK WILLIAMS

Jack blames a girl for his downfall because he had robbed to maintain her. When he was captured and sent to Newgate, he wrote to his girl for comfort, but she coldly replied, "I hate thievish company". In some versions he is to be transported to Botany Bay; in others, he is sentenced to be hanged but escapes.

> I am a boatman by trade,
> Jack Williams is my name,
> And by a false deluding girl
> Was brought to guilt and shame.

Eddy, 171, 10 (O.). Gardner, 333, 6½, m. (Mich.). Mackenzie, 291, 8 (N.S.). Pound, 152, 8 (Neb. from ms.). *JAF* 35, 378, 10 (O.) Refs. *JAF* 52, 16, 7½, m. (Ky. via Wis.).

JFSS VIII, 13, 2 (Middlesex).

Broadsides: (B) Bebbington, 4d (Harvard X, 108). Such, 4d. No imprint, 10 sts. Songsters: (A) *The American Songster*, Phila. 1850, p. 74 (K). *The Forget Me Not Songster*, Phila., 160, 10 sts. The same, N.Y., 112, 10 sts.

L 18

VAN DIEMAN'S LAND

Three poachers are caught by the keepers and are transported to Van Dieman's Land for fourteen years. The prisoners are sold to planters and are yoked to plows. They live miserably, dreaming of their homes and families. A fellow prisoner, Susan Summers, is married by a planter after he has bought her freedom. She treats the men well. The ballad ends with a warning against poaching.

> Come all you gallant poachers, that ramble free from care,
> That walk out on moonlight nights, with your dog, gun, and snare,
> The jolly hares and pheasants, you have at your command,
> Not thinking that your last career is to Van Dieman's Land.

Ashton, 361, 8d. Colcord, 172, 4d. Creighton, 131, 6d, m. (N.S.). Leach, 708, 5d (Nfld.). Mackenzie, 304, 6d (N. S.) Refs.

Greig, xxxiii, 8d (Scot.). Ord, 384, 8d (Scot.). Williams, 263, 6d and 1d (a composite text). *JFSS* I, 142, 8d, m. (Sussex).

Broadsides: (B) Cadman, 8d (Harvard VI, 299). Harkness, 9d (Harvard VI, 98). Gilbert, Newcastle, 9d (Harvard IV, 111).

"The English first colonised Van Dieman's Land (now Tasmania), in 1803. From 1804 to 1853 convicts were transported to the island." (Note from Broadwood, *Eng. Trad. Songs*, p. 113).

L 19

I AM A WILD YOUNG IRISH BOY

The transported convict complains that being an ex-sailor he didn't understand farming. Instead he became an outlaw, but he never committed unprovoked murder and he robbed only the rich. In attempting to hold up a wagon of gold, he is surrounded by six policemen of whom he kills five. He lets the sergeant go for the sake of his wife and children. He distributes his riches among the farmers so that they may have fine horses and wagons. On his deathbed he generously reveals his identity to a newsboy so that the boy's mother may receive the bounty for his capture.

> Sure I am a wild young Irish boy and from Dublin town I came,
> Transported out to Van Dieman's Land; of it I ain't ashamed.
> Sure, I'll have you all to know, me byes, that wherever I may be,
> I'll die at my post like an Irish lad, or a wild colonial boy!

Doerflinger, 270, 14d, m. (N.Y.).

L 20

THE WILD COLONIAL BOY

Dolan goes from Ireland to Australia where he robs the rich squires and destroys their farms but helps the poor. Three troopers, Kelly, Davis, and Fitzroy, ride to capture him and call on him to surrender. He chooses to fight with his two pistols and shoots Kelly, but the other two shoot him dead.

> There was a noted hero, Jack Dolan was his name;
> Brought up by honest parents, he was reared near Castlemain.
> He was his father's only pride and his mother's only joy,
> And dearly did his parents love their wild Colonial boy.

Beck, 239, 7d (Mich.). Barry, 63, 6d, m. (Me.). Flanders and Brown, 130, 3½d, m. (Vt.). Gardner, 326, 7d, m. (Mich.) ; 7d (Mich. from ms.). Lomax, *Cowboy Songs,* 167, 7d (Mo. A cowboy variant, "The Wild Montana Boy"). Lomax, *Our Singing Country,* 320, 6d, m. (Mich.). Mackenzie, 317, 6d (N.S.).

"According to *Notes and Queries* 159: 101, Jack Dowling was an Australian bushranger of the 1870's". (Note from Barry, p. 100).

L 21

JOHNNY TROY

Troy, who was born in Dublin, is convicted of robbing a widow and is sentenced to seven years in New South Wales. As he and other prisoners are being taken ashore in a launch guarded by six armed policemen, the convicts, under Troy's leadership, overpower the guards and escape. Johnny becomes an outlaw, robbing the rich and helping the poor. He intends to rob an old man but gives him fifty pounds instead when he learns that his victim was once a transported convict and is the father of a large family. Eventually Johnny is hanged at Sydney.

> Come all ye daring bushrangers
> And outlaws of the land,
> Who scorn to live in slavery
> Or wear a convict's band.
>
> Come listen to my story,
> To that most solemn lay,
> Of those most mournful days,
> The days of Johnny Troy.

Gardner, 329, 16 (Cal. via Mich.) Stanzas one and two are given above. Beck, 235, 8d (Mich.). Henry, *Folk-Songs,* 178, 15 (Ga.).

L 22

JACK DONAHUE

Jack Donahue is banished from Ireland for life but continues his career as a highwayman in Australia. After being arrested, he escapes and terrorizes the countryside. He and four companions are surprised by the horse-police. His comrades surrender, but rather than face the gallows, Jack engages in a gun-fight with the police and kills five of them before dying with a ball in his heart.

> Come all you gallant bushrangers and outlaws of disdain,
> Who scorn to live in slavery or wear the brands of chains.
> Attention pay to what I say, and value it if you do.
> I will relate the matchless fate of bold Jack Donahue.

Mackenzie, 306, 12d (N.S.) Notes and refs. Beck, 237, 11 (Mich.). Hudson, 241, 9 (Miss.). Lomax, *Cowboy Songs,* 209, 10d and ref. (Tex). Pound, 158, text reprinted from Lomax. Wells, 304, 12d, m. (Vt.).
Broadside: (A) Wehman no. 751 (M). Songsters: (A) O'Conor, 22, 10d. *617 Irish Songs,* 74, 10d; 111, 4d.
Jack Donahoe, age 23, a native of Dublin, was killed in a gun battle with police near Sydney, Australia, Sept. 1, 1830. For details see G. C. Ingleton, *True Patriots All,* Sydney [1952], p. 130, which contains a newspaper account of the bushranger's death, along with a text of this ballad in seven double stanzas and chorus. (Interestingly enough, none of the police were killed or injured when Donahoe was slain).

BALLADS OF FAMILY OPPOSITION TO LOVERS (M)

M   1   Early, Early in the Spring
M   2   Johnny Doyle
M   3   Charming Beauty Bright
M   4   The Drowsy Sleeper
M   5   Henry Connors
M   6   Erin's Lovely Home
M   7   William and Harriet
M   8   Riley's Farewell (Riley to America)
M   9   William Riley's Courtship
M 10   William (Willie) Riley (Riley's Trial)
M 11   My Father's Servant Boy
M 12   The Apprentice Boy
M 13   Locks and Bolts (I Dreamed of My True Love)
M 14   The Bonny Laboring Boy
M 15   The Iron Door
M 16   Mary Acklin (The Squire's Young Daughter)
M 17   Mary Neal
M 18   Pretty Betsy
M 19   Young Sailor Bold I (The Rich Merchant's Daughter)
M 20   Betsy Is a Beauty Fair (Johnny and Betsy)
M 21   The Merchant's Only Son
M 22   The Bonny Sailor Boy (Jolly Young Sailor Boy)
M 23   Gay Girl Marie
M 24   The Jolly Plowboy (Little Plowing Boy)
M 25   The Banks of Dundee (Undaunted Mary)
M 26   The New River Shore (The Red River Shore)
M 27   The Bold Soldier
M 28   The Tan-Yard Side
M 29   Beautiful Susan
M 30   Farewell, Dear Rosanna
M 31 A & B   William and Dinah A and Villikins and His Dinah (William and Dinah B)
M 32   The Bramble Briar (In Bruton Town; In Seaport Town; The Merchant's Daughter).
M 33   The Constant Farmer's Son
M 34   Edwin in the Lowlands Low
M 35   Lovely Willie
M 36   American Woods
M 37   The *Nightingale*
M 38   Nancy of Yarmouth (Jemmy and Nancy)
M 39   Sir Neil and Glengyle.

M 1

EARLY, EARLY IN THE SPRING

The sailor keeps writing to the girl who has promised to marry him but gets no answer. When he returns, her father announces her marriage to another man. She blames her father for keeping the sailor's letters from her. Although she wants him to stay ashore and find another girl, he is determined to go back to sea. He gives instructions for his burial and reminds her that she will be the cause of his death.

> Early, early in the spring
> I was pressed on board to serve my king;
> And leaving my dearest dear behind,
> Who often told me her heart was mine.

Henry, *Folk-Songs,* 233, 11 (Va.) ; 7 (Ga.). Belden, 163, 8½ (Mo.) ; 6½ (Mont. via Mo.) Refs. Brown, 290, 10; add. sts.; 8 (N.C.). Cambiaire, 55, 11 sts. Cox, 358, 11; 11; 8½ (W. Va.). Creighton and Senior, 154, 5d, m. (N.S.). Henry, *Songs Sung,* 144, 11 (Va. Same text as above). Hudson, 155, 9 (Miss.). Randolph I, 333, 6, m. (Mo.) ; 7 (Ark.) ; 4; 10, m. (Mo.) ; 1 (Ark.). Scarborough, 328, 8; 7; 4 (Va.). Sharp II, 151, 6; 7 (N.C.) ; frags. with tunes. *SFQ* V, 175, 9 (Ind.).

Greig, cxxviii, 10 (Scot.). Sharp and Marson III, 44, 5, m. (Somerset).

Broadsides: (B) Ashton, *Real Sailor Songs,* 56, 10 ("The Sailor Deceived"). Logan, 29, 11 ("The Disappointed Sailor").

M 2

JOHNNY DOYLE

The girl is about to elope with Johnny, but her mother discovers their intention, confines the girl to her room, and forces her to dress for another wedding. With a large retinue she is taken to the parson and forced to marry another man. When she finds that the girl is sick and broken-hearted, her mother offers to send for Johnny, but her daughter says it is too late, wishes him well, and dies.

> I am a fair maiden all tangled in love.
> My fate I will make known to the great God above;
> I thought it a credit yet I feared it a crime
> For to roam this world over with my own Johnny Doyle.

Flanders-Barry, 248, 11d, m. (Vt.) Notes. Brown, 365, 15d couplets (N.C.). Eddy, 187, 5, m. (O.). Gardner, 69, 10d, m. (Mich.). Henry,

Folk-Songs, 162, 12 (Ga.). Hudson, 159, 8d (Miss.). Mackenzie, 106, 9d (N.S.). Morris, 331, 6d, m.; 7d (Fla.). Randolph I, 350, 9d, m. (Mo.); 8½d (Ark.); 7d, m. (Mo.). Scarborough, 248, 8d (N.C.). Sharp II, 27, 6½d, m. (N.C.); 1d, m. (Va.). *JAF* 24, 340, tune only. *JAF* 46, 32, 8d (N.C.).

Greig, cii, 13d (Scot.). *JFSS* V, 142, 6d, m. (Sussex) Notes.

Broadsides: (B) Bebbington, 10d (Harvard X, 98). Such, no. 310 (Harvard XIII, 3) (M). (A) DeMarsan (M). Songsters: (A) *617 Irish Songs,* 27, 10d. O'Conor, 16, 10d.

M 3

CHARMING BEAUTY BRIGHT

When the girl's parents hear that she and the narrator are in love, they confine her to her room, but she promises to be faithful to him until death. He is pressed to sea or goes into the army. After serving the king for seven years he returns to find that the girl has died for love of him. He wishes he, too, were in his grave. In some texts he goes mad and is sent to "New Bedlam".

> Once I courted a fair beauty bright,
> And on her I placed my whole heart's delight;
> I courted her for love, and her love I did obtain.
> Do you think I've any reason of love to complain?

Sharp II, 106, 8d, m. (Ky.); 103, 6d, m. (N.C.); 4d, m., (Tenn.); frags. with tunes from N.C. and Va. Belden, 164, 8d, (Kan.) Refs. Brewster, 196, 7d (Ind.). Arnold, 16, 5d, m. (Ala.). Brown, 293, 5d; 4½d; add. sts.; 8d (N.C.). Chappell, 130, 1½, m.; 6½d (N.C.). Cox, 342, 6 (Va. via W. Va.); tune, p. 529. Refs. Eddy, 113, 7d, m. (O.). Fuson, 136, 5d (Ky.). Morris, 343, 3d, m.; 12d couplets (Fla.). Owens, 87, 7d, m. (Tex.). Randolph I, 346, 5½d, m. (Mo.); 6d, m. (Ark). Scarborough, 311, 5d (Va.) Sturgis, 22, 5d, m. (Vt.). *JAF* 26, 176, 6d (Mass.). *JAF* 28, 147, 6d (Miss. from ms.). *JAF* 29, 184, 8d (Ind.). *JAF* 30, 334, 5d, m. (Ky.). *JAF* 35, 388, 1d, m. (O.). *JAF* 52, 33, 6d, m. (Ky. via Wis.). *JAF* 60, 216, 6d (Ill. from ms. of 1866). *SFQ* III, 203, 26d lines (Ind. from ms.).

JFSS II, 81, 1d, m. (Lincs.)

M 4

THE DROWSY SLEEPER

Though obviously in love with the man who calls at her bedroom window, the girl asks him to leave. Both her mother and father are violently opposed to her marrying him; in fact, her father is lying in wait with a weapon to kill him. The ballad has various endings. In some versions the girl expects to die of grief, in others she plans to forsake her parents, and in still others both lovers commit suicide.

> "Awake, awake, you drowsy sleeper!
> Awake, awake, it is almost day!
> How can you bear to lie and slumber
> When your true lover is a-going away?"

Belden, 120, 7, m.; 119, 2 (Mo.); 5½ (Ark.); 7 (Mo. from ms.); 6 (Kan.); 8; 8 (Mo.). Refs. Barry, 83, 7, m. (Me.). Brewster, 170, 7; 9, m.; frag. with tune (Ind.). Brown, 255, 4d; 6; add. sts. (N.C.). Cox, 348, 5; 6 (W. Va.) Refs. Doerflinger, 314, 7, m. (N.B.). Eddy, 92, 3, m.; 6, m.; 2, m.; 8, m. (O.). Gardner, 86, 8, m.; frags. with tunes (Mich.). Greenleaf, 55, 7, m. (Nfld.). Henry, *Folk-Songs,* 190, 1 (N.C.). Hudson, 161, 9 (Miss.). Mackenzie, 99, 8 (N.S.). Morris, 362, 6, m. (Fla.). Pound, 51, 7 (Neb. from ms.); 6½ (Utah). Randolph I, 244, 7½, m.; 6 (Mo.); 5 (Ark.) 8, m.; 7; 7, m. (Mo.). Ritchie, 219, 8, m. (Ky.). Sharp I, 358, 7, m.; 8, m.; 6, m. (N.C.); 1, m.; 6, m.; 7, m.; 6, m. (Va.); frags. with tunes. Thompson, 390, 8 (N.Y.). Scarborough, 139, 6; 6 (N.C.); 6 (Va.); 7 (N.C. from ms.). Sturgis, 30, 9, m. (Vt.). *JAF* 20, 260, 9 (Ky.). (Reprinted by Leach, 728). *JAF* 29, 200, 22 lines (Ga.). *JAF* 30, 340, 9 (Ky.); 6 (Mich.) Refs. *JAF* 35, 356, refs. *JAF* 60, 223, 8 (Ill. from ms.).

Christie I, 224, 7d, m. (Scot. A more polished variant entitled "I Will Put my Ship in Order") (Reprinted by Leach, 728). Sharp and Marson IV, 56, 10, m. (Somerset). *JFSS* I, 269, 2, m.; 5 (Sussex). *JFSS* II, 7d, m., reprinted from Christie. *JFSS* III, 78, 2, m.; 5, m. (Dorset).

Broadside: (A) Kittredge (in *JAF* 30) refers to a broadside of this piece published by H. J. Wehman, which "shows admixture of 'The Silver Dagger' ", a ballad presumably of American origin.

This ballad is mentioned in C. R. Baskervill's "English Songs on the Night Visit", *PMLA* 36 (1921), 565-614.

M 5

HENRY CONNORS

Henry, a servant, falls in love with his master's daughter. Aided by the girl's mother, the lovers plan to marry and go to Scotland. But her father plants evidence to indicate that Henry is a thief and has him transported.

> My name is Henry Connors from the green Castle Dawson;
> That village I'll never set my eyes on again.
> I'm transported for life in the height of vigor,
> Which causes my parents to blush for my shame.

Greenleaf, 191, 8d (Nfld.).
Cf. "Erin's Lovely Home".

M 6

ERIN'S LOVELY HOME

The young servant falls in love with his employer's daughter, and, at the girl's suggestion, they plan to leave Ireland together. They board a ship at Belfast where the girl's father has the youth arrested and returned to jail in County Tyrone. He is sentenced to be transported for seven years. His sorrowful sweetheart says she will wait for him.

> When I was young an' in my prime, at th' age of twenty-one
> I acted as a servant unto a gentleman,
> I served him true an' honest, as the truth's to you's well known,
> In cruelty he banished me from Erin's lovely home.

Randolph I, 356, 7d, m. (Mo.). Mackenzie, 117, 7d (N.S.) Refs. Greig, xlvii, 9d (Scot.). Ord, 106, 9d (Scot.). Sharp and Marson II, 24, 6d, m. (Somerset). *JFSS* I, 117, 3d, m. (Sussex). *JFSS* II, 167, 1d, m.; add. tune (Norfolk); 211, 1d, m.; add. tune (Wilts.). *JIFSS* I, 11, 7d, m. (Devon).

Broadsides: (B) Such no. 31, 8d. J. Gilbert, 8d (Harvard IV, 170). Ryle, 8d (Harvard V, 217). Songsters: (A) O'Conor, 25, 8d. *617 Irish Songs*, 92, 8d. *Delaney's Irish Song Book No. 1*, p. 19.

M 7

WILLIAM AND HARRIET

To escape from her father, who is trying to prevent their marriage, William and Harriet go to sea together. Their ship sinks and they are cast upon an island where they die of exposure and starvation.

> There was a rich merchant, in London did dwell,
> He had an only daughter, the farmer loved well;
> Because she was so handsome, he liked her so well;
> Her father he wanted her to bid him adieu.

Cox, 343, 6d (W. Va. "The Rich Merchant"). Refs. *PTFLS* X, 157, 2 brief sts. (Tex.).

JFSS VIII, 267, 10d, m. (Suffolk. "Harriet and Young William").

Broadsides: (B) Such, 10d. Ryle, 10d (Harvard V, 162). W. R. Walker, 10d (Harvard IV, 29). No imprint, 10d.

M 8

RILEY'S FAREWELL
(*Riley to America; John Riley*)

To escape being shot by his girl's disapproving father, Riley leaves Ireland for America with one thousand pounds donated by the girl's mother. Having bought some land, he returns for the girl and they sail together. The ship is wrecked and both die. She leaves a note written in blood blaming her father for their tragedy.

> As I roved out one evening down by a riverside,
> I heard a maid complaining great, and the tears stood in her eyes.
> "This is a dark and stormy night," these words I heard her say.
> "My love is on the raging sea, bound for Ameriky."

Greenleaf, 182, 8d (Nfld.). Chappell, 66, 14, m. (N.C.). Creighton and Senior, 171, 8d, m. (N.S.). Mackenzie, 126, 7d (N.S.). Refs. Pound, 89, 6 (Eng. via Neb.). Thomas, *Devil's Ditties*, 167, 5d; 1d, m. (Ky.). *JAF* 52, 31, 3d m. (Ky. via Wis.). *JAF* 67, 127, 8d, m. (Nfld.).

JFSS I, 256, 16d couplets (Knaresborough. "Young Riley the Fisherman"). *JFSS* II, 214. 1d, m. (Gravesend). *JFSS* V, 147, 8d, m. (Sussex). *JIFSS* I, 5, 2d, m. ("One Evening Fair").

Broadsides: (B) Ashton, 390, 8d. Cadman. Such. W. R. Walker, 8d (Harvard IV, 17). (A) DeMarsan (M). Wehman (M). Songsters: (A) *Delaney's Irish Song Book No. 3*, p. 24. O'Conor, 49, 8d.

M 9
WILLIAM RILEY'S COURTSHIP

Willie falls in love with the girl at first sight and she returns his affection but warns him against her severe father. To be near her, Willie works for her father and at last asks for her hand. He is discharged at once and told to leave town, whereupon he and the girl elope on horseback. Her father's men pursue and capture the couple, and Riley is sent to jail.

> 'Twas on a pleasant evening all in the bloom of Spring,
> When as the cheerful songsters in concert sweet did sing,
> The primrose and the daisy bespangled ev'ry lawn,
> It was in her father's arbor I spied my Colleen Bawn.

Randolph I, 418, 3d, m. (Mo.). Pound, 86, 13d (Neb. from ms.). Creighton, 152, 26, m. (N.S.).

Hayward, 96, 11d (Ireland).

Songsters: (A) *The Forget Me Not Songster*, Phila., 243, 13d. The same, N.Y., 181. *The American Songster*, Phila., 1836, 13d.

M 10
WILLIAM (WILLIE) RILEY
(*Riley's Trial*)

The eloping couple is pursued by the girl's father and captured. Riley is thrown into Sligo jail to await trial for kidnapping the girl and stealing her jewels. His "Colleen Bawn" pleads successfully in his behalf, and instead of being hanged, as her father has demanded, or transported, he is freed. Most versions end with Riley about to leave the country, wearing one of the girl's diamond rings for remembrance.

"O, rise up Willy Reilly, and come along with me.
I mean for to go with you and leave this counteree,
To leave my father's dwelling house, his houses and free land."
And away goes Willy Reilly, and his dear Colleen Bawn.

Greenleaf, 184, 15d, m. (Nfld.). Belden, 289, 14d (Mo. from ms.). Brewster, 260, 12d (Ind.). Brown, 363, 16 (N.C.). Cox, 336, 18d, (W. Va.). Creighton, 152, 26, m. (N.S.). Leach, 741, 14d (Nfld.); 743, a *cante-fable* variant containing 20 lines of verse, reprinted from *PMLA* 29, 476. Randolph I, 419, 2d, m. (Ark.). Sharp II, 81, 7d, m. (Ga.); 1d, m. (N.C.). Thomas, *Devil's Ditties,* 166, 2d, m. (Ky.).

Greig, cxliii, 15d (Scot.). Hayward, 99, 14d (Ireland). *JFSS* III, 133, 26d lines, m. (Dorset). Notes.

Broadsides: (B) No imprint, 14d ("William Riley and Colinband". Reprinted in *JFSS* III, 134). Catnach, 14d (Harvard V, 154). Ross, 14d (Harvard IV, 146). (A) Deming, Boston, 15d (Harvard). 42 N. Main St., Providence, 12d (Harvard). N. Coverly, Jr., 52d lines (Thomas Coll., II, 53). Songsters: (A) *Forget Me Not Songster,* Phila., 246, 12d (with "Riley's Courtship" and "Riley's Releasement"). *The American Songster,* Phila., 1836, 182. *Delaney's Irish Song Book No. 3,* p. 12.

Note: "The event commemorated in this ballad occurred towards the end of the eighteenth century, and the scene is near Bundoran, beside the boundaries of the three counties, Donegal, Fermanagh, and Sligo, where the ruined house of the great Squire Folliard is still to be seen. The proper family-name is Ffoliott, but the people always pronounce it Folliard. The whole story is still vividly remembered in the district; and Carleton has founded on it his novel of 'Willie Reilly'. The penal laws were then in force, and it was very dangerous for a young Catholic Irishman to run away with the daughter of a powerful Protestant local Squire." (Note from Joyce, *Old Irish Folk Music and Song,* p. 230.

In American song books "Willie Riley" usually appears as the second of three ballads telling a continuous but slightly overlapping story: "William Reily's Courtship", "Reily's Trial", and "Reily's Answer, Releasement, and Marriage with Coolen Bawn". The first ballad is M 9 above. In the third, which has not, so far as I know, been recorded from tradition, Riley is sentenced to be transported and is freed through his own petition to the Lord Lieutenant in time to rescue the girl from Bedlam and marry her.

M 11

MY FATHER'S SERVANT BOY

The girl upsets her father's plans to have her marry a gentleman and elopes with a servant, They go to Belfast and find a ship's captain who will take them to America. In Philadelphia they are supported by a "true Irish friend" until the youth finds employment. The girl feels she is better off than at home.

> Come all you old, both great and small, attend unto my fame;
> There's none of you will pity me but those who felt the same.
> I lived between Duncannon and the town of Duncalloy,
> And now I'm in America with my father's servant boy.

Mackenzie, 119, 5d (N.S.) Refs.
Broadsides: (B) Such, no. 346 (Harvard XIII, 39) (M). Pitts. Catnach, 32d lines ("The Servant Boy").

M 12

THE APPRENTICE BOY

When the lady's parents hear of her love for the apprentice boy, they send him away. The boy becomes waiting-man and eventually steward to a merchant in a foreign country. Then he wins twenty thousand pounds in a lottery and returns to England with his riches. His true-love rejects him at first, thinking him a duke or other nobleman, but when she learns his identity she flies into his arms. A marriage follows.

> As down in Cupid's garden for pleasure I did walk,
> I heard two loyal lovers most sweetly for to talk.
> It was a brisk young lady and her prentice boy,
> And in private they were talking, for he was all her joy.

Mackenzie, 88, 8d (N.S.) Refs. Chappell, 125, 13 (N.C.). Creighton, 92, 8d, m. (N.S.) Pound, 74, 8d (Ind. from ms. of 1844). Randolph I, 429, 13 (Ark. via Mo.).
JFSS II, 195, 8d, m. (Sussex).
Broadsides: (B) Pitts (M). (A) N. Coverly, 8d (Thomas Coll., I, 88). No imprint, 8d. Andrews (L of C). Songsters: (A) *The American Song-ster*, Phila., 248, 8d. *The Forget Me Not Songster*, Phila., 178, 8d.

M 13

LOCKS AND BOLTS
(*I Dreamed of my True Love*)

Disapproving of her love for the narrator, a man without money, the rich girl's parents send her away from home. Her lover finds her locked in her uncle's house, breaks the locks and bolts, and escapes with her after a battle. The devoted lovers marry. (Traditional texts are usually rather incoherent).

I dreamed of my true love last night,
All in my arms I had her,
But when I woke it was a dream;
I was forced to lay without her.

Sharp II, 18, 7, m.; 17, 7, m. (N.C.); frags. Arnold, 62, 9, m. (Ala.).
Belden, 168, 2 (Mo.). Brewster, 300, 5 (Ind.). Brown, 285, 6½ (N.C.).
Henry, *Folk-Songs*, 253, 4 (Ga.); 8; 4 (Tenn.). Randolph I, 413, 6, m.
(Mo.); 5 (Ark.). Sandburg, 149, 4, m. (Ia.). Thompson, 399, 5 (N.Y.)
JAF 49, 236, 8, m. (Ky.). *JAF* 52, 13, 1, m. (Ky. via Wis.).

Brewster points out that a related ballad may be found in Rollins' edition
of the Pepys Ballads, II, 201, 8d, under the title "The Constant Wife",
Part I, which dates from 1631. This ballad, which Brewster reprints, p. 301,
is apparently the original from which the more modern piece was rewritten.

M 14

THE BONNY LABORING BOY

Her parents object to the rich girl's love for a laboring boy and try to
prevent their marriage by confining the girl to her room and sending the
youth to some foreign land. The lovers flee to Belfast where they plan to
take ship to America.

As I walked out one evening fair, it was in the month of early spring,
I met a beautiful damsel fair, most grievously did sing,
Saying, "Cruel was my parents, they did me so annoy.
They would not let me marry with my bonny laboring boy.

Gardner, 180, 8d (Ind. via Mich.).
Broadsides: (B) Ryle, 9d (Harvard V, 215). Cadman, 12d (Harvard VI,
204). O'Lochlainn, 18, 6d, m. Refs. Songster: (A) O'Conor, 84, 9d.

M 15

THE IRON DOOR

When Mary Ann falls in love with her servant man, her infuriated father
builds a dungeon with an iron door and confines her therein on bread
and water. Her lover contrives to enter the dungeon, allows her to escape
in some men's clothes he has brought, and awaits her father. When the
old man promises to spill his blood, the youth offers to let him do so but
insists on his love for the girl. The father has a change of heart and gives
the couple his blessing, "since love can enter an iron door".

It's of a damsel, neat, tall and handsome,
Those lines are true as I've been told,
On the banks of Shannon in a lofty mansion
Her father claimed great stores of gold.

Creighton, 181, 14d, m. (N.S.).

Broadwood, *Eng. Trad. Songs,* 38, 7 8-line d. sts., m. (Sussex).

Broadsides: (B) No imprint, 7 8-line d. sts. (Harvard VI, 168. "Mary Ann and her Servant Man"). Such, no. 95, 7 8-line d. sts. ("Cruel Father and Affectionate Lover").

M 16

MARY ACKLIN

(*The Squire's Young Daughter*)

A disapproving father secretly listens to a pledge of love between his daughter and the narrator. The girl gives her lover a ring, whereupon her father confines her to her room and has the youth arrested for robbery. Mary pleads in his behalf at the trial. Instead of being transported, the young man is freed, marries Mary, and settles down with her on the banks of the Shannon.

> Ye tender young lovers draw near me, the truth unto you I'll unfold,
> In grief I am left here bewailing, no pleasure I have to behold.
> Six months in a sad situation, bound down in strong irons it's true,
> For nothing but loving a fair one, I'm afraid I must bid her adieu.

Greenleaf, 189, 8d (Nfld. "The Squire's Young Daughter" or "Mary Acklin"). Barry, 54, 7d, m. (Me.). Gray, 82, 12 (Me. "Mary Aclon"). Mackenzie, 120, 10 (N.S. "Mary Riley"). Mackenzie says, " 'Mary Riley' is probably a modified version of that most popular of Irish folk-songs, 'Willy Reilly' ".

Hayward, 110, 6d (Co. Down. "Mary Acklin"). *JFSS* VIII, 14, m. (Ont.).

M 17

MARY NEAL

When the narrator is tried for kidnapping Mary, she pleads in his defense and he is set free. The lovers meet secretly and plan to escape to Quebec. Mary steals her clothes and some of her father's money, and the two are married. Their sea voyage almost ends in disaster when many of the passengers including Mary are washed overboard, but her husband manages to rescue her. Later he scorns her father's offer of half his land if they will return home.

> I am a bold undaunted youth; my name is John McCann;
> I'm a native of sweet Donegal, convenient to Strawval.
> For stealing of an heiress I lie in Wexford jail,
> And her father swears he'll hang me for his daughter Mary Neal.

Greenleaf, 187, 9d with several lines missing (Nfld.). Creighton, 173, 12d, m. (N.S.).

Joyce, 123, 1d, m. (Donegal). *JFSS* III, 129, 3d, m. (Dorset).

Broadsides: (B) Such, no. 313, 12d ("Charming Mary Neal." Harvard XIII, 6). Bebbington, 11d (Harvard IX, 117).

M 18

PRETTY BETSEY

Betsey's father beats her so viciously for loving William that she is near death. With her mother's help William is able to pay a last visit to the girl. She dies in his arms.

> There was a young lady in London did well.
> She had a true lover most wonderful well;
> And when her old father this news came to know
> He beat her so fearfully, he beat her so sore
> Till Betsey was thrown in the bed to rise no more.

Brown, 262, 23d lines (N.C.).

M 19

YOUNG SAILOR BOLD I
(*The Rich Merchant's Daughter*)

The rich merchant threatens to kill William, his daughter's lover. She disguises herself as a sailor, warns him of his danger, and says she'll meet him in London. Her father mistakes her for William and kills her. When he discovers his error, he falls on his sword and dies, and William, too, dies of grief.

> It's of a rich merchant in London I'm told
> Had a beautiful daughter most elegant to behold,
> Forty thousand bright guineas was her fortune in gold.
> And she fell in love with a young sailor bold.

Creighton and Senior, 219, 10d, m.; 218, frag. of 9 lines; add. tune (N.S.). Gardner, 112, 10d (Mich. from ms.). Thompson, 392, 5½d (N.Y.). *JFSS* I, 222, 10d, m. (Sussex).

Broadsides: (B) Ashton, 388, 10d ("The London Merchant"). Pitts, 10d.

M 20

BETSY IS A BEAUTY FAIR
(*Johnny and Betsy; The Lancaster Maid*)

A young man's mother overhears him making love to her young servant girl. She spirits the girl away and has her transported to Virginia as a bound servant. The boy pines away and dies of grief and the mother regrets her unkindness.

> Betsey Evans, a beauty fair,
> Has lately landed on the Yankee shore,
> A bound servant all for to be
> More fitter for some higher degree.

Eddy, 218, 14 (O.). Brown, 254, 9 (N.C. "The Lancaster Maid") Refs. Creighton, 62, 13, m. (N.S.). Flanders and Olney, 9, 10, m. (R.I.). Gardner, 114, 13, m. (Mich.). Pound, 66, 45 lines (Neb.). Randolph I, 235, 12, m. (Mo.). *JAF* 12, 245, 8d (Mass. from ms.); 3d (Mass.). *JAF* 19, 130, 9 (Cal.). *JAF* 56, 107, 11½ (Pa. via Ia.).

Greig, lxxx, 11 (Scot.).

Broadside: (B) Pitts (Reprinted in Firth, *An American Garland,* pp. 69-71, 12 sts. "The Betrayed Maiden").

Note: This ballad is probably a rewriting of "Love Overthrown," Rollins, *The Pepys Ballads,* VII, 137, 14 sts.

M 21

THE MERCHANT'S ONLY SON

To prevent his marriage to a girl of low degree, a youth's parents send him to America to seek his fortune. His ship is sunk, but he manages to get to shore. There he meets a rich, handsome girl who suggests marriage. When he tells her of his love for the girl at home, she gives him 500 guineas and tells him to return to his true-love.

> I am a merchant's only son; my age it is twenty-two.
> I fell in love with a handsome girl, the truth I will tell to you.
> Because I had money plenty and she of a low degree,
> Which caused my parents for to frown and proved my destiny.

Gardner, 198, 8d, m. (Mich.).

M 22

THE BONNY SAILOR BOY

The rich girl's father overhears his daughter making love to a sailor in the garden. He threatens to have the youth transported, but she swears to remain faithful to him.

> Come all you lads and lasses I pray you will attend
> Unto those few lines I am now going to pen,
> It is of a brisk young sailor and he a prentice bound,
> He fell in love with a lady gay worth thirty thousand pounds.

Creighton and Senior, 179, 4d, m. (N.S. "Jolly Young Sailor Boy").

M 23

GAY GIRL MARIE

A love letter meant for Marie is delivered to her father, who banishes her from home. The narrator searches for her in Ireland and elsewhere. After a long separation the lovers are reunited.

> I am a young lover and sorely oppressed,
> For the loss of a fair maid I can take no rest,
> She's handsomely featured in every degree,
> She's the pride of all beauty, my gay girl Marie.

Randolph I, 433, 10d (Mo.). Flanders-Barry, 34, 11d, m. (Vt. from ms. of ca. 1800. "Sweet Gramachree").

"A different version is found on a broadside by Harkness, printed in the middle of the last century." (Note from Flanders-Barry, p. 36). " 'My gay girl Marie' can reasonably be guessed to be a corruption of 'mo gradh geal mo chroidhe' (Bright heart's love)." (Note from Professor Samuel P. Bayard).

M 24

THE JOLLY PLOWBOY

(Little Plowing Boy; The Simple Plowboy)

When the rich girl's father hears that she loves a plowboy, he has a press-gang take the youth away. The girl dresses in men's clothes and follows her lover. She rows a boat out to his ship, pays the captain generously in gold, and returns to shore with the youth.

> A little plowing boy was a-plowing in the field,
> And his horse was standing in the shade.
> He whistled and he sung, it was as he plowed along,
> Until at length he spied a charming maid, maid, maid,
> Until at length he spied a charming maid.

Brown, 322, 7d; 2d (N.C.). Chappell, 127, 7d (N.C.). Creighton and Senior, 176, 9d, m. (N.S.). Mackenzie, 130, 7d (N.S.) Refs. Sharp I, 369, 4½d, m. (Va.) Refs.

Baring-Gould and Sharp, 60, 7d, m. Sharp and Marson V, 20, 8d, m. (Somerset). Ford II, 150, 8d, m. (Scot.). Greig, cxvii, 8d (Scot.). Ord, 233, 8d (Scot.). *JFSS* I, 132, 6d, m. (Sussex). *JFSS* II, 146, 1d, m. (Essex). *JFSS* IV, 303, 8d, m.; 8d, m.; add. tunes (Essex). *JFSS* VIII, 268, tune (Norfolk), 1d, m. (Lancs.). Joyce, 223, 5d, m. (Limerick).

Broadsides: (B) Paul. Catnach. Fortey, 4 8-line d. sts. Harkness, 8d (Harvard II, 133). Pitts (reprinted in part in *JFSS* II, 146, 1 d. sts.).

M 25

THE BANKS OF DUNDEE
(*Undaunted Mary*)

Because Mary loves the plowboy rather than the squire whom he wants
her to marry, her uncle has a press-gang come for the boy. A bitter fight
ensues in which Willie is wounded. When the squire attempts to make
violent love to Mary, she grabs his weapons and shoots him dead. Her
uncle threatens to kill her, and she shoots him, too. Before he dies he leaves
his gold to Mary, "who fought so manfully". Mary sends for Willie and
the lovers are married.

> 'Twas of a farmer's daughter most beautiful I'm told,
> Her father died and left to her a large amount of gold,
> She lived with her uncle, the cause of all her woe,
> But soon you'll hear this lady fair she proved his overthrow.

Creighton and Senior, 128, 11d. m.; 10d (N.S.). Belden, 137, 5d (Reprinted by Leach, 740). 7d, m. (Mo.). Chappell, 102, 16 (N.C.). Cox,
379, 9d; 8½d (W. Va.). Eddy, 155, 11 (O.). Gardner, 187, 11d, m.; 1d
(Mich.). Mackenzie, 84, 9½d (N.S.). Randolph I, 275, 10d, m.; (Mo.);
8d, m. (Ark.). Stout, 44, 3 (Ia.). Thompson, 394, 20 (N.Y.). Sharp I,
399, 9d, m.; 1d, m. (Ky.); 1d, m. (Tenn.). *JAF* 35, 354, 11 (O.) Detailed
refs. by Kittredge, *JAF* 52, 9, 7d, m. (Wis.).

Broadwood, 116, 10d, m. (Berks.). Ford I, 78, 11d, m. (Scot.). Greig,
lxvi, 11d (Scot.). Ord, 406, 11d (Scot.).

Broadsides: (B) Catnach (Harvard VII, 117). Geo. Walker, 11d (Harvard II, 36). Kidson, 54, 8d, m. (words from a Catnach broadside with
two stanzas omitted). Johnson, *Pop. Brit. Ballads* II, 217, 10d (partly from
a broadside). (A) Wehman no. 274 (K). Andrews (K). Deming, 10d
(L of C). Songsters: (A) O'Conor, 68, 10d. *617 Irish Songs*, 39, 10d.
Wehman's Irish Song Book No. 1, 117 (K).

A sequel to the present ballad recounts the adventures of William, who
finally returns home in disguise to test Mary's love. See Christie I, 258
("The Banks of Sweet Dundee", 5 8-line d. sts.) or a broadside by Ross,
Newcastle, ("An Answer to Undaunted Mary", 10d. Harvard IV, 184).

M 26

THE NEW RIVER SHORE
(*The Green Brier Shore; The Red River Shore*)

The narrator courts a girl but is forced to leave her, in some texts because her parents have him sent to war. She writes and asks him to return.
When he does so, he is met by a band of some twenty armed men hired
by the girl's father to kill him. He disposes of them in battle and wins
the girl.

And when her old parents came this for to hear,
They swore they'd deprive her of her own dearest dear.
They selected an army, full twenty or more,
To fight her own true love on the green brier shore.

Sharp II, 188, 7d, m. (Ky.) Stanza five is given above. Brown, 286, 11
(N.C.). Lomax, *Cowboy Songs,* 181, 10d, m. ("The Red River Shore".
A composite text). Mackenzie, 138, 7d. (N.S. "The New River Shore").
Detailed notes and refs. *PTFLS* VI, 158, 6d, m. (Okla. "The Red River
Shore"). *Bulletin* no. 2, p. 8, 6½d, m. (Me. "The Low River Shore").

Note: "The Red River Shore" is an American cowboy variant of this
ballad.

M 27

THE BOLD SOLDIER

A father threatens to end his daughter's life because she insists on marrying a soldier. He sends seven armed men against his daughter's lover, but
the soldier fights fiercely and kills two of them. The terrified father quickly
changes his mind and offers him the girl with a large dowry, but his
daughter says the portion is too small. With that the old man makes him
the heir of all his lands and money.

I'll tell you of a soldier that lately came from war,
He courted a lady so rare and so fair,
Her riches was so great that they scarcely could be told,
But still she loved her soldier because he was so bold.

Randolph I, 303, 8d, m. (Mo.); 12 (Ark.); 6½d, m. (Mo.); 7 (Ark.).
Barry, Eckstorm, and Smyth, 377, 9d; 6d, m.; 8d (Me.). Belden, 103, 8d,
(Mo. from ms.) Refs. Brown, 287, 5½ d; 7d; 5d; 4d (N.C.). Chappell,
88, 3d, m. (N.C.). Cox, 375, 6½d (W. Va.) Refs. Creighton, 25, 7d, m.
(N.S.). Davis, *Traditional Ballads,* 92, 28d lines (Va.). Flanders and
Brown, 232, 8d, m. (Vt.). Gardner, 380, 8d (Mich.). Henry, *Folk-Songs,*
185, 13 (Tenn.); 7d (Ga.). Pound, 68, 6d (La.). Scarborough, 201, 6½d
(Va.). Sharp I, 333, 6d, m. (N.C.); frags. with tunes; 13, m. (Va.). *JAF*
23, 447, 9d (N.J. from ms.). *JAF* 35, 414, 1d, m. (O.). *JAF* 60, 215, 9d
(Ill. from ms.). *JAF* 68, 202, 9d (N.Y.). Flanders, *A Garland,* 60, 9d, m.
(Vt.).

Williams, 115, 6d (Oxford. "The Bold Dragoon"). *JFSS* I, 108, 3½d, m.
(Sussex. "Come All You Maids of Honour").

Broadsides: (B) Belden speaks of 19th century stall prints of this piece
and mentions one by Such. (A) N. Coverly, Jr., 9d (Thomas Coll., II. 67).

Belden says, "The likeness of the story here told to that of *Erlinton,* Child
No. 8, has been noted by previous collectors," and Davis includes the ballad
as an appendix to "Earl Brand" (Child No. 7). Belden further traces the
story to a 17th century broadside about a gamekeeper and a lord's daughter

entitled "The Master-piece of Love Songs" (*Roxburghe Ballads*, VI, 229 and Ashton, *A Century of Ballads*, p. 164). Norman Cazden in "The Bold Soldier of Yarrow," *JAF* 68, 201-209, relates the piece to Child no. 214 and no. 215.

M 28
THE TAN-YARD SIDE

After a year of courtship the narrator is about to marry his girl, but her cruel father has him sent to sea. He says that he will make her his bride, if he ever returns.

> I am a rambling hero,
> With life I am ensnared,
> Near to the town of bonny Glas
> There dwells a comely maid.
> She is fairer than Diana bright,
> She is free from earthly pride,
> She's a lovely girl, and her dwelling place
> Lies near the tan-yard side.

Creighton, 165, 5d, m. (N.S.). Shoemaker, 238, 5d (Pa. ca. 1880).
Broadsides: (B) O'Lochlainn, 82, 5d, m. Such, no. 411, 5d (Harvard XIII, 105). Songsters: (A) O'Conor, 25, 5d. *617 Irish Songs*, 38, 5d.

M 29
BEAUTIFUL SUSAN

Because her true-love William is far away, Susan's parents inform her that he is dead and force her to marry another man. When William returns to England he sends her a letter and she commits suicide. Her ghost appears to William; he goes to Plymouth, kisses her, and falls on his sword.

> In Plymouth town there lived a fair virgin,
> And beautiful Susan was her name.
> Right straight off to court her
> The ship carpenter steering came.

Brown, 252, 54d lines (N.C.).

M 30
FAREWELL, DEAR ROSANNA

Rosanna's parents, disapproving of her suitor, send him away and have her marry a squire. Alamander, her lover, goes to sea; his ship strikes a rock and all but one are lost. The survivor takes the bad news to England, and Rosanna commits suicide with a sliver dagger. The ballad ends with a denunciation of parental cruelty.

Farewell, dear Rosannie, and shall I no more
Behold your fair face as I have done before.
I'll stand at your window both early and late,
So hard is my fortune and troubles so great.

Sharp II, 243, 8d, m. (Ky.). Combs, 196, 10d couplets (Ky.). Ritchie,
131, 6d, m. (Ky.).

M 31 A
WILLIAM AND DINAH A

When Dinah's father stubbornly insists upon her marrying a man she
does not love, the girl goes to a grove, writes a note to her lover, takes
poison, and dies. William finds her body and falls on his sword.

In Cumberland city I've often heard say,
There lived a fair damsel both gallant and gay;
Her name was Diana, scarce sixteen years old,
Yet she had for her fortune a large sum of gold.

. . . .

That evening, as it happened, Sir William walked out,
He walked the groves all around and about,
Till he came to the place where Diana lay dead,
Saying, "Heaven, dear gracious! Here lies my love dead."

Eddy, 149, 9d, m. (O.) Stanzas 1 and 8 are given above. (Reprinted by
Leach, 768). 150, 9d (O.). Creighton, 34, 9d, m. (N.S.). Fuson, 90, 3d
(Ky.). Gardner, 395, 29d lines, m. (Mich.). *NYFQ* V, 91, 9d (N.Y.).
JAF 35, 418, 9d (O.); 7d (N.Y.) Refs.
Broadsides: (B) Catnach, 8d. W. King, Oxford, 8d.
This typical romantic broadside was revised as a comic stage song. See
M 31 B.

M 31 B
VILIKINS AND HIS DINAH
(*William and Dinah* B)

In this variant, when he finds Dinah dead, Vilikins also drinks the "cold
pizen" and dies. In most traditional texts her father is reprimanded by the
ghosts of the two lovers. A gay refrain of the "tura-li-ura-li-ay" type is
sung with the comic text, the most characteristic stanza of which is the
second given below.

There was a rich merchant in London did dwell,
Who had for his daughter a very fine girl;
Her name it was Dinah, just sixteen years old,
Had a very large fortune in silver and gold.

. . . .

As Vilikins was walking the garden around,
He saw his dear Dinah lying dead on the ground,
And a cup of cold pizen a-laying by her side,
And a billet-doux a-stating 'twas of pizen she died.

Cox, 344, 7d (W. Va.) Stanzas 1 and 5 are given above. Belden, 147,
9 (Mo.) Refs. Brown, 483, 9d and chor. (N.C.). Creighton, 36, 6d and
chor., m. (N.S.). Flanders & Brown, 48, 5d and chor. (Vt.). Fuson, 90,
3d, (Ky.). Gardner, 397, 7d and chor. (Mich.). Linscott, 301, 7d and
chor., m. (Mass.). Morris, 339, 5d, m. (Fla.) A text like Stout's below
in which the girl, Katrina, chokes to death on a sausage. Randolph I,
331, 7d and chor.; 1d (Mo.). Stout, 54, 8d (Reprinted by Leach, 769).
30 lines (Ia. Rewritten texts in comic "Dutch" dialect). JAF 29, 190,
1d (La.). Refs. JAF 66, 45, 8d (N.Y. Another Dutch text).
    Broadsides: (B) Bebbington, 7d (Harvard VI, 230). Ryle, 7d (Har-
vard V, 202). (A) Andrews, 7d "Sung nightly by Charley White with
Shouts of Applause at 49 Bowery, N.Y.". Wehman, no. 627 (K). De-
Marsan (K). Sheet Music: (Dichter, p. 27, item 461) "Vilikins and His
Dinah." Comp. by John Parry. Bost. Oliver Ditson. ca. 1855."

M 32

THE BRAMBLE BRIAR
(The Merchant's Daughter; In Bruton Town, etc.)

A rich merchant's daughter falls in love with a servant. To prevent a
marriage, her two brothers invite him to go hunting, murder him in a
lonesome valley, and return home. Her lover appears to the girl in a dream,
weeping and covered with blood, and says that he has been murdered.
She searches for him, finds his corpse, kisses it repeatedly, and stays with
his body for three days. Hunger drives her home. She accuses her brothers,
who flee in a ship and are drowned.

In Smithford Town there lived a merchant
Who had two sons and a daughter fair
And an apprentice bound for to be his servant,
Who enraptured fell with the Lady Claire.

Brewster, 193, 13, m. (Ind.). Belden, 109, 13; 32 lines (Mo.) Refs.
Brown, 229, 12; 12 (N.C.). Cox, 305, 11 (Va. via W. Va.); 12 (W. Va.).
Eddy, 85, 15, m. (O.). Gardner, 59, 18 (Mich. from ms.). Henry, Folk-
Songs, 161, 7 (Tenn.). Owens, 83, 7, m. (Tex.). Pound, 53, 32 lines
(Belden's B text); 16 (Ky.). Randolph I, 381, 10, m. (Ark). Sharp I,
310, 12, m.; 1, m.; 1, m. (N.C.); 13, m. (Ky.); frags. JAF 29, 168, 1
(O.). JAF 35, 359, 1, m. (O.). JAF 46, 13 (N.C.) (Reprinted by Leach,
705). SFQ V, 176, 7½ (Ind. "In Seaport Town"). PTFLS II, 6, 10, m.
(Tex.).

Sharp, *One Hundred*, 4, 4 8-line sts., m. Notes. Sharp and Marson, I, 24, 5, m. (Somerset). *JFSS* II, 42, 32 lines, m. (Somerset). *JFSS* V, 123, 12, m. (Herts.); 9, m. (Somerset) Notes.

Broadside: (A) Wehman (K).

For a detailed study of this ballad and its literary relations see H. M. Belden, "Boccaccio, Hans Sachs, and *The Bramble Briar*", *PMLA* 33 (1918), 327-395.

M 33

THE CONSTANT FARMER'S SON

To prevent their sister's marriage to a farmer's son, two young men invite him to spend the day with them and then murder him. They tell their sister that her lover has run off with another girl. In a dream, Mary sees her love dead. She finds his body, weeps over it for a night and a day, and then returns home and accuses her brothers. They are executed and she dies of grief.

> Long time this couple courted and fixed the wedding day,
> Her parents they consented, but her brothers they said nay,
> "There is a lord who pledged his word and him she shall not shun,
> For we'll betray and then will slay her constant farmer's son."

Creighton and Senior, 141, 9d, m. (N.S.) Stanza two is given above. Mackenzie, 90, 9d (N.S.). Pound, 76, 8d (Neb.). *NYFQ* V, 96, 7d N.Y.).

Broadwood, *Eng. Trad. Songs*, 28, 9d, m. (Sussex). *JFSS* I, 160, 8d, m. (Sussex). *JFSS* VIII, 1d, m. (Essex).

Broadsides: (B) Forth, 9d (Harvard IV, 211). Cadman, 9d (Harvard V, 32). J. Gilbert, 9d (Harvard IV, 58).

M 34

EDWIN (EDMUND, EDWARD, ETC.) IN THE LOWLANDS LOW

Edwin returns to the girl he loves after seven years at sea. He shows her his gold, and she says he can spend the night at her father's public house, but she cautions him against revealing his identity. That night her father murders him for his gold and throws his body into the sea. The girl discovers the crime and informs against her father. The murderer is hanged, and the ballad ends with the girl's lament.

> Come all you wild young fellows and listen to my song,
> Concerning gold as we've been told that led so many wrong,
> Young Emily was a servant girl, she loved a sailor bold
> Who ploughed the main much gold to gain down in the
>   lowlands low.

Creighton and Senior, 220, 9d, m. (N.S.). Belden, 127, 8 (Mo.) Refs. Brewster, 202, 7d (Ind.). Brown, 267, 13; 8½ (N.C.). Cox, 345, 6½d

(W. Va.). Flanders and Brown, 106, 8d, m. (Vt. from ms.). Gardner, 62, 12 (Mich.). Henry, *Folk-Songs*, 164, 8; 10 (N.C.). Mackenzie, 92, 12 (N.S.). Morris, 345, 8 (Fla.). Randolph II, 59, 6d, m. (Mo.). Sharp I, 350, 5d, m. (N.C.); 8, m. (Tenn.); 5d, m.; 1, m. (Ga.); 12, m. (N.C.); frags. Thompson, 392, 6d (N.Y.). *Bulletin* no. 12, 12, 5d, m. (Me.); 2d (Vt.) Notes. *JAF* 20, 274, 9d couplets (Ky.) Refs. *JAF* 35, 421, 10 (Ky.) (Reprinted by Leach, 704). Refs. *JAF* 40, 230, 10, m. (O. via Ky.). *JAF* 52, 25, 7, m. (Ky. via Wis.). *JFSS* VIII, 227, 19 (Ont.).

JFSS I, 124, 1d, m. (Sussex). *JFSS* III, 266, 8d, m. (Hants.) (Reprinted by Leach, 703. *JFSS* III, 24, 2d, m. (Ireland).

Broadsides: (B) Pitts, Such, no. 228, 10d. Gilbert, Newcastle (Harvard IV, 109). Forth, 10d (Harvard IV, 209).

M 35

LOVELY WILLIE

A girl who is courted by men of high rank falls in love with Willie, who is of lower degree. When her father hears of their love he stabs the boy to death. Willie is laid in his grave and his grieving sweetheart looks forward to death.

> On last Monday evening, as I went to a ball,
> I met my own Jamie, so proper and tall;
> I asked him to go with me a piece down the road
> I'd show him my father's garden and where I abode.

Barry, 35, 5d, m. (Me. "Lovely Jamie"). Gardner, 103, 6d (Mich.). Randolph I, 417, 3d, m. (Mo.) Refs.
O'Lochlainn, 110, 6d, m. (Belfast).

M 36

AMERICAN WOODS

Young William, a blood relative of a Highland girl named McFarlan, is pressed into the military service by her disapproving parents. She gives him a ring and he goes to America. Near Fort Niagara in the year '69 he is murdered by some Indians, who cut off his ring finger. At this moment his ghost appears to Mary in Scotland, tells of his murder, and says he'll wander until she is with him. The girl expires within a week.

> Come, all ye loyal lovers, I pray lend an ear
> To a sad, dismal story, and soon you shall hear.
> 'Tis of a young couple that lived in the North
> And upon the high mountains that stands by your fort.

Creighton, 214, 15d, m. (N.S.).

M 37

THE *NIGHTINGALE*

Disapproving of their daughter's lover, her parents have him pressed into naval service on the *Nightingale*. On the night his ship sinks in a gale, his ghost appears to the girl blaming her parents for his death. The ghost says that his body lies in the Bay of Biscay with his shipmates.

> Both old and young, I pray lend an ear
> To a lovesick maiden in deep despair,
> Whose heart was light, but whose courage failed,
> When her true love sailed in the *Nightingale*.

Doerflinger, 304, 6, m. (N.S.). Korson, *Penna. Songs,* 49, 3, m. (Pa.). Greig, cviii, 7 (Scot.). Kidson, 61, 2, m. (Yorks.).

Broadsides: (B) Catnach, 7 (Harvard V, 177). R. Taylor, 7 (Harvard III, 23). W. R. Walker, 7 (Harvard IV, 164). Songsters: (A) *The Forget Me Not Songster,* Phila., 230, 17 sts. The same, N. Y., 107.

M 38

NANCY OF YARMOUTH

(*Jemmy and Nancy; The Barbadoes Lady*)

Because Nancy is rich, her father objects to her marrying a meanly bred man. He promises, however, that when Jimmy returns to Yarmouth after a voyage on one of his ships the youth may wed his daughter. Jimmy goes to Barbadoes where another rich lady falls in love with him and commits suicide because he will not marry her. When Jimmy is about to return home, Nancy's father orders the boatswain to murder him. He does so by throwing Jimmy overboard. That night Jimmy's ghost appears to Nancy and asks her to follow him into the deep. She joins her lover in death, the boatswain is hanged, and Nancy's father dies of a broken heart.

> Lovers, I crave, lend an ear to my story,
> Take an example by this constant pair,
> It is of a young couple who love out of measure,
> Beautiful Nancy of Yarmouth we hear.

Creighton, 81, 13d, m. (N.S.). Brown, 223, 55½d (N.C. from ms.). Sharp I, 379, 12d, m. (N.C.). *JAF* 26, 178, refs.

Christie II, 282, tune only. *JFSS* II, 113, 4d, m. (St. Leonard's-on-Sea). Notes and refs.

Broadsides: (B) Ashton, *Real Sailor Songs,* after p. 64, 56d ("The Constant Lovers' Garland"). In a chapbook by C. Randall, Stirling, 56d (Bell Coll. no. 51). Harkness, 55d. (A) Deming, Boston ("Jemmy and

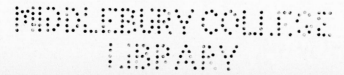

Nancy"). Songsters: (A) *The American Songster*, Phila., 1836, p. 193, 184. lines. *The Forget Me Not Songster*, Phila., 220, 28 8-line d. sts. The same, N. Y., 86.

M 39

SIR NEIL AND GLENGYLE

Lady Ann MacVaugh is wooed by Sir Neil and later by Glengyle. Ann's brother, hearing the false rumor that Sir Neil has slandered his sister, challenges the young man to a duel. Despite his reluctance to fight, Sir Neil accidentally causes MacVaugh's death. Glengyle appears and threatens Sir Neil, who tries to prevent further slaughter but is killed in an unguarded moment. Lady Ann grieves at the tragedy, calls Glengyle a traitor, and vows to die a maid.

> In yonder isle beyond Argyle
> Where flocks and herds were plenty,
> Lived airy squire whose sister fair
> Was the flower of all that country.
>
> The knight Sir Neil had wooed her long,
> Expecting soon to marry.
> A Highland laird his suit preferred,
> Young, handsome, brisk, and airy.

Mackenzie, 76, 29 (N.S.) Refs.

Buchan, *Ancient Ballads* (1828) II, 16, 15d. Christie I, 82, 11d, m. (Scot. "Sir Neil and MacVan"). Greig, cix, 13½ ("Sir Neil and M'Van").

Broadside: (B) In a chapbook without imprint, "Sir Neil and Glengyle, the Highland Chieftains." (Item 1094 in the Harvard Catalogue).

BALLADS OF LOVERS' DISGUISES AND TRICKS (N)

N 1 The Duke of Argyle

N 2 The Paisley Officer (India's Burning Sands)

N 3 Female Sailor Bold

N 4 The Female Warrior (Pretty Polly)

N 5 The *Lady Leroy*

N 6 Disguised Sailor

N 7 Jack Monroe (Jackie Frazier; The Wars of Germany)

N 8 William and Nancy I (Lisbon; Men's Clothing I'll Put On I)

N 9 The Banks of the Nile (Men's Clothing I'll Put On II)

N 10 The Silk Merchant's Daughter

N 11 William Taylor

N 12 The Maid in Sorrow (Short Jacket)

N 13 The Handsome Cabin Boy (The Female Cabin Boy)

N 14 Polly Oliver

N 15 The Noble Duke

N 16 The Rose of Britain's Isle

N 17 Caroline and Her Young Sailor Bold (Young Sailor Bold II)

N 18 The Prince of Morocco (The Sailor Boy II)

N 19 The Blaeberry Courtship

N 20 The Golden Glove (Dog and Gun)

N 21 The Female Highwayman

N 22 Kate and Her Horns

N 23 The Half-Hitch

N 24 Katie Morey

N 25 Love in a Tub (The Merchant Outwitted)

N 26 The Lawyer Outwitted

N 27 The Blind Beggar's Daughter of Bednall Green

N 28 Willie and Mary (Little Mary, the Sailor's Bride)

N 29 A Seaman and His Love (The Welcome Sailor)

N 30 William Hall (The Brisk Young Farmer)

N 31 Waterloo II

N 32 The Plains of Waterloo I

N 33 Lovely Nancy I

N 34 Janie on the Moor

N 35 The Dark-Eyed Sailor (Fair Phoebe and Her Dark-Eyed Sailor)

N 36 John (George) Riley I

N 37 John (George) Riley II (Young Riley)

N 38 The Mantle so Green

N 39 MacDonald's Return to Glencoe (The Pride of Glencoe)

N 40 The Banks of Claudy

N 41 The *Lady of the Lake* (The Banks of Clyde)

N 42 Pretty Fair Maid (The Maiden in the Garden)

N 43 Johnny German

N 1

THE DUKE OF ARGYLE

Miss Gordie accompanies Alexander to battle on the banks of the Nile. Her lover is slain, but she continues to fight for the king. True to Alexander, she rejects a duke's advances.

> The Duke of Argyle he came courting this lady,
> Where she's dressed in men's attire, and he's going to
> salute her.
> But still she cries "No! Though you are our commander,
> No man I'll enjoy since I lost Alexander."

Greenleaf, 88, 6d, m. (Nfld.) The last stanza is given above.
"The Duke of Argyle's Courtship to an English Lady", which appears in Ord, p. 197, and on several broadsides (items 785, 786, etc., in the Harvard Catalogue) is an entirely different ballad.

N 2

THE PAISLEY OFFICER
(India's Burning Sands)

Henry, the Paisley officer, falls in love with Mary. When his regiment is called to India they marry, and she disguises herself as a recruit and accompanies him. He is fatally wounded in battle and she is killed while caring for him. "They closed their eyes, no more to rise on India's burning shore."

> Way down in bonny Scotland where the blue bells they do grow
> There lived a farmer's daughter down by the lowlands low,
> She watched the flocks the whole day long down by the banks of Clyde,
> Though Mary's cot was neat and clean, she was called the village pride.

Creighton and Senior, 192, 8d; 8d (N.S.). Doerflinger, 308, 8d, m. (N.Y.); 11d (N.B.). Flanders-Barry, 19, 8d, m. (N.H.). Gardner, 222, 16 (Mich. "The Village Pride"). Gray, 85, 18 (Me.). Mackenzie, 143, 16; 12 (N.S.). *Bulletin* no. 4, p. 15, 7d, m. (Me.).
Broadsides: (B) W. R. Walker, 17d couplets (Harvard IV, 101). Bebbington, 6d (Harvard IX, 119).

N 3

FEMALE SAILOR BOLD

Jane Thorton, a Gloucester girl whose father lived in Ireland, disguises herself as a sailor to seek her fiancé, a sea captain. Arriving in New York, she learns that the captain is dead. After thirty-seven months of service on several ships, she returns to London. There her sex is discovered and her story is unfolded.

> Come, all ye good people, and listen to my song,
> While I relate a circumstance that down to love belong,
> Concerning a pretty maid who ventured we are told
> Across the briny ocean as a female sailor bold.

Creighton, 68, 12d, m. (N.S.).

Broadsides: (B) J. Gilbert, 12d (Harvard IV, 70). Ross, 12d (Harvard IV, 140). Spencer, 12d (Harvard I, 119). Songsters: (A) *The Forget Me Not Songster,* Phila., 125, 12d ("Gallant Female *Sailor"*). The same, N.Y., 104, 12d.

Notes: "The incident of a girl going to sea disguised in sailor's attire during the last century's naval wars was really not an uncommon one; there are many such recorded." (Kidson, p. 102, makes this observation in connection with another ballad).

"There is a well-authenticated instance (see *Times,* November 4, 1799) of a Miss Talbot, who followed her lover as a seaman, and after quarrelling with him, she enlisted in the army; but her love of the sea was unconquerable, and she joined the Navy, being present on board Earl St. Vincent's ship on February 14, and again under fire at Camperdown." (Ashton, *Modern Street Ballads,* p. 259, in a note to "Bold William Taylor").

N 4

THE FEMALE WARRIOR
(*Pretty Polly*)

After learning the mariner's art, a damsel dresses in men's clothing and ships on board a British warship as mate. During a fierce battle with a French ship, the captain is slain. The girl takes his place, leads the crew to victory, and returns to England, where she is rewarded by the Queen and marries her true love.

> A story, a story to you I will tell,
> 'Tis of a fair damsel in London did well.
> The truth of the story I mean you shall hear,
> How she ventured her life for the sake of her dear.

Gardner, 220, 13d (Mich. from ms. "Pretty Polly"). Doerflinger, 143, 6d, m. (N.S.). Eddy, 145, 6d (O.). Mackenzie, 223, 5d (N.S. "As We Were A-Sailing") Refs. *JFSS* VIII, 222, 10d, m. (Ont.) Notes and refs.

Christie II, 176, 5 8-line d. sts. (Scot. "The Bold Damosel"). Kidson, 100, 5d, m. (Yorks.). Williams, 261, 6d (Wilts. "Aboard the *Resolution").* *JFSS* III, 180, 6d, m. (Lincs. *"The Rainbow"*) Notes.

Broadside: (B) Harris, 7d ("Down by the Spanish Shore"). Songster: (A) *The American Songster,* Phila., 1836, 245, 6d.

N 5

THE *LADY LEROY*

To escape the wrath of her father, a girl disguises herself as a man, buys a ship, the *Lady Leroy,* from him, and sails away with her lover. The angry father sends another ship after them and a sea battle ensues in which the girl's ship is victorious. She sends the prisoners and their ship back to her father with a message that the lovers will not be parted. The young couple sail on, usually to Boston.

> She dressed herself up in a suit of men's clothes;
> Straightway to her father disguised she goes.
> She purchased a vessel, paid down his demand,
> But little thought he 'twas from his daughter's hand.

Gardner, 174, 14d (Mich from ms.) Stanza 3 is given above. Belden, 180, 12d (Mo. from ms.). Cox, 377, 9½d (Ireland via W. Va.). Dean, 33, 9d (Minn.). Flanders & Brown, 137, 10d, m. (Vt.). Greenleaf, 220, 9d (Nfld.). Sharp II, 210, 4d, m. (Ky.). Shoemaker, 72, 10d (Pa.). Stout, 32, 12d (Ia.). Thompson, 399, 4d (N.Y.). *JAF* 29, 180, 8d (Ill.). *JFSS* VIII, 218, 9d m. (Ont.).

N 6

DISGUISED SAILOR
(*The Sailor's Misfortune and Happy Marriage; The Old Miser*)

The merchant objects to his daughter's love for a sailor and tries to dissuade her from marrying him. When she remains adamant, her father pretends to agree to a wedding but has the youth pressed to sea. The girl follows him in disguise and becomes his bunkmate. After a while she tells the downhearted sailor his fortune and reveals her identity. The lovers return home to find that her father has died and are married.

> It's of a rich merchant, I can't call his name,
> He had but one daughter and a daughter of fame,
> She courted a great many but slighted them all,
> For the sake of a sailor both handsome and tall.

Creighton and Senior, 146, 10d, m. (N.S.) A confused text.
JFSS II, 181, 7d. m. (Essex. "It's of an Old Lord"). *JFSS* VIII, 9, 8d, m. (Somerset. "The Press Gang"); VIII, 265, 8d, m. (Norfolk. "The Old Miser").
Broadsides: (B) Ashton, *Real Sailor Songs,* 55, 15d ("The Sailor's Misfortune and Happy Marriage"). Haly, Cork, 11d ("The Constant Lovers"). (A) DeMarsan, 10d ("The Farmer's Daughter").

N 7

JACK MONROE

(*Jackie Frazer; The Wars of Germany*)

To get rid of his daughter's unwelcome suitor, a sailor named Jackie Frazer, the wealthy merchant has him sent to the wars of Germany. Polly dresses in men's clothes, enlists under the name of Jack Monroe, and goes to battle. She finds her lover wounded, has him cared for, reveals her identity, and marries him.

> She went into a tailor shop
> And dressed in men's array
> And waited for an officer
> To carry her away
>   O to carry her away.

> 'Your face is not familiar;
> Your name I do not know.'
> She answered in a low sweet voice:
> 'They call me Jack Monroe.
>   O they call me Jack Monroe'.

> 'Your waist it is too slender,
> Your fingers are too small.
> Your face it is too delicate
> To face a cannon ball'.

Belden, 176, 22 (Mo.) Stanzas 6-8 are given above. 171, 7 (Mo.); 16; 25 (Mo. from ms.) Notes and refs. Brewster, 206, 4; 14, m.; 12 (Ind.). Brown, 314, 10d couplets; add. sts.; 6 (N.C.). Cox, 330, 14; 6d; 11d couplets (W. Va.). Eddy, 106, 1, m; 33 (O.). Gardner, 165, 6d, m. (Mich.). Henry, *Folk Songs*, 208, 3 (N.C.). Hudson, 147, 13 (Miss.). Korson, *Penna Songs*, 53, 19, m. (Pa.). Lomax, *Our Singing Country*, 170, 9, m. (Va.). Morris, 353, 20, m. (Ga. via Fla.). Randolph I, 217, 11 (Mo.); 15 (Mo. from ms.). Sharp I, 385, 7, m. (N.C.); 18, m. (Ky.); 14, m. (Ga.); 17 fragments with tunes from Va., N.C., Ky., and Tenn. Wyman, 38, 14, m. (Ky.). *PFLST* X, 150, 13, m.; 9; 7 (Tex.). *JAF* 20, 269, 14; 16 (Ky.). *JAF* 12, 249, 8 (N.C. "Pretty Polly"). *JAF* 46, 38, frag. of 4 sts. (Tenn. "Jacky Frazer"). *JAF* 46, 48, frag. of 4 sts. (Tenn.). *JAF* 35, 377, frags. with tunes (O.) Refs. *JAF* 66, 46, 21, m. (tune from N.Y. tradition; text from a songbook).

Broadsides: (B) In a chapbook by J. Morren, Edinburgh. (Item 1615 in the Harvard Catalogue). Walker, Durham, 14d. (A) Elton, N.Y., 22 sts. Songster: (A) *The American Sailor's Songster*, N.Y., 172 (B).

N 8

WILLIAM AND NANCY I
(*Lisbon; Men's Clothing I'll Put On I*)

When William is called away to war, the girl begs to disguise herself as a sailor and go with him. He says, "Your waist it is too slender, love,/Your fingers are too small," but she disagrees and promises to be brave. Touched by her devotion, he decides to let her accompany him. They marry and sail away together.

> 'Twas on one Monday morning
> Just at the break of day,
> Our ship she slipped her cable
> And boldly sailed away.
>
> The wind it being northeast
> For Lisbon she was bound.
> The hills and dales were covered
> With pretty girls around.
>
> .   .   .   .
>
> "Then I'll put off these yellow locks,
> Men's clothing I'll put on,
> And like some gallant sailor
> I'll go with you along.

Gardner, 169, 15 (Mich.) Stanzas 1, 2, and 7 are given above. Belden, 178, 9d (Cal. via Mo.) ; 2 (Mo.) Notes and refs. Chappell, 120, 13 (N.C.). Creighton and Senior, 156, 6d, m.; 7½d, m. (N.S.). Combs, 208, 12 (Ky. "I'm Going to Join the Army"). Fuson, 104, 4d; 7d (Ky.). Henry, *Folk-Songs,* 167, 12 (Ga.). Mackenzie, 109, 15 (N.S.) Notes and refs. Randolph I, 217, 2d (Ark.) ; 3½d; 2d, m. (Mo.) Refs., p. 215; see also p. 224. Sharp II, 139, 10, m. (N.C.) ; 10, m. (Va.) ; 1, m. (Ky.). Stout, 47, 1d (Ia.).

JFSS II, 22, 4d, m. (Somerset) ; 191, 6d, m. (Sussex). *JFSS* VI, 17, 6d, m. (Surrey). *JFSS* VII, 50, 5½d, m. (Dorset).

Broadside: (B) Harkness, 7d.

N 9

THE BANKS OF THE NILE
(*Men's Clothing I'll Put On II*)

When William is called to Egypt, Molly begs to go with him, saying she will cut off her yellow locks and put on men's clothes. He replies that no woman may go because of the climate and bids her a sad farewell.

Hark th' drums are beatin', no longer can I stay,
I hear th' trumpets soundin', my love, I must away,
We are ordered from Fortsmouth for many long miles,
To j'ine th' British Army on th' banks of th' Nile.

Randolph I, 126, 6d, m. (Mo.). Dean, 105, 7d (Minn.). Mackenzie,
111, 10 (N.S.). Notes and refs.

Greig, xxv, 7d (Scot.). Ord, 298, 7d (Scot.).

Broadsides: (B) Ross, 7d (Harvard IV, 130). No imprint, (Harvard V,
42). Such, no. 191, 7d. Brereton, 7d.

Note: "The Banks of the Nile" is clearly related to "William and Nancy"
(N 8). In addition to their similar subject matter the two pieces have
several phrases in common, but they are sufficiently different to be treated
separately. Presumably the generalized older ballad was rewritten to apply
to an event of current interest. Randolph (I, 216) observes that Ord con-
nects the ballad with the battle of Aboukir, Egypt, in 1801. Several decades
later, "The Banks of the Nile" was itself recomposed. Mackenzie, 113,
prints a Civil War adaptation in 12 sts. under the title "Dixie's Isle", which
begins as follows:

> "We're ordered down to New Orleans
> To that unfruitful soil,
> To fight those Southern soldiers
> Way down upon Dixie's Isle".

N 10

THE SILK MERCHANT'S DAUGHTER

A girl's parents discharge a porter to prevent his marrying their daughter.
She dresses in men's clothes and follows her lover. On her way she kills
one of two heathens who attempt to murder her. She finds the porter and
with him joins the crew of a ship which later springs a leak and sinks.
After many days in a lifeboat, the crew casts lots to see who shall be killed
for food. The girl is chosen and her lover is designated executioner. She
reveals her identity by producing a broken ring, and he offers to die in
her place, but a ship is sighted, all are saved, and the lovers marry.

> 'Tis of a silk merchant in London I write;
> He had a fair daughter, his heart's chief delight.
> She loved a young porter, and to prevent the day
> Of marriage they forced this young man away.

Gardner, 176, 10d (Mich. from ms.). Brewster, 239, 22d (Ind.) In
this version, which seems almost completely rewritten, the young man scorns
the girl's advances and goes to sea to avoid her. Brown, 332, 16½d; 4
(N.C.). Cox, 334, 4d lines (W. Va.). Doerflinger, 296, 6, m. (Ont. via

N.Y.) ; 297, Gardner's text. Greenleaf, 57, 6d, m. (Nfld.). Hudson, 148, 10d (Miss. from ms.). Morris, 395, 12d, m. (Fla.). Randolph I, 222, 14d, m. (Mo.). Sharp I, 381, 16d, m. (N.C.) ; frags. with tunes. Stout, 21, 1d (Ia.). *JAF* 28, 160, 15½d (N.C. from ms.).

Ord, 63, 11d, m. (Aberdeenshire). *JFSS* VIII, 186, 26d lines (Dorset).

Broadside: (A) "Sold near Liberty-pole, 1794", 30d ("The Constant Lovers; or, The Valiant Young Lady").

N 11

WILLIAM TAYLOR

When Willie is impressed, his true-love dresses as a man and follows him to sea. During a battle, the buttons fly off her jacket and reveal her sex. She tells the captain her story, and he reports that William is false to her and is about to be married. She goes searching for him with a pistol and kills him and his new love. Pleased by her forthright conduct, the captain offers her command of his sailors; in some versions, he marries her.

> Willie Taylor was a brisk young sailor,
> Courted by a lady gay.
> A little before they were to be married,
> Pressed he was, and sent to sea.

Mackenzie, 133, 9; 132, 11 (N.S.) Discussion, xxxii-xxxiii. Belden, 182, 10 (Mo.) In this the girl commits suicide. Cox, 382, 10 (W. Va.) Detailed refs. Greenleaf, 49, 11, m. (Nfld.). Flanders and Brown, 152, 12 and ref. (Vt.). Randolph I, 295, 7, m. (Mo.). Sharp I, 373, 4, m. (N.C.) ; 4d, m.; 10, m. (Ky.). *JAF* 22, 380, 9, m. (Co. Tyrone via Mass.). *JAF* 28, 162, 11½ (N.C.). *JAF* 52, 21, frag. of 20 lines, m. (Ky. via Wis.).

Christie II, 208, 6d, m. ("Billy Taylor"). Greig, ci, 11 ("Billy Taylor"). Joyce, 235, 10d couplets, m. (Kilkee). *JFSS* I, 254, 1, m. (Whitby). *JFSS* III, 214, 12, m.; add. tune (Lincs.) Notes. *JFSS* V, 68, 1, m. (Somerset) ; add. tunes. *JFSS* V, 161, 10, m. (Herts.) ; 1, m. (Sussex).

Broadsides: (B) Hodges, 10 sts. ("Billy Taylor"). Such, 11 (Harvard XIII, 37). Catnach, 11 ("Bold William Taylor", reprinted in *JFSS* I, 255.). Ashton, 259, 11 "Bold William Taylor", a text different from the preceding. (A) Deming, Boston, 10 (L of C).

N 12

THE MAID IN SORROW
(*Short Jacket*)

A girl dresses in men's clothes and goes to sea as a sailor to seek her true-love. The captain is attracted by her and wishes his young sailor were a maid. She puts him off saying there are handsome girls ashore. As she leaves the ship she reveals that she is a girl.

I am a maid in sorrow, in sorrow to complain,
And it's all for the sake of my Jimmy I crossed the raging main;
And if I do not find him, I'll more contented lie;
It's all for the sake of my Jimmy a maid I'll live and die.

Gardner, 401, 5d, m. (Mich.). Greenleaf, 100, 5d, m. (Nfld. "Short Jacket").

N 13

THE HANDSOME CABIN BOY
(*The Female Cabin Boy*)

The captain discovers the sex of his disguised cabin boy and has an affair with her. One night the ship's crew is awakened by the groaning of the girl. When the doctor examines the patient, he discovers that she is about to have a child. The crew all drink to her success, and even the captain's wife joins in the merriment.

It is of a pretty female
As you shall understand;
She had a mind for roving
Unto some foreign land;
All dressed in sailor's clothing,
This fair maid did appear;
She engaged with a captain,
O his cabin boy to be.

Gardner, 399, 5d, m. (Mich.).
Ord, 160, 8d (Scot.).
Broadsides: (B) Such. Todd. W. R. Walker, 8d (Harvard III, 201).
(A) DeMarsan, 8d.

N 14

POLLY OLIVER
(*Pretty Polly*)

When Polly's parents come between her and her love she dresses in men's clothes and follows her captain. She meets him in an inn and gives him a letter from Polly containing a guinea to buy drinks and toast her. The captain offers to share his bed with the young recruit, but she demurs and goes to another room. The next day she appears in her own clothing and is joyfully greeted by the captain. The lovers marry, and her parents mourn for her at home.

It was a fair damsel in London did dwell,
She was courted by a captain who loved her real well,
And when her old parents those tidings did hear
He banished pretty Polly far far from her dear.

Creighton and Senior, 197, 12d, m.; 195, 11d, m. (N.S.) Belden, 183, 8d (Mo. from ms.); 10d (Mo.) Refs. Brown, 312, 16d couplets (N.C.). Cox, 387, 9d (W. Va.) Refs. Gardner, 167, 9d (Mich.). Greenleaf, 51, 9d (Nfld.). Linscott, 273, 4d, m. (Mass.). Mackenzie, 151, frag. of 3d (N.S.). Sharp I, 344, 3d, m. (N.C.); 9½, m. (Ky.); 11d, m. (Va.). Shoemaker, 185, 9d (Pa.). Stout, 22, 1 (Ia.). *JAF* 12, 248, 9½d (N.C.). *JAF* 22, 75, tune only. *JAF* 24, 337, 8d, m. (Ire. via Mass.).

Kidson, 116, frag. of 5d from a broadside with two tunes.

Broadsides: (B) Such, no. 369, 8d ("Polly Oliver's Rambles"). No imprint (Harvard VII, 150). Bebbington, 8d (Harvard X, 16).

N 15

THE NOBLE DUKE

The girl follows her lover, who has been pressed to sea, and, disguised as a duke, arrests him for stealing her treasure. He denies robbing any man, the girl reveals her identity, and the two are happily reunited.

> She dressed herself like any Duke
> With a star upon her breast;
> She said she'd kill the captain
> If he did her molest;
> The officers stood a-gazing
> This Noble Duke to see;
> They thought he was a-coming
> Their commander for to be.

Thomas, *Devil's Ditties,* 76, 6d, m. (Ky.) Stanza 2 is given above. *JAF* 28, 163, 6d (N.C. from ms. "The Damsel Disguised").

N 16

THE ROSE OF BRITAIN'S ISLE

When Jane falls in love with her father's servant boy, the youth is sent to sea. Jane follows him, disguised as a man, and is wounded in battle. Edward, her lover, then marries her and the couple return home to find her father in a generous and forgiving mood.

> Come all you people far and near,
> It's quickly you shall hear;
> It's of a lady tall and slim
> That lived in Cankershire.

> Her cheeks like blooming roses
> All in her face did shine;
> This maiden's name was lovely Jane,
> She was the rose of Britain's Isle.

Mackenzie, 115, 13½ (N.S.) Refs. Greenleaf, 65, 10 and chor., m. (Nfld.).

Broadsides: (B) George Walker, Jr., 8d (Harvard II, 9). Harkness, 11d ("The Blooming Rose of Fair Britain's Isle").

In connection with another ballad, Ebsworth observes, "Love-sick Serving-Men were generally successful in ballads, but the writers purveyed the food that was acceptable to their patrons, and domestics were good purchasers." (*Roxburghe Ballads, VI,* 264).

N 17

CAROLINE AND HER YOUNG SAILOR BOLD
(*Young Sailor Bold II*)

Although the sailor tries to discourage the rich girl who has fallen in love with him, she follows him to sea and becomes a sailor herself. At last she returns home and gets her father's consent to their marriage.

> There lived a rich nobleman's daughter,
> So comely and handsome and fair,
> Her father possessed a great fortune,
> Full thirty-five thousand a year.
> She being his only daughter,
> Caroline is her name we are told,
> One day from her drawing-room window
> She espied there a young sailor bold.

Creighton, 66, 7d, m. (N.S.). Brown, 321, 5d (N.C.).
Greig, clxiii, 14 (Scot.).
Broadsides: (B) No imprint, 7d (Harvard I, 80). W. R. Walker, 7d (Harvard IV, 18). Ross, Newcastle (Harvard IV, 126).

N 18

THE PRINCE OF MOROCCO
(*The Sailor Boy II*)

To outwit her disapproving father and gain his lady's hand, the poor sailor (or farmer) disguises himself as the Prince of Morocco and woos her. The couple are married with the old man's blessing. After the father has given the girl twelve thousand pounds, the youth reveals his identity.

> There was a poor sailor with courage brave and bold.
> He courted a fair lady worth thousands of gold.
> And then up speaks her father saying, "If this is your intent,
> To marry with that sailor boy, I'll never give consent."

Flanders-Barry, 38, 7½, m.; add. sts. (Vt. "The Poor Sailor Boy"). Brown, 232, 13d (N.C.). Randolph I, 354, 9d, m. (Ark. "The Sailor Boy"). Good notes to all texts.

Broadsides: (B) Saxton, 11d, "Father Deceived; or the Crafty Farmer" (Harvard). "The Crafty Ploughman's Garland, or The Young Farmer's Policy to Gain a Fair Lady", Percy Coll., I, 23 (Harvard Catalogue, item 1926). Also in Harvard Catalogue, item 1925.

N 19
THE BLAEBERRY COURTSHIP

Despite her father's disapproval, the Lowland girl finally accepts her poor suitor's invitation to pick blueberries in the Highlands. The engaged couple travel on foot, and the girl is near exhaustion by the time they reach his home. His servants welcome him and provide her with the best bed in the house. The next day he shows her his rich lands and possessions and identifies himself as Sandy, the poor schoolboy she had befriended many years before. With a large retinue, the lovers return to her parents to help provide for them.

> "Will ye gang to the Highlands, my jewel, wi' me?
> Will ye gang to the Highlands my flock for to see?
> It is health to my jewel to breathe the fresh air,
> And to pu' the blaeberries in the forest sae fair."

Mackenzie, 69, 25d; 14d (N.S.). Refs. *JAF* 35, 345, 12d couplets (Scot. via Ill.) Refs.

Christie I, 150, 8 8-line d. sts., m. (Scot.). Ford II, 77, 32d (Scot.). Greig xliii, 31d (Scot.). Ord, 190, 8-8-line d. sts. (Scot.).

Broadsides: (B) Stephenson, Gateshead (Item 698 in the Harvard Catalogue). George Walker, 32d (Harvard II, 50). In a chapbook by T. Johnston, Falkirk, 32d (Item 697 in the Harvard Catalogue).

Note: "The Blaeberry Courtship" is a modernization of the story told in "Lizie Lindsay" (Child no. 226). The broadside text of 32 double stanzas has itself been condensed into a more artistic piece of 16 double stanzas. (The latter variant is printed by Christie and by Ord).

N 20
THE GOLDEN GLOVE
(*Dog and Gun*)

The lady sees a farmer who is to take part in her wedding to the squire and falls in love with him. Using illness as an excuse, she calls off the wedding. She goes hunting in men's clothes, and in conversation with the farmer discovers that he loves her. She then hands him a gold-decorated glove, saying she has found it. At home again, she announces that she will marry the first man who finds her glove. The farmer brings it to her, and after their marriage she tells him of the trick she has played.

> A lofty young squire from Portsmouth he came,
> And courted a nobleman's daughter so fair,
> The day was appointed a wedding to be,
> The farmer was chosen to give her away.

Thomas, *Devil's Ditties,* 170, 9d, m. (Ky.). Belden, 229, 11d, m.; add. sts. (Mo.). Brown, 475, 7½ (N.C.). Chappell, 106, 8d, m. (N.C.). Cox, 385, 12d, m. (W. Va.) Refs. Creighton and Senior, 148, 10d, m.; 10d (N.S.). Eddy, 173, 6d; 12d (O.). Flanders & Brown, 117, frag. with tune (Vt.). Flanders-Barry, 29, 4d, m. (N.H. from ms.). Gardner, 195, 10½d (Mich.). Hudson, 158, 9d (Miss.). Mackenzie, 80, 10½d (N.S. Tune, p. 395). Scarborough, 228, 9d (Ky. Same singer as in Thomas). Sharp I, 377, 5d, m. (N.C.); tune from Va. Thompson, 416, 11d (N.Y.). Randolph I, 308, 9d, m.; 8½d (Mo.). Wyman, 49, 8d, m. (Ky.). *SFQ* II, 149, 10½d, m. (Ky.). *JAF* 29, 171, 10½d (Pa. via Kan.); *JAF* 52, 36, 2d, m. (Ky. via Wis.); *JAF* 60, 228, 10d (Ill. from ms.).

Greig, xcv, 11d (Scot.). Kidson, 49, 12d, m.; add. tune. *JFSS* VI, 29, 10½d, m. (Surrey); add. tunes.

Broadsides: (B) Forth, 11d (Harvard III, 128). Gilbert, 11d (Harvard IV, 115). No imprint, 11d (Harvard V, 52). (A) Kittredge in *JAF* 29, 172, writes, "An American broadside of the early nineteenth century is in the Harvard College Library, 25242.5.10(211)."

N 21
THE FEMALE HIGHWAYMAN

To test her lover, a girl disguises herself as a highwayman and robs him of his watch and gold. When he refuses to yield the diamond ring she has given him, she rides away satisfied. Later he discovers the plot and expresses concern that he might have shot her.

> As Zillah on a certain day
> She dressed herself in men's array;
> With sword and pistol by her side,
> To meet her true love away did ride.

Mackenzie, 318, 7; 7 (N.S.) Refs. Creighton, 51, 7, m. (N.S.). Flanders and Brown, 133, 6, m. (Vt.). Greenleaf, 61, 8, m. (Nfld. "Wexford City"). Shoemaker, 180, 8 (Pa.). *JFSS* VIII, 225, 9, m. (Ont.).

Sharp and Marson II, 10, 8, m. (Somerset. "Sovay, Sovay"). *JFSS* III, 127, 1, m.; 7, m.; 2, m. (Dorset). JFSS VIII, 227, 1, m. (Sussex).

Broadsides: (B) Pitts (M). Jackson ("Sylvia's Request and William's Denial") (M). Such, no. 548, 9 sts.

N 22

KATE AND HER HORNS

Kate finally consents to marry the clothier, whereupon he leaves her for a rich lawyer's daughter. The jilted girl obtains a cowhide from a tanner, wraps herself in it, and confronts her false lover at night in a lonely field in the guise of the devil. To escape Lucifer's clutches, the clothier promises to return to Kate, does so, and they marry. At her lying-in she reveals her trick and everyone laughs about it.

> A damsel sweet in Colchester,
> And there a clothier courted her
> For three months' space, both night and day,
> But yet the damsel still said nay.

Mackenzie, 325, 20 (N.S.) Refs. Belden, 231, 9 and chor. (Mo.). Combs, 157, 10 (Ky.). Creighton and Senior, 184, 19, m. (N.S.). Gardner, 387, 10, m. (Eng. via O. and Mich.); 15 (Mich.). Sharp I, 405, 8, m. (Ky.). Thompson, 413, 20 (N.Y. Partly from ms.).

Broadsides: (B) *Roxburghe Ballads* VIII, 430, 22d couplets ("Crafty Kate of Colchester; or, The False-hearted Clothier frighted into Good Manners"). (A) No imprint, 20 sts. N. Coverly, Jr., 20 sts. (Thomas Coll., I, 47). Songsters: (A) *The Forget Me Not Songster*, Phila., 212, 20 sts. The same, N.Y., 145, 20 sts.

For a ballad which tells a similar story see "The Politick Maid of Suffolk; or, The Lawyer Outwitted", items 2006 and 2007 in The Harvard Catalogue. See also "The Jealous Husband Outwitted", 18 sts., Logan, 384.

N 23

THE HALF-HITCH

To test her fiancé, a girl pretends fickleness and refuses to marry him. Vastly annoyed he swears to marry the next woman he meets. The girl dresses like a beggar, "with her petticoats hoisted upon the half-hitch", and contrives to cross his path. An amusing dialogue ensues in which his sense of honor compels him to propose to her. He takes her home and she behaves atrociously at the wedding feast. When, however, he follows her to bed, he finds his true-love dressed in fine clothes and looking beautiful.

> There was a rich merchant in Plymouth did dwell;
> He had a fair daughter, a beautiful girl.
> A handsome young man with riches supplied
> He courted this lady for to be his bride.

He courted her long and had gained her love,
And the lady intended the young man to prove.
A time she set to him, and then she denied;
She told him right off she would not be his bride.

Thompson, 417, 23d plus 10 spoken lines (N.Y.). Flanders and Olney, 33, 20½d plus 9 spoken lines, m. (Vt.). Barry, Eckstorm, and Smyth, 384, 16d (Me. "The Loathly Bride"); 18d (Vt.). "The Half-Hitch". Reprinted from Sturgis, p. 50).

The New England editors speak of this ballad as a secondary form of Child no. 31 ("The Marriage of Sir Gawain"). While the old motif of the knight and the loathly lady may be recognized here in comic form without the supernatural element, the ballads have no other demonstrable relationship to one another.

N 24

KATIE MOREY

The narrator attempts to seduce Katie by inviting her to pick grapes with his sisters in a bower. She goes with him and when they are alone he threatens to kill her if she will not comply. She seems willing but says her father is near and tells the youth to climb a tree until he has passed by. When he reaches the top, she speaks insultingly to him and runs away. At first furious, the young man decides later that the girl is to be admired for her virtue and marries her.

Come all you sly and tricky lads,
Come listen to my story.
I'll tell you how I fixed my plans
To 'spoil young Katie Mory.

Thompson, 411, 14 (N.Y. from ms.). Gardner, 393, 10, m. (Mich. Two sts. omitted). Lomax, *Our Singing Country*, 122, 12, m. (Ky. via N.Y.). Sharp II, 119, 6, m. (Tenn.); 6, m.; 1, m. (N.C.) All with refrains. Shoemaker, 130, 12 (Pa.). *JAF* 35, 385, 9 and ref., m, (O.). *JAF* 49, 232, 8, m. (Ky. "Catherine Moore").

Broadside: (A) " 'Katy Mory' in fifteen stanzas, the last two quite free in their nature, occurs in an American broadside of about 1830 (no imprint): 'Katy Mory, and Poll and Mistress' (Harvard College)." (Note from Kittredge, *JAF* 35, 387).

Tolman and Eddy, *JAF* 35, 385, point out a similarity between this piece and "The Baffled Knight", Child no. 112. Child neatly summarizes the plot of that ballad as follows: ". . . A knight, coming upon a damsel at a distance from her home, desires to have his will of her. She asks him to take her to her father's hall, where he shall be gratified. Reaching the house, she slips in and leaves the knight without. She jeers at him for not using his opportunity." (Child II, 480).

N 25

LOVE IN A TUB
(*The Merchant Outwitted*)

A vintner falls in love with a merchant's daughter. To be sure of her dowry, he must get her father's consent to their marriage. The girl hides in one of the merchant's wine casks, and the vintner offers to buy whatever it contains. Because the cask seems empty when tapped, the merchant insists that the bargain be kept. When his daughter is revealed, the merchant admits defeat, gives his consent, and awards the girl a large dowry.

> In the city of London a lady did dwell;
> A very rich merchant was known very well.
> He had but one daughter, a beauty so bright.
> And on her he placed his chief joy and delight.

Belden, 233, 17d (Mo.) Stanza two is given above.

Broadsides: (B) In two chapbooks without imprint and in one by James Magee, Belfast, 1764. (Items 1925, 1976, and 694 in the Harvard Catalogue). Broadside, Bow Church Yard, London, "Love in a Tub; or, the Miser Outwitted". (Item 1977 in the Harvard Catalogue. (A?) No imprint, 21d sts. "Love in a Tub, or, The Merchant Outwitted by a Vintner", Thomas Coll., II, 4.

N 26

THE LAWYER OUTWITTED

The lawyer's daughter falls in love with the squire's youngest son. Fearing her father's disapproval, he consults him professionally without revealing his identity. The lawyer advises a quick trip to the parson on a horse provided by the girl, so that the youth will not be accused of kidnapping. The elopement is carried out, and the couple return for her father's blessing. He is enraged but admits that he has been outwitted.

> 'Tis of a young councilor I write
> Who had one only daughter,
> And she was of the beauty bright.
> Now mind what follows after.
> She had five hundred pounds a year,
> In gold and silver ready.
> Courted was she by lords and peers
> But there's none could gain this lady.

Flanders-Barry, 121, about 7d, m. (Vt.) Notes. Creighton, 47, 11d, m. (N.S. "Rich Counsellor"). Henry, *Folk-Songs*, 303, 7½ (Tenn.). Sharp I, 402, 18, m. (Tenn.). Shoemaker, 295, 11d (Pa.).

Sharp and Marson II, 32, 6d, m. (Somerset). Greig, xv, 20 sts.

Broadsides: (B) *Coll. of Old Ballads* II, 234, 11d. W. Dicey, Northampton, "The Crafty Lover; or, The Lawyer Outwitted" (item 1920 in Harvard Catalogue). No imprint (item 1921). Aldermary Church Yard, (item 1922). Bebbington, 11d (Harvard X, 181). (A?) No imprint, Thomas Coll. I, 14.

N 27

THE BLIND BEGGAR'S DAUGHTER OF BEDNALL GREEN

The beggar's comely daughter is wooed by such men as a lord, a merchant, a capain, and a squire, each of whom offers his riches if she will reveal the identity of her father. When she does so the others scornfully reject her, but the squire still seeks her hand. On hearing this, the beggar provides her with a handsome dowry.

> There was a blind beggar, he lost his sight;
> He had a daughter most beautiful and bright;
> "Shall I seek my fortune, dear father," says she;
> The favor was granted to pretty Bet-see.

Eddy, 83, 11d (O.). Flanders and Olney, 107, 9d, m. (Me.). Greenleaf, 71, 8d (Nfld.) Refs. Sharp I, 308, 2, m. (N. C.). *JAF* 35, 357, refs. *JAF* 52, 61, 1d, m. (N.J.).

Williams, 255, 13d (Wilts.). *JFSS* I, 202, 11d, m. (Surrey) (Reprinted by Leach, 694).

Early broadsides: (B) *A Coll. of Old Ballads* II, 202, Part I, 34d; Part II, 29d. Child IV (1857), 161. Hales and Furnivall, *Bishop Percy's Folio Manuscript* II, 281, 65d. Hindley, *Roxburghe Ballads* I, 38, 64d. Late broadsides: (B) W. Dicey, Northampton. Forth, Pocklington, 10d (Harvard III, 142). Catnach, 12d (Harvard VII, 61). Songsters: (A) *The Forget Me Not Songster*, Phila., 237, 11d. The same, N.Y., 129, 11d.

Notes: According to Hales and Furnivall, "The ballad was certainly not written later than Queen Elizabeth's reign." The traditional texts are derived from the late broadsides, which tell a story less than one-fifth the length of the original. In Part II of the longer broadsides, the beggar appears at the sumptuous wedding feast which he has provided and reveals that his name is Montford, that he is of high birth, and that he became a beggar after being blinded while fighting in France.

N 28

WILLIE AND MARY

(Mary and Willie; Little Mary, the Sailor's Bride)

Three years after Willie has gone to sea, a beggar with a patch over one eye appears at Mary's door, asks for charity, and offers to tell her fortune. She inquires about Willie and is told that he was shipwrecked,

is living in poverty, and will not return to her. She says she would welcome him in any condition, whereupon the beggar reveals that he is
Willie and that he was testing her love. He has returned wealthy and
plans to marry her at once.

> Mary and Willie sit by the sea shore
> Their last farewell to take.
> Says Mary to Willie: "You're now going to sea;
> I fear that my fond heart will break."
>
> "Oh, don't be despairing," young Willie then said,
> And pressed his fair maid to his side;
> "My absence don't mourn, for when I return
> I'll make little Mary my bride."

Belden, 152, 10 (Mo. from ms.) Sts. 1 and 2 are given above. Barry, 24,
10, m. (text from a song book, tune from Me.). Brewster, 356, 2 (Ind.).
Flanders and Brown, 150, 7 (Vt. "The Single Sailor"). Flanders-Barry,
25, 5d, m. (Mass.). Henry, *Folk-Songs*, 172, 9 (Tenn.). Hudson, 153, 5d
(Miss.). Randolph I, 264, 6, m.; 2 (Mo.).
Barrett, 58, 1, m. (Cheshire); 3 (Bedfordshire).
Broadsides: (B) Catnach. Such, no. 357, 5d (Harvard). Pitts, 5d
(Harvard). Barrett, 59, reprints seven stanzas of this piece from a broad-
side by J. Evans.

N 29

A SEAMAN AND HIS LOVE
(*The Welcome Sailor*)

The sailor learns from the weeping girl that her lover has been away
at sea for seven years and that she fears he is dead. He produces a token
which he says her lover sent before he died, with the request that she
marry its bearer. When she says she can only mourn for the rest of her
life, the sailor reveals that he is her lover and a happy reunion follows.

> One dark and gloomy night all clouded over,
> Where rivers running by and ships a-sailing,
> A pretty maid I spied, weeping and wailing.
> I stepped up to her and asked her, "What doth
>   grieve thee?"
> The answer that she made, "None can relieve me.

Gardner, 152, 6d (Mich. A confused text).
Broadsides: (B) Pitts, 7d ("The Welcome Sailor"). *Roxburghe Ballads*
III, 127, 17 sts. (A 17th century broadside which names Cuthbert Birket
as the author).

N 30

WILLIAM HALL
(*The Brisk Young Farmer*)

William Hall's parents, disapproving of his love, send him to sea. When he returns he finds that his girl does not recognize him and attempts to court her. She describes her lover, and he says he was killed at sea by a French cannon ball. When she weeps, he reveals his identity and produces the ring she gave him. The happy couple are married, "whether their parents are willing or no."

> I will tell you of a brisk young farmer.
> He is a credit to any man,
> He courted a fair and a handsome lady,
> She did dwell in a Western town.

Thomas, *Devil's Ditties,* 84, 12, m. (Ky.). Belden, 156, 10 (Mo. from ms.); 9; 11 (Mo.). Cox, 326, 9; 3 (W. Va.) tune, 528. Henry, *Folk-Songs,* 180, 9 (Ga.). Hudson, 154, 11 (Miss.). Gardner, 153, 11, m. (Mo. via Mich.). Morris, 350, 6, m.; 8 (Fla.). Pound, 71, 10 (Neb. from ms.). Randolph I, 231, 11, m. (Mo.). Scarborough, 264, 10 (N.C. This version begins as "A Pretty Fair Maid" and ends as "William Hall"). Sharp II, 239, 10, m. (Va.); 8, m. (N.C.); frags. Owens, 79, 11, m. (Tex.). Wyman, 100, 7, m. (Ky.).

N 31

WATERLOO II

The narrator asks the girl to describe Willie and then says he saw him die from five bayonet wounds. The girl falls half fainting into his arms, whereupon he shows his scars, reveals that he is Willie, and says he'll marry her.

> As a fair maid was walking down by the banks of Clyde,
> The tears runned down her rosy cheeks as she passed by
>   my side.
> I saw her heaving bosom, her words were good and true,
> Saying, "I fear, I fear my Willie's slain on the fields of
>   Waterloo."

Gardner, 227, 6d (Mich. "Bloody Waterloo"). Greenleaf, 178, 5d; 3d (Nfld.). *JAF* 67, 134, 5d, m. (Nfld. "Lonely Waterloo"). All the Newfoundland texts end with the girl grieving at the news of Willie's death.

N 32

THE PLAINS OF WATERLOO I

The soldier tells Sally that William Smith, his comrade, died at Waterloo after sending her a farewell message. He then brings out his half of a broken token and reveals that he is Willie.

As I did rove out on a fine dewy morning,
It was down by the banks of a clear running stream,
And who did I spy but my own charming Sally,
As I lay in ambush to hear what she say,
Where the song that she sang made the valleys to ring,
While the poor feathered songsters around her they flew,
Saying, "The wars are all over and peace is now proclaimed,
And my Willie's not returned from the plains of Waterloo."

Greenleaf, 172, 5 8-line d. sts., m. (Nfld.). Mackenzie, 183, 7d (N.S.)
Detailed notes.

N 33

LOVELY NANCY I

When the sailor asks the girl what she is doing so far from home, she
replies that she is seeking her true-love, who has been away for three years.
After she describes him in glowing terms, he pulls his half of their broken
ring from his bosom and says he wants to marry her and stay at home.

As I rode out one fine summer evening
To view the stars and to take the air,
It was there I spied a fair lovely damsel
And for her beauty I did her adore.

Creighton and Senior, 187, 9d, m. (N.S.).

N 34

JANIE OF THE MOOR

The narrator chats with Janie and then makes love to her and proposes
marriage, but she remains faithful to Dennis Ryan (or Riley) from New
York. He tells her that Dennis fell in battle and shows her the young
man's ring. She faints but revives when he reveals that he is Dennis.

One morn for recreation, as I strayed by the sea-side,
While the hills and valleys round me, with flowers were
  decked with pride,
'Twas there I spied a pretty fair maid, as she roamed
  along the shore;
Like the rose in bloom, red was the cheek of Janie
  of the Moor.

Barry, 82, 7d, m. (Me.). Mackenzie, 175, 7d; 7d (N.S.) Refs.
Broadsides: (B) Such, no. 121, 8d ("Jenny of the Moor"). Disley (M).
Fortey (M). (A) Partridge, Boston (the source of all but six lines of
Barry's text). DeMarsan (M). *Delaney's Irish Song Book No. 4,* p. 22 (M).

N 35

THE DARK-EYED SAILOR
(*Fair Phoebe and her Dark-Eyed Sailor*)

A sailor tries to woo a girl, but she remains faithful to her dark-eyed sailor, William. Seven years before he broke a gold ring in two and gave her half of it. The young man finally identifies himself by producing his half of the ring, and marriage follows. The couple settle in a cottage by the sea.

> As I roved out one evening fair,
> To view the fields and to take the air,
> I meet a maiden all on my way,
> And I paid attention,
> And I paid attention to what I heard her say.

Greenleaf, 81, 6 (Nfld.). Barry, 42, 9, m. (Text from the *Rough and Ready Songster*, N.Y., 1848; tune from trad. in Maine). Cox, 319, 7 (W. Va.) Detailed refs. Creighton, 58, 8, m. (N.S.). Brown, 310, 9 (N.C.). Creighton and Senior, 144, 8, m.; 7 (N.S.). Doerflinger, 300, 8 m. (N.S. Tune from Flanders-Barry). Flanders-Barry, 36, 8, m. (Vt.). Gardner, 160, 8 (Mich. from ms.); 1, m. (Mich.). Gray, 108, frag. (Me.). Lomax, *Our Singing Country*, 218, 8, m. (O. "Dark-Eyed Canaller"). Mackenzie, 172, 7 (N.S.). Scarborough, 267, 5 (Va.). *Bulletin* no. 6, p. 9, 9, m.; 2, m. (Me.).

Greig, cxii, 8 (Scot.). O'Lochlainn, 10, 7, m. (Ireland). Ord, 323, 9, m. (Scot.). JFSS IV, 129, 9, m. (Lincs.); five frags with add. tunes. Notes.

Broadsides: (B) Walker, Newcastle, 9 sts. (Harvard IV, 98). No imprint, 9 sts. Such, 9 sts. Ashton, *Real Sailor Songs*, 71, 9 sts. (A) Wehman, No. 406 (C). J. Andrews, 9 sts. (L of C). *Home Sentimental Songster*, N.Y., p. 160 (C).

N 36

JOHN (GEORGE) RILEY I

A sailor asks a maiden to forget about her lover, but she continues to grieve for him. He then tells her that Riley was his messmate aboard the *Belflew* and was killed by a French cannon ball in a battle between Rodney and DeGrasse. Finally he puts an end to the girl's grief by revealing that he is Riley.

> On one bright summer's morning, the weather being clear,
> I strolled for recreation down by the river fair.
> I overheard a damsel most gracious-like complain
> All for an absent lover who plowed the raging main.

Thompson, 215, 10d (N.Y.). Brewster, 215, 10d (O. via Ind.). Cox,

323, 14d (W. Va.) Refs. Eddy. 114, 14d (O.). Sharp II, 23, 7d, m. (Va.). *SFQ* III, 211, 9 (Ind.).

Greig, cxxxviii (M).

Broadsides: (A) No imprint, 12d (Boston Public Library). Songsters: (A) *The American Songster,* Phila., p. 40, 14d. *The Forget Me Not Songster,* Phila., 200, 14d. The same, N.Y., p. 150.

See Mackenzie, 182-183 for a discussion of the relationship between this ballad, his "Waterloo" and "The Mantle So Green".

N 37

JOHN (GEORGE) RILEY II
(*Young Riley*)

A sailor tries to persuade a girl to marry him, but she announces her loyalty to John Riley. He suggests sailing to Pennsylvania, but again she refuses. He then reveals himself as Riley, says he is now rich, and proposes a quick marriage.

> As I walked out one mornin' early,
> To take the cool an' pleasant air,
> There I saw a beautiful creature,
> She appeared to me like lillies fair.

Randolph I, 262, 9, m.; 6 (Mo.). Cambiaire, 95, 7 sts. Cox, 323 refs. Flanders and Brown, 135, 8, m. (Vt.). Lomax, *Our Singing Country,* 168, 9, m. (Ky.). Ritchie, 230, 7, m. (Ky.). Sharp II, 22, 6, m.; 1, m. (N.C.); frags. and tunes. Thomas, 104, 7, m. (Ky.). Wyman, 34, 7, m. (Ky.). Brown, 306, 7 (N.C.). Scarborough, 268, 7 (Ky. Same text as Thomas's).

According to Cox, this is a modified form of the "Young Riley" ballad found on broadsides by Catnach, Such, no. 83, and Fortey, no. 341 (Harvard VI, 186).

N 38

THE MANTLE SO GREEN

Meeting a girl in the meadows, a young man proposes marriage, but she tells him she is faithful to William O'Reilly, whose name is embroidered on her mantle. After telling her that O'Reilly died at Waterloo, he reveals himself as her long absent lover, and the two are married.

> When I was a-roving one morning in Spring
> To view the sweet flowers and the meadows so green
> I met a young damsel, she appeared like a queen
> With her costly fine robes and her mantle so green.

Randolph I, 371, 9d, m. (Mo.) Refs. Belden, 151, 9d (Mo.). Creighton, 60, 11d, m. (N.S.). Gardner, 157, 4 8-line d. sts., m. (Mich.). Greenleaf,

175, 8d; 8d (Nfld.). Thompson, 401, 8d (N.Y.). *NYFQ* V, 80, 7d (N.Y. from ms.).

Broadsides: (B) Such, no. 197, 11d. Cadman, 11d (Harvard V, 40). (A) DeMarsan (M). Wehman, no. 438 (M). Songsters: (A) O'Conor, 38, 11d. *617 Irish Songs,* 120, 11d. *Delaney's Irish Song Book No. 3,* p. 7.

N 39

MACDONALD'S RETURN TO GLENCOE
(*The Pride of Glencoe*)

The narrator meets a fair damsel in Glencoe and makes love to her, but she rejects him, saying she is loyal to MacDonald, the pride of Glencoe, who went to war ten years before. When he suggests that her lover may have forgotten her, she denies the possibility and says she'll remain single if she never sees him again. The speaker then produces the glove she had given him as a love token and reveals himself as MacDonald.

> As I went out walking one evening of late
> Where flowers gay mantle did the fields decorate,
> I carelessly wandered where I did not know,
> To the foot of a mounting that lies near Glencoe.

Gardner, 225, 10d (Mich. from ms.). Greenleaf, 174, 7d (Nfld.). Mackenzie, 180, 8d (N.S.) Refs. Randolph I, 435, 1d (Mo.).

Greig, lv, 11d (Scot. "Glencoe"). Ord, 65, 11d (Scot.). *JFSS* II, 171, tune only (Essex). *JFSS* V, 100, 11d, m. (Waterford).

Broadsides: (B) Gilbert, Newcastle, 11d (Harvard IV, 113). Forth (Harvard IV, 181. Dalton Pub. Library, York (Harvard III, 172). (A) DeMarsan, 11d. Wehman, no. 437 (M). Songsters: (A) O'Conor, 136, 10d. *617 Irish Songs,* 103, 11d.

N 40

THE BANKS OF CLAUDY

The narrator finds a downhearted girl seeking her lover on the banks of Claudy. At first he tells her that Johnny is false. She denies this, saying he is away at war. He then says that Johnny's ship has been wrecked on the coast of Spain. After the girl has wrung her hands and torn her hair, he reveals that he is Johnny.

> As I walked out one evening
> In the pleasant month of May,
> Down by yon flowery meadow
> So carelessly did stray,
> I overheard a damsel
> Most grievously complain,
> Saying, "On the banks of Claudy
> My darling doth remain."

Belden, 154, 8d (Mo. from ms.). Chappell, 124, 8d (N.C.). Cox, 321, 8d (W. Va.) Refs. Eddy, 157, 6d, m. (O.). Gardner, 191, 6d, m. (Mich.). Hudson, 152, 6d (Miss.). Mackenzie, 185, 7d (N.S.). Owens, 72, 7d, m. (Tex.). Pound, 73, 8d (Ind. from ms.). Randolph I, 233, 8d, m.; 3 (Mo.). Scarborough, 266, 6 (Va.) *JAF* 26, 362, Pound's text. Refs. *JAF* 35, 352, 1d, m. (O.) Refs.

Christie II, 70, 8d, m. (Scot.). Ford II, 211, 8d, m. (Scot.). Greig, xlviii, 8d (Scot.). Kidson, 89, 6d, m. (Scot. Partly from a London broadside). Ord, 130, 8d (Scot.).

Broadsides: (B) J. Gilbert, 8d (Harvard IV, 33). Livsey, 7d (Harvard II, 13). Ross (Harvard IV, 125). (A) Johnson, Phila. 7d (L of C). Partridge, Boston, 7d (L of C). Wehman, no. 414 (K). Songsters: (A) O'Conor, 38, 4 8-line d. sts. *Delaney Irish Song Book No. 1,* p. 8.

N 41

THE *LADY OF THE LAKE*
(*The Banks of Clyde*)

Concealing his identity, the narrator questions his true-love, Eliza Gray, about the cause of her weeping. She fears that her Willie Brown has died with nearly three hundred other emigrants in the shipwreck of the *Lady of the Lake* off the coast of Newfoundland. He confirms her fears, describes the wreck, and gives her Willie's final message before revealing that he is Willie.

> One evening as I chanced to stray along the banks of
>   Clyde,
> Near to the town of sweet Dundee a bonnie lass I spied.
> She sighed and sobbed and thus did say: "Oh, may I
>   rue the day
> My sailor lad left Brinnecay to cross the raging sea!"

Doerflinger, 302, 12d (N.S.). Mackenzie, 178, 7d (N.S.) Reprinted from *JAF* 25, 185.

Greig, lxxxviii, 12d (Scot.).

Broadsides: (B) Cadman, 12d (Harvard VI, 202). Bebbington, 12d (Harvard IX, 166).

N 42

PRETTY FAIR MAID
(*The Maiden in the Garden; The Broken Token*)

A girl expresses her devotion to a lover who has been at sea for seven years and refuses to marry a sailor who attempts to woo her. The sailor removes a gold ring (or half a ring) from his pocket, and she recognizes it as the token she had given him. A happy reunion follows. (Some texts mention their marriage).

A pretty fair maid all in a garden,
A young sailor boy came riding by;
He drew his rein close down beside her,
Saying "Pretty fair maid, won't you marry me?"

Belden, 150, 7, m. (Mo.); 148, 7 (Va. via Mo.); 7 (Mo.) Refs. Brown, 305, 7 (N.C.). Cambiaire, 64, 9 sts. Chappell, 122, 6 m. (N.C.). Cox, 316, 7; 9 (W. Va.) Refs. Creighton, 56, 7, m. (N.S.). Creighton and Senior, 134, 8, m.; 9; 10; 8; 10 (N.S.). Eddy, 152, 7, m. (O.). Henry, *Folk-Songs*, 201, 6 (N.C.); 8 (Tenn.); 7 (Ga.). Hudson, 150, 7 (Ky. via Miss.). Mackenzie, 168, 12; 8 (N.S.) Refs. Morris, 346, 9, m. (Ga. via Fla.); 7, m. (Fla.). Owens, 91, 6, m. (Tex.). Sandburg, 68, 7, m. Scarborough, 260, 7; 7; 3; 7 (Va.); 6 (N.C.). Randolph I, 258, 7, m.; 4½; 3, m.; 1; 6 (Mo.). Sharp II, 70, 7, m.; 7, m. (N.C.); frags. with tunes. Wyman, 88, 8, m. (Ky.). *JAF* 22, 67, 7 (Ky.) (Reprinted by Leach, 702). *JAF* 22, 379, 7, m. (Co. Tyrone via Mass "The Test of Love"). *JAF* 29, 201, 5 (Ga.). *JAF* 52, 8, 4, m. (Ky. via Wis.). *PTFLS* VI, 194, 7 (Tex. A cowboy variant). *PTFLS* X, 155, 9, m. (Tex.).

Christie I, 264, 6½d, m. (Reprinted by Leach, 701); II, 200, 4d, m. (Scot.). Greig, xxiii, 11 sts. (Scot.). O'Lochlainn, 4, 4½d, m. (Ireland). Ord, 326, 11 (Scot.). *JFSS* IV, 127, 9, m. (Hampshire); tunes from Surrey and Herts.

Broadsides: (B) Catnach, 9 sts. (Harvard III, 60). Such, 10 sts. ("Young and Single Sailor". Harvard XI, 126).

N 43
JOHNNY GERMAN

The sailor learns from the girl that she is sad because her lover has been away a long time. When he hears her lover's name, he reports that Johnny died months before. The girl takes to her bed in grief, whereupon the sailor dresses in scarlet, returns to her and reveals himself as Johnny.

Last time I was in London
I heard some certain news,
And I'll relate it unto you
If you will not refuse.
It was of a jolly sailor,
A merry hearted lad,
Who meets a country fair girl
Whose countenance was sad.

Sharp II, 256, 8d, m. (Ky.). Belden, 155, 8d (Mo.). Brown, 307, 19; 13 (N.C.). Cox, 328, 8d (W. Va.). Gardner, 155, 9d, m. (Mich.). Mackenzie, 173, 14 (N.S.). *NYFQ* V, 79, 9d (N.Y. from ms.). *PFLST* X, 156, 35 lines (Tex. "Jack the German").

Broadside: (A) Belden refers to a Boston broadside of about 1840 in the Harvard Library containing this piece and "The Lexington Miller".

BALLADS OF FAITHFUL LOVERS (O)

O 1 The Black Water Side

O 2 The Brown Girl

O 3 The Foggy Dew

O 4 The Gypsy Maid (The Gypsy's Wedding Day)

O 5 Ellen the Fair

O 6 The Lass of Glenshee

O 7 Cupid the Plowboy

O 8 The Sailor and the Shepherdess

O 9 Branded Lambs

O 10 Pretty Betsy the Milkmaid (Blackberry Fold)

O 11 Two Rigs of Rye

O 12 Robin Tamson's Smiddy

O 13 The Jolly Young Sailor and the Beautiful Queen

O 14 Pretty Polly (Moll Boy's Courtship)

O 15 The Green Mossy Banks of the Lea

O 16 King David Had a Pleasant Dream (The Slighted Soldier)

O 17 Seventeen Come Sunday

O 18 The Bonny Wee Window

O 19 Rich Amerikay

O 20 When a Man's in Love

O 21 Barney and Katie

O 22 Two Lovers Discoursing

O 23 When Will Ye Gang Awa' (Huntingtower)

O 24 The Bold Fisherman

O 25 The Lady of Carlisle

O 26 The Turkish Lady (The Turkish Rover)

O 27 Jolly Roving Tar

O 28 Black-Eyed Susan (Dark-Eyed Susan)

O 29 Erin's Flowery Vale (The Irish Girl's Lament)

O 30 Jimmy and His Own True Love

O 31 Soldier Boy

O 32 The Bold Privateer

O 33 The Girl Volunteer

O 34 Burns and His Highland Mary

O 35 A-Growing (He's Young but He's A-Growing; The Trees They Do Grow High)

O 36 Molly Bawn (Shooting of His Dear)

O 37 The Silvery Tide

O 38 Fair Fanny Moore

O 39 The Sheffield Apprentice

O 40 The Lady and the Farmer's Son

O 41 The Constant Lovers

O 1

THE BLACK WATER SIDE

The youth begs the girl to marry him, but she says she is poor and not fit to be his bride. He insists that he loves her but says he will not propose again. She gets her mother's consent and the two are married.

> On a bright summer's morning as I went a-walking
> Viewing the streams that gently did flow,
> As the bright sun arose, the hills did adorn
> Surrounding the banks of the Black Water Side . . .

Flanders and Olney, 39, 5 8-line d. sts. m. (Ireland via Vt. The first half of st. 1 is given above.)
Broadside: (B) Such no. 596, 8d.

O 2

THE BROWN GIRL

Young Delaney returns to the girl he loves and reminds her that her parents' disapproval of his low estate had caused the lovers to part. She promises to marry him, and he offers to deck her in jewels.

> When first to this country I came as a stranger
> I placed my affections on a handsome young girl,
> She being young and tender, her waist slim and slender,
> She appeared like an angel or some gypsy queen.

Creighton and Senior, 139, 6d, m.; 6d, m. (N.S.). Dean, 75, 5d (Minn.).
Broadsides: (B) Bebbington, 5d ("Bonny Brown Girl", Harvard X, 168). Hodges, 5d.

O 3

THE FOGGY DEW
(*The Bugaboo*)

The narrator takes the pretty maid to bed with him to keep her from the foggy dew (or the bugaboo). The next morning they part. She has a son later in the year. In some texts he marries her and makes her a virtuous wife.

> When I was young and in my prime
> I followed the ramblin' trade,
> And the only wrong I ever done
> Was I courted a fair young maid.

227

> I courted her one summer long
> And part of the winter too,
> I often rolled her in my arms,
> For the love of foggy dew.

Randolph I, 394, 9, m.; 1 (Mo.). Combs, 214, 10 (Ky.). Henry, *Folk-Songs*, 182, 7 (Tenn.). Morris, 160, 8, m. (Fla.). Sandburg, 460, 2d, m. Sharp II, 174, 7, m. (Va.). Thompson, 421, 8 (N.Y.).

Kidson, 167, 1d (Yorks.). Sharp and Marson I, 34, 3d (Somerset). *JFSS* I, 134, 1d, m. (Sussex); tune only (Hants.).

Broadside: (B) Such, 5d (Harvard XI, 40).

O 4

THE GYPSY MAID
(*The Gypsy's Wedding Day*)

The Gypsy maid meets a handsome young lawyer who asks her to tell his fortune. She reads his palm and tell him that, although he has courted many fair ladies, a gypsy maid will be his bride. He takes her to his mansion and marries her.

> My father was a chieftain
> Of a Gypsy tribe you know,
> My mother died and left me
> Some counting for to do.

> With my knapsack on my shoulder
> I bid them all farewell,
> I took me a trip to London
> Some fortunes for to tell.

Randolph I, 437, 8, m. (Mo.). Cox, 335, 5d (W. Va.) Refs. Eddy, 224, 3d and ref., m. (O. "The Gypsy's Wedding Day").

Roxburghe Ballads, VIII, 853, 4d (Lincs. A racier traditional text than the others.) *JFSS* I, 231, 1, m. *JFSS* III, 220, 4d, m. (Lincs.).

Broadsides: (B) Such, no. 238, 7d (Harvard XII, 84). Jackson and Son, Birmingham (ref. from *JFSS* III). Songsters: (A) *American Star Songster*, N.Y., 1851, p. 45 (Randolph).

O 5

ELLEN THE FAIR
(*Helen the Fair*)

The wealthy narrator, a nobleman's son, gazes enraptured upon the flower seller, decides to marry her, and eventually does so. The ladies at court are envious of her beauty.

Fair Ellen one morn from her cottage had strayed;
To the next market town tripped the beautiful maid.
She looked like a goddess, so charming and fair.
"Come buy my sweet posies!" cried Ellen the Fair.

Mackenzie, 122, 6d (N.S.) Refs.
Broadsides: (B) Cadman, 6d (Harvard V, 4). Kendrew, 6d (Harvard III, 89). Dodds, 6d (Harvard III, 129). Deming, Boston, 6d (L of C). Songsters: (A) *The Forget Me Not Songster,* Phila., 24, 6d. The same, N.Y., 141, 6d.

O 6

THE LASS OF GLENSHEE

The narrator makes love to the Scottish shepherdess and offers to make her his lady and provide her with a carriage and servants. She replies that she is content with her crook and her herd but consents to go with him. Marriage and years of happiness follow,

It was on a day when the heather was bloomin',
The hieland hills hummed wi' the sair laden bee.
I met a fair maid as hame I was ridin';
Was herdin' her sheep on the hills of Glenshee.

Gardner, 202, 7d (Mich.). Flanders and Brown, 131, 21d lines (Vt.). Ford I, 12, 12d (Scot.). Ord, 75, 12d (Scot.). *JFSS* V, 106, 1d, m. (Aberdeenshire); add. tune.
Broadsides: (B) No imprint, 11d (Harvard IV, 114). Harkness, 12d. George Walker, 12d (Harvard II, 72).
"I do not know a more popular song than this. It has been sung in nearly every farmhouse, cottage, and bothy in Scotland for the past seventy or eighty years. The author of it was a shoemaker named Andrew Sharpe, a native of Perth, who died there on 5th February, 1817." (Note from Ord).

O 7

CUPID THE PLOUGHBOY

The lady falls in love with the ploughboy who is breaking up clods. She refers to him as Cupid, and fancifully imagines that his farming tools are arrows. He offers to be a true husband, and the two are married.

As I roved out one May morning,
The Mays were all in bloom;
I roved into some sweet flowery field
To taste the sweet perfume.
I roved in to some meadows
To turn my eyes awhile;
There I saw Cupid the plowboy,
Who did my heart beguile.

Greenleaf, 162, 5d (Nfld.). Randolph I, 344, 5d, m, (Ark.) Refs.

Baring-Gould, 158, 4d, m. (W. of Eng.). Barrett, *Eng. Folk-Songs,* 29, 6d, m. (Eng.). *JFSS* III, 109, 5d, m. (Dorset). *JFSS* IV, 336, 2 tunes (Yorks.); 1d, m. (Horsham).

Broadsides: (B) Catnach, 6d (Harvard V, 216). Forth, 6d (Harvard III, 191).

O 8
THE SAILOR AND THE SHEPHERDESS

Seeing a shepherdess asleep on the grass, the sailor kisses her. Startled, she begins to cry, but he offers her his love and his fortune, and the two are married.

> It's of a bonny shepherdess
> A watching of a flock,
> Down by the seaside all alone;
> Chance there came that way
> Was a bright young sailor gay,
> And he fain would make her his bride.

Mackenzie, 148, 7 6-line sts (N.S.) Refs.

Broadsides: (B) No imprint, 7d. Harkness, 7d. Forth (M). Catnach (M).

O 9
BRANDED LAMBS

A girl asks Johnny if he has seen her branded lambs, and he tells her that they are down in a distant meadow. She goes to seek them and Johnny follows her. Her flock is not there but Johnny makes love to her—"and the lambs they were sporting all in the morning dew". A wedding follows, with the lovers planning to combine their flocks.

> As Johnny rode out one fair summer's morn
> He being quite wearied threw himself underneath a thorn,
> He had not been long there when a damsel did pass by
> And on this lovelie Johnny she cast a longing eye.

Creighton and Senior, 133, 6d, m. (N.S.).

Joyce, 180, 4d, m. (Ireland. An incomplete text).

O 10
PRETTY BETSY THE MILKMAID
(*Blackberry Fold*)

The squire offers to marry the milkmaid, but she asks him not to make fun of her poverty. He breaks a ring and gives her half as a token of sincerity. Later when they are walking in the blackberry fold, he attempts to seduce and then to rape her, but she wounds him with her scissors. When he recovers, the two are married. Six years later the squire dies, leaving her with two babies. She concludes that it pays to be honest.

> The squire and his sister were a-sitting in the hall,
> A-singing together they heard someone call.
> As they were a-singing their morning song,
> Pretty Betsy the milkmaid came trippling along.

Moeran, 8, 5d, m. (Suffolk. "Blackberry Fold." An abbreviated version which omits the central part of the story).

Neely and Spargo, 153, 11d (Ill.).

JFSS VI, 35, 11d, m. (Sussex. "Squire and Milkmaid or Blackberry Fold".) ; 269, 1d, m. from Moeran's text.

Broadside: (B) Such, 10d (Harvard XII, 116.)

O 11

TWO RIGS OF RYE

The girl tells her lover that her family is opposed to their marriage but she is true to him. At first he seems unwilling to accept her without a dowry, but when she appears sad he says he was just teasing her. He assures her that they will never be parted.

> 'Twas on a morning in sweet July,
> Just as the sun had reach'd the sky;
> It was between two rigs of rye
> I heard two lovers talking.
> Said he, "Why such a cheerful lass
> Should seem to be in heaviness—
> I wonder what can be amiss."
> Then off from her he wandered.

Christie II, 224, 5d, m. (Eng. "The Rigs o' Rye").

Gardner, 163, frag. of 4 sts., m. (Scot. via Mich.). *Bulletin* no. 1, 8, 7, m. (Me.).

Ord, 31, 9 (Aberdeen).

O 12

ROBIN TAMSON'S SMIDDY

While having the mare shod at Robin's smithy, the narrator woos the smith's "bonnie dochter". At first the girl objects to his old breeches, but he argues that she can care for them if she will elope with him and become his wife.

> Ah, me mither ment me auld breeks,
> An' ae, but they were diddy-o.
> She sent me to git shod the mare,
> At Robin Tamson's smiddy-o.
> The smiddy stands ayont the burn,
> As it gangs through the clachan-o;
> I never yet gae by the door,
> But aye I fa' a-laughin'-o.

Gardner, 182, 6d and chor., m. (Scot. via Mich.). Broadwood, *Eng. County Songs,* 4, 6d (Can. via Northumberland).

Ford I, 194, 6d, m. (Scot.). Logan, 366, 6d; notes. Greig, cxxxix, 6d (Scot.). Kidson, 8, 6d, m.

Broadsides: (B) No imprint, 6d and chor. (Harvard VI, 191). Livsey, 6d (Harvard II, 101). In chapbook by E. Johnstone, Stirling, (Item 1309 in the Harvard Catalogue).

This ballad was written by the Scottish poet Alexander Rodgers (1784-1846) and was published in the third series of *Whistle-Binkie,* 1842, under the title "My Auld Breeks, air the Corn Clips". (Note condensed from Greig and from Kidson).

O 13

THE JOLLY YOUNG SAILOR AND THE BEAUTIFUL QUEEN

Smitten by his charms, a rich girl asks a sailor many questions and then says that he should stay ashore and perhaps find a rich girl to marry. At first reluctant to give up rambling, he changes his mind when she offers him her hand and her wealth.

> As I was a-walking in the sweet month of May
> A jovial young sailor by chance passed that way,
> He was stalwart and handsome as he passed by,
> I beckoned unto him and bade him draw nigh.

Creighton and Senior, 180, 7d, m.; 6d, m.; 7d; 6d, m.; 6d (N.S.). Creighton, 76, 7d, m. (N.S. "It is of a Rich Lady"). Doerflinger, 298, 9d (N.S. Tune from Creighton) Refs.

JEFDSS VI, 90, 7d, m. (N.S. Creighton and Senior's A text above).

O 14

PRETTY POLLY
(*Moll Boy's Courtship*)

The girl refuses her suitor's proffered gifts and love because he is already married. He offers to kill his wife, but she begs him not to do so. Instead she will wait for him for seven years. Just before the time expires, the suitor's wife conveniently dies and the two lovers marry.

"Good morning, pretty Polly, we have met in good time,
A question for to ask you which I hope is no crime;
Come, sit you down beside me, and married we will be,
And learn how to love me, my charming Polly.

Eddy, 159, 11d (O.). Gardner, 185, 8d (Mich. from ms. "The Charming
Moll Boy"). Morris, 340, 4d (Fla. "Charming Nancy").
Johnson, *Pop. Brit. Ballads* II, 215, reprints "Sir Arthur and Charming
Mollee", 8d sts., from Bell's *Ancient Poems, Ballads, and Songs. JFSS* VIII,
177, 7½d, m. (Dorset. "Noble Lord Hawkins").
Broadsides: (B) Logan, 348, 9½d ("Moll Boy's Courtship". Source not
indicated.) Logan refers to a copy of this ballad called "Honest Mall Boye"
in *The Dairy Maid; a Vocal Miscellany*, Edinburgh, 1784. In a chapbook
without imprint in the Boswell Coll.: "Honest Mall Boye". This is item
1976 in the Harvard Catalogue.

O 15

THE GREEN MOSSY BANKS OF THE LEA

The young man immediately falls in love with a girl he meets by chance.
When her father appears, the youth says he has a large fortune and offers
to marry her. The couple are happily united, and the American lives with
his bride on the banks of the Lea.

When first from my country, a stranger, curiosity caused me to roam,
Over Europe I resolved to be a stranger, when I left Philadelphia my home.
I quickly sailed over to Ireland, where forms of great beauty doth shine.
It was there I beheld a fair damsel, and I wished in my heart she was mine.

Mackenzie, 135, 6d (N.S.) Refs. Creighton, 167, 6d, m. (N.S.). Gardner,
190, 6 (Mich.). *JAF* 22, 81, tune only.
JFSS II, 150, 12, m. (Essex. Text partly from a Such broadside). *JFSS*
IV, 91, 1d, m. (Norfolk). *JFSS* VII, 24, tune only (Norfolk). Sharp and
Marson III, 34, 4d, m. (Somerset).
Broadsides: (B) No imprint, 12 sts. Catnach, 12 (Harvard V, 168).
Ross, 6d (Harvard IV, 20). (A) Wehman, no. 924 (M). *Delaney's Irish
Song Book No.* 5, p. 24, 6d. *Wehman's Irish Song Book No.* 1, p. 9 (M).

O 16

KING DAVID HAD A PLEASANT DREAM

The soldier overcomes the girl's prejudices against men of his profession
by telling the story of David, who started as a shepherd but slew Goliath
and became both king and soldier. His girl decides to kiss him despite her
mother's warnings.

A soldier and a comely maid, as they walked forth one day,
Many a handsome compliment he unto her did say:
"And shall I kiss your ruby lips? 'Twould make me somewhat bolder."
But "O no, sir; my mamma says I must not kiss a soldier."

Belden, 170, 6d (Ark.). Sharp II, 247, 5d, m. (Tenn. "The Slighted Soldier").

O 17
SEVENTEEN COME SUNDAY

The youth questions the pretty girl, who says she is running an errand for her mother. He asks her age and she replies "seventeen come Sunday". She agrees to let him visit her that night. In some versions her mother does not hear him arrive; in others she does and gives the girl a beating.

> As I walked out one morning in May
> Just as the day was dawning,
> There I spied a pretty little Miss
> So early in the morning.

Sharp II, 156, 7, m.; 3, m.; 5, m.; 1, m. (Va.). Cox, 394, 4 (W. Va.) Refs. Creighton & Senior, 164, 6 and ref., m.; fragments (N.S.). Eddy, 188, 7 and ref. (O.); 8 (O. from ms.).
Sharp, One Hundred, 138, 6 and ref., m. Sharp and Marson II, 4, 7 and ref., m. (Som.). JFSS I, 92, 6, m. (Sussex). JFSS II, 9, 8, m.; 1 and ref., m. (Som.); II, 269, 2 frags. and 3 tunes (Yorks.). JFSS IV, 291, 1, m. (Sussex); 2, m. (Scot.).
Broadsides: (B) No imprint, 9 sts. (Harvard V, 21). Such, no. 249. Bebbington (reprinted with 2 sts. deleted in JFSS II, 270).

O 18
THE BONNY WEE WINDOW

One evening Johnny is visiting Nellie through the window. When he kisses her goodnight, his head sticks in the empty frame. Hearing the sound of his cursing and the girl's laughter, her grandmother rushes out and beats Johnny with a poker. Finally he escapes with the frame around his neck.

> There was a brave lass and her name was Nell,
> Who lived in the house where her granny did dwell,
> The house being small, the windows were less,
> They had but four panes and one needed a glass.

Randolph I, 431, 7d and chor. (Mo.).
Ford I, 20, 11d (Scot.). Greig cxxiii, 11d (Scot.). Ord, 99, 11d and chor. (a Scottish text in dialect).
Broadside: (B) No imprint, 11d and chorus ("Kissing at the Window").

O 19

RICH AMERIKAY

A rich lady is saying goodbye to a farmer's son, who is leaving Ireland for America. She begs him not to go to the savage shore, but he says that Ireland is now a land of poverty. Finally her love overcomes her fear and she consents to go with him.

Ye roving blades of Ireland
Who guards the ancient plain,
Ye gentle and you muses
That do resort the plains,
I roved for recreation
On charming Uras Quay,
When as this pier in steamers bright
Bound for Amerikay.

Greenleaf, 195, 8d, m. (Nfld.) A confused text.

O 20

WHEN A MAN'S IN LOVE

The lover asks to be admitted to the girl's chamber, but she persuades him instead to sit by the fireside. He tells her that he has courted her long against her parents' will and now he is leaving for America. She suggests that they marry, and the wedding takes place.

When a man's in love sure he feels no cold
Like I not long ago,
Like a hero bold for to seek my love
I set out through frost and snow,
The moon had gently shone her light
O'er the dark and lonesome way,
When I arrived at her sweet cot
Where all my treasure lay.

Creighton and Senior, 214, 6d, m. (N.S.).

O 21

BARNEY AND KATIE

Barney calls on Katie and asks to be taken in out of the cold. Katie replies that no one else is at home and that he should consider her reputation. He returns home cheered by the thought of his love's virtue.

'Twas a cold winter's night and the tempest was snarly,
The snow like a sheet covered cabin and sty;
Barney went over the hills to his darling,
And rapped at the window where Katie did lie.

Eddy, 309, 6d, m. (Co. Limerick via O.). Flanders and Olney, 222, 6d, m. (Conn.).

Cf. "Barney Brallaghan's Courtship", Moffat, 292, 6d, m.

O 22

TWO LOVERS DISCOURSING

Mary reminds the young man of his promise to marry her and accuses him of courting Nancy. He insists that he is devoted to her but seems reluctant to marry. When she complains that the small birds are kinder to each other than he is to her, she wins him over and the two are married.

> As I rode out one evening down by a river side,
> I heard two lovers talking, and the fair one she replied:
> "You're the most onconstant young man that ever I did know.
> You promised for to marry me, why did you not do so?"

Doerflinger, 316, 7d, m. (N.B.).

O 23

WHEN WILL YE GANG AWA'?
(Huntingtower)

In this dialogue Jamie promises to bring Janie first a new gown and then a gallant gay, but she wants only Jamie. He teasingly says he has a wife and three bairns, but when she appears upset he promises to marry her.

> When will ye gang awa' Jamie,
> Far across the sea laddie,
> When will ye gang to Germanie,
> What will ye bring to me laddie.

Creighton and Senior, 217, 9, m. (N.S.) Notes.

Kinloch, *Ancient Scottish Ballads*, 170, 15 ("Was taken down from the recitation of an Idiot boy in Wishaw". "The Duke of Athol").

Broadside: (B) No imprint, no. 636, 12 sts.

Child (IV, 299) quotes Aytoun's statement that "Richie Story" (Child, no. 232) was recomposed in a romantic form under the title "Huntingtower", was widely printed, and passed into tradition. "When Will Ye Gang Awa'?" is a traditional version of "Huntingtower", as in Kinloch's "The Duke of Athol", which Child reprints. Child refers to various printings of "Huntingtower".

O 24

THE BOLD FISHERMAN

The fisherman tells the lady that he has come for her sake. He pulls his boat on shore and takes her by the hand. When he takes off his cloak, she sees three gold chains hanging from his neck and falls to her knees, begging his pardon for mistaking him for a fisherman. He says he is not offended, takes her to his father's house, and marries her.

> As I rode out on May morning
> Down by a river side
> There I espied a young fisherman,
> A fishing on the tide . . .

Creighton and Senior, 113, 8, m.; 2 (N.S.) Notes. Flanders and Olney, 218, 6, m. (Me.).

Broadwood, 110, 6, m. (Herts.). Sharp, *One Hundred*, 96, 6, m. Sharp and Marson III, 42, 9, m. (Somerset. A composite text). *JFSS* I, 138, 5½, m. (Sussex). *JFSS* V, 132, 8, m. (Herts.) (Reprinted by Leach, 692); Detailed notes. *JFSS* VII, 21, 7d couplets, m. (Norfolk). *JFSS* VII, 36, 7d couplets; 2d couplets, m. (Dorset). Notes.

Broadsides: (B) Catnach, 3d (Harvard VII, 34). Such, no. 455, 3½d (Harvard XIII, 147).

This ballad is discussed in detail by Lucy E. Broadwood in *JFSS* V, 133-135 and *JFSS* VII, 37-40. Miss Broadwood believes that it is an ancient bit of religious symbolism. "To students of Gnostic and Early Christian mystical literature," she writes, (p. 133), "The River, the Sea, the royal Fisher, the Three Vestures of Light (or Robes of Glory), the Recognition and Adoration by the illuminated humble Soul, the free Pardon, the mystical Union of the Bride to the Bridegroom in the House of the Father (or Father-House), are familiar elements, and we can find them all, certainly, amongst the variants of this ballad."

O 25

THE LADY OF CARLISLE

The lady decides to choose between the two brothers who love her by determining which is the braver. She tosses her fan into a lions' den and asks the brothers to retrieve it. After the lieutenant's refusal, the sea captain recovers the fan and gains a bride. His brother looks forward to nothing but loneliness and death.

> Down in Carlisle there lived a lady,
> She was both beautiful and gay,
> She was determined to live a lady
> That none on earth could her betray.

Sharp I, 396, 12, m.; frags. with tunes (Ky.). Brewster, 279, 12 (Ind.).
Brown, 296, 9; 15 (N.C.). Creighton, 87, 5d, m. (N.S.). Flanders-Barry,
67, 12, m. (Vt.) Notes. Flanders, *A Garland,* 54, 12, m. (Vt.). Flanders
and Olney, 207, 10, m. (Conn.). Hudson, 140, 11 (Miss.). Lomax, *Our
Singing Country,* 162, 11, m. (Ky.). Mackenzie, 82, 11 (N.S.) Refs. *JAF*
49, 227, 11, m. (Ky.). *JAF* 51, 41, 14 (O. from ms.).

Christie II, 126, 7d, m. Ord, 393, 7d (Scot.). *JFSS* V, 114, tune only.
JFSS V, 258, 11, m.

Broadsides (B): "The oldest version (*Percy Broadsides,* I, 69, Harvard
Univ. Library) bears the title 'The Distressed Lady, or A Trial of True
Love. In Five Parts.' It is a long-winded piece— the five acts of a romantic
drama." (Note from Flanders-Barry). Chapbook no. xxi in Bell Coll, by
J. Morren, Edinburgh, 19 sts. ("The Bostonshire Lady"). Catnach, 64
lines ("The Faithful Lover; or The Hero Rewarded", L of C). Rewritten
version, "The Bold Lieutenant": Ashton, *Real Sailor Songs,* 54, 7d and
Hodges, 7d.

See Shearin and Kittredge, "The Ballad of *The Den of Lions*", *MLN*
26, 113 and 167, with a text from Ky. of 12 sts.

O 26

THE TURKISH LADY

A merchant ship from Bristol is captured by a Turkish rover and all its
men are made slaves. The narrator is cruelly treated, along with the others,
until the lady who owns him offers to relieve his misery if he will become
a Turk and marry her. He refuses, saying that he would rather die at the
stake than forsake his God. After brief indecision she turns Christian and
marries the slave.

> Young virgins all I pray draw near,
> A pretty story you shall hear.
> 'Tis of a Turkish lady brave,
> Who fell in love with an English slave.

Mackenzie, 67, 12; 11 (N.S.). Creighton, 26, 12, m. (N.S.). Creighton
and Senior, 123, 8, m. (N.S.).

Christie I, 246, 6d, m. (Scot.). *JFSS* I, 113, 2, m. (Sussex).

Broadsides: (B) Swindells, 10 sts ("Turkish Rover"). Elias Keys, 6d.
Logan, 16, 14 sts. Extended notes and comments. Songster: (A) *The Forget Me Not Songster,* N.Y., 169, 12 sts. Reprinted in *JAF* 23, 450.

Child mentions this ballad in his discussion of "Young Beichan" (no. 53),
I, 463.

O 27

JOLLY ROVING TAR

Susan remembers the happy evenings she has spent with her love and decides to see that her father's ships are well stocked for him and his mates. She bids farewell to the maids of London and announces that she will cross the ocean for her jolly roving tar.

It was in the city of London town, was there by the highway.
I espied a lovely damsel fair and she alone did stray,
She did appear like a Venus or some bright lovely star
As she strayed the beach lamenting for her jolly roving tar.

Creighton and Senior, 178, 4d, m. (N.S.).
Broadsides: (B) Pitts, 6d. W. R. Walker, 4d (Harvard IV, 74). Ryle, 6d (Harvard VII, 94.).

O 28

BLACK-EYED SUSAN
(Dark-Eyed Susan)

Susan comes on board a ship seeking William. Hearing her voice, he slides down a rope to the deck, kisses away her tears, and promises to be faithful to her wherever he goes. The ship prepares to leave, and Susan waves a sad farewell from her boat.

All in the downs the fleet lay moored
The streamers waving in the wind,
When dark-eyed Susan came on board,
Oh where may I my true love find,
Oh tell me my dark-eyed sailor bold
Does my sweet William,
Does my Sweet William sail among your crew.

Creighton and Senior, 132, 5, m.; 6, m. (N.S.). (The ballad is usually printed in six-line stanzas).
Broadsides: (B) No imprint (Harvard II, 8). Gilbert, 8 sts. (Harvard IV, 75). (A) No imprint, 7 sts. (Thomas Coll. I, 113. "Sweet William's Departure". The second column contains a continuation in 7 sts. called "Susan's Lamentation"). DeMarsan, 7 sts. Harris, Phila., 8 sts. (L of C). Songster: (A) *The American Songster*, Phila. 1836, 207, 8 sts.
" 'Black-Ey'd Susan, or Sweet William's Farewell' was written by Gay, the author of the 'Beggar's Opera', and is included among his published poems. The music was composed by Richard Leveridge, a genial, jovial individual, who published a collection of his songs in 1727. 'Black-Ey'd Susan' was not issued till 1730." (Note from S. J. Adair Fitzgerald, *Stories of Famous Songs*, Phila., and London, J. B. Lippincott, 1906, II, 19).

O 29

ERIN'S FLOWERY VALE
(*The Irish Girl's Lament*)

The narrator hears two young lovers talking. The youth is about to sail for America, and the girl is afraid he will forget her. He promises to be faithful, and the two bid each other a tearful farewell.

> One evening fair when Venus bright her radiant beams displayed,
> And Flora in her verdant gale those fragrant hills arrayed,
> As I did rove throughout each grove, no cares did me assail,
> 'Til a pair I spied by a river side, on Erin's flowery vale.

Doerflinger, 318, 8d, m. (N.B.).

O 30

JIMMY AND HIS OWN TRUE LOVE

Annie bids Jimmy a tearful farewell as he leaves for a voyage to the West Indies and gives him diamond rings as a token of devotion. He promises to remain faithful and to return to her.

> As Jimmy and his own true love went walking out one day
> To view the hills and the valleys, for they were young and gay,
> It was in the spring when the birds did sing, and the larks sang
>   loud on high,
> It was so sweet and charming to hear their melody.

Mackenzie,128, 6d (N.S.) Refs.
Broadsides: (B) (Mackenzie's refs.) J. Jennings (Harvard 25242.4, II, 63). 60 Old Street. Pitts (Harvard 25242.4, II, 62).

O 31

SOLDIER BOY

The departing soldier explains to Sally that he must go to India to fight along with a thousand other Irish boys. She bids him a tearful goodbye and wishes him well.

> As I roved out one evening in the springtime of the year,
> Through flowering fields and sweet latels my course I did steer;
> There I see all the young soldiers and a pretty maid,
> Sat gazing on each other's company in the shade.

Greenleaf, 164, 5½d (Nfld.).

O 32

THE BOLD PRIVATEER

Molly begs Johnny to stay at home with her instead of risking his life at sea. He replies that her friends dislike him and her brothers would take his life. He offers to exchange rings with her and, if his life is spared in' the war, to return and marry her.

O my dearest Molly,
It's you and I must part;
I'm going across the sea, my love,
I leave you with my heart.

The ship now is waiting,
So fare you well, my dear;
I'm going on board the vessel,
A bold privateer.

Sharp II, 175, 8, m. (Va.). Eddy, 196, 6 (O.). *SFQ* III, 4d (Ind. from ms.).

Kidson, 101, 5d, m. (Yorks.).

Broadsides: (B) Catnach, 4d (Harvard VII, 178). Pitts, 4d, Bebbington, no. 185 (Harvard IX, 179) (K). (A) Wm. K. Wood, Boston, 4d. Harris, Phila., 4d (L of C). J. Andrews (K). Songsters: (A) Kittredge in *JAF* 35, 357-358 gives references to various American songsters including *The Ethiopian Serenader's Own Book*, p. 23 and *The American Dime Song Book*, Phila., 1860, p. 20.

O 33

THE GIRL VOLUNTEER

The girl pleads with her lover to go with him to war. At first he says no, adding that her rosy cheeks would fade away on guard duty in winter. She says that she'll offer his captain bright guineas to release him. In some texts Johnny finally says she may go.

The war is a-raging;
Poor Johnny he must fight.
For I want to be with him
From morning till night.

Brown, 317, 7; 2d; 2d (N.C.). Belden, 180, 6d couplets (Mo.). Fuson, 104, 4d (Ky.).

O 34

BURNS AND HIS HIGHLAND MARY

Burns meets Mary by the banks of the Ayr. The lovers swear to be true to each other, and Mary promises not to stay long in the Highlands. They part in sadness and Mary goes away only to die and be buried "in Greenoch Kirkyard on the banks of the Clyde".

> In green Caledonia, there ne'er were two lovers
> So fairly enraptured in each other's arms,
> As Burns, the sweet bard, and his own Highland Mary
> How fondly and sweetly he sang of her charms.

Creighton and Senior, 159, 14d (N.S.). Doerflinger, 312, 13d, m. (N.B. Tune from Me.) Notes.

Christie I, 62, 5 8-line d. sts., m. (from a broadside with the first eight lines omitted). Ford I, 124, 7 8-line d, m. (Scot.). Greig, lxxvi, 13d (Scot.). Ord, 354, 14d, m. (Scot.).

Broadsides: (B) No imprint, 7 8-line d. Walker, Durham, 7 8-line d. Bebbington, 7 8-line d (Harvard X, 185).

" 'Burns and His Highland Mary' has long enjoyed the highest popularity over broad Scotland among rural singers, while the poet's own songs about Mary are seldom heard except among those who pretend to some musical culture and skill." (Note from Greig). "Mr. Walter Towers . . . informs me that the song was written about sixty years ago by a West of Scotland police constable named Thomson, who subsequently emigrated to Canada." (Note from Ord).

O 35

A-GROWING
(He's Young But He's Daily A-Growing)

The girl complains to her father that he has married her to too young a boy, but he reminds her that the boy is daily growing. She says that she will make him a fine shirt with ribbons so that the girls will know he is married. She watches her husband playing ball with other school boys and considers him the fairest of them all. Soon after she bears his son, the youth dies and she sadly buries him.

> The trees are growing high and the leaves are growing green,
> And many's the happy days that I have seen,
> It's lying alone of a cold winter's night,
> He's young but he's daily a-growing.

Creighton and Senior, 108, 7d, m.; 5 add. lines; 4d (N.S.). Flanders and Olney, 196, 6d, m. (Conn.). Sharp I, 410, 4d, m. (Ky.) Refs. Sturgis, 3, 7d, m. (Vt.) Notes.

Christie II, 212, 3d, m. (Scot. "Young Craigston"). Ord, 112, 7d (Scot.). Sharp and Marson I, 30, 6d, m. (Somerset). Johnson, *Pop. Brit. Ballads* II, 225, 12d ("The Trees they are so High"). Note, p. xix: "The following version of this ballad is the complete original from which Mr. Baring-Gould composed that in *Songs of the West.*" Baring-Gould, 8, 8d, m. (W. of Eng.) Notes, p. xiv. *JFSS* I, 214, 6d, m. (Surrey). *JFSS* II, 44, 6d, m.; 6d. m. (Som.); II, 95, 1d, m. (Devon); 1d, m. (Som.); II, 206, 1d, m. (Essex); II, 274, 1d, m. (Yorks.); add. tune, (Dorset). *JFSS* V, 190, 7d, m. (Herts.); add. tunes (Lancs.).

Broadsides: (B) Disley, 7d (Harvard XIV, 42). Such, 7d (Harvard XI, 63.) Such's broadside is reprinted in *JFSS* II, 275. (A) Sturgis reports that this ballad was printed about 1880 by Wehman.

Note: This ballad was rewritten by Robert Burns as "Lady Mary Ann". For a text, see Johnson, *Pop. Brit. Ballads* III, 42, 5d sts.

O 36

MOLLY BAWN

(*Shooting of his Dear*)

Jimmy goes hunting at dusk and mistakenly shoots his true-love Molly, who has taken refuge from a shower in a grove. The youth fears that he will be hanged, but the girl's father promises to aid him. At the trial Molly's ghost appears and asks that Jimmy be freed, explaining that he had mistaken her white apron for a swan.

In the county of Derry where I was bred and born,
And ev'ryone called me a roving young man . . .

Lovely Molly went walking, there came a shower of hail;
She went under a green bower, herself to conceal.

Her true-love being a-fowling, he shot in the dark,
But oh and alas, he did not miss his mark.

Gardner, 66, 18d couplets, m. (Mich.) Couplets 1, 3, and 4 are given above; 10d couplets (Mich. from ms.). Brown, 263, 6; frag. (N.C.). Chappell, 101, 2 (N.C.). Cox, 339, 6d (Ohio via W. Va.); 5d; 4d; tune, p. 529 (W. Va.). Eddy, 194, 13d couplets (O.). Hudson, 145, 9d couplets (Miss.); 13 lines (Ky. via Miss.). Korson, *Penna. Songs,* 46, 15d couplets, m. (Pa. "Molly Banding"). Linscott, 274, 5d, m. (Mass. "Polly Van"). Morris, 398, 5d, m. (Fla.); 5d (Ga. via Fla.); 6d (Fla.). Pound, 78, 13d couplets (Ky.). Randolph I, 254, 6½d, m.; 2½ (Mo.); 1 (Mo. from ms.); 1½ (Mo.); 1; 3 6-line sts. (Ark.). Scarborough, 116, 4½d (Va.). Sharp I, 328, 7½, m. (N.C.); 1, m. (Tenn.); 5½, m. (Ky.); 8, m. (Va.); 1d, m.; 1d, m. (Ky.). *Bulletin* no. 10, 12, 1d, m.; 9d lines (Me.) Notes. *JAF* 22, 387,

4d (Me.). *JAF* 30, 359, 5½d (Mass.); 19d lines (Ky.). *JAF* 52, 32, 1d, m. (Ky. via Wis.); *JAF* 52, 56, 7d couplets; 7d couplets, m.; add. tune and frag. (N.J.).

JFSS II, 59, 5d, m. (Somerset); 2, m. (Kent.). *JFSS* VII, 17, 4d, m. (Norfolk) Notes. *JIFSS* III, 25, 5d couplets (Ireland). Joyce, 220, 5d, m. (Ireland).

Broadsides: (B) Pitts. Jennings, 6½d ("Molly Whan").

O 37

THE SILVERY TIDE

During Henry's absence a nobleman courts Molly, but she remains loyal to her lover. The nobleman threatens to drown her if she will not marry him. When she remains adamant, he binds her with a handkerchief and throws her into the ocean. Henry returns from sea and hears from her parents that Molly has committed suicide. He dreams that she is walking by the ocean, goes to the shore, and finds her floating corpse. He recognizes the ring on her hand and finds the murderer's handkerchief with his name on it. The nobleman is hanged, and Henry mourns until his death.

> It's of a fair young creature
> Who lived by the sea side,
> Whose pretty form and feature
> Was called the village pride.
> Young Henry a sea captain
> Whose heart Molly did gain,
> Which proved true to young Henry
> Who's on the silv'ry tide.

Randolph I, 368, 9d, m. (Tenn. via Mo.) Refs. Belden, 126, 15 (Mo. from ms.). Creighton and Senior, 207, 8d, m.; 10d, m. (N.S.). Doerflinger, 282, 10d (N.S. from ms.). Eddy, 166, 5d, m. (O.). Gardner, 73, 10d (Mich.). Mackenzie, 147, 5d (N.S.) Refs.

Ord, 472, 10d (Scot.). Sharp and Marson, V, 24, 10d, m. (Somerset. A composite text). *JFSS* I, 216, 10d, m. (Sussex).

Broadsides: (B) W. R. Walker, 10d ("Poor Mary of the Silvery Tide". Harvard IV, 74). Catnach (Harvard VII, 57). Such no. 303, 10d (Harvard XII, 148) (M).

O 38

FAIR FANNY MOORE

Fanny is loved by two men, Randolph, who is rich and haughty, and Henry, a farmer of low degree. She chooses the latter and marries him. One day when her husband is absent, Randolph comes to her cottage and demands either her love or her life. When she refuses to yield, he stabs her to death. He is hanged for his crime, and Henry, distracted with grief, wanders until he dies and is buried beside his bride.

> Go down to yonder cottage all dark and alone,
> The walks once were gravel, but now are o'ergrown.
> Go there and you will find one dark spot on the floor,
> Alas! 'tis the blood of the fair Fanny Moore.

Randolph II, 68, 9d (Ark. from ms.) ; 65, 14, m. (Mo.) ; 9d, m. (Ark.) Refs. Belden, 139, 9d; 8d (Mo.). Brown, 264, 8d (N.C.). Cox, 441, 7d (Ky. from ms.). Dean, 85, 7½d (Minn.). Flanders and Brown, 58, 8d (Vt.). Flanders-Barry, 233, 8d, m. (Vt.). Morris, 130, 9d (Fla.). Owens, 74, 7d, m. (Tex.). Pound, 206, 9d (Mont.). Shoemaker, 71, 9d (Pa.).

O 39

THE SHEFFIELD APPRENTICE

The apprentice runs away from his master in London and goes to Holland as servant to a lady who later proposes marriage. He refuses her, saying that he is engaged to Polly, her chambermaid. His indignant mistress slips a gold ring into his pocket and has him arrested and condemned to death as a thief. About to be hanged he bids a sad farewell to Polly.

> I was brought up in Sheffield not of low degree,
> My parents doted on me, having no child but me,
> I rolled about in pleasure just where my fancy led,
> Till I was bound a prentice and all my joys were fled.

Creighton and Senior, 203, 10d, m.; 5d; 9d (N.S.). Belden, 131, 8d (Mo.). Cambiaire, 80, 10d. Brown, 354, 7d; add. st. (N.C.). Cox, 294, 8½d (W. Va.). Brewster, 274, 8d (Ind.). Dean, 18, 11d (Minn. "The Apprentice Boy"). Flanders and Brown, 94, 15, m. (Vt. "In the Town of Oxford"). Gardner, 71, 8d (Mich.). Gray, 90, 20 (Me.) Refs. Henry, *Folk-Songs,* 183, 15, m. (Tenn.). Sharp II, 66, 7d, m.; 8d, m. (N.C.) ; add. tunes from N.C. and Tenn. *JAF* 28, 164, 7d (N.C.).

Christie II, 67, 5 8-line d. sts., m. (Scot.). Greig, xlv, 10d (Scot.). Ord, 421, 10d, m. (Scot.). *JFSS* I, 200, tune from Surrey; *JFSS* II, 169, 2 frags with tunes (Norfolk).

Broadsides: (B) Walker, Durham, 10d. Cadman, 10d (Harvard V, 15). Such no. 333, 10d, reprinted in *JFSS* I, 200. (A) Deming, Boston, 40d lines. Songster: (A) *The Forget Me Not Songster,* N.Y., 244, 10d.

O 40

THE LADY AND THE FARMER'S SON

When the lady tells the youth that she intends to be his wife, he explains that he is bound by oath to marry Sally, her chambermaid. The lady arranges a boat trip and tosses the maid overboard. Conscience-stricken, she confesses the crime and is confined to jail. The youth loses his mind and is sent to Bedlam.

> Young lovers all, I pray draw near
> And a relation you shall hear
> Of how a lady was undone
> By loving of a farmer's son.

Flanders and Olney, 170, 12, m. (Vt.).

O 41

THE CONSTANT LOVERS

The sailor says he'll be faithful to his girl, make one more trip, and marry her on his return. When his mother threatens to disinherit him, he reminds her that his father raised her station from that of servant maid and swears to be loyal to the girl.

> A sailor courted a farmer's daughter,
> He lived convenient to the Isle of Man,
> But mark, good people, what followed after,
> A long time courting but little won.
> A long time courting, and yet discoursing
> Of things concerning the ocean wide,
> He says, "My dearest, at our next meeting
> If you'll consent I'll make you my bride."

Creighton, 99, 4½d, m. (N.S.).
Broadside: (B) Catnach, 5d.

BALLADS OF UNFAITHFUL LOVERS (P)

P   1 A & B   The Girl I Left Behind
P   2   The Green Bushes
P   3   No Sign of a Marriage
P   4   The Sailor and the Tailor
P   5   William and Nancy II (Courting Too Slow)
P   6   Pretty Susan, the Pride of Kildare
P   7   The Foot of the Mountain Brow
P   8   The Gray Mare (Rogers the Miller)
P   9   A Rich Irish Lady (The Fair Damsel from London)
P 10   The Rejected Lover
P 11   Nancy I
P 12   Nancy II (The Rambling Beauty)
P 13   Peggy and the Soldier (The Lame Soldier)
P 14   The Nightingale (One Morning in May)
P 15   Rinordine
P 16   The Dawning of the Day
P 17   Blow the Candle Out
P 18   Pretty Little Miss
P 19   Tripping Over the Lea
P 20   The Fatal Snowstorm
P 21   Mary of the Wild Moor
P 22   The Lovely Banks of Boyne
P 23   Bold Lover Gay
P 24   The Butcher Boy
P 25   Love Has Brought Me to Despair
P 26   The Bonny Young Irish Boy
P 27   Caroline of Edinburgh Town
P 28   Bessie of Ballington Brae
P 29   The Lily of the West
P 30   Oxford City
P 31   The Nobleman's Wedding (The Faultless Bride; The Love Token)
P 32   A Gentleman of Exeter (The Perjured Maid)
P 33   Susannah Clargy
P 34 A & B   The Sailor's Tragedy (The Sailor and the Ghost A) and
       Handsome Harry (The Sailor and the Ghost B)
P 35   The Wexford Girl (The Oxford Girl; The Cruel Miller)
P 36 A & B   The Cruel Ship's Carpenter A (The Gosport Tragedy) and
       The Cruel Ship's Carpenter B (Pretty Polly)
P 37   The Old Oak Tree
P 38   James MacDonald
P 39   Pat O'Brien
P 40   Jessie Munroe

P 1 A

THE GIRL I LEFT BEHIND (A)
(*The Maid I Left Behind*)

The girl fears that the narrator will forget her when he crosses the main, but he promises to be faithful. He travels to Glasgow, where he meets other girls, and then to Dumfries, where Jennie Ferguson offers to give him gold if he will forget his loved ones. After marrying her, he is haunted by thoughts of his parents and his girl, who have died of broken hearts.

> My parents reared me tenderly, they had no child but me.
> My mind was bent on rambling, but with them I could not agree,
> Until I became a rover bold; it grieved their hearts full sore.
> I left my aged parents that I never shall see any more.

Brown, 378, 8d; 18d couplets (N.C.). Chappell, 137, 18, m. (N.C.). Cox, 300, 10d (W. Va.). Doerflinger, 305, 9d with tune from Gardner (N.S. from ms.). Gardner, 98, 8d, m. (Mich.). Randolph I, 283, 9d, m. (Mo.). *JAF* 67, 128, 6d, m. (Nfld.).

Greig, lxxxiii, 12d (Scot.).

Broadsides: (B) No imprint, 9d (Harvard V, 63). Songster: (A) *The Forget Me Not Songster,* Phila., 149, 10d ("The Maid I Left Behind").

P 1 B

THE GIRL I LEFT BEHIND (B)

The girl promises to be true to her lover, who is crossing the plains. One day in Salt Lake City (or some other town) he receives a letter by mail coach saying that she has married another man. The narrator regrets that he did not marry the girl while he had the chance. (In some versions he refuses the hand of Peggy Walker before learning of his girl's unfaithfulness).

> One day as I was riding across the public square,
> The mail-coach came in and I met the driver there;
> He handed me a letter which gave me to understand
> That the girl I left in Texas had married another man.

Thorp, *Songs of the Cowboys,* 134, 6d ("The Rambling Cowboy"; "author supposed to have been K. Tolliver".) Stanza five is given above. Brown, 381, 5½d; 10d couplets (N.C.); 12d couplets (N.C. from ms. This is Sharp's A text); 6d (N.C.). Belden, 199, 5½; 12 (Mo.); 8 (Mo. from ms. "Peggy Walker"). Cambiaire, 47, 9d. Dean, 9d (Minn.). Henry, *Folk-Songs,* 354, 9d (Tenn.); 356, two songs with some stanzas in common with this ballad. Lomax, *Cowboy Songs,* 187, 15d ("Lackey Bill". A long composite text with stanzas not found elsewhere); 192, 6d, m. ("The Rambling Cowboy"). Randolph I, 285, 14 (Ark.); 5½; 7 (Mo.). Wyman, 76, 7d couplets, m. (Ky.). *JAF* 28, 161, 12d couplets (N.C.). *JAF* 52, 38, 5d, m. (Ky. via Wis.).

Ord, 45, 12d, m. (Scot.) In this text the narrator marries Peggy Walker after learning that his former love is already married. *JFSS* VIII, 262, 4d and chor., m. (Suffolk. "All Frolicking I'll Give Over").

Broadsides: (B) Such. Bebbington, no. 306 (Cox). George Walker, Jr., 7½d (Harvard).

P 2
THE GREEN BUSHES

A man makes love to a girl he meets by chance on an evening walk and offers her fine clothes if she will be his bride. She refuses the gifts but is willing to marry him and forsake her true love. They leave together just as her former lover comes to meet her by the green bushes. He speaks bitterly of the falseness of women.

> As I was a-walking for pleasure one day,
> For sweet recreation one evening in May,
> I spied a fair damsel and sweeter sang she,
> "Down by the green bushes where he thinks he'll meet me."

Greenleaf, 67, 7d, m. (Nfld.) Refs. Creighton, 38, 6, m. (N.S.). Flanders and Brown, 246, 7d (Vt.). Sharp II, 155, 5, m. (Va.).

Ord, 147, 6d (Scot.). Sharp, *One Hundred*, 92, 6d, m. Kidson, 47, 7d, m. *JFSS* V, 177, 6d, m. (Kent). *JFSS* VIII, 112, tune only (Cornwall); VIII, 209, 1d, m. (Dorset).

Broadsides: (B) Such., no. 345, 5d. No imprint, 6d. Cadman, 5d (Harvard VI, 152). (A) Andrews, 4d (L of C). (The following refs. are from Greenleaf, p. 68): Songsters: (A) *The Pearl Songster*, p. 108. *The Shamrock*, N.Y., 1862, p. 7. *Lloyd's Song Book*, 1st Ser. (1846), p. 19.

P 3
NO SIGN OF A MARRIAGE

When the girl observes that she has been waiting a long time, her suitor complains that marriage is too confining and suggests that she find another husband. She does so quickly and invites him to her wedding. Dismayed at losing her, he tries unsuccessfully to get her to change her mind.

> Away in the north country there lived a young couple,
> A man and a maid both gallant and gay.
> A long time a-courting and no sign of a marriage,
> No sign of a marriage to be.

Brown, 481, 7d; 7d (N.C.).

P 4

THE SAILOR AND THE TAILOR

A sailor and his girl agree to marry when he returns from sea. After several years he arrives home to learn that the girl is about to marry a tailor. He waits for the couple in the churchyard and persuades the girl to change her mind.

> There was a rich merchant in Bristol did dwell.
> He had a fine daughter; she was courted excell,
> And courted she was by a sea-faring man,
> A brisk young Tarpolian whose name it was John.

Thompson, 403, 10d (N.Y.). Creighton and Senior, 167, 8d, m. (N.S.) A corrupt text.

Sharp, *One Hundred,* 164, 6d, m. ("The Watchet Sailor").

P 5

WILLIAM AND NANCY II
(*Courting Too Slow*)

Although he loves Nancy and courts her, William leaves the girl and sails away. When he writes to her he learns that she has married someone else. William becomes sick with grief and Nancy arrives to comfort him. Both almost immediately die of broken hearts.

> I courted lovely Nancy till her favours I won;
> Straight after some other away I did run.
> It was the height of my practice and the greatest of woe.
> I lost lovely Nancy by courting too slow.

Sharp II, 21, 7d, m. (Ky.); Stanza two is given above; 20, 5d, m. (N.C.) Belden, 196, 7d couplets (Mo.). Scarborough, 317, 5½d (Va.). Thomas, *Devil's Ditties,* 96, 6d, m. (Ky.). *JAF* 20, 273, 6d (Ky.). *JAF* 49, 225, 7d, m. (Ky.).

Logan, p. 364, 5d, prints a semi-humorous related piece entitled "Courting Too Slow".

Professor Kittredge (*JAF* 20, 273) has this to say of the ballad: "This song is much disordered. The first three stanzas are a fragment of a version of 'Courting Too Slow' (Logan, 'A Pedlar's Pack', p. 364). The others belong to some stall-ballad of love and death and give an unfittingly tragic outcome to the composite. The break in sense, style, and tendency is obvious. The whole affords a first-rate example of the freakishness of oral tradition." Since all the texts later collected from tradition have been tragic, and since the first three stanzas are unfitting only when considered as part of Logan's variant, perhaps oral tradition is not so freakish as Kittredge thought it.

P 6

PRETTY SUSAN, THE PRIDE OF KILDARE

Susie rejects the sailor because he is poor and gives her love to a wealthy man. The grieving sailor returns to sea; he never finds another beauty like Susie.

> Her keen eyes they glistened like the bright stars of night,
> The robe she was a-wearing it was costly and white.
> Her fair neck was shaded by her long raven hair.
> Her name it was Pretty Susie, the pride of Kildare.

Brown, 368, 5d (N.C.) Stanza two is given above.
JFSS VI, 11, 5d, m. (Surrey) Notes.
Broadsides: (B) Catnach, 6d (Harvard V, 212). Gilbert, 6d (Harvard IV, 110). No imprint, 6d (Harvard I, 36). Such, no. 326, 6d.

P 7

THE FOOT OF THE MOUNTAIN BROW
(*The Maid of the Mountain Brow*)

Jimmy woos Polly and says he will work hard for her. He shows her his crops, his horses, and his men and says they are all for her. But she criticizes his habits, saying he spends too much time and money at the inn. After reminding her that his money is his own and that she has none, he leaves her. The girl regrets her hasty words.

> Come all young lads and lasses, come listen to my song;
> I hope you'll pay attention, it won't detain you long.
> It's all about a young couple I'm going to tell you now,
> That lately began a-courting at the foot of the mountain brow.

Greenleaf, 153, 7d, m. (Nfld.). Dean, 83, 6d (Minn. "The Maid of the Logan Bough"). Gardner, 122, 6d (Mich.). Mackenzie, 124, 7d (N.S.).
O'Lochlainn, 38, 6d, m. ("The Maid of the Sweet Brown Knowe". The editor reports that his text comes partly from a ballad sheet.).

P 8

THE GRAY MARE

Despite having gained Kate's hand and her dowry of five thousand pounds, the miller says he won't marry her unless he gets her father's gray mare. Enraged, the old man says he'll get nothing and turns him out. Much later the sorrowful but greedy miller meets Kate. When he tries again to woo her, she refers to him as the man who came courting her father's mare and indicates that she will have nothing more to do with him.

> Young Jimmy the miller he courted of late
> A farmer's fair daughter called beautiful Kate.
> She had for her portion fine jewels and rings,
> Gay gold and silver, and many fine things.
>> She had for her portion
>> She had for her portion full fifty fine things.

Belden, 235, 8 6-line d. sts. (Kan. from ms.). Eddy, 172, 7d, m. (O.). Flanders and Brown, 62, 6 6-line d. sts., m. (Vt.). Gardner, 392, 7d (Mich.). Greenleaf, 59, 7d (Nfld.). Pound, 80, 10d couplets (Neb. "My Father's Gray Mare"). *JAF* 12, 251, 7 6-line d. sts. (Mass. from ms.). *JAF* 35, 372, 1d, m. (O.) Refs.

Baring-Gould, 110, 6d, m. (W. of Eng.). Greig, lxvii, 1d. (Scot.). Kidson, 79, 8d, m. (Yorks.).

Broadsides: (B) Such, no. 156 (Harvard XII, 3) (K). Harkness 14d sts. (Harvard II, 152). (A) "Corner Cross and Fulton Sts.", Boston, 8 6-line d. sts. L. Deming, Boston. N. Coverly, Jr., 8 6-line d. sts. (Thomas Coll. I, 37).

P 9

A RICH IRISH LADY
(*The Fair Damsel from London; Sally and Billy; The Sailor from Dover; Pretty Sally, etc.*)

Some time after the rich girl has expressed a complete lack of love for her suitor, she sends for him and announces that her feelings have changed. Although she is dying for love of him, he now treats her with scorn and says he will dance on her grave. She gives him three diamond rings to wear while dancing, bids him farewell, and dies.

> A rich Irish lady from London there came,
> A beautiful damsel called Sally by name.
> Her riches were more than the Queen could possess,
> And her beauty was more than the gold at its best.

Belden, 114, 9d, m.; 112, 10d; 11d couplets; 9 d, m. (Mo.) Notes and refs. Barry, Eckstorm, and Smyth, 419, 8d, m. (Me.); 9 d, m. (Me. from ms.). Brewster, 164, 6d (Ind.). Brown, 300, 10d (N.C. from ms.); 7d couplets (N.C.); 8½d (N.C.) Notes and refs. Cambiaire, 119, 8d. Chappell, 74, 10d, m. (N.C.). Cox, 366, 10½d; 9d; 8d (W. Va.). Davis, *Trad. Ballads*, 538, 8d.; 15d couplets; 5d; 9d couplets; 6 frags. inc. 2 with tunes (Va.) Notes. Flanders & Brown, 244, 12d (Vt. from *The Green Mountain Songster*, 1823). Henry, *Folk-Songs*, 134, 7 (Tenn.). Hudson, 128, 10d; 7d (Miss.). Morris, 330, 7d (Fla.). Randolph I, 205, 17½, m.; 5d m. (Mo.); 2d (Ark.); 7½d (Mo.). Sharp I, 295, 6d, m. (Reprinted by Leach, 680); 4d; 1d, m.; 1d, m.; (N.C.); 1d, m. (Va.); 9d (Ga.); 12d, m. (Ky.);

11d, m. (Va.); 10d, m. (N.C.); 8, m. (Va.); 1d, m. (Ky.). *JAF* 27, 73, 11d with tune from Mass. (Kan. from ms.). *JAF* 32, 502, 23d lines (W. Va.). *JAF* 52, 12, 3½d, m. (Ky. via Wis.) *JAF* 63, 260, 8, m. (Va.).

Christie II, 240, 9d, m. ("The Bold Sailor"). *JFSS* VIII, 5, 10d, m. (Somerset. "Pretty Sally").

Broadsides: (B) Such ("Sally and Her True Love"). Ashton, *Real Sailor Songs,* 70, 9d ("Sally and Billy"). Barry, Eckstorm, and Smyth, 422, print a text of 9d sts. from a broadside at Yale without imprint. (A) 424, a text of 12d sts. from a Brown Univ. broadside with the imprint of E. Mills, 6 Market Square, Boston.

The ballad seems to exist in two closely related broadside forms. In the first the young man is mentioned in the opening line. Later he asks the girl if her pain is in her head or her side. In the second the rich girl is described throughout the opening stanza. Later the man asks if he is the doctor she has sent for, and she replies that he can kill or cure her. For a broadside of the first type, see Ashton; for the second type, which may be American, see Flanders and Brown. Both types are widely distributed in this country, and traditional texts vary considerably.

Note: This ballad is printed by some editors as a variant of "The Brown Girl" (Child, no. 295). In "The Brown Girl" the situation is reversed. The man is scornful of the girl because she is so brown, but later his feelings change and he calls her to him. She laughs at his plight and says she'll dance on his grave. Aside from various differences in narrative details, the Child piece is in ballad meter while the broadsides approach iambic tetrameter. Under the circumstances, "A Rich Irish Lady" should be considered a separate ballad, though it is clearly related to Child no. 295.

P 10

THE REJECTED LOVER

The girl tells the young man that she won't be tied down and asks him not to return. Six months later she changes her mind, but he says that his love for her has died. In the final stanza the girl warns others against her mistake.

> Once I had a true love, I loved her as my life,
> And with my heart and with my hand I couldn't make her
>   my wife,
> She looked on me with scorn and her suit she did disdain,
> And the answer that she gave to me was not to come again.

Sharp II, 98, 6d, m. (N.C.); 96, 7, m. (N.C.); 6, m. (Tenn.); 3, m. (Va.); 100, frags. with tunes from Ky. and Va.

P 11

NANCY I

The young man says he's not rich but offers Nancy his love. She coolly rejects him but later changes her mind. This time he announces that he has found another love. The girl warns others against slighting their true loves.

> It was down in yon green valley in the pleasant month of June,
> The birds were sweetly singing, all nature was in tune,
> It was there I first saw Nancy, she's the girl I adore,
> For she was my only fancy and I could love no more.

Creighton and Senior, 189, 7d, m. (N.S.).

P 12

NANCY II
(*The Rambling Beauty*)

The narrator is treated scornfully by Nancy, who refuses to marry him. He hopes she'll find trouble if she ever marries, and she does, for she marries a man who pays little attention to her. Some years later, when he is wealthy, the narrator has the satisfaction of giving the now destitute girl some money. She regrets her former attitude toward her constant lover.

> Once on a time with boyish fancy,
> When life was fair and I was young,
> I loved a girl whose name was Nancy;
> I loved her more than the common run.

Belden, 191, 5 (Mo.?) ; 5; 8 (Mo. from ms.). Sharp II, 226, 8, m. (Va.) ; 5, m. (Ky. "Loving Nancy"). *Bulletin* no. 1, 7 (B).
Christie II, 7, 5d, m. (Scot.). Greig, cxlii, 10 (Scot.).

P 13

PEGGY AND THE SOLDIER
(*The Lame Soldier*)

Peggy leaves her husband and her baby and goes to sea with a soldier with whom she soon quarrels. He beats her and tells her to return to her cuckold. When she arrives home, she looks through the window and sees her husband singing to their baby. She begs to be taken in, but he will have nothing more to do with her.

Oh, it's of an old soldier, he's just come from sea,
He's going up to London to pay off his fee;
A beautiful damsel appeared in his eye,
Oh, on pretty Peggy he cast his bright eye.

"My gold and my silver, oh, all shall be thine,"
Oh, he said, "my dear jewel, if you will be mine;
Likewise I will treat you with cakes and strong beer,
If you will go oversea with a soldier."

JFSS VIII, 196, 7d, m. (Dorset) Stanzas 1 and 2 are given above. Notes.
Lomax, *Our Singing Country,* 164, 8d, m. (Ind. "The Lame Soldier").
SFQ III, 216, 6½d (Ind.) ; *SFQ* V, 179, 6d (Ind.). *JAF* 49, 223, 5½d
chor., m. (Scot. via Ky. "Poor Peggie").

Miss Ann Gilchrist found the tune to "Peggie is Over Ye Sie Wi' Ye
Soldier" in an edition of the Skene MS., a collection of 17th century Scottish
airs for the lute. She says that black-letter copies of "Peggy" have been
discovered, and she dates the ballad from 1620-1629. (*JFSS* VIII, 197-
198).

P 14

THE NIGHTINGALE
(*One Morning in May*)

A solider meets a pretty girl and chats with her. After a while he draws
his fiddle from his knapsack and plays her a tune. She asks him to play
more, but he says it's time to leave. When she asks him to marry her, he
says he has a wife and six children in London. The ballad ends with a
lament and a warning against men who leave girls to rock the cradle alone.

One morning, one morning, one morning in May
I spied a fair couple a-making their way.
One was a lady so bright and so fair,
And the other was a soldier, a gay cavalier.

Belden, 242, 8d, m. (Reprinted by Leach, 744) ; 7d; 3d couplets; 6d, m.;
frag.; (Mo.) Notes and refs. Cambiaire, 92, 6d. Flanders and Olney, 164,
6d, m. (Mass.). Henry, *Folk-Songs,* 200, 6d (Tenn.). Lomax, *Cowboy
Songs,* 183, 8d, m. (Tex. A composite text). Morris, 360, 3d, m. (Fla.) ; 4d
(Ireland via Fla.). Randolph I, 266, 2d, m.; 5d; 4d (Mo.) ; 1d (Ark. from
ms.) ; 9d, m. (Mo.). Sandburg, 136, 6d, m. Scarborough, 310, 6d; 5d (Va.).
Sharp II, 192, 6d, m. (Tenn.) ; frags. with tunes (Ky.). Thomas, *Devil's
Ditties,* 112, 1d, m. (Ky.). Wyman, 68, 6d, m. (Ky.). *PTFLS* 7, 167, 6d,
m. (Tex. A cowboy variant).

JFSS VIII, 194, 6d, m.; add. tune (Dorset).

P 15

RINORDINE

A man makes love to a girl he meets by chance in the mountains. When she asks his name, he cautions her against telling her parents, who would cause his death, and says that his name is Rinordine and that he has a castle in the forest. The ballad ends with a warning to maidens against walking at night and meeting Rinor.

> One evening as I rambled two miles below Pomroy,
> I met a farmer's daughter all on the mountains high,
> I said, "My pretty fair maiden your beauty shines most clear,
> And in these lofty mountains I'm glad to meet you here."

Thomas, *Devil's Ditties*, 108, 7d, m. (Ky.). Belden, 286, 12 (Kan.); equiv. of 10 (Mo.). Combs, 165, 8 (W. Va.). Chappell, 84, 13, m. (N.C.). Eddy, 192, 14 (O.). Gardner, 96, 19 lines, m. (Mich.). Flanders-Barry, 64, 6, m. (Vt. A different text with its literary source reprinted). Mackenzie, 102, 7d (N.S.) Detailed refs. Randolph I, 379, 1d, m. (Ark. from ms.).

JFSS I, 271, 2d, m. (Sussex).

Broadsides: (B) Bebbington, 7d ("Mountains High". Harvard IX, 117). Such, 7d ("The Mountains High" Reprinted in *JFSS* I, 271). (A) N. Coverly, Jr., Boston (Thomas Coll. I, 55, "The Soldier and His Fair Maid", 6d and I, 64, "Ranordine", 7d). Songsters: (A) *The American Songster*, Phila., 1836, 191, 7d. *The Forget Me Not Songster*, Phila., 18, 7d. The same, N.Y., 199.

P 16

THE DAWNING OF THE DAY

The narrator seduces a reluctant milk-maid at the dawning of the day and then leaves her. Seven months later she meets him again and asks him to marry her, but he replies haughtily that he has just married a rich girl. The tearful milk-maid warns other girls against deceivers.

> As I walked out one morning fair all in the month of June,
> Each bush and tree was decked in green and the flowers were in
>   their bloom.
> Returning home all from a walk through a field I took my way;
> I chanced to see a pretty fair maid at the dawning of the day.

Mackenzie, 152, 9d (N.S.) Refs. Thompson, 384, 12d (N.Y. from ms.). Moffat, 16, 3d, m. Ord, 163, 3d (Scot.).

Broadsides: (B) Such, no. 232, 10d. Forth, 11d (Harvard III, 57). Gilbert, Newcastle, 11d (Harvard IV, 139). (A) Deming, Boston, 12d (L of C). Songsters: (A) *The Forget Me Not Songster*, Phila., 240, 10d. The same, N.Y., 178.

P 17
BLOW THE CANDLE OUT

The young man asks the girl to blow the candle out, reminds her that her father and mother are embracing in a nearby room, and suggests that they do the same. Nine months later she has a child, "And she damned the very hour / That she blowed the candle out."

> Come all ye jolly boatsman boys
> That go to see your dear;
> The moon is shining bright,
> And the stars a-twinkling clear.
>
> I dropped at my love's window
> To ease her of her pain;
> So quickly she rose and let me in,
> And went to bed again.

Combs, 161, 10 (Ky. "The Jolly Boatsman") Stanzas 1 and 2 are given above.

Ord, 95, 5d (Scot.).

Broadsides: (B) Catnach, 7d. J. Gilbert (Harvard IV, 30). Harkness, 7d (Harvard III, 47).

Note: see also the comic and risqué "Blow the Candle In," Catnach, 8d (Harvard VII, 97).

P 18
PRETTY LITTLE MISS

After talking of marriage the young man takes the girl to bed with him. In the middle of the night he dresses to leave. When she reminds him of his promise, he tells her that she has only herself to blame. The ballad ends with several stanzas of lament.

> As I walked down by the river
> I met a nice young girl,
> I said to her: My pretty fair Miss,
> Won't you sit with me awhile?
>
> O no, kind sir, she answered me,
> O no, kind sir, I am too young.
> The younger you are the better for me,
> For I want a wife and a son.

Sharp II, 91, 11, m. (Ky.); 9, m. (N.C.).

JFSS III, 296, frag. of 4 sts., m. (Hampshire). *JFSS* IV, 281, 4, m. (Sussex. "Down by the Greenwood Side").

Notes: Sharp's B version has stanzas in common with "Home, Dearie, Home". Like other pieces in which the lyrical note is strong and the narrative relatively weak, the ballad displays much textual instability.

P 19

TRIPPING OVER THE LEA

After seducing the girl he meets by chance, the young man says he has no intention of marrying her. The girl sadly awaits the birth of her baby.

> As I walked out on a May morning,
> On a May morning, as it happened to be,
> The prettiest lass that ever I did see,
> She came linking o'er the lea to me.

Barry, *JAF* 22, 382, 4 sts. and chorus, m. (Co. Tyrone via Mass.).

Johnson, *Scots Musical Museum*, 1839, IV, 410, 8 sts., m., ("As I Went Out Ae May Morning").

P 20

THE FATAL SNOWSTORM

The young woman with an infant in her arms speaks of the cruelty of her parents and of the young man who "sold his heart for gold". She warns fair maids against deceivers, kisses her baby's cold lips, lies down beside her, and dies.

> 'Twas on a winter evening,
> When the frost came down like snow
> Over hill and valley,
> Where wintry winds do blow.
>
> I spied a female form
> All in a depth of snow
> With an infant in her arms;
> She knew not where to go.

Mackenzie, 166, 10 (N.S.) Stanzas 1 and 2 are given above.

Mackenzie refers to a Pitts broadside at Harvard called "The Fatal Snowstorm" by John Embleton, which he says is related to this ballad. The broadside is a sentimental and flowery piece in 24 long lines.

P 21

MARY OF THE WILD MOOR

Mary's father does not hear her at the door but finds her dead the next morning, with her child still alive in her arms. He dies of grief and the baby follows him to the grave, leaving a vacant cottage.

> One night when the wind it blew cold,
> Blew bitter across the wild moor,
> Young Mary she came with her child,
> Wand'ring to her own father's door,

Crying, "Father, oh pray let me in;
Take pity on me I implore,
Or the child at my bosom will die
From the winds that blow o'er the wild moor.

Morris, 397, 4d (Fla.). Belden, 207, 4d (Mo.) Refs. Brewster, 246, 7
(Ind.). Brown, 266, 8 (N.C.). Cox, 437, 8 (W. Va.). Eddy, 209, 4d, m.
(O.). Henry, *Folk-Songs,* 372, 4 (N.C.). Mackenzie, 164, 7 (N.S.) Refs.
Neely, 149, 5 (Ill.). Pound, 81, 4d (N.Y. via Neb.). Randolph I, 311, 7,
m. (Mo.); 5, m. (Ark.); 8, m. (Mo.). Sandburg, 466, 5 lines, m. (Ind.).
Scarborough, 335, 8 (Va.). Owens, 75, 6, m. (Tex.). Shoemaker, 114, 4d
(Pa.). Stout, 28, 4d (Ia.) (Reprinted by Leach, 734). Sturgis, 36, 3d, m.
(Vt.). *JAF* 26, 355, 2d (Neb.). *JAF* 35, 1d and two tunes (O.) Refs.
Kidson, 77, 8, m. (Leeds). Williams, 312, 4d (Cirencester).
Broadsides: (B) Such, no. 73 (M). Bebbington (M). Cadman, 4d (Harvard V, 54). (A) Partridge, Boston, no. 145, 4d. DeMarsan, 4d. J. H.
Johnson, Phila. (K). Doyle, Baltimore, 4d (L of C). Songsters: (A)
Wehman's Song Book No. 3, p. 17 (K). *Delaney's Song Book No. 2,* p.
8 (K).

P 22

THE LOVELY BANKS OF BOYNE

Jimmy promised to wed the narrator but deserted her after gaining her
favors. She hears he has gone to London and has married a fair lady there.
The disconsolate girl must remain in Dublin far from her home on the
banks of the Boyne.

I am a gay young lassie and I love my Jimmy well.
My heart was ever true to him, far more than tongue can tell.
'T was at my father's castle where he gained this heart of mine,
And he causes me to wander from the lovely banks of Boyne.

Mackenzie, 384, 5d (N.S.).
Broadside: (B) Such, no. 333, 7d.

P 23

BOLD LOVER GAY

The lover woos May with promises of an easy life and silk and satin dresses.
He takes her to his home across the sea. A year later she is pining for home,
has no fine dresses, and is pregnant.

Ho, ho, pretty lassy, ho, ho, you sweet little dear,
Come sit you on my lap and do not fear.
Why those rosy blushes, why those blushes, I say?
All on account of a bold lover gay!

Belden, 208, 6 irreg. sts. (Mo.).

P 24

THE BUTCHER BOY

When the butcher boy leaves his girl for one who has more gold she hangs herself in her bedroom. Her father discovers her body and a note saying she is foolish to hang herself for the butcher boy. She asks that her grave be dug wide and deep and that a turtle dove be placed on her breast to show the world she died for love.

> In Jersey City where I did dwell
> Lived a butcher boy that I loved so well,
> He courted me my heart away,
> And now with me he will not stay.

Randolph I, 229, 8, m.; 226, 6½, m.; 4; 4; 1 (Mo.); frag. (Ark.). Arnold, 66, 8, m. (Ala.). Belden, 203, 7, m.; 8, m. (Mo.); 6 6-line (S.C. via Mo); 1, m. (Wis.) Extended notes and refs. Brewster, 198, 7; 8; 5 (Ind.). Cox, 430, 8; 5½ (W. Va.) tune, p. 530. Creighton, 33, 7, m. (N.S.). Eddy, 129, 9, m.; 9, m. (O.). Flanders & Brown, 115, 8, m. (Vt.). Gardner, 117, 10; 1; 1 (Mich.). Henry, *Folk-Songs*, 195, 7 (Ga. via Tenn.); 8 (Tenn.); 5; 5; 2 (N. J.); 1 (Ind.). Hudson, 160, 8 (Miss.). Brown, 272, 9; 9; add. sts.; 7; add. sts.; 13; 6; 5 (N.C.). Linscott, 179, 4½d, m. (Mass.). Mackenzie, 157, 9; 10 (N.S.). Morris, 334, 4 (Ky. via Fla.); 9 (Fla.) Refs. Neely, 146, 6½, m.; 7; 4½; 13 lines (Ill.). Owens, 89, 7, m. (Tex.). Pound, 60, 7½ (Wyo.). Sandburg, 324, 7. Scarborough, 282, 1; 9; 7; 6 (Va.); 3; 5½; 5 (N.C.). Stout, 37, 7; 8; frags.; 4 8-line; 6 (Ia.). Thompson, 387, 8 (N.Y.) *JAF* 29, 169, 8 (O.) (Reprinted by Leach, 738); Many refs. to this and related pieces. *JAF* 35, 360, tunes and refs. Sharp II, 76, 8, m. (Ga.); 1, m. (N.C.); 1, m. (Va.); 1, m. (N.C.).

JFSS II, 159, 8, m. (Essex. "In Jessie's City").

Broadsides: (A) J. H. Johnson, Phila., 4 8-line sts. (The text begins "In Jersey City . . . "). DeMarsan. Wehman. Songsters: (A) *Wehman Bros. Good Old-Time Songs No. 3*, p. 72. *Delaney's Song Book No. 18*, p. 24. (The last four refs. are from Kittredge, *JAF* 35, 361).

See also Anne Lutz, "The Ballad of the Butcher Boy in the Ramapo Mountains," *NYFQ* III, 28-34. 29, 9 sts.; frags. and tunes (N.Y.).

According to Kittredge, *JAF* 29, 170, this ballad "appears to be an amalgamation of 'The Squire's Daughter' (also known as 'The Cruel Father, or, Deceived Maid') with 'There is an Alehouse in Yonder Town' (well known as a student song in this country under the title 'There is a Tavern in the Town')." For the former text he refers to a broadside in the Harvard Library, 25242.5.5 (147), no. 7, by Shelmerdine, Manchester. For the latter, see the following piece.

Cf. the concluding stanzas in "The Sailor Boy I".

P 25

LOVE HAS BROUGHT ME TO DESPAIR

The narrator overhears a girl complaining that her false lover has brought her to despair. She goes to the meadow to find a flower to ease her mind, but none of them does so. After making a bed of flowers she lies down. She asks for a marble stone at her head and a turtle dove on her breast, and then she dies for love.

> In Oxford Town in Halifax fair
> As I walked out to take the air,
> I viewed the hills and the valleys 'round,
> And at length I heard a doleful sound.

Brewster, 276, 7, m. (Ind.); 6 (Ill.).

JFSS II, 155, 1, m. (Essex. "A Bold Young Farmer"); 158, 6 sts. and 2 tunes (Essex. "Died for Love"). *JFSS* V, 181, 5, m. (Westmoreland. "A Brisk Young Sailor Courted Me; or, Died for Love".) This is non-narrative and begins "There is an ale-house in the town." The singer's fourth stanza is the familiar plaint:

> I wish my baby it was born,
> Set smiling on its nurse's knee,
> And I myself was in my grave
> And the green grass growing over me.

JFSS V, 183, 2, m. (Lancs.); 184, 1, m. (Herts.); 184, 10, m. (Herts.) This begins "There is an ale-house", includes a stanza similar to that just above and proceeds with the gathering of flowers and the girl's death and burial. Notes and refs.

P 26

THE BONNY YOUNG IRISH BOY

Much in love with her Irish boy, the girl is deeply hurt when he leaves her to cross the ocean. She follows him to Boston (or elsewhere), finds that he is married, and falls sick. Before her death of a broken heart, she asks to be buried in Ireland.

> O first I came a-courted by a bonny young Irish b'y,
> He called me all of his jewels, his sweetheart, pride, and j'y.
> 'Twas in fair Dubelin city, a place so old and fair,
> When first I came a-courted by a bonny young Irish b'y.

Greenleaf, 192, 5d, m. (Nfld.) Refs. *JAF* 67, 131, 8d,m. (Nfld.) In this text the girl finds her faithful lover and marries him.

Greig, xlviii, 6d (Scot.). Kidson, 152, 4d, m. (Scot.). Ord, 162, 11 (Scot.).

Broadsides: (B) Greenleaf refers to broadsides by Bebbington and Such. Ryle, 6d (Harvard V, 143).

P 27

CAROLINE OF EDINBURGH TOWN

To escape her parents' criticism of her Highland suitor, Caroline goes with him to London where they are married. After six months her husband treats her harshly and then leaves her to go to sea. In parting he tells her that she can beg her way back to Edinburgh. She wanders awhile, goes to the ocean to watch the ships, and finally plunges to death in the sea.

> Come all young men an' maidens, attend unto my rhyme,
> 'Twas of a young damsel who had scarcely reached her prime,
> She beat the blushin' roses an' admired by all around,
> Was comely young Caroline of Edinborough town.

Randolph I, 240, 8d, m.; 8d, m. (Mo.) Refs. Brown, 359, 9d; add. sts. (N.C.). Cox, 262, 9d (W. Va.). Dean, 53, 8d (Minn.). Eddy, 165, 11 (O.). Flanders-Barry, 79, 10d, m.; frag. of 28 d. lines (Vt.) Notes. Hudson, 143, 19 (Miss.). Gardner, 64, 11d (Mich. from ms.). Linscott, 183, 11d, m. (Mass.). Mackenzie, 94, 8½d (N.S.). Sharp I, 404, 1d, m. (Ky.). Shoemaker, 210, 10d (Pa.). Thompson, 383, 11d (N.Y.). *JAF* 35, 362, 2 (O.) Detailed refs. *JAF* 52, 14, 5½d, m. (Ky. via Wis.).

Greig, lxx, 11d (Scot.). Ord, 186, 11d (Scot.).

Broadsides: (B) Such no. 359, 11d (Harvard XIII, 53) (K). Brereton, 10d. Gilbert, 11d (Harvard IV, 110). (A) J. Andrews, N.Y., (Brown Univ.) (K). Bonsal, Baltimore, 11d (L of C). Songsters: (A) *Delaney's Scotch Song Book No.* 1, p. 2 (K). *The American Songster, Phila.,* 1850, p. 44 (K). *The Forget Me Not Songster,* Phila., 104, 11d. The same, N.Y., 175. Note: A complete text of this ballad is given in Chapter IV.

"Another broadside ballad recounts the well-deserved 'Fate of Young Henry in Answer to "Caroline of Edinburgh Town"' (Pitts). He is twice shipwrecked, and the second disaster ends with his drowning." (Note from Kittredge, *JAF* 35, 363.). There is another print by T. Batchelar, 8 d. sts.

P 28

BESSIE OF BALLINGTON BRAE

Bessie appears to the young lord as he lies dreaming, says he has led her astray, and that she is dead. He hurriedly rides to Bessie's cottage where her grieving father confirms her death. The lord reveals himself as her betrayer but says he had promised to marry her. He commits suicide by piercing his heart with his sabre and asks to be placed beside Bessie.

> Come all you young men and maidens so fair,
> Come list to a tale of two lovers so dear—
> Charming young Bessie of Ballydubray
> And the Lord of the Moorlands who led her astray.

Flanders-Barry, 90, 8½d, m. (Vt.). Dean, 44, 32d lines (Minn.).
Gardner, 104, 9d, m. (Mich. "Jessie of Ballington Brae"). Mackenzie, 101,
frag. of 5½ lines (N.S.).

Joyce, 150, 1 6-line d. st., m. (Ireland, "Ballindown Braes").

Broadside: (B) No imprint, 40d lines ("Answer to Betsy of Ballantown
Bray").

The broadside referred to above indicates that this ballad is the sequel
or "answer" to a piece which Mackenzie describes as "a lament by a deserted
maiden who is going back to Ballenden Braes to die." He refers to a broadside text of "Sweet Ballenden Braes" without imprint at Harvard.

P 29

THE LILY OF THE WEST

The narrator courts Mary (or Flora) only to have her slight him for
another man. In a fit of jealous rage, he stabs his rival to death. He is
sentenced for his crime, and although he blames Mary for depriving him
of his liberty, he says he still loves her.

> I just come down from Louisville
> Some pleasure for to find,
> A handsome girl from Michigan
> So pleasing to my mind.
> Her rosy cheeks, her rolling eye,
> Like arrows pierced my breast.
> They call her handsome Mary, the Lily of the West.

Sharp II, 199, 6d, m. (Ky.). Belden, 132, 6d (Mo.). Creighton, 84, 7d,
m. (N.S.). Eddy, 147, 5d, m.; 6d (O.). Randolph II, 76, 5, m. (Ark.); 6d
(Ark. from ms.); 1d (Ark.); 6d, m. (Mo.). *JAF* 35, 368, 1d, m. (O.)
Detailed refs.

Baring-Gould, rev. ed., 118, 4d, m.; 120, add. tune.

Broadsides: (B) No imprint (Harvard V, 61). Such no. 35, 6d. Catnach,
7d (Harvard V, 201). O'Lochlainn, 184, 6d, m. (A) Andrews, 6d. De-
Marsan (Brown Univ.) (K). Songsters: (A) *Beadle's Dime Song Book
No. 5*, N.Y., 1860, p. 48 (K). *Uncle Sam's Army Songster*, Indianapolis,
1862, p. 20 (K).

P 30

OXFORD CITY

The servant proposes to the lady but she puts him off, saying that they
are too young to marry. She goes to a dance and dances with someone else,
and the youth, in a fit of jealousy, poisons her wine. Feeling ill, she asks
him to take her home, and he tells her that they have both drunk the
poisoned wine. They die in each other's arms.

In Oxford City there lived a lady,
The truth to you, I will make known;
She was courted by a servant boy;
Oftimes he told her he loved her well.

Flanders and Brown, 92, 10, m. (Vt.). Gardner, 75, 7, m. (Mich.).
JAF 30, 356, 10 (Eng. via N.B.) Refs.
Greig, cxxxvii, 10 (Scot.). *JFSS* II, 37, 2 and chor., m. (Somerset. "Down
in the Groves"); II, 157, 7, m. (Essex. "Newport Street"); II, 200, 8, m.
(Sussex). *JFSS* VII, 41, 1, m.; 8 ("Although my Name it is Maria"); 7
("In Midfordshire") (Dorset) Notes.
Broadsides: (B) Such. No imprint, 11 sts. (Harvard V, 48). Catnach,
11 sts (Harvard IV, 92).

P 31

THE NOBLEMAN'S WEDDING
(*The Faultless Bride; The Love Token*)

A man returns home in time to attend, in disguise, the wedding reception
of the girl he loves. He reminds her in song of her unfaithfulness and says
he will return her gold love token. Stricken with remorse, she collapses,
and asks to spend the night at her mother's home. The next morning she
is found dead.

I was of late at a noble wedding,
The wedding of one that proved unkind
To him that I loved her but was forsaken,
And now the thoughts of him filled her mind.

Belden, 165, 11d (Mo. from ms. "The Faultless Bride"). Greenleaf,
155, 10d, m. (Nfld.) Refs. Sharp II, 83, 7d, m. (Ga. "The Awful Wedding"). *JAF* 24, 339, 6d, m. (Me. from ms. "The Love Token").
Colum, 5, 6d. Joyce, 224, 7d, m. Ord, 132, 12d, m. (Scot.). *JFSS* VIII,
4, 4d, m. (Somerset); VIII, 202, 5d and ref., m. (Dorset) Notes.
See Johnson, *Pop. Brit. Ballads* IV, 248, for William Allingham's rewritten version of this ballad in 8d sts.

P 32

A GENTLEMAN OF EXETER
(*The Perjured Maid*)

A girl and a sea captain fall in love, break a gold token, and vow always
to be true to one another. Soon after he goes to sea, however, she becomes
engaged to another man. When the captain returns she treats him with
scorn. On the day of her wedding he dies, and that evening appears to
her as a ghost and takes her away to sleep with him in the clay.

A gentleman of Exelter,
He had but one only daughter dear.
When she was scarce sixteen years of age,
Was courted by young lords and squires.

Flanders-Barry, 5, 17, m. (Vt.) Notes. Henry, *Folk-Songs,* 147, 16 (Tenn.).

Broadside: (B) Henry, *Folk-Songs,* 149, prints a 36 stanza text of this ballad, under the title "The Perjured Maid", from a Scottish chapbook. (Item 1013 in the Harvard Catalogue).

P 33

SUSANNAH CLARGY

Susannah falls in love with a widow's son and vows to be faithful. They break a gold ring in token of their love. Twenty-four weeks later the girl agrees to marry another man. Her first lover goes to see her but is rejected. He commits suicide, and that night his ghost comes to claim the new bride.

There was a lady lived in Cain,
Susannah Clargy were her name;
Courted were she by a widow's son,
And he soon became her fav'rite one.

Sharp II, 261, 7, m. (Va.).

This piece is almost identical in plot with "A Gentleman of Exeter" ("The Perjured Maid").

P 34 A

THE SAILOR'S TRAGEDY

(*The Sailor and the Ghost A*)

A pregnant girl deserted by her lover hangs herself in a grove. She leaves a note asking that her body be kept above ground as a warning to fair maidens, and she promises her false lover no rest. He goes to sea to escape her spirit, but she appears in a boat and demands to see him. Coached by the young man, the captain says that the sailor has died, but the ghost threatens a violent storm unless he is produced. The captain complies, the girl denounces her lover, and the boat sinks in flames with him aboard. The ghost reappears with a warning to sailors against proving false to womankind.

It's of a sailor of whom I write,
And to the seas he took great delight,
When a fair maiden he did beguile
When this fair maiden he had with child.

Creighton and Senior, 151, 15, m.; 9, m.; 7 (N.S.). Mackenzie, 243, 12 (N.S.) Notes and refs. Kittredge, *JAF* 26, 179, 16 (N.J. from ms.) Detailed notes and refs.

JFSS VII, 46, 10, m. (Dorset. "The Man and Two Maidens").

Broadsides: (B) Kittredge, *JAF* 26, 177, reports copies of "The Sailor's Tragedy" in garlands printed at Stirling in 1825 by W. Macnie. (These are items 1076 and 1077 in the Harvard Catalogue). Songster: (B): *Universal Songster*, London, 1834, II, 273, 17 sts. ("The Sailor and the Ghost of his Deserted Lady").

"On March 25, 1805, Laurie and Whittle (London) published an engraved and illustrated broadside containing a full text of the . . . song: 'The Sailor and the Ghost: A Whimsical Ballad.—As sung by Mr. Moody, Mr. Suett, and Mr. R. Palmer.' Thus it appears that the ballad was a favourite on the English stage in the latter part of the eighteenth century." (Note from Mackenzie, p. 243.).

P 34 B

HANDSOME HARRY

(*The Sailor and the Ghost B*)

This rewritten version contains various proper names including those of the two women, Kate and Ruth, whom the sailor has seduced. The phrasing has been largely reworked, and the full text is seven stanzas longer than 'The Sailor's Tragedy".

> Handsome Harry he was called;
> In Southampton he did dwell.
> To the Betsey Ship most famous
> He belonged, 'tis full well to know.

Brown, 250, 12 (N.C.) Stanza three is given above. (This text ends with the suicide note.). Davis, 44, refers to a fragment of three stanzas collected in Virginia.

Broadsides: (A) Kittredge, *JAF* 26, 177, reports three broadsides at Harvard. These are items 2424-2426 in the Harvard Catalogue. The third bears the imprint of Nathaniel Coverly, Jr.; (Thomas Coll. I, 20, 96 lines, is the same item). Songster: (A) *The Forget Me Not Songster*, N.Y., 133, 25 sts.

"As this version is to be found only in American broadsides and songsters, it is to be presumed that it originated in the United States." (Note from Mackenzie, 243.).

P 35

THE WEXFORD GIRL

(The Oxford, Lexington, or Knoxville Girl; The Cruel Miller, etc.)

The miller's apprentice invites his fiancée for a walk to discuss their wedding day. When they reach a lonely spot, he pulls a stake from a fence and hits her with it. She begs him not to murder her, but he beats her to death and throws her body into the river. He returns home and explains that his clothes are bloody because of a nosebleed. When the murder is discovered, the youth is sentenced to be hanged.

> My tender parents brought me up—provided for me well.
> It was in the city of Lexington, they placed me in a mill.
> It's there I met a pretty fair maid; on her I cast my eye;
> I promised her I'd marry her, and she believed a lie.

Henry, *Folk-Songs,* 219, 5½d (N.C.) (Reprinted by Leach, 785); 214, 18; 11 (Tenn.). Belden, 134, 12 (Mo. from ms.); 13½ (Mo.) Notes and refs. Brewster, 204, 13 (Ind.). Brown, 240, 12; add. sts.; 12; add. sts.; 6; add. st. (N.C.). Cox, 311, 6d; 5½d (W. Va.). Doerflinger, 288, 2, m. (N.B.); 15 (N.S. from Mackenzie). Flanders and Brown, 88, 12, m. (Vt.). Gardner, 77, 7d; frag. of 21d lines (Mich.). Hudson, 141, 15 (Miss.). Lomax, *Our Singing Country,* 174, 13, m. (Va.). Mackenzie, 293, 15 (N.S.). Morris, 337, 12 (Fla.). Neely, 150, 4 (Ill.). Owens, 81, 12, m. (Tex.). Randolph II, 93, 11, m.; 1; 4, m.; 8½d; 1d; frag.; 14, m. (Mo.); 2 (Ark.); 4½d, m. (Mo.); 1d; 8 (Ark.); 7½, m. (Mo.). Scarborough, 160, 12 (N.C.); 10 (Va.); 11 (from ms.). Sharp I, 407, 11, m. (Ky.); frags. with tunes from Ky. and Va. *NYFQ* V, 95, 11 sts. (Ireland(?) via N.Y.). *SFQ* III, 208, 13 sts. (Ind. "The Printer's Boy"); 12 (Ind.). *JAF* 42, 247, 6d (N.C.); 290, 5½d (N.C.). *PTFLS* VI, 213, 11, m. (Tex.).

Greig, cxxxvii, 12 (Scot. "The Butcher Boy"). *JFSS* VII, 23, 12d couplets, m. (Norfolk. "Hanged I Shall Be"); 44, 6d, m. (Dorset. "The Prentice Boy").

Broadsides: (B) Such, no. 622, 9d. No imprint, 9d ("The Cruel Miller". Harvard VII, 45). "London: Printed and Sold in Stonecutter-street, Fleet-Market", 44 sts ("The Berkshire Tragedy, or the Wittam Miller"). *Roxburghe Ballads* VIII, 629, 22d (the same). (A) A Boston broadside without imprint, 11½d ("The Lexington Miller") Reprinted in *JAF* 42, 249 and by Leach, 786.

The variants of this ballad are discussed in Chapter IV, where complete texts are given.

P 36 A

THE CRUEL SHIP'S CARPENTER A
(*The Gosport Tragedy*)

William, the carpenter, makes love to Mary (or Molly) and promises to marry her. She becomes pregnant and they meet, supposedly to arrange the wedding. He lures her to a lonely place and announces that he has spent all night digging her grave. Despite her pleas he stabs her to death and throws her body into the grave. The carpenter then escapes to sea, but the girl's ghost, with an infant in its arms, appears to one of the crew and vanishes when he tries to embrace it. The captain demands to know the identity of the murderer on board. The carpenter confesses and "raving distracted he died that same night". The girl's parents hear the news, find her body, and bury it in the Gosport churchyard.

> In Gaspard of late a young damsel did dwell,
> For wit and for beauty few did her excell,
> A young man did court her for to be his dear,
> And he by his trade was a ship carpenter.

Mackenzie, 96, 23d (N.S.). Brewster, 298, 7d; 3 couplets (Ind.). Brown, 235, 25d (N.C. Probably copied from print). Creighton and Senior, 115, 20½d, m.; 118, 2d, m. (N.S.); 119, a text of 9d sts. described as a parody of this ballad. Greenleaf, 120, 14 lines (Nfld.). Henry, *Folk-Songs*, 231, 6d (Ga.). Morris, 341, 8½d (Fla.). Randolph II, 113, 2d; 7d (Mo.). Scarborough, 129, 3½d; 7d (N.C.); 6d (Va.). Sharp I, 317, 7d (N.C.); 10d (Tenn.); 7d (Ky.); frags. with tunes.

Christie II, 98, 6d, m. (Scot.). Sharp and Marson IV, 8, 10d, m. (Somerset).

Broadsides: (B) Ashton, *Real Sailor Songs*, after p. 86, 34d sts. In a chapbook, "The Gosport Tragedy; or, The Perjured Ship Carpenter" (Item 871 in the Harvard Catalogue). Broadside in the Percy Coll. with imprint "Bow Church Yard, London." (Item 872 in the Harvard Catalogue). *Roxburghe Ballads* VIII, 143, 11d sts. (part of garland text; reprinted by Leach, 698). *Roxburghe Ballads* VIII, 173, 23d sts. ("the remainder" of the ballad, from a broadside). (A) Deming, Boston, 27d sts. (L of C).

Songsters: (A) *The Forget Me Not Songster*, Phila., 153, 27d. The same, N. Y., 232.

Note: A comic parody on this ballad entitled "Molly the Betrayed, or The Fog Bound Vessel" appears on a ballad sheet in the Harvard Library. The eighth and ninth of ten stanzas read as follows:

> Then he calls up his men vith a shout and a vhoop,
> And he orders young Villiam to stand on the poop;
> There's summat not right, says he, 'mongst this here crew,
> And blowed if I don't think young Villiam it's you.

Then Villiam turned red, and then vite, and then green,
Vhile Molly's pale ghost at his side it vos seen;
Her buzzom vos vite, the blood it vos red,
She spoke not, but wanished, and that's all she said.

P 36 B
THE CRUEL SHIP'S CARPENTER B
Pretty Polly

This is a much reduced variant which preserves the essentials of the
story. The original phrasing is frequently altered, and some new details
are added, such as that of the spade standing by the new-made grave.
The girl, who is now Polly, gets direct and violent revenge: "She stript
him and tore him, she tore him in three . . ." The two address each other
here as "O William, O William" and "O Polly, O Polly".

It was early next morning before it was day,
He went to his Polly these words he did say,
O Polly, O Polly you must go with me,
Before we are married my friends for to see.

Broadside, Such, 11d, reprinted in *JFSS* I, 172. Stanza three is given
above.

A further reduction of this text has resulted in a briefer traditional
form in which the girl is called Pretty Polly and in which William, or
Willie, says, "I was digging your grave the best part of last night". (In
the other texts the line reads, "For all the long night I've been digging
your grave").

Pretty Polly, pretty Polly,
Come, go along with me;
Before we get married
Some pleasure to see."

Henry, *Songs Sung*, 53, 6 (N.C.) Stanza two is given above.

Because there is some crossing over between these variants I am listing
them together.

Brown, 238, 9d; 5d couplets; 9d lines (N.C.). Cox, 308, 8d couplets;
4d; 3½d (W. Va.). Creighton and Senior, 117, 12d (N.S.). Fuson, 69,
10d couplets (Ky.). Henry, *Folk-Songs*, 229, 15; 6d couplets (Ky.). Leach,
699, 6d couplets (Va. ". . . as sung to Alan Lomax"). Lomax, *Folk Song
U.S.A.*, 304, 10d couplets, m. Lomax, *Our Singing Country*, 172, 12d
couplets, m. (Va., Ky. via N.Y. A confused composite containing some
verses from A). Randolph II, 112, 6d, m.; 2d (Mo.); 7d (Mo. from ms.).
Scarborough, 128, 11d couplets (N.C.); 13d couplets; 9d couplets (Va.).
Sharp I, 321, 7d couplets, m. (Ky.); frags with tunes. Wyman, 79, 11d
couplets, m. (Ky.). *JAF* 20, 262, 15; 9 (Ky.) Refs. *JAF* 42, 276, 14½
(Ky.).

Broadsides: (B) Catnach. Cadman, 11d (Harvard V, 45). Dalton's Pub. Lib., York, 11d (Harvard III, 175). Gilbert, Newcastle, 11d (Harvard IV, 13).

P 37

THE OLD OAK TREE

Betty leaves home to meet her lover and does not return. Unable to find her, her mother dies of grief. During a fox hunt the hounds come upon the grave of the missing girl "down by the old oak tree". Her wounds bleed afresh in the presence of the squire whose knife is found in her side. He confesses that he has murdered the girl rather than marry her and then commits suicide and is buried by the oak tree.

> These hounds begin to sniff and snort
> And then to dig the clay;
> 'Twas more than those three men could do
> To keep those hounds away.
> When these three men they gathered round,
> They called for picks and spade
> And dug the ground and there they found
> This missing, murdered maid.

Greenleaf, 116, 10d, m. (Nfld. "Squire Nathaniel and Betsy") Stanza five is given above. Doerflinger, 283, 8d (N.S. Tune from Greenleaf). Flanders-Barry, 74, 20, m. (Quebec via Vt.) Refs. Gardner, 107, 9d, m. (Mich.).

Cf. *JFSS* I, 186, "The Poor Murdered Woman Laid on the Cold Ground", a ballad in 8 d. sts. from Surrey with some details in common with "The Old Oak Tree".

" 'The Old Oak Tree' is of Irish origin: the earliest record of it in print is an Irish broadside in the Boston Public Library". (Note from Flanders-Barry, p. 77).

P 38

JAMES MacDONALD

James says that he will marry Annie, who is about to bear his child, and tells her to meet him secretly. When he has her alone in a dark place he announces that he will murder her. Despite her pleas, he wounds her fatally and departs. She is found the next morning, tells what has happened, and dies. James is arrested and sentenced to death.

> Come, all good people, old and young,
> I pray you lend an ear,
> It is of a true story
> As ever you did hear,

>Young James he courted a comely maid
>Until her he had beguiled,
>And for to take her precious life
>He planned his scheme in time.

Creighton, 42, 9d, m. (N.S.). Flanders-Barry, 71, 8d, m. (Vt.) Notes and ref. to a text in Ord, 477.
JFSS IV, 65, 7d, m.
Broadside: (B) Bebbington, 11d ("James MacDonald, who was executed in Longford for the murder of Anne O'Brien". Harvard IX, 150).

P 39

PAT O'BRIEN

Pat O'Brien asks Nancy to meet him in a grove, decides not to marry her, and stabs her to death despite her pleas. Her ghost reports the deed to her mother. The girl's body is found and Pat is arrested, but he does not confess until the ghost has appeared to him repeatedly in his jail cell.

>Come all you loyal lovers, wherever that you be,
>And likewise pay attention and listen unto me;
>It's of two loyal lovers, all in their youthful bloom;
>One was cruelly murdered and the other was hung in June.

Bulletin no. 10, p. 14, 15d, m. (Me.). Flanders-Barry, 131, about 9½d, m. (N.H.); add. sts. (Vt.) from "The Sorrowful Lamentation of Pat O'Brine", reprinted by Helen H. Flanders in the Springfield, Mass., *Union*, Dec. 4, 1932. Notes.

P 40

JESSIE MUNROE

Entranced by Jessie, a blacksmith's daughter, Johnny proposes to her, saying that he has fine buildings and land. When she replies scornfully that his buildings are "shattery" and that she wants a handsomer laddie, he decides to return to his less bonny Betsy.

>One fine summer's evening as I was a-walking
>Down by Leicester market I chanced for to go,
>I spied a fair damsel, she attracted by attention,
>I'll tell you about her as far as I know.

Creighton, 169, 5d and chor., m. (N.S.).

HUMOROUS AND MISCELLANEOUS BALLADS (Q)

Q 1   Father Grumble
Q 2   The Old Woman of Slapsadam
Q 3   Johnny Sands
Q 4   Devilish Mary
Q 5   The Dumb Wife
Q 6   The Holly Twig
Q 7   A Rich Old Miser
Q 8   The Boatsman and the Chest
Q 9   Will the Weaver
Q 10   The Major and the Weaver
Q 11   The Dog in the Closet
Q 12   The Sea Captain and the Squire
Q 13   The Oyster Girl
Q 14   The Monkey Turned Barber
Q 15   The Love-of-God Shave
Q 16   Courting in the Kitchen
Q 17   Finnegan's Wake
Q 18   The Irish Wake
Q 19   Doran's Ass
Q 20   Duncan Campbell (Erin-Go-Bragh)
Q 21   The Miller's Will
Q 22   Skewball
Q 23   Creeping Jane
Q 24   Pat Malloy
Q 25   Tom O'Neill
Q 26   The Bad Girl's Lament
Q 27   Erin's Green Shore
Q 28   The Soldier's Poor Little Boy
Q 29   The Fisherman's Boy
Q 30   The Farmer's Boy
Q 31   The Lost Lady Found
Q 32   The Romish Lady
Q 33   The Lake of Cool Finn (Willie Leonard)
Q 34   The Children in the Wood
Q 35   The High Blantyre Explosion
Q 36   The Miner's Doom
Q 37   The Factor's Garland
Q 38   The Valiant London Prentice
Q 39   The Building of Solomon's Temple

Q 1

FATHER GRUMBLE

When the old man criticizes his wife's efficiency, she agrees to let him do the housework while she follows the plow. She gives him a list of instructions, including milking the cow, feeding the pigs, washing the clothes, and churning the cream. Her husband forgets about half his assignments and is kicked by the cow, permits the fat to go up in flames, and otherwise has a bad day. When she returns he willingly admits her superiority.

> There was an old man lived under the hill,
> As you may plainly see, see.
> He said he could do more work in a day
> Than his wife could do in three, three,
> He said he could do more work in a day
> Than his wife could do in three.

Belden, 225, 14; 2; 10; 9; (Mo.).; 10 (Va. via Mo.) Notes and refs. Brewster, 217, 12; 9 (Ind.); 5d (Scot. via Ind. This is the Scottish "John Grumlie"). Cox, 455, 11 (O. via W. Va.); 11; 10; 10; 9; 7; 11 (W. Va.). Eddy, 135, 10, m. (O.). Flanders, *A Garland,* 50, 8 and ref., m. (Vt.). Flanders and Brown, 104, 11 (Vt.). Gardner, 415, 12 (Mich.). Hudson, 175, 10 (Miss.). Linscott, 248, 5d, m. (Mass.). Owens, 228, 7, m. (Tex.). Pound, 82, 9 (Kan.) Reprinted from *JAF* 26, 364. Randolph I, 318, 10; 11 (Mo.); 13 6-line sts., m. (Ark.). Scarborough, 243, 10 (N.C.). Brown, 446, 66 lines (a related piece entitled "Darby and Joan"); 447, 10 (N.C.). *JAF* 26, 364, 9 (Kan.) (Reprinted by Leach, 747); 3 (Kan.) Refs. *JAF* 29, 173, 10 (Va.); 13 (Ind.); 12 (Ind.). *JAF* 35, 366, 2 frags. and tunes (O.). *JAF* 49, 237, 11, m. (Ky.).

Cunningham II, 123, 5 d ("John Grumlie"). Baring-Gould and Sharp, 6, 5d, m. ("The Old Man and His Wife". This text is similar to those traditional in America). Ford II, 46, 6d (Scot. "John Grumlie").

See Arthur K. Moore, "Types of the Folk Song 'Father Grumble' ", *JAF* 64 (1951), 89-94. The author points out that this ballad, in the form familiar in American tradition, was published in 1842 by J. O. Halliwell-Phillipps in *The Nursery Rhymes of England* (Percy Soc., IV), p. 32.

Q 2

THE OLD WOMAN OF SLAPSADAM

(The Wily Auld Carle; The Old Woman in Dover, etc.)

The old woman feeds her husband marrow bones to make him blind. He then says he will drown himself and asks her to push him into the water. As she runs forward to do so, he steps aside and she falls in. When she calls for help he reminds her that he cannot see to aid her.

> There was an old woman of Slapsadam,
> In Slapsadam did dwell;
> She loved her old man dearly,
> But another twice as well.

Eddy, 90, 8 and ref. (O.). Belden, 238, 7 and ref. (Mo.) Notes and refs. Brewster, 281, 8 (Ind.). Brown, 450, 8 and ref.; 9 and ref. (N.C.). Chappell, 79, 6, m. (N.C.). Cox, 464, 8d couplets (W. Va.) Refs. Linscott, 255, 10, m. (Me. "The Old Woman in Dover"). Lomax, *Our Singing Country*, 176, 9, m. (Tex. A Negro version). Neely, 151, 7½ (Ill. "The Old Woman from Slab City") Owens, 207, 7 and ref., m. (Tex. "The Old Woman from Ireland"). Randolph IV, 248, 4d, m. (Ark.). Scarborough, 239, 7 and ref. (Va.). Sharp I, 348, 7, m. (N.C.) frags. with tunes from Va. and N.C. *JAF* 29, 179, 8 (O.). *JAF* 40, 40, frag. of 4 sts. (O.). *PTFLS* X, 165, 8, m. (Tex.).

Greig, xiii, 12 ("The Wily Auld Carle").

See also the following piece.

Q 3

JOHNNY SANDS

Johnny announces that he is tired of life and has decided to drown himself. His wife agree to run downhill and push him into the water. At his request she ties his hands in case he should try to save himself. When she comes down the hill, he steps aside and she plunges into the water. She calls for help, but he reminds her that she has tied his hands.

> A man whose name was Johnny Sands
> Had married Betty Hague;
> Although she brought him gold and lands,
> She proved a terrible plague;
> She proved a terrible plague.

Morris, 368, 8, m. (Fla.); 5 (Ga. via Fla.). Belden, 238, 6 (Mo.) Notes and refs. Brewster, 262, 8; 1, m. (Ind.). Brown, 448, 6; add. sts. (N.C.). Eddy, 89, 8 (O.). Hudson, 198, 8 (Miss.). Neely, 175, 6, m. (Ill.). Pound, 114, 4d (from ms.); 3d (Wyo.). Randolph IV, 246, 8, m. (Mo.). Stout, 65, 32 lines, m. (Ia.). *JAF* 28, 174, 7 (Miss. from ms.). *JAF* 29, 179, refs. *JAF* 35, 385, refs. *JAF* 49, 235, 4d (Ky.). *JAF* 60, 204, equiv. of 4 sts. (Ill. from ms.). *PTFLS* VI, 223, 4d, m. (Tex.).

Ord, 93, 4d (Scot.).

Broadsides: (B) Ryle, 8 (Harvard V, 195). Bebbington (Harvard X, 216) (K). (A) J. A. Johnson, Phila., (K). Andrews, 4d (L of C). Harris, 4d (L of C). Songsters: (A) *Uncle Sam's Army Songster,* Indianapolis, 1862, p. 17 (K). *Dan Kelly's Songster,* N.Y., 1869, p. 55 (K). *Delaney Irish Song Book No. 2,* p. 22, 4d.

See also the preceding piece.

Q 4
DEVILISH MARY

The narrator marries Mary after a quick courtship. She soon decides to wear the breeches. She hits him with a shovel, fills his bath with switches, and otherwise torments him. When he tells her they should part, she leaves without a word. The next time he marries, he'll find a girl who can't wear the breeches.

> I went up to London Town
> To court a fair young lady;
> I inquired about her name
> And they called her Devilish Mary.

Lomax, *Our Singing Country,* 136, 7 and ref. (A composite text from La. and Fla.). Randolph III, 187, 6 and ref., m. (Ark.); 2 and ref., m.; 3½ and ref. (Mo.); 6 and ref., m. (Ark.) Refs. Sharp II, 200, 1 and ref., m.; 1, m. (Ky.).

Q 5
THE DUMB WIFE
(*Dumb, Dumb, Dumb*)

The new bride is talented in all household arts but is unable to speak. Her husband gets a doctor to cure her of her dumbness only to find that his wife is a constant talker and a scold. The doctor says that nothing can now be done to make her hold her tongue.

> There was a jolly blade
> And he married him a maid,
> And safely conducted her home, home, home;
> She was neat and she was smart,
> And she pleased him to the heart,
> But alack, and alas, she was dumb, dumb, dumb.

Morris, 380, 6; 4, m. (Fla.). Brown, 453, 9; 6 (N.C.) Refs. Eddy, 214, 12 3-line sts., m. (O.). Korson, *Penna. Songs,* 56, 6, m. (Pa.) Randolph III, 119, 6, m. (Mo.) *SFQ* V, 181, 5 (Ind.) reprinted in *JAF* 57, 282.

JAF 62, 62, 5 (Pa.). *JAF* 66, 48, 6, m. (N.Y.) Refs.
Ford I, 30, 9 (Scot.). Greig, xiii, 8 (Scot.)
Broadsides: (B) Belden (Brown, 452) notes that in *Roxburghe Ballads*
IV, 357-359, Ebsworth prints both the 17th century broadside and a mod-
ern stall-ballad form of this piece. Ashton (*A Century of Ballads*, 319, and
Humor, Wit, and Satire of the 17th Century, 99) prints the late 17th cen-
tury broadside of 10 sts., 'The Dumb Maid; or, The Young Gallant
Trapann'd", "To a new tune call'd 'Dum, dum, dum,' or, 'I would I were
in my own Countrey'." Cadman, 8 (Harvard V, 5). Catnach. (A) J. G.
and H. Hunt, Boston. N. Coverly, Jr., Boston (Thomas Coll. I, 66, 8 sts.)
Andrews, 6 sts. (L of C).

Q 6

THE HOLLY TWIG

The man discovers that he has married a terrible scold. He goes to the
woods and cuts a twig with which he gives his wife such a beating that
he sends her soul to hell. A little devil comes for her and he is at peace
once more. (All the events take place on succeeding days of the week).

> When I was a bachelor bold and young
> I courted me a girl with a clattering tongue.
> She promised she'd marry me, she didn't say when.
> The kisses I gave her were a hundred and ten,
> The kisses I gave her were a hundred and ten.

Hudson, 174, 7 (Miss.). Brown, 455, 7; 6 (N.C.) Refs. Chappell, 77, 7,
m.; 7 couplets (N.C.). Henry, *Folk-Songs*, 154, 9 (Ga.). Randolph III,
367, 6, m. (Mo.). Sharp I, 341, 6½, m.; 7, m.; 1, m. (Va.).
JFSS III, 315, 7, m. (Hants.).
"I have a reference (now mislaid) that this was sung by Grimaldi the
clown, circa 1820, and I am possessed of a printed copy of that period."
(Note from Frank Kidson in *JFSS* III, 316).

Q 7

A RICH OLD MISER

The miser is extremely jealous of his young bride and beats her black
and blue for no good reason. One morning she retaliates by breaking a
ladle over his head and thereby tames him.

> A rich old miser courted me;
> His age it was three score and three;
> And mine it was scarce seventeen.
> I wish his face I ne'er had seen.

Gardner, 422, 5 and ref., m. (Mich.); 2 (Mich. from ms.).

Q 8

THE BOATSMAN AND THE CHEST

The boatsman returns home suddenly when his wife is being visited by the tailor. She tells her lover to hide in a chest. Feigning ignorance of its contents, the boatsman has the chest carried from the house to his ship. When he opens it, he tells the tailor he will take him to sea (or throw him into the sea) to keep him away from his wife.

> There was a little boatsman, wherever he did dwell,
> And he had a little wife and the tailor loved her well,
> And he could not step more than one inch out of the way
> Till a trick upon his wife the little tailor he would play.
> Singing fol de dol the day long.

Sharp I, 338, 6d, m. (N.C.); 17d couplets, m. (Ky.). Eddy, 143, 11 (Ohio. "Jolly Boatman"). Greenleaf, 112, 9d and ref. (Nfld. "The Boatswain and the Tailor"). Henry, *Folk-Songs*, 191, 2 lines and ref. (Ga.). Morris, 371, 13d couplets and ref. (Fla.). *JAF* 52, 64, 16, m. (N.J.).

Broadsides: Harkness, no. 325 and Pitts, 12d ("The Bold Boatswain of Dover").

Morris observes the similarity between this ballad and Boccaccio's *Decameron*, novel 10, 4th day.

Q 9

WILL THE WEAVER

Informed that Will is visiting his wife, the newly married man returns home suddenly. Will climbs upon the chimney pole to escape detection, but the husband sees him, builds a fire, smokes him out, and sends him away with black eyes.

> "Mother, mother, now I'm married
> And I wish I'd longer tarried,
> For my wife doth now declare
> That the breeches she will wear."
>
> . . . .
>
> "There I saw Will the Weaver
> And your wife stood close beside him;
> At the threshold by the door
> They went in, I saw no more."

Brewster, 360, 9, m. (Ind.) Sts. 1 and 4 are given above. Henry, *Folk-Songs*, 304, 11, m. (Ga.). Mackenzie, 328, 11 (N.S.) References. Sharp II, 207, 7, m. (Ky.); 13, m. (Ky.). Shoemaker, 135, 14 (Pa.). *JAF* 46, 22, 14 (N.C.) *JAF* 63, 265, 10, m. (Va.).

Williams, 106, 15 (a composite text).

Broadsides: (B) W. Armstrong, 56 lines. In Scottish chapbooks, items 1254 and 1309 in the Harvard Catalogue. (A) N. Coverly, Jr., 14 sts. (Thomas Coll. I, 78).

Q 10

THE MAJOR AND THE WEAVER

When the weaver comes home suddenly, the major is forced to hide under the bed. Later the weaver dresses to leave home and puts on the major's breeches by mistake. He discovers what he has done when he finds a gold watch and twenty guineas. He returns home claiming that he has as much right to wear the breeches as his wife does to be with the major.

> The weaver had a wife
> And the major loved her dearly;
> And to her bed side
> He appeared both late and early.

Henry, *Folk-Songs,* 306, 10 (Ga.) A somewhat confused text.

Q 11

THE DOG IN THE CLOSET
(*The Old Dyer*)

When the husband returns home unexpectedly, his wife tells the hatter to hide in a closet. The suspicious husband locks the closet door and goes away for help. His wife finally frees her lover and puts a dog in his place. When her husband returns with friends, opens the closet, and discovers the dog, the friends think him a fool, and he begs forgiveness of his wife.

> "There was an old farmer near London did dwell,
> He had a handsome wife and she loved the hatter well
> The old farmer got jelos not without a cause
> It was the young hatter that gave him the cause
>   So it was

Flanders-Barry, 123, 11d (Vt. from ms.). Brown, 445, 5d and ref. (N.C.).

Q 12

THE SEA CAPTAIN AND THE SQUIRE

After the sea captain has gone away, a neighboring squire seduces the captain's bride. Nine months later the captain comes home, notices his wife's stoutness, and calls a doctor when she complains of colic. That night the cook, the maids, and the captain's wife all have babies. Her husband forgives her "for the joke's sake", and she tells him about the squire and says that his servants got her maids with child.

There was a sea captain who was married of late,
He courted a lady to gain her estate;
He was a sea captain, and was bound for the sea,
And before he was bedded he was call-ed away,
With his fol dee die addy, fol dee die addy die ay.

Combs, 159, 13d with 6 lines missing (W. Va.).

Q 13
THE OYSTER GIRL

The oyster girl willingly accepts the scheming narrator's invitation to discuss his purchase in a private room at an inn. Soon after their arrival she picks his pocket, jumps out the window, and disappears, leaving him with a kettle of oysters and the landlord's bill to pay.

I was a-walking down over Chestnut Street,
A fine little oyster girl I chanced for to meet,
And into her kettle so slightly did peep
And asked her did she have any oysters.

Chappell, 86, 7d (N.C.).
Greig, xcvi, 11 (Scot.).
Broadsides: (B) Cadman, 6d (Harvard V, 45). Such, no. 105, 7. Bebbington, 6d (Harvard IX, 142). Hodges, 7 (L of C).

Q 14
THE MONKEY TURNED BARBER

When Pat asks for a shave, a monkey dressed like a man gives a wink and a nod and sets to work. Pat roars with pain and the monkey disappears up the chimney. The barber returns and Pat accuses his father of cutting him. The barber protests that his father is dead, and Pat discovers the truth.

I am a wild Irishman just lately come to town
To view the fine cities of fame and renown.
I stopped at a barber shop for to get shaved,
Where a big ugly beast was to me ill-behaved.

Beck, 223, 8d (Mich. "Irishman's Lumber Song"). Belden, 249, 6d and ref.; 7 and ref. (Mo.). Creighton and Senior, 239, 8d and ref. (N.S.). *JAF* 54,, 173, 5d (Ia.).
Sharp and Marson II, 46, 8d and ref. (Somerset).
Broadsides: Forth, 9d (Harvard III, 1). W. R. Walker, 9d (Harvard IV, 52). Cadman, 9d (Harvard V, 35).

Q 15

THE LOVE-OF-GOD SHAVE

(*Lather and Shave*)

When Pat asks for a shave on credit, the barber uses the old razor he keeps for such people. Unable to stand the torture, Pat rushes out of the shop, saying he'd rather be shaved by a brick. A few days later he hears a jackass bray just as he is passing the barber shop and he assumes that some other poor devil is being given a love-of-God shave.

> A barber kept a razor
> Full of notches and rust
> To shave the poor divils
> Who came there for trust.
>
> .   .   .   .
>
> He looked at the barber
> And then lay down his hod,
> Saying, 'Can you trust me for a shave
> For the love-sake of God?'

Belden, 251, 8 (Mo.) Stanzas one and three are given above. Beck, 225, 8d (Mich. "Lather and Shave"). Henry, *Folk-Songs*, 409, 8d (Tenn.). Shoemaker, 134, 3d and ref. (Pa.).

Broadsides: (B) Harkness (Harvard VI, 55). No imprint, 8d (Harvard I, 8). W. Midgley (Harvard I, 31). Such, no. 424, 8d ("Lather 'Em, Shave 'Em). (A) Andrews, 8d. Songster: (A) *617 Irish Songs*, 111, 8d.

Q 16

COURTING IN THE KITCHEN

Miss Bell treats the narrator to refreshments and then sits on his lap. When her employer returns home suddenly, the girl turns on her suitor and claims that he has come uninvited and has forced his attentions on her. He is sentenced to six months in jail for courting in the kitchen.

> Come all you belles and beaux,
> I pray you give attention.
> For love, it plainly shows,
> Is the devil's own invention.
> Once in love I fell
> With a maid who smiled bewitching;
> Miss Henrietta Bell,
> Lived in Captain Phipps's kitchen.

Mackenzie, 355, 9d and chor. (N.S.).

O'Lochlainn, 64, 9d, m. (Ireland. Text partly from *Wisehart's Comic Songster*).

Songster: (B) *The Sprig of Shillelah,* "compiled by Dinny Blake", London, 1852, p. 214 (M).

Q 17

FINNEGAN'S WAKE

Tim Finnegan falls from a ladder and cracks his skull. His wife takes his "corpse" home and holds a wake, which turns into a free-for-all. When some whiskey is spattered on Tim, he sits up and shows some resentment at being thought dead.

> Tim Finnegan lived in bankers' street;
> He's an Irish gentleman, mighty odd;
> He's a beautiful brogue, so rich and sweet,
> And by profession he carried a hod.
> But you see, he'd a sort of tipsy way;
> With a love for liquor poor Tim was born,
> And to help him through with his work each day
> He'd a drop o' the creature every morn.

Gardner, 409, 5d and ref. (Mich.). Creighton, 185, 5d and ref., m. (N.S.). Eddy, 312, 1d and ref., m. (O.).

O'Lochlainn, 180, 5d and ref., m. (Ireland).

Broadside: (A) Partridge, Boston, no. 920, 5d and ref. Songsters: (A) *617 Irish Songs,* 29, 5d. *Delaney's Irish Song Book No. 1,* p. 10.

Q 18

THE IRISH WAKE

At his wife's suggestion, Pat decides to play dead in order to collect his life insurance. He can't keep still, however, when he smells the whiskey at his wake or when the hearse driver demands payment. Only when the clods are falling on his coffin does Pat realize the consequences of his actions. He jumps from the coffin and flees.

> Times was hard in Irish town,
> Ev'rything was going down,
> And Pat Malone was pushed for ready cash,
> He'd for life insurance spent
> All his money to a cent,
> And so all of Pat's affairs had gone to smash.

Randolph III, 236, 8½ irreg sts., m. (Mo.); 1 st. (Ark.).

Q 19

DORAN'S ASS

On his way to meet Biddy, Pat, who is drunk, lies down to sleep. A jackass lies beside him, and Pat, thinking he is caressing the girl, is horrified to be awakened by a loud braying. He runs to Biddy's home, and she calms his fears by explaining that the creature was Doran's ass.

> One Paddy Doyle lived in Killarney
> He courted a girl called Biddy O'Toole.
> Her tongue was tipped with a bit of the blarney;
> The same to Pat was a golden rule . . .

Mackenzie, 338, 6 8-line sts. and chor. (N.S.) Refs. Creighton, 163, 6 8-line sts. and chor., m. (N.S.). Dean, 38, 6 8-line sts. and chor. (Minn.).

Broadsides: (B) O'Lochlainn, 166, 217, 7 8-line sts., m. (from a ballad sheet). Bebbington, 6 8-line sts. (Harvard X, 70). Such. (A) Partridge, Boston, no. 995, 7 8-line sts. Wehman no. 413 (M). Songsters: (A) 617 *Irish Songs,* 55, 7 8-line sts. O'Conor, 43, 7 8-line sts.

Q 20

DUNCAN CAMPBELL

(*Erin-Go-Bragh*)

When he goes to the city, the man from Argyle is mistaken for an Irishman by a policeman. He starts to beat the policeman and then escapes in a river boat before anyone harms him.

> My name is Duncan Campbell from the town of Argyle.
> I've travelled this country for manys the long mile;
> I've travelled this country, old England and all,
> And the name that I go by is Erin go bragh.

Mackenzie, 330, 7d (N.S.) Notes and refs.

Ford I, 47, 9d, m. (Scot.). Greig, cxxvii, 8d (Scot.). Ord, 387, 9d (Scot.). Joyce, *Ancient Irish Music,* 86, 6d, m. (An Irish variant).

Broadsides: (B) No imprint, 9d (Harvard III, 55). Fordyce, 9d. (A) DeMarsan (M). Songster: (A) *Delaney's Irish Song Book No. 3,* p. 9 (M).

Q 21

THE MILLER'S WILL

(*The Miller's Three Sons*)

To decide which of his three sons should be left the mill, the dying miller asks each how much toll he would take. Heck answers that he would take a peck from each bushel and Ralph says he'd steal half. The miller is displeased until the youngest son says he would take three pecks and leave one. His father says he has learned his trade well and gives him the mill.

> There was an old miller and he was well known;
> He had three sons who were well nigh grown;
> He came to die—to make his will;
> He had nothing to give but an old tub mill

> *Refrain*
> Fa-de-re-de-ri-you-die-you-die.
> Fa-de-re-de-ri.

Henry, *Folk-Songs,* 192, 10 (N.C.); 10 Tenn.?). Belden, 244, 8; 7; 8 (Mo.) Refs. Brown, 441, 10 and ref.; 8; add. sts. (N.C.). Chappell, 183, 4 (N.C.). Cox, 450, 7½ and ref.; 7 and ref. (W. Va.) Tune, p. 531. Creighton and Senior, 234, 10, m. (N.S.). Creighton, 203, 10 and ref., m. (N.S.). Eddy, 167, 9, m.; 10, m. (O.). Flanders-Barry, 11, 10, m. (Vt.) Notes and refs. Gardner, 247, 10, m. (Mich.). Morris, 381, 7, m.; 2 (Fla.). Randolph I, 359, 7, m.; 2; 1 (Ark.); 20 couplets and ref., m. (Mo.). Scarborough, 240, 9 (Ky.); 7 (N.C.). Sharp II, 221, 11, m. (Ky.); 10, m. (N.C.). Thomas, *Devil's Ditties,* 80, 9, m. (Ky.). *JAF* 35, 390, 9 and ref., m. (O.) Refs. *JAF* 46, 11 (N.C.).

Baring-Gould, 24, 5d, m. (W. of Eng.). Greig, xli, 10 sts. (Scot.). Williams, 192, 10 (Wilts.).

Broadsides: (B) No imprint, "The Miller's Advice to his Three Sons, in Taking of Toll." (Item 1988 in the Harvard Catalogue). *Roxburghe Ballads* VIII, 611, 10 sts. (Aldermary Churchyard).

Q 22

SKEWBALL

On the plains of Kildare, Skewball and the gray mare race before a large crowd which has bet heavily on the mare. Half way around the course, Skewball speaks to his rider and promises to win much money for his master. He easily beats the mare and drinks a toast to the victory with his rider.

> Ye gallyants and nobles, I pray listen all
> While I sing the praises of famous Sku-ball
> That has lately come over as you may understand
> By the great Artumaro, the peer of the land.

Flanders-Barry, 172, 7d, m. (Vt.) Notes and refs. Brown, 371, 2 7-line frags. of Negro variants (N.C.) Refs. Lomax, *American Ballads,* 68, 20d couplets ("Stewball". A Negro variant).

Broadsides: (B) G. Walker, Jr., Durham, 10d (Harvard II, 20). Forth, 11d (Harvard III, 166). No imprint, 11d ("Skew Ball"). Songster: (A)

The Songster's Museum, Hartford, 1826, p. 3, 7d. (Reprinted in Flanders-Barry, p. 173).

"The oldest known version of this ballad of the race on the Kildare, Ireland, track between Sku-ball and Sir Ralph Gore's mare, Miss Portly, was printed in *The Vocal Library* (London, 1822), p. 526, and reprinted in Scarborough, *On the Trail of Negro Folk Songs,* pp. 61-62. . . .

"Skewbald, or skewball, is applied to a horse having a coat marked with blotches of bay on a white ground . . . ." (Notes from Flanders-Barry, pp. 174-175).

Q 23

CREEPING JANE

Creeping Jane had no reputation as a race horse, but after a slow start she managed to win a race. She was then as fresh as ever, while the other horses were exhausted. The ballad ends with a report of Jane's death and a plea to keep her body from the hounds.

> O when she came the racecourse along,
> The gentlemen they viewed her all around,
> Saying, "She's not able for to gallop the racecourse along,
> She's not able to gallop o'er the ground, fal de ray.
> Fal de ral de ray,
> She's not able for to gallop o'er the ground, fal de ray."

Gardner, 250, 4, m. (Mich.).

Baring-Gould and Sharp, 40, 6, m. Sharp and Marson, I, 51, 6 and ref., m. (Somerset). *JFSS* I, 233, 1, m. (Yorks.).

Broadside: (B) Such, no. 317, 7 sts.

Q 24

PAT MALLOY

Finding thirteen children hard to provide for, Pat's mother sends him away with her blessing. He goes to England and America, makes some money, and sends all of it home. At last he is about to return to Ireland and to Molly, the girl he loves.

> At sixteen years of age I was
> My mother's fair-haired boy.
> She kept a little huckster's shop,
> Her name it was Malloy.

Scarborough, 334, 11 (S.C.).

Broadsides: (A) DeMarsan, 6d. Partridge, Boston, no. 969, 3 8-line d. sts. Songsters: (A) O'Conor, 136, 3 8-line d. sts. *617 Irish Songs,* 3 8-line d. sts.

A continuation in 6 d. sts. entitled "Molly's Welcome to Pat Malloy" is found on a broadside by Partridge (no. 1016). A DeMarsan printing of the same piece (L of C) is called "The Return of Pat Malloy."

Q 25

TOM O'NEILL

Tom decides to become a priest and goes to college. Later he is ordained and sent home for a visit. When a rich girl tries to have him give up the priesthood and marry her, he firmly refuses. Shortly thereafter the girl claims that Tom has seduced her and made her pregnant. Brought to trial, Tom is sentenced to be transported. Then a man rides up and clears the priest's name by declaring that he is the baby's father and that the girl gave him one thousand pounds for his share in the plot.

> There was a widow lived in this place
> Who had three darling sons,
> Their father died and left them
> When they were very young.
> A long time she endeavoured
> To maintain her darling sons,
> Her youngest one became a man
> At the age of twenty-one.

Creighton, 187, 19d, m. (N.S.).

Broadsides. (B) No imprint, 9 8-line d. sts. (Harvard X, 18. "Father Tom O'Neale"). Such, no. 271 (Harvard XII, 116). Songsters: (A) *617 Irish Songs*, 42, 19d. O'Conor, 8, 19d.

Q 26

THE BAD GIRL'S LAMENT

(St. James' Hospital; The Young Girl Cut Down in Her Prime)

The bad girl tells of her descent from the ale-house and the dance-hall to the poorhouse and finally almost to the grave. She asks pity for her mother and a prayer from the minister. She requests roses for her coffin and asks that it be carried by young sailors.

> As I walked out of St. James' Hospital,
> St. James' Hospital one early morn,
> I spied my only fairest daughter
> Wrapped up in white linen as cold as the clay.
>
> *Chorus:*
> So beat your drums and play your pipes merrily,
> And play the dead march as you bear me along.
> Take me to the churchyard and throw the ground o'er me;
> I'm a young maiden. I know I've done wrong.

Mackenzie, 301, 5d (N.S.) Refs. Cox, 242, refs. to this and related ballads. Creighton, 219, 5d, m. (N.S.). Cf. Sandburg, 228, "Those Gambler's Blues". Sharp II, 164, 4d, m. (Va. "St. James' Hospital" or "The Sailor Cut Down in his Prime". In this text the victim is a young man). *JAF* 25, 277, 2d and ref. (N.S. "The Maiden's Lament").

JFSS IV, 325, 6d, m. (Hants. "The Young Girl Cut Down in Her Prime"); 1d, m. (Oxon.); 1d, m. (Somerset). *JFSS* V, 193, 4d, m. (Herts.).

Note: "The Bad Girl's Lament", like the American ballad "The Cowboy's Lament" (B 1 in *Native American Balladry*) is derived from a British broadside called "The Unfortunate Rake" or "The Unfortunate Lad". Kidson in *JFSS* I, 254 gives one stanza of the ballad, which he says "will scarcely bear reprinting in its entirety". For "The Unfortunate Lad" see a broadside without imprint of 7 d. sts. (Harvard V, 119). The most explicit stanza reads as follows:

> Had she but told me when she disordered me,
> Had she but told me of it in time,
> I might of got salts and pills of white mercury
> But now I'm cut down in the height of my prime.

Q 27

ERIN'S GREEN SHORE

The narrator dreams of a beautiful damsel in a green mantle decorated with shamrocks and roses. She tells him she has come to awaken her countrymen, "who slumber on Erin's green shore." The dreamer awakens and wishes success to this "Goddess of Freedom."

> One morning in June as I rambled
> By the shores of a clear purling stream,
> I lay down on a bank of primroses,
> I quickly fell into a dream.
> I dreamt I beheld a fair damsel,
> Her equal I ne'er saw before.
> She sighed for the wrongs of her country,
> As she strolled along Erin's green shore.

Greenleaf, 142, 5d. m. (Nfld.). Belden, 282, 7 (Kan.). Cox, 442, 4d; 4d; equiv. of 4d (W. Va.) Refs. Creighton, 171, 5d, m. (N.S.). Korson, *Penna. Songs,* 45, 4d, m. (Pa.). Randolph I, 324, 4d, m. (Mo.). Thomas, *Devil's Ditties,* 176, 4d, m. (Ky.).

Broadsides: (B) Cadman, 6d (Harvard VI, 146). George Walker, Durham (Harvard II, 97). Bebbington (C). Songsters: (A) *Delaney's Irish Song Book No. 1,* p. 7. O'Conor, 38, 4d.

Q 28

THE SOLDIER'S POOR LITTLE BOY

The poor boy asks to be sheltered from the storm, saying that his mother is dead and his father is away at war. The lady gladly takes him in and says he may stay as long as she lives, for her own son has fallen in battle.

> The snowflakes fast were falling,
> The howling winds did roar,
> When a little boy, half-naked,
> Came up to a lady's door.

Eddy, 297, 8 (0). Belden, 273, 4d (Mo. from ms.) ; 4d; 3½d, m. (Mo.). Brewster, 304, 4d; 4d (Ind.). Brown, 396, 4d; 5 (N.C.). Cox, 275, 6; 8 (W. Va.) Refs. Greenleaf, 201, 8 (Nfld.) Refs. Shoemaker, 74, 8 (Pa.). Stout, 117, 4d; 2 6-line sts. (Ia.).

Broadsides: (B) Cox refers to broadsides by Such, Ryle, and Pitts, and says "This is a version of 'The Soldier's Homeless Boy', a song ascribed in a Philadelphia broadside (J. H. Johnson) to Charles Bender." (A) De-Marsan, 4d. Wehman (C).

Q 29

THE FISHERMAN'S BOY

The boy's mother has died at home and his father in a storm at sea. He wanders alone until a kind lady takes him in and persuades her father to find work for him. He serves his master faithfully until he becomes a man.

> Down in the lowlands a poor boy did wander,
> Down in the lowlands a poor boy roamed,
> By his friends he was deserted, he looked so dejected,
> Cries the poor little fisherman so far away from home.

Eddy, 178, 7d (O.). Greenleaf, 200, 6d (Nfld.). *JAF* 35, 366, 7d (O. from ms. of 1852). Refs. *PTFLS* VI, 30, 2d, m. (Tex.).

Greig, lii, 7d (Scot.). *JFSS* VIII, 38, 1d, m. (Sussex).

Broadsides: (B) W. R. Walker, 7d (Harvard IV, 36). Catnach, 7d (Harvard V, 151). Such, 7d. Songster: (A) *Marsh's Selection, or, Singing for the Million*, II, 197, (K).

For related pieces see the preceding ballad; 'The Fisherman's Girl", *JAF* 35, 367, with Kittredge's refs. to other texts; and "The Poor Smuggler's Boy", Ashton, p. 240.

Q 30

THE FARMER'S BOY

The boy asks to be given employment, or at least to be sheltered over-night from the cold. The farmer's wife and daughter persuade him to

keep the lad. When the farmer dies, he leaves the boy, who has worked
loyally for many years, both his land and the hand of his daughter.

> The sun went down one dreary day,
> Across yon dreary moor.
> Both ragged and lame a poor boy came
> Up to a farmer's door.
> "Can you," said he, "tell me of any
> That will give to me employ?
> I can plow, I can sow, I can reap and mow
> And be a farmer's boy.

Flanders & Brown, 118, 4d (Vt.). Belden, 272, 4d (Wis.) Refs. Creighton & Senior, 158, 3d, m. (N.S.). Pound, 69, 5d (Eng. via Wyo.) Stout, 27,
5d (Ia.). *JAF* 51, 38, 6 (O. from ms. of 1855). *JAF* 52, 37, 7, m. (Ky.
via Wis.) *NYFQ* V, 90, 3 (N.Y.).

Broadwood, 134, 5d, m. (Sussex); 1, m. (Leeds); 1, m. (Yorks.). Kidson, 63, 5d, m. (Yorks.)

Broadsides: (B) Pitts. Catnach. Such, reprinted in Johnson's *Popular
British Ballads* II, 260, 5d. (A) Wehman. Wrigley. DeMarsan, 5d. Brown,
Baltimore, 5d (L of C).

Q 31
THE LOST LADY FOUND

Because his niece has been stolen by gypsies, a man is accused of her
murder and is sentenced to death. Her lover finds the girl in Dublin and
tells her of her uncle's predicament. She promises to marry the youth and
give him much money if he will take her back to England. He does so and
her uncle's life is saved.

> It's of a rich lady in England did dwell.
> She lived with her uncle, I know it right well.
> It's down in the valley by lowlands so sweet
> The gypsies betrayed her and stole her away.

Mackenzie, 86, 9d (N.S. A confused text). Refs.

Barrett, 74, 9d (London); tune from Cheshire. Broadwood, *Eng. Trad.
Songs*, 86, 9d, m. (Lincs.). *JFSS* II, 99, 9d, m. (Lincs. Text from a Such
broadside).

Broadsides: (B) Catnach, 9d (Harvard VII, 185). Fortey, 9d. T.
Batchelar, 9d.

Q 32
THE ROMISH LADY

A young lady secretly reads her Bible and refuses to worship angels
and pictures. Her mother reports her to the priests, who throw her into

a dungeon and later bring her to trial before the Pope. Because she refuses to recant, she is condemned to be burned, and the execution is carried
out. She blames her mother for her ruin but asks pardon for all her
tormentors.

> There was a Romish lady brought up in Popery;
> Her mother always told her the priest she must obey.
> "Oh, pardon me, dear mother, I humbly pray thee now,
> For unto these false idols I can no longer bow".

Eddy, 220, 11d (O.). Arnold, 19, 5d, m. (Ala.). Belden, 450, 8½d;
11d (Mo. from ms.); 8d; 17 (Mo.) Refs. Brewster, 257, 13; 4 (Ind.).
Brown, 213, 11d (N.C.) Refs. Gardner, 363, 9d (Mich. from ms.). Hudson, 137, 16 (Miss.). Morris, 388, 22 (Fla.). Owens, 284, 7d, m. (Tex.).
Pound, 63, 22 (Ind. from ms.). Randolph IV, 32, 7d, m. (Mo.). Scarborough, 176, 22 (Va.). *JAF* 52, 1½d, m. (Ky.). *JAF* 60, 11d (Ill. from
ms.). *SFQ* V, 147, 11d (N.C.).

Broadsides: (B) Evans I, 135, 12d. *Roxburghe Ballads* I, 35, 24 (reign
of Charles II). (A) A broadside of ca. 1850 pub. in N. Y. Lomax, *Our
Singing Country*, 40-43, reprints a text of 11d sts. and a tune from a
reprint of *The Southern Harmony*, Phila., 1854.

Note: The first line of this ballad, and perhaps more, is sung by Merry-
thought in Fletcher's *The Knight of the Burning Pestle*, 1613, V, iii.

Q 33

THE LAKE OF COOL FINN
(*Willie Leonard*)

Willie persuades his comrade to take a morning swim. He dives into
the lake first and reaches an island but warns his friend against following
him. In attempting to return to shore, Willie disappears. His sister dreams
that he has drowned, and his uncle finds the body. Twenty-four young men
assist in burying Willie, while his loved ones grieve.

> Young Willie stripped off to swim the lake round;
> He swam to an island, and came to dry ground,
> Saying, "Comrade, my comrade, don't venture to come in,
> For there's deep and false water in the Lake of Cool Finn."

Barry, 26, 9d, m. (Me.) Stanza three is given above. Notes. Flanders-
Barry, 32, 8½d, m. (Vt.) Notes. *Bulletin* no. 8, p. 9, 8d, m. (Me.) (Reprinted by Leach, 733) Notes.

Joyce, 227, 6d, m. (text revised by the editor). Johnson, *Pop. Brit. Ballads* IV, 166, 5d (as revised by Joyce).

Broadsides: (B) Such, no. 369, 8d (Harvard XIII, 63. "The Lake of
Cold Finn"). Catnach, 8d. Songsters: (A) *617 Irish Songs*, 99, 8d.
O'Conor, 15, 6d.

"Willie was not 'drowned'; he was taken away to *Tir fa Tonn,* 'Fairyland-under-wave', by a water woman who had fallen in love with him". (Note from Flanders-Barry, p. 33).

Q 34

THE CHILDREN IN THE WOOD

(*The Babes in the Woods*)

A gentleman of Norfolk and his wife die suddenly, leaving a boy of three and a younger girl. The father leaves his fortune to the children when they come of age. In the meantime, they are to be cared for by his brother, who will inherit the money should the children die. A year later the uncle hires two ruffians to murder them in the woods. One of the murderers relents, and a fight ensues in which he kills the other. He then deserts the children, and after a while they die in each other's arms. The robins cover their bodies with leaves. The wrath of God falls upon the uncle in the form of fires, crop failures, and financial loss. His two sons die on a voyage to Portugal. Finally his crime is revealed, and he confesses, goes to prison, and dies.

> Now ponder well, you parents dear,
> These words which I shall write;
> An awful story you shall hear
> In time brought forth to light.

Morris, 401, 40 (Fla.). Gardner, 343, 19d (Mich. from ms.). Flanders-Barry, 234, 12, m. (Vt.) Notes and refs. The editors quote Addison's praise of this ballad from the *Spectator,* no. 85. *JAF* 35, 348, refs.

Christie I, 142, 13d, m. (Text condensed from Percy's *Reliques*).

Broadsides: (B) The Harvard Library has eleven or more English, Irish, and Scottish broadsides and chapbooks containing this ballad under various titles, e. g., "The Babes in the Wood; or, The Norfolk Gentleman's Last Will and Testament," Belfast, 1769 (Item 640 in the Harvard Catalogue); "The Two Babes in the Wood," J. Neilson, Paisley, 1812, 39½ sts. (Item 642); "The Children in the Wood," Bow Churchyard, London (Item 644). Percy's *Reliques,* ed. Wheatley, III, 172, 20 d. sts. *Roxburghe Ballads* II, 216, 20d; notes, 214. Catnach, a large two-penny broadside of the piece with eight woodcuts (K). (A) N. Coverly, Jr., Boston, 76 couplets (Thomas Coll. II, 9). W. and J. Gilman, Newburyport.

Notes: This ballad was entered in the *Stationers' Register* under the title "The Norfolk Gent, his Will and Testament . . ." on October 15, 1595. It may have been based on an old play. See the discussion in Percy's *Reliques,* ed. Wheatley, III, 169-172.

A three stanza lament on the fate of the children called "The Babes in the Wood" is widely known in American tradition, but the long ballad is rarely met with.

A comic parody of the ballad may be found in Ashton, p. 124, and on a broadside by Bebbington (Harvard X, 148).

Q 35

THE HIGH BLANTYRE EXPLOSION

The young woman tells the narrator that her fiancé, John Murphy, a youth of twenty-one, was killed in the mines of High Blantyre on October 22nd, with more than 200 others. She sadly reflects that she'll never more walk with him and pull daisies on the banks of the Clyde. She will transplant the daisies onto his grave and water them with her tears.

> On Clyde's bonny banks as I lately did wander,
> To a village High Blanter I chanced for to roam.
> I saw a young female all dressed in deep mourning,
> And sadly lamenting the fate of her love.

Korson, 44, 6d, m. (Pa. "The High Blanter Explosion").
Lloyd, 78, 5d (a composite Scottish text).
"The disaster occurred at Messrs. Dixon's colliery, High Blantyre, near Glasgow, on October 22nd, 1877." (note from Lloyd, 136).
Henderson, *Victorian Street Ballads,* p. 45, prints another piece on this disaster entitled "Fearful Colliery Explosion in Scotland."

Q 36

THE MINER'S DOOM

The miner is killed when the elevator rope breaks as he is returning to the surface. His wife dies of grief and their three children are left alone.

> At five in the morning as jolly as any,
> The miner doth rise to his work for to go;
> He caresses his wife and his children so dearly,
> And bids them adieu before closing the door;
> And goes down the deep shaft at the speed of an arrow,
> His heart light and gay without fear or dread,
> Has no thoughts of descending to danger and peril—
> But his life is depending on one single thread.

Korson, *Penna. Songs,* 388, 4 8-line d. sts., m. (Wales via Pa.). Korson, *Minstrels,* 203, 4 8-line d. sts. (Pa.).
Lloyd, 71, 4 8-line d. sts., m. (Wales).

Q 37
THE FACTOR'S GARLAND

The kind-hearted factor pays a dead Christian's duties so that he can be buried and then ransoms a girl who is about to be hanged for striking a Turkish lady. The grateful girl returns to England with him as his maid. On his next trip, to an unnamed country, he takes as a present to the emperor a garment embroidered by the girl. Overjoyed, the emperor recognizes his daughter's work and offers the factor her hand if he will bring her safely home. On his return trip the factor is tossed overboard by the captain, who hopes to marry the princess. When she reaches home, the grieving princess agrees to marry the captain after mourning for forty days. In the meantime the factor has been rescued from an island by an old man in a canoe, who asks as payment the couple's first baby. The factor arrives at court and accuses the captain, who commits suicide. The factor then marries the princess, they have a son, and the old man later comes for him. He reveals himself as the spirit of the body the factor had had buried, expresses his gratitude, and allows them to keep their child.

> I'll tell you a ditty, a truth and no jest,
> Concerning a young gentleman in the east,
> Who by his great gaming came to poverty,
> And afterwards went many voyages to sea.
>
> He was well educated and one of great wit;
> Three merchants in London they all thought it fit
> To make him their Captain and Factor also;
> So for them a voyage he to Turkey did go.

PTFLS VI, 59, 54d (Tex.) Stanzas 1 and 2 are given above. Brown, 220, 86d lines (N.C.). Flanders and Brown, 81, frag. of 4 sts., m. (Vt.). Gardner, 479, a reference to a text in manuscript in the Mich. collection. *JAF* 66, 54, a corrupt frag. of about 19d lines recited with the rest of the story summarized in prose.

Greig, cxx, 47d (Scot.).

Broadsides: (B) *A Coll. of Old Ballads* III, 221, 58d. London, Bow Church Yard ("The Turkey Factor"). Turner, Coventry. (Items 814 and 815 in The Harvard Catalogue, which also lists four chapbooks containing this piece under the title "The Factor's Garland"). (A) No imprint. N. Coverly, Boston ("Tune 'Paul Jones' Victory' ").

Q 38
THE VALIANT LONDON PRENTICE

The London prentice is sent by a merchant to be a factor in Turkey. There he keeps asserting the superiority of Queen Elizabeth over all other rulers. Annoyed, the Turkish king asks his son to stop the youth's boasting, whereupon the prentice breaks the prince's neck. Condemned to be torn apart by two lions, the prentice thrusts his arms down their throats and tears out their hearts. Finally convinced of English superiority, the Turkish ruler acknowledges the virtues of England's queen and gives the prentice his daughter in marriage.

> 'Tis of a wealthy prentice my purpose is to speak,
> And tell his bold adventures done for his country's sake,
> Search all the world about you and you will hardly find
> A man in valour to exceed this gallant prentice mine.

Creighton and Senior, 124, 17d, m. (N.S.).

Broadsides: (B) *Osterley Park Ballads,* p. 213, 18d (from a print of ca. 1675). Richard Hill, London, 1681 (Harvard). *A Collection of Old Ballads,* I, 199, 18d. Dicey, Northampton (Item 950 in the Harvard Catalogue). (A?) No imprint, 36 sts. (Thomas Coll., II, 86).

"This ballad was originally published in the reign of Elizabeth about 1595 . . ." (note from Fawcett, *Osterley Park Ballads,* p. 215).

Q 39

THE BUILDING OF SOLOMON'S TEMPLE

This Masonic ballad describes in detail Solomon's hiring of thousands of workmen and the careful construction of a magnificently adorned temple in Jerusalem. The ballad ends with two stanzas dealing with modern Freemasonry.

> In history we read of a freemason king,
> The glory of Israel, his praise let us sing!
> He who built a great fabric, as we understand,
> On the Mount Moriah in Jerusalem.

Mackenzie, 381, 17d (N.S.) Notes and refs.

Greig, cxlviii, 20d (Scot.).

Broadsides: (B) Bloomer, Birmingham, 56d lines.No imprint, 11d (L of C). (A) Marshall and Hanover Sts., Boston, ("Solomon's Temple") (M). *Howe's One Hundred Old Favorite Songs,* p. 262 (M).

Appendix II

SOME BRITISH BALLAD PRINTERS OF THE NINETEENTH CENTURY

H. Andrews, 27 St. Peter's St., Leeds. (Formerly Barr).

W. Armstrong, Banastre St., Liverpool.

Richard Barr, Leeds. (See also H. Andrews).

T. Batchelar or Ann Batchelar, Little Cheapside; later, 14 Hackney Road Crescent, London.

J. Beaumont, 176 York St., Leeds.

John O. Bebbington, 31 Oldham Road; later, 26 Goulden St., Manchester.

T. Birt, 39 Great St. Andrews St., Seven Dials, London.

T. Bloomer, 10 High St., Birmingham.

P. Brereton, 1 Lower Exchange St., Dublin.

Brock, Bristol.

J. Cadman, 152 Great Ancoats St., Manchester.

W. Carbutt, Tadcaster.

James Catnach, 2 & 3 Monmouth Court, Seven Dials, London.

C. Croshaw, Coppergate, York.

Dalton's Public Library, 96 Walmgate, York.

J. Davenport, 6 George Court, London.

B. W. Dickinson, High Petergate, York.

Henry Disley, 57 High St., St. Giles, London. (Formerly with Catnach).

Matthew S. Dodds, 33 & 34 Quayside, Newcastle.

J. Easton, York.

J. Evans and Sons, 42 Long Lane, London.

R. Evans, Foregate St., Chester.

T. Evans, 79 Long Lane, London.

W. and T. Fordyce, 15 Grey St., Newcastle.

Wm. S. Fortey, 2 & 3 Monmouth Court; later, 4 Great St. Andrews St., Seven Dials, London. (Formerly Catnach.)

J. Forth, Pocklington.

W. Forth, Bridlington and Hull.

John Gilbert, Newcastle.

Haly, Hanover St., Cork.

John Harkness, 121 Church St., Preston.

W. Harris, 179 Deritend, Birmingham.

Henson, Northampton.

Hill, Lambeth, London.

Hillat and Martin, London.

E. Hodges, 31 Dudley St.; later 26 Gratton St., Seven Dials, London.
(Formerly Pitts).

Howard and Evans, London.

Hurd, Shaftesbury.

Jackson and Son, 21 Moor St.; later, 69 Digbeth, Birmingham. (Formerly
J. Russell).

George Jacques, Oldham Road Library, Manchester.

F. Jennings, Sheffield.

J. Jennings, 13 Water-lane, Fleet Street, London.

J. Kendrew, 23 Colliergate, York.

Elias Keys, Devonport.

W. King, Oxford.

John Livsey, 43 Hanover St., Shudehill, Manchester; also, 12 Whittle St.,
Oldham St., Manchester.

W. McCall, Liverpool.

Mason, Belper.

W. Midgley, Russell St., Halifax.

Nichols, Wakefield.

J. Pannell, 24 Byron St., Liverpool.

C. Paul, 18 Great St. Andrews St., London.

James Paul and Co., 2 & 3 Monmouth Court, Seven Dials, London. (Formerly Catnach.)

T. Pearson, 6 Chadderton St., Oldham Rd., Manchester.

Charles Pigott, 52 Compton St., Clerkenwell, London.

G. Pigott, 60 Old Street, London.

John Pitts, 6 Great St. Andrews St., Seven Dials, London.

Pitts, Jackson, and Co., Birmingham. (Formerly J. Russell).

"The Poet's Box", Glasgow.

H. Pratt, Birmingham.

William Pratt, 82 Digbeth, Birmingham.

J. V. Quick, 42 Bowling Green, Clerkenwell, London.

John Ross, Newcastle.

J. Russell, Birmingham.

Ryle and Co., 2 & 3 Monmouth Court, Seven Dials, London. (Formerly
Catnach).

Sanderson, Edinburgh.
W. Shelmerdine, Deansgate, Manchester.
Spencer, Broadstones, Bradford.
W. Stephenson, 8 Bridge St., Gateshead
Henry Parker Such, 123 Union St.; also, 177 Union St., London.
S. Summerside, 58 Whitechapel, Liverpool.
Swindells, Manchester.
Taylor, 14 Waterloo Road, London.
R. Taylor, Bedale.
W. Taylor, Brick Lane, Spitalfields, London.
J. Todd, Easingwold.
John Turner, Coventry.
George Walker and George Walker, Jr., 46 Sadler St., Durham.
R. Walker, near the Duke's Palace, Norwich
W. R. Walker, Newcastle.
J. Wheeler, White St. or 10 Well St., Shude-Hill, Manchester.
White, Manchester.
John Whiting, 134 Moor St., Birmingham.
Willey, London.
Williamson, Newcastle.
W. Wright, Lichfield and Birmingham.

SOME AMERICAN BALLAD PRINTERS OF THE NINETEENTH CENTURY

J. Andrews, 38 Chatham St., New York.
A. W. Auner, 10th & Race Sts., or 110 N. 10th St., or 11th & Market Sts., Philadelphia.
Bell and Co., 639 Kearny St., San Francisco.
Louis Bonsal, Baltimore and Frederick Sts., Baltimore.
T. C. Boyd, Montgomery St., corner of Pine, San Francisco.
George W. Brown, 319 N. Gay St., Baltimore.
Nathaniel Coverly, Boston.
Nathaniel Coverly, Jr., Milk St., Boston.
H. DeMarsan, 38 Chatham St., New York (formerly J. Andrews).
L. Deming, 1 Market St., or 62 Hanover St., Boston.
Thomas G. Doyle, 297 Gay St., Baltimore.
Elton, 134 Division St., New York.
W. and J. Gilman, Middle St., Newburyport, Mass.
Harris, S. E. corner 4th and Vine Sts., Phila.

J. G. and H. Hunt, N. E. corner of Fanueil Hall, Boston.

Jackson, 190 Houston St., New York.

J. H. Johnson, 7 N. 10th St., Phila.

J. Magee, 316 Chestnut St., Phila.

Charles Magnus, 12 Frankfort St., New York.

Horace Partridge, 37 Hanover St., or 105 Hanover St. and 54 Friend St.,
    Boston.

Wehman Bros., 158 Park Row, or H. J. Wehman, 130 Park Row, New York.

William K. Wood, 108 Court St., Boston.

J. Wrigley, 27 Chatham St., New York.

Corner of Marshall and Hanover Sts., Boston.

25 High St., Providence, R. I.

42 N. Main St., Providence, R. I.

Appendix III

SOME AMERICAN RECORDINGS OF
BRITISH BROADSIDE BALLADS

(List derived from Ben Gray Lumpkin's *Folksongs on Records,* Issue Three, and the *Check-List of Recorded Songs* published by the Library of Congress).

	Lumpkin's Item no.	*Check-List no.*
The Bad Girl's Lament		Fla. 956B3
		Tex. 2637A3
The Banks of Claudy		Mich. 2281A2
The Banks of Dundee		N.J. 1774B1
		Ariz. 3324A
Bay of Biscay	620	
Black-Eyed Susan	183	N.Y. 1836B4 & 5
		Ky. 1998A-10 in.
The Blind Beggar's Daughter		Mich. 3396A2
The Boatsman and the Chest		N.Y. 3665A1
The Bold *Princess Royal*		Mich. 2274B
The Bold Soldier	265	N.H. 3701B
		3702A1
The Bonny Irish Boy		N.Y. 3665A2 & B1
		Mich. 2290A
The Bonny Wee Window	233	
The Boston Burglar	120, 336, 550, L.C.A. 14	N.Y. 826A1 Mo. 3224A2
Brennan on the Moor	265	D.C. 1636A1 & B1
		Mich. 2280B2
The Butcher Boy	60, 336	N.Y. 827B1
		Ky. 1446A1
Caroline of Edinburgh Town	L.C.A. 14	Mich. 2298A3
Charming Beauty Bright		N.Y. 2541A
		Ky. 1486A1
The Constant Farmer's Son		Mich. 2285A
Creeping Jane	577	

	Lumpkin's Item no.	*Check-List* no.
The Croppy Boy	415	
The Dark-Eyed Sailor	148	
Devilish Mary	27	La. 18B1
		Fla. 955B1
The Drowsy Sleeper	85, 228	Tex. 6684
		N.Y. 1789B2
The Drummer Boy of Waterloo		N.C. 2850A2
Edwin in the Lowlands Low		Cal. 3818B3
Erin-Go-Bragh	229	Cal. 4210A3
		Ind. 1719B2
Erin's Green Shore		Ky. 1441A
Fair Fanny Moore		3759B
The Farmer's Boy		N.Y. 1789A2
		Tex. 915A1
Father Grumble	L.C.A. 14	Va. 3432A
Finnegan's Wake		Cal. 4212A3
The *Flying Cloud*		Cal. 4202B1
		Mich. 2281B2, 2288B3
The *Flying Dutchman*		N.Y. 2529B, 2530A
The Foggy Dew	265, 444, 521	Miss. 2986A2, B1
		Ind. 1752A1
A Gentleman of Exeter		3756A
The Girl I Left Behind	325	
The Golden Glove		O. 1696A1
		N.Y. 2574A & B
Green Beds		Miss. 3102B2
		Tenn. 2903B1
The Green Bushes	155, 156, 442	
The Green Mossy Banks of the Lea	43	
The Greenland Whale Fishery	9	Mich. 2325A
Henry Connors		Mich. 2297B1
High Barbary	10, 522, L.C.A. 21	Mich. 3401A2
The Holly Twig		Tenn. 2909B1
Jack Donahue	433, 465	Cal. 4113A
Jack Monroe		Miss. 3102A & B1
		Ky. 1386A2
Jack Williams		N.H. 3706B2
James Ervin		Tex. 57A2

	Lumpkin's Item no.	Check-List no.
James MacDonald		Vt. 3712B
Johnny Doyle		N.C. 2855A3
Johnny Troy		Ky. 1401B
Kate and Her Horns	27	Ind. 1721A
		Vt. 3736B
Katie Morey		Mich. 2413A2
		N.C. 2844A1
The *Lady Leroy*		Ky. 1484B1 & 2
		Mich. 3401A1
The Lady of Carlisle		Ky. 1587B
		Ind. 1754A1
The *Lady of the Lake*		Ark. 849A1
The Lily of the West		Va. 2744B4
		Va. 2823A2
Locks and Bolts		Ky. 1442B3, 1445A1
MacDonald's Return to Glencoe	410	Mo. 3223A1
McCollister		Cal. 4196B2
The Major and the Weaver		Mich. 2262A4 & 5
Mary O' the Dee		Cal. 3812B2
Mary of the Wild Moor		N.C. 2866A1
		Va. 2824A1
The Miller's Will		N.Y. 2553B
		O. 1695B1
The New River Shore		Tex. 625B1
The Nightingale	426	Mo. 3223B2
		Conn. 73B1
The Old Woman of Slapsadam	54, 478	N.J. 1773B
		Mich. 2264A2
The Oyster Girl		N.Y. 3668A2
Patrick Sheehan	405	3745B2, 3741A1
Peggy and the Soldier		Ky. 2773B2, 2774A1
Polly Oliver	448	
Pretty Fair Maid	L.C.A. 21	Tenn. 2940B1
The Rambling Boy		Miss. 2979A2
A Rich Irish Lady		Miss. 2953B
		N.Y. 1787B1
Rinordine		Tex. 63A2
		Va. 2784B2, 2785B1
Robin Tamson's Smiddy		Mich. 2286B2, 2287A1

	Lumpkin's Item no.	Check-List no.
The Romish Lady		Ky. 1492B2
		Tex. 916B1
The Sailor and the Tailor		Fla. 957B2
The Sailor Boy I		Miss. 3103B2,
		3104A1. Vt. 3747A3
Saly Monroe		Mich. 2283A
Sam Hall	485, 517	
The Sheffield Apprentice		Ind. 1751B
		Vt. 3724B
The Silk Merchant's Daughter		Ill. 3266B1
		Fla. 984B
The Silvery Tide		N.C. 3786B2
		Mich. 2276B, 2281A
Skewball	311	Miss. 736B
		Va. 831A
The Tan Yard Side	156	
The Three Butchers		N.C. 2850B2
The True Paddy's Song		N.J. 1776A1
		Mich. 2353A1
The Turkish Lady		Va. 2787B2
Villikins and His Dinah	54	Vt. 3735B
The Wexford Girl		Mich. 3401B
		Mo. 2282A
Will the Weaver		Conn. 157B2
		Vt. 3740A1
William Hall		N.Y. 2551B
		Ky. 306A
William Riley		O. 1008B1
		Mich. 2413B1 & 2
William Taylor		Cal. 3814A3
		N.H. 3707A 2 & 3,
		3708A
The Yorkshire Bite		Tenn. 2905A 4

See also *A List of American Folksongs Currently Available on Records*. Washington: Library of Congress, 1953. This is useful but far from complete.

Selected Bibliography

(Editors' last names are used in Appendix I to designate collections here marked with the asterisk.)

The American Songster. Philadelphia: John Kenedy, 1836.

The American Songster. New York: Nafis & Cornish, 1847.

*Arnold, Byron. *Folksongs of Alabama.* University, Alabama: University of Alabama Press, 1950.

Ashton, John. *A Century of Ballads.* London: Elliot Stock, 1887.

Ashton, John. *Chapbooks of the Eighteenth Century.* London: Chatto and Windus, 1882.

Ashton, John. *Humour, Wit, and Satire of the Seventeenth Century.* London: Chatto and Windus, 1883.

*Ashton, John. *Modern Street Ballads.* London: Chatto and Windus, 1888.

*Baring-Gould, S. and Cecil J. Sharp. *English Folk-Songs for Schools.* London: J. Curwen and Sons, [1906].

*Baring-Gould, S. and H. Fleetwood Sheppard. *Songs and Ballads of the West.* Four parts in two volumes. London: Methuen and Co., 1895. Revised ed., 1905.

*Barrett, Wm. Alexander. *English Folk-Songs.* London: Novello and Co., [1891].

*Barry, Phillips. *The Maine Woods Songster.* Cambridge, Mass.: The Powell Printing Co., 1939.

*Barry, Phillips, Fannie Hardy Eckstorm, and Mary Winslow Smyth. *British Ballads from Maine.* New Haven: Yale Univ. Press, 1929.

*Beck, Earl Clifton. *Songs of the Michigan Lumberjacks.* Ann Arbor: University of Michigan Press, 1941.

*Belden, Henry Marvin. *Ballads and Songs Collected by the Missouri Folklore Society.* Columbia: *The University of Missouri Studies,* XV (No. 1), 1940.

The Bell Collection. *Ballads Collected by John Bell, Newcastle.* (One volume containing 109 chapbooks. Harvard Library no. 25252.19.).

Bell, Robert. *Ancient Poems, Ballads, and Songs of the Peasantry of England.* London: John W. Parker and Sons, 1857.

Black-Letter Ballads. *A Collection of Seventy-Nine Black-Letter Ballads and Broadsides Printed in the Reign of Queen Elizabeth.* London: Joseph Lilly, 1867.

*Brewster, Paul G. *Ballads and Songs of Indiana.* Indiana University Publications, Folklore Series No. 1, Bloomington, 1940.

*Broadwood, Lucy E. and J. A. Fuller Maitland. *English County Songs.* London: The Leadenhall Press, 1893.

Broadwood, Lucy E. *English Traditional Songs and Carols.* London: Boosey and Co., 1908.

*Brown, Frank C. *Folk Ballads from North Carolina.* Edited by Henry M. Belden and Arthur Palmer Hudson. Durham: Duke Univ. Press, 1952. (Vol. II of *The Frank C. Brown Collection of North Carolina Folklore.*)

Bulletin of the Folk-Song Society of the Northeast. Cambridge, Mass., 1930-1937. (Cited as *Bulletin.*)

302

California Folklore Quarterly see *Western Folklore.*

*Cambiaire, Celestin Pierre. *East Tennessee and Western Virginia Mountain Ballads.* London: The Mitre Press, [1934].

Chambers, Edward K. "Popular Narrative Poetry and the Ballad", *English Literature at the Close of the Middle Ages.* Oxford: The Clarendon Press, 1945, pp. 122-184.

*Chappell, Louis W. *Folk-Songs of Roanoke and the Albemarle.* Morgantown, W. Va.: The Ballad Press, 1939.

*Child, Francis James. *The English and Scottish Popular Ballads.* 5 vols., Boston and New York: Houghton, Mifflin and Co., 1898.

*Christie, W. *Traditional Ballad Airs.* 2 vols., Edinburgh: Edmonston and Douglas, 1876, 1881.

Clark, Andrew. *The Shirburn Ballads: 1585-1616.* Oxford: The Clarendon Press, 1907.

Coffin, Tristram P. *The British Traditional Ballad in North America. Publications of the American Folklore Society: Bibliographical Series, Vol. II,* Phila., 1950. X

*Colcord, Joanna C. *Songs of American Sailormen.* New York: W. W. Norton and Co.,[1938].

A Collection of Old Ballads. 3 vols., London: J. Roberts, 1723-1725 (19th century reprint).

*Colum, Padraic. *Broad-Sheet Ballads.* London and Dublin: Maunsel and Co., [n. d.]

*Combs, Josiah H. *Folk-Songs du Midi des Etats-Unis.* Paris: Les Presses Universitaires de France, 1925.

*Cox, John Harrington. *Folk-Songs of the South.* Cambridge: Harvard University Press, 1925.

*Creighton, Helen. *Songs and Ballads from Nova Scotia.* Toronto and Vancouver: J. M. Dent and Sons, 1933.

*Creighton, Helen and Doreen H. Senior. *Traditional Songs from Nova Scotia.* Toronto: The Ryerson Press, 1950.

Croker, T. Crofton. *The Popular Songs of Ireland.* London: Henry Colburn, 1839.

Cunningham, Allan. *Songs of Scotland, Ancient and Modern.* 4 vols., London: John Taylor, 1825.

*Davis, Arthur Kyle, Jr. *Folk-Songs of Virginia: A Descriptive Index and Classification* . . . . Durham: Duke Univ. Press, 1949.

Davis, Arthur Kyle, Jr. *Traditional Ballads of Virginia.* Cambridge: Harvard Univ. Press, 1929.

*Dean, Michael C. *The Flying Cloud and One Hundred and Fifty Other Old Time Songs and Ballads.* Virginia, Minnesota: The Quickprint, 1922.

Dean-Smith, Margaret. *A Guide to English Folk Song Collections, 1822-1952.* The University Press of Liverpool in association with the English Folk Dance and Song Society, 1954.

Delaney's Song Books. Published by Wm. W. Delaney, 117 Park Row, New York.

Dichter, Harry. "Handbook of American Sheet Music". Phila., 1947. (A priced catalogue).

Dobie, J. Frank see under Publications of the Texas Folklore Society.

*Doerflinger, Wm. Main. *Shantymen and Shantyboys: Songs of the Sailor and Lumberman.* New York: The Macmillan Co., 1951.

Duffy, Charles Gavin. *The Ballad Poetry of Ireland.* 39th ed., Dublin and London: James Duffy, 1866.

Ebsworth, J. Woodfall see under Roxburghe Ballads.

*Eckstorm, Fannie Hardy and Mary Winslow Smyth. *Ministrelsy of Maine.* Boston: Houghton, Mifflin and Co., 1927.

*Eddy, Mary O. *Ballads and Songs from Ohio.* New York: J. J. Augustin, [1939].

Entwistle, William J. *European Balladry.* Oxford; The Clarendon Press, [1951] (reprint).

Evans, Thomas and R. H. Evans. *Old Ballads, Historical and Narrative, with Some of Modern Date.* 4 vols., London: R. H. Evans, 1810.

*Finger, Charles J. *Frontier Ballads.* New York: Doubleday, Page and Co., 1927.

Firth, C. H. *An American Garland: Being a Collection of Ballads Relating to America,* 1563-1759. Oxford: B. H. Blackwell, 1915.

Firth, C. H. *Naval Songs and Ballads.* (*Publications of the Navy Records Society,* Vol. XXXIII), London, 1908.

*Flanders, Helen Hartness. *A Garland of Green Mountain Song.* (*Green Mountain Pamphlets, No. 1*), Northfield, Vt., [1934].

*Flanders, Helen Hartness, Elizabeth Flanders Ballard, George Brown, and Phillips Barry. *The New Green Mountain Songster: Traditional Folksongs of Vermont.* New Haven: Yale Univ. Press, 1939. (Cited as Flanders-Barry).

*Flanders, Helen Hartness and George Brown. *Vermont Folk-Songs and Ballads.* Brattleboro, Vermont: Stephen Daye Press, [1931].

*Flanders, Helen Hartness and Marguerite Olney. *Ballads Migrant in New England.* New York: Farrar, Strauss, and Young, 1953.

Ford, Robert. *Auld Scots Ballants.* Paisley and London: Alexander Gardner, 1889.

*Ford, Robert. *Vagabond Songs and Ballads of Scotland.* First and second series, Paisley and London: Alexander Gardner, 1899, 1901.

Ford, Worthington C. *Broadside Ballads . . . Printed in Massachusetts, 1639-1800.* (*Massachusetts Historical Society Collections,* LXXV), Boston, 1922.

Ford, Worthington C. *The Isaiah Thomas Collection of Ballads.* Worcester: The American Antiquarian Society, 1924.

The Forget Me Not Songster, New York: Nafis and Cornish, [n.d.].

The Forget Me Not Songster. Phila. and Baltimore: Fisher and Bros., [n.d.].

*Fuson, Harvey H. *Ballads of the Kentucky Highlands.* London: The Mitre Press, [1931].

*Gardner, Emelyn E. and Geraldine J. Chickering. *Ballads and Songs of Southern Michigan.* Ann Arbor: Univ. of Michigan Press, 1939.

Gerould, Gordon Hall. *The Ballad of Tradition.* Oxford: The Clarendon Press, 1932.

Gillington, Alice E. *Songs of the Open Road.* London: J. Williams, 1911.

Gordon, Robert W. *Folk-Songs of America.* New York: National Service Bureau, 1938.

*Gray, Roland Palmer. *Songs and Ballads of the Maine Lumberjacks.* Cambridge: Harvard Univ. Press, 1924.

*Greenleaf, Elizabeth B. and Grace Mansfield. *Ballads and Sea Songs from Newfoundland.* Cambridge: Harvard Univ. Press, 1933.

*Greig, Gavin. *Folk-Song of the North-East.* Peterhead: "Buchan Observer" Works, 1914.

Greig, Gavin and Alexander Keith. *Last Leaves of Traditional Ballads and Ballad Airs.* Aberdeen: The Buchan Club, 1925.

Gummere, Francis B. *The Popular Ballad.* Boston and New York: Houghton, Mifflin & Co., 1907.

Hale, Edward Everett and His Children. *New England History in Ballads*. Boston: Little, Brown & Co., 1903.

Hammond, H. E. D. *Folk-Songs from Dorset*. London: Novello, 1908.

The Harvard Catalogue see under Welsh.

*Hayward, H. Richard. *Ulster Songs and Ballads*. London: Duckworth, [1925].

*Henderson, W. *Victorian Street Ballads*. London and New York: Charles Scribner's Sons, 1938.

Hendren, J. W. *A Study in Ballad Rhythm*. (Princeton Studies in English), Princeton University Press, 1936.

Henry, Mellinger E. *A Bibliography for the Study of American Folk-Songs*. London: The Mitre Press, [n.d.].

*Henry, Mellinger E. *Folk-Songs from the Southern Highlands*. New York: J. J. Augustin, 1938.

*Henry, Mellinger E. *Songs Sung in the Southern Appalachians*. London: The Mitre Press, [1934].

Herd, David. *Ancient and Modern Scottish Songs, Heroic Ballads, etc.* Reprinted from the ed. of 1776. 2 vols. Glasgow, 1869.

Hindley, Charles. *Curiosities of Street Literature*. London: Reeves and Turner, 1871.

Hindley, Charles. *The Life and Times of James Catnach, (Late of Seven Dials), Ballad Monger*. London: Reeves and Turner, 1878.

Hindley, Charles. See under Roxburghe Ballads.

Hodgart, M. J. C. *The Ballads*. London: Hutchinson's University Library, 1950.

*Hudson, Arthur Palmer. *Folk Songs of Mississippi*. Chapel Hill: Univ. of North Carolina Press, 1936.

Hughes, Herbert, *Irish Country Songs*. London: Boosey and Co., 1915.

Hustvedt, Sigurd Bernhard. *Ballad Books and Ballad Men*. Cambridge: Harvard Univ. Press, 1930.

Johnson, James. *The Scots Musical Museum*. 6 vols., Edinburgh: James Johnson, 1839.

Johnson, R. Brimley. *Popular British Ballads, Ancient and Modern*. 4 vols., London: J. M. Dent & Co. and Phila.: J. B. Lippincott Co., 1894.

Johnson, R. Brimley. *A Book of Popular British Ballads*. Everyman's Library, no. 572. London and New York: Dent and Dutton, 1912. (A one volume abridgement of *Popular British Ballads*.)

Journal of American Folklore. Published by the American Folklore Society, 1888—. (Cited as *JAF*.)

Journal of the Folk-Song Society. Published by the Folk-Song Society, London, 1899-1931. (Cited as *JFSS*.)

Journal of the English Folk Dance and Song Society. Published by the English Folk Dance and Song Society, London, 1932—.(Cited as *JEFDSS*.)

Journal of the Irish Folk Song Society, London. London: The Irish Folk Song Society, London; 1904-1939.

Joyce, Patrick Weston. *Ancient Irish Music*. Dublin and New York: Longmans, Green and Co., 1906.

*Joyce, Patrick Weston. *Old Irish Folk Music and Song*. New York: Longmans, Green and Co., 1909.

Keith, Alexander see under Greig.

Kidson, Frank. "The Ballad Sheet and Garland," *Journal of The Folk-Song Society* II, 70-78.

Kidson, Frank. *A Garland of English Folk Songs*. London: Ascherberg, Hopwood, and Carew, Ltd., [1926].

*Kidson, Frank. *Traditional Tunes*. Oxford: Charles Taphouse and Son, 1891.

Korson, George. *Coal Dust on the Fiddle: Songs and Stories of the Bituminous Industry*. Phila.: Univ. of Penna. Press, 1943.

Korson, George. *Minstrels of the Mine Patch: Songs and Stories of The Anthracite Industry*. Phila.: Univ. of Penna. Press, 1938.

*Korson, George. *Pennsylvania Songs and Legends*. Phila.: Univ. of Penna. Press, 1949.

Laws, G. Malcolm, Jr. *Native American Balladry: A Descriptive Study and a Bibliographical Syllabus*. (*Publications of the American Folklore Society, Bibliographical Series*, Vol. 1), Phila., 1950.

*Leach, MacEdward. *The Ballad Book*. New York: Harper and Bros., 1955.

Library of Congress. *Check-List of Recorded Songs in the English Language in the Archive of American Folk Song to July, 1940*. 2 vols., mimeographed, Washington, D.C., 1942.

*Linscott, Eloise Hubbard. *Folk Songs of Old New England*. New York: The Macmillan Co., 1939.

*Lloyd, A. L. *Come All Ye Bold Miners: Ballads and Songs of the Coalfields*. London: Lawrence and Wishart, 1952.

*Logan, W. H. *A Pedlar's Pack of Ballads and Songs*. Edinburgh: Wm. Paterson, 1869.

Lomax, John A. and Alan Lomax. *American Ballads and Folk Songs*. New York: The Macmillan Co., 1934.

Lomax, John A. and Alan Lomax. *Cowboy Songs and Other Frontier Ballads*. (Revised and enlarged), New York: The Macmillan Co., 1938.

Lomax, John A. and Alan Lomax. *Folk Song U. S. A.* New York: Duell, Sloan, and Pearce, [1947].

Lomax, John A. and Alan Lomax. *Our Singing Country*. New York: The Macmillan Co., 1941.

Lumpkin, Ben Gray. *Folksongs on Records, Issue 3*. Denver: Alan Swallow, 1950.

*Mackenzie, W. Roy. *Ballads and Sea Songs from Nova Scotia*. Cambridge: Harvard Univ. Press, 1928.

*Moeran, E. J. *Six Suffolk Folk-Songs*. London: J. Curwen and Sons; New York: G. Schirmer, Inc. [1932].

Midwest Folklore. Bloomington, Indiana: Indiana Univ., 1951—.

*Moffat, Alfred. *The Minstrelsy of Ireland*. 4th ed., London: Augener Ltd., [1897].

*Morris, Alton C. *Folksongs of Florida*. Gainesville: Univ. of Florida Press, 1950.

*Neely, Charles and John W. Spargo. *Tales and Songs of Southern Illinois*. Menasha, Wisconsin: George Banta Pub. Co., 1938.

Neeser, Robert W. *American Naval Songs and Ballads*. New Haven: Yale Univ. Press, 1938.

New York Folklore Quarterly. Ithaca, N. Y.: Cornell Univ. Press for the New York Folklore Society, 1945—.

*O'Conor, Manus. *Irish Com-All-Ye's and Ballads of Ireland*. New York: The Popular Pub. Co., [1901].

The Old Forget Me Not Songster. Boston: Locke and Dubier, [n.d.]. (The same as *The Forget Me Not Songster*, N. Y., Nafis and Cornish).

*O'Lochlainn, Colm. *Irish Street Ballads*. (Revised ed.), Dublin: The Sign of the Three Candles, [1946].

*Ord, John. *The Bothy Songs and Ballads of Aberdeen, Banff & Moray, Angus and the Mearns.* Paisley: Alexander Gardner, 1930.

Osterley Park Ballads. *Broadside Ballads of the Restoration Period from the Jersey Collection known as the Osterley Park Ballads.* Ed. F. Burlington Fawcett, London: John Lane, 1933.

*Owens, William A. *Texas Folk Songs.* (*Publications of the Texas Folk-Lore Society No. XXIII*), Dallas, Texas, 1950.

Pepys Ballads see under Rollins.

Percy, Thomas. *Reliques of Ancient English Poetry.* Ed. H. B. Wheatley, 3 vols., London: Swan Sonnenschein and Co., 1889.

*Pound, Louise. *American Ballads and Songs.* New York: Charles Scribner's Sons, 1922.

Pound, Louise. *Poetic Origins and the Ballad.* New York: The Macmillan Co., 1921.

Publications of the Texas Folk-Lore Society. Vols. II, VI, VII, and X, ed. J. Frank Dobie. (Cited as *PTFLS*). See also under Owens.

Ramsay, Allan. *The Tea-Table Miscellany: A Collection of Choice Songs Scots and English.* Reprinted from the 14th ed., 2 vols., Glasgow: John Crum, 1871.

*Randolph, Vance and Floyd C. Shoemaker. *Ozark Folksongs.* 4 vols., Columbia: The State Historical Society of Missouri, 1946-1950.

Richardson, Ethel Park. *American Mountain Songs.* New York: Greenberg, [1927].

*Rickaby, Franz. *Ballads and Songs of the Shanty-boy.* Cambridge: Harvard Univ. Press, 1926.

*Ritchie, Jean. *Singing Family of the Cumberlands.* New York: Oxford Univ. Press, 1955.

Ritson, Joseph. *Ancient Songs and Ballads from the Reign of King Henry the Second to the Revolution.* 3rd ed., rev. by W. Carew Hazlitt, London: Reeves and Turner, 1887.

Ritson, Joseph. *Northern Garlands: A Collections of Songs Edited by Joseph Ritson (1784-1793).* Edinburgh: E. and G. Goldsmid, 1887.

Roberts, John S. *The Legendary Ballads of England and Scotland.* London and New York: Frederick Warne and Co., 1887.

Rollins, Hyder E. *An Analytical Index to the Ballad-Entries (1557-1709) in the Registers of the Company of Stationers of London.* Chapel Hill: University of North Carolina Press, 1924.

Rollins, Hyder E. "The Black-Letter Broadside Ballad," *PMLA* 34 (1919), 258-339.

Rollins, Hyder E. *Old English Ballads, 1553-1625.* Cambridge University Press, 1920.

Rollins, Hyder E. *The Pack of Autolycus, or Strange and Terrible News of Ghosts, Apparitions, Monstrous Births . . . (etc.) 1624-1693.* Cambridge: Harvard University Press, 1927.

Rollins, Hyder E. *The Pepys Ballads.* 8 vols., Cambridge: Harvard University Press, 1929-1932.

Rollins, Hyder E. *A Pepysian Garland: Black-Letter Broadside Ballads of the Years 1595-1639.* Cambridge University Press, 1922.

The Roxburghe Ballads. 9 vols. Edited by J. Woodfall Ebsworth and William Chappell, Hertford: Printed for the Ballad Society by S. Austin and Sons, 1871-1899.

(*The Roxburghe Ballads.*) *A Book of Roxburghe Ballads.* Edited by John Payne Collier, London, 1847.

The Roxburghe Ballads. 2 vols. Edited by Charles Hindley, London: Reeves and Turner, 1873, 1874.

*Sandburg, Carl. *The American Songbag.* New York: Harcourt, Brace and Co., [1927].

Sargent, Helen Child and George Lyman Kittredge. *English and Scottish Popular Ballads.* Cambridge: Houghton, Mifflin Co., [1904]. (One-volume edition of the Child ballads).

*Scarborough, Dorothy. *A Song Catcher in Southern Mountains.* New York: Columbia Univ. Press, 1937.

Sharp, Cecil J. *English Folk-Song: Some Conclusions.* London: Simpkin, [1907].

*Sharp, Cecil J. *English Folk-Songs from the Southern Appalachians.* Ed. Maud Karpeles. 2 vols., London: Oxford Univ. Press, 1932.

*Sharp, Cecil J. *One Hundred English Folksongs.* Boston: Oliver Ditson Co., [1916].

*Sharp, Cecil J. and Charles Marson. *Folk-Songs from Somerset.* Five series, London: Simpkin and Co., 1910-1919.

*Shay, Frank. *American Sea Songs and Chanteys.* New York: W. W. Norton and Co., [1948].

*Shoemaker, Henry W. *Mountain Minstrelsy of Pennsylvania.* Phila.: Newman F. McGirr, 1931.

Six Hundred and Seventeen Irish Songs and Ballads. New York: Wehman Bros., [n.d.].

Southern Folklore Quarterly. Gainesville, Florida: The University of Florida in Cooperation with the Southeastern Folklore Society, 1937——. (Cited as *SFQ*).

Spaeth, Sigmund. *Read 'Em and Weep: The Songs You Forgot to Remember.* New York: Doubleday, Page and Co., 1927.

Spaeth, Sigmund. *Weep Some More, My Lady.* New York: Doubleday, Page and Co., 1927.

Stanier, John. *Catalogue of English Song Books Forming a Portion of the Library of Sir John Stanier.* London, 1891.

*Stout, Earl J. *Folklore from Iowa.* (*Memoirs of the American Folklore Society,* Vol. XXIX), New York, 1936.

*Sturgis, Edith B. and Robert Hughes. *Songs from the Hills of Vermont.* New York: G. Schirmer, Inc., 1919.

*Thomas, Isaiah. "Songs, Ballads, etc. Purchased from a Ballad Printer and Seller in Boston, 1813." 3 vols. of broadsides in the American Antiquarian Society, Worcester, Mass. (Cited as Thomas Coll.).

Thomas, Jean. *Ballad Makin' in the Mountains of Kentucky.* New York: Henry Holt and Co., 1939.

*Thomas, Jean. *Devil's Ditties: Being Stories of the Kentucky Mountain People with the Songs they Sing.* Chicago: W. W. Hatfield Co., 1931.

*Thompson, Harold W. *Body, Boots, and Britches.* Phila.: J. B. Lippincott Co., 1939.

*Thorpe, N. Howard. *Songs of the Cowboys.* Cambridge: Houghton, Mifflin Co., 1921.

Wehman's Song Books. Published by Wehman Bros., 158 Park Row, New York.

Weiss, Harry B. *A Book about Chapbooks: the People's Literature of Bygone Times.* Trenton, N. J., 1942.

Welsh, Charles, et al. *Catalogue of English and American Chapbooks and Broadside Ballads in Harvard College Library.* (*Bibliographical Contributions* No. 56) Cambridge: Library of Harvard University, 1905. (Cited as the Harvard Catalogue).

The Universal Songster or Museum of Mirth. 3 vols., London: George Routledge and Sons, [n.d.].

Wells, Evelyn K. *The Ballad Tree: A Study of British and American Ballads, Their Folklore, Verse, and Music.* New York: The Ronald Press Co., 1950.

Western Folklore (formerly *California Folklore Quarterly*), Berkeley and Los Angeles: Univ. of California Press for the California Folklore Society, 1942—. (Cited as *WF*).

*Wheeler, Mary. *Kentucky Mountain Folk-Songs.* Boston: The Boston Music Co., [1937].

*Williams, Alfred. *Folk-Songs of the Upper Thames.* London: Duckworth and Co., [1923].

Winn, Cyril. *A Selection of Some Less Known Folk-Songs.* vol. 2. Arranged by Cecil Sharp, R. Vaughan Williams and Others. London: Novello and Co., 1930.

Winslow, Ola Elizabeth. *American Broadside Verse from Imprints of the 17th and 18th Centuries.* New Haven: Yale Univ. Press, 1930.

*Wyman, Loraine and Howard Brockway. *Lonesome Tunes: Folk Songs from the Kentucky Mountains.* New York: H. W. Gray Co., [1916].

Index of Ballads

References to Appendix I are printed in italics.